LET US WATCH
RICHARD WILBUR

Let Us Watch Richard Wilbur

A BIOGRAPHICAL STUDY

Robert Bagg

AND

Mary Bagg

University of Massachusetts Press

Amherst and Boston

Copyright © 2017 by University of Massachusetts Press
All rights reserved
Printed in the United States of America

ISBN 978-1-62534-224-9 (paper); 223-2 (cloth)

Designed by Jack Harrison
Set in Adobe Garamond Pro
Printed and bound by Sheridan Books, Inc.

Cover design by Jack Harrison
Cover art: Richard Wilbur, c. 1947. Unknown photographer.
Courtesy of Richard Wilbur.

Library of Congress Cataloging-in-Publication Data
A catalog record for this book is available from the Library of Congress.

British Library Cataloguing-in-Publication Data
A catalog record for this book is available from the British Library

To the memory of
Charlee Wilbur (1922–2007)

Contents

vii

LET US WATCH
RICHARD WILBUR

Prologue

Richard Wilbur published his first book of poems, *The Beautiful Changes,* in 1947. He was twenty-six years old. Reviewing the book for the *New Yorker,* the American poet Louise Bogan, who was also an acute critic, concluded with a prediction. "Let us watch Richard Wilbur," she wrote. "He is composed of valid ingredients."[1] Not quite ten years later, Wilbur won the first of his two Pulitzer Prizes for poetry. Unlike the Nobel Prize winners, who receive a rousing phone call from Stockholm in the middle of the night, Wilbur did not hear the good news firsthand.

On the day of the announcement, May 6, 1957, Wilbur's duties as an associate professor at Wellesley College included a welcome assignment. Marianne Moore, the grand dame of American poetry and a friend of Robert Frost and William Carlos Williams, was to read her poems that evening on campus. Wilbur would introduce her, and that afternoon he had written out and polished his remarks.

Moore and Wilbur had already developed both affection and respect for each other. In 1948, for instance, Wilbur had sent Moore a drawing of a swan reflected in a lake, which he thought was relevant to her poem "See in the Midst of Fair Leaves." He felt bold enough to include his image of the "double swan," along with his perception of how it related to her poem, because he had read somewhere that she liked to accompany her poems with small drawings.[2] Moore responded kindly that the swan intensified and enhanced her poem, more than she thought the poem deserved.[3]

Moore's reading at Wellesley was scheduled for seven o'clock. John Malcolm Brinnin, a poet, teacher, and critic who had become a close friend during Wilbur's post–World War II graduate-school and teaching years at Harvard, arrived to pick up Wilbur's wife, Charlee, at the couple's home in

South Lincoln, Massachusetts, and drive her to the reading. In his diary he recorded what happened next:

> Downstairs, waiting for Charlee to finish dressing upstairs, I flip on the radio. It's Pulitzer Prize day—the award goes to Richard Wilbur. . . . I yell up, Charlee hurries down; we fall in to an embrace and do a little dance around the coffee table. Later, as we are driving toward the campus, she says, "*You* tell him."
>
> "I don't think I should—wouldn't he be happier hearing it from you?" [I say].
>
> "No—you tell him, I want you to," [she says].
>
> As we enter the lecture hall, Dick is just approaching the podium to announce Marianne Moore. Charlee and I find seats together and somehow induce ourselves to pay attention. The reading is brief, interspersed with (calculated?) ramblings that always end, or seem to end, bull's-eye on targets no one had supposed were even there. When it's over, I start down the steps at the side of the auditorium and Dick starts up the steps. I shake his hand as hard as I can and simply nod. [He asks,] "Do you mean it?" Without saying a word, I nod again, and Charlee breaks through to confirm it.
>
> To celebrate we head for a steak house on Route 9, drink to the fates, the world, the weather, the day we met. Back on the campus about nine, we find Marianne in the sunroom of a faculty apartment where a welter of Wellesley girls has gathered at her feet. Her tricorne is firmly on her head and her stockings are grey.[4]

The Wilburs went home, and Brinnin headed back to his apartment in Cambridge. Close to midnight, as Brinnin reports, using details he learned the next day, Wilbur received a telegram: "YOUR BEAUTIFUL POEMS WILL LIVE FOREVER. JOHN BERRYMAN." Wilbur, writes Brinnin, went to bed without suspecting that Berryman intended the hyperbole in his telegram as sarcasm.[5] Not only had the Pulitzer committee just passed over Berryman's *Homage to Mistress Bradstreet* in favor of Wilbur's *Things of This World,* but just two months earlier the National Book Award committee had also bestowed its annual prize on Wilbur. Berryman was not a gracious loser.

The next day, Wilbur sent Berryman a note expressing his gratitude for the telegram. Some weeks later—regretting the ill will he had intended and anticipating Wilbur's ire—Berryman sent back a long, abashed, ranting apology he'd begun to write before he'd even read what Wilbur had to say. That letter, quoted in chapter 10, exemplifies the charged and tense atmosphere of the poetry world in the mid-twentieth century, a small world in which Wilbur was fully immersed.

Berryman's rant represented his "painful and dreadful" competitive spirit, as Wilbur described it, one even more intense than Robert Lowell's or Theodore Roethke's.[6] Berryman would eventually receive universal and lasting praise for *Mistress Bradstreet*—now widely recognized as the finest long poem by an American since T. S. Eliot's *The Wasteland*—and in 1965 he won his Pulitzer for *77 Dream Songs*. (In 1969 Berryman's *His Toy, His Dream, His Rest* won both the National Book Award and the Bollingen Prize for poetry.) His anguished response to Wilbur's first Pulitzer contrasts with Lowell's and Elizabeth Bishop's silence. By 1957 both had already received their Pulitzers (Lowell in 1947, Bishop in 1956). Neither formally wrote to congratulate Wilbur, nor did they write to each other about his success that year.[7]

For Wilbur, sweeping the major poetry prizes of 1957 improved his chances for earning tenure at Wesleyan University, where he began to teach in the following fall. As the father of three (soon to be four) children, he was grateful for the position and the prizes. Yet he has said that prizes don't make a difference to a serious poet who is devoted to writing, and he downplays winning them when he does—a modest attitude that he seems to have inherited from his father. "I don't remember my father saying a bragging thing," Wilbur told us in 2007, "and he was the sort of person who is good at everything he does."[8]

Born in 1921, Wilbur became a member of what Tom Brokaw has named the Greatest Generation. He served in World War II as a cryptographer with the 36th Texas Division, which joined the invasion on the Anzio beachhead on May 15, 1943, and entered Rome on June 5, 1944, the day when Mark Clark's Fifth Army captured the city. The 36th engaged in combat for longer than any other division did during the European campaign. After the war, Wilbur returned to civilian life to join a generation of formidable poetic peers—the most accomplished group since the heyday of Robert Frost and Wallace Stevens—including Lowell, Berryman, Bishop, and Roethke as well as Anthony Hecht, Randall Jarrell, James Merrill, Karl Shapiro, and Delmore Schwartz.

Wilbur has been prolific, publishing ten volumes of poetry, four books for children of all ages, and fifteen translations of widely performed plays by Molière, Jean Racine, and Pierre Corneille. His theatrical interests and talents, however, reach beyond the classical French plays he has rendered into English. He collaborated with Lillian Hellman and Leonard Bernstein on the Broadway production of *Candide,* a project that was both rewarding and frustrating. Also, in his two books of literary essays (which follow the American school of practical and appreciative criticism rather than the more pontifical criticism of, for instance, Eliot), he provides a counterpoint to the New Critical and close-reading approaches in vogue during the mid-twentieth century. Throughout this book, we quote excerpts from those essays to illuminate how he has applied his critical practice to composing his own poetry.

In addition to the two Pulitzers and the National Book Award, Wilbur has earned every major American literary accolade, including election to the National Institute of Arts and Letters in 1957, appointment as U.S. Poet Laureate in 1987–88, and two Bollingen prizes—one for poetry, one for translation.[9] The critic David Orr, who has called Wilbur "A Grand Old Man of American Poetry," praises *Anterooms* (2010), Wilbur's slender volume of recent poems, in part because "it asks something slightly unusual from the contemporary reader. It asks us to value poetry that is happy to be read as solid and static, rather than unstable and in flux."[10]

In response to a few influential critics, who over the years have been less impressed by Wilbur's body of work or have failed to respond to or even grant its philosophical, visionary, and religious depth, Dana Gioia described his poetic effort as an "ironic achievement." Wilbur excels, Gioia says, "at precisely those literary forms that many contemporary critics undervalue," those being "metrical [and stanzaic] poetry, verse translation, comic verse, song lyrics, and perhaps foremost among these unfashionable but extraordinary accomplishments, religious poetry."[11]

Certain critics, while acknowledging Wilbur's wit, metaphoric élan, and formal resourcefulness, find his work merely accomplished or pleasing or elegant. Yet others have seen, within that elegance, a fierce intellectual energy. The qualities that various critics have identified as Wilbur's attributes—his "ingredients," as Bogan called them—have evoked a striking diversity in the literary profession's evaluation of his achievements.

Bruce Michelson, for instance, has called Wilbur's work "mannered," "amiable," and "safe," whereas Hecht has seen it as "chilling," "unfeigned," and "kinetic" (the latter quality inspired by Wilbur's study of Edgar Degas). Wilbur possesses, according to Hecht, "a philosophical bent and a religious temper, which are by no means the same thing, but which here consort comfortably together." William Logan has called Wilbur "clever as a cat," "coolly detached," and "complacent," though "honorable." Joseph Bennett has deemed his poetry "durable"; to John Ciardi, it is "calm" and "melodic." Leslie Fiedler, writing in 1964, assessed Wilbur at the start of an era in which to "cut loose" and "challenge authority" was applauded: "There is no personal source anywhere, as there is no passion and no insanity; the insistent 'I,' the asserting of sex, and the flaunting of madness apparently considered in equally bad taste."[12] Wilbur faced the challenge raised by Fiedler's implication—that there's something wrong with being sensible and restrained (for either the poet or the poetry) or something suspect in appearing to be normal—at a time when many of his peers, suffering from mental illnesses and suicidal depression, focused their poetry on angst and despair. He never felt an impulse to write confessional poetry; he sensed that the genre was undignified for a man who believes that complaining, by its nature, is a weakness.

Throughout this book, we examine how Wilbur has remained true to his own poetic identity, refusing to develop fashionable, and usually transitory, styles. Yet in his recent collection *Anterooms,* he has taken a different tack: more than half of the poems he has composed speak in the first person, and in them he examines his life more directly, with grace and dignity, as he contemplates its end. As Orr notes, remaining solid and not in flux is "especially tricky if you're writing about death, as Wilbur is in the strongest poems here."[13]

In this biography we invite readers to watch Wilbur's life unfold, in chapters both chronological and thematic, as we look ahead to (or reflect upon) how certain events and attitudes surface in his work. We begin with the early influences and the often-solitary interests of his childhood, particularly his fascination with codes, drawing, and spontaneous pranks that disconcerted adults. He attended Amherst College at a time when the country was debating and then preparing to enter World War II. His own entry into the military, which tested his pacifist principles and his assumption that free speech was sacred even during a war, began with a nearly disastrous accusation of disloyalty to his country. But a moment of good fortune restored him to active duty and the code work he was trained to do. His experiences during the European campaign had a life-changing impact on his future as they moved him to write his first serious poems.

Postwar, at Harvard, a Junior Fellowship liberated Wilbur from pursuing a purely scholarly career and allowed him to travel to Paris and Rome. Each city provided subjects, attitudes, and inspiration for his writing. During the

Vietnam era his antiwar beliefs and activism conflicted with his veteran's sense of duty to the nation, which he believed required his sons to accept the draft.

Contrary to the perception of fans and the general public, Wilbur's personal life was not free from emotional hardship, especially when his and Charlee's fourth child, Aaron, was diagnosed as autistic in the early 1960s. While at the Camargo Institute in the mid-1980s, as mounting mental stress affected both Wilbur and Charlee, they became addicted to Valium and struggled with the aftereffects for years. Charlee's physical health became increasingly fragile in the early 2000s, thus preventing the Wilburs from returning to their cherished winter getaway in Key West. Her death in 2007 left Wilbur without the companionship and literary partnership that had sustained him for sixty-five years. Yet his resilience and faith allowed him to produce more French translations, this time of Corneille, and the acclaimed poems of *Anterooms*.

We supplement our discussions of Wilbur's poetic oeuvre with critical analyses by others and with excerpts from his published prose and translations for the theater. We quote passages from interviews we conducted with Wilbur between 2005 and 2015 and with Charlee from 2005 until her death. In unpublished journals, Wilbur has consistently recorded his thoughts on everything from philosophy to religion to literature as well as on his ambitions and fears, and he has granted us permission to use this material.

In May 1973, Wilbur was two years away from retirement at Wesleyan; immediately thereafter he would become a writer in residence at Smith College. The following passage from his journal, written during that month, shows him assessing his present state of mind. At the time he was gearing up to plant his garden in Cummington, Massachusetts, and anticipating getting back to work on the "The Mind-Reader," a poem that occupied him for nearly twenty years. Written amid these transitions, the passage perfectly captures his lifelong spirit and sense of purpose:

> I have noticed that I am happiest when taken out of myself, either by the desire to say or write or do something better than my ordinary lumpish self could do it, or by going out to others in aid or sympathy. No doubt I am conditioned to feel so by such religious training as has truly rubbed off on me, and by my society's high estimation of work and achievement.[14]

1

Childhood in North Caldwell, New Jersey

"Back where safety was"

Growing up in North Caldwell in what amounted to a little British colony, it was understood that anything British was better than anything American, at least contemporaneously. Of course we felt that George Washington was better than George III.

—RICHARD WILBUR, interview by the authors, April 4, 2006

A memory from childhood opens each of the three stanzas of "This Pleasing Anxious Being," a poem that Richard Wilbur wrote at the age of seventy-seven. In each stanza Wilbur pauses for a moment in the remembered scene and then feels time pulsing him forward, inevitably toward death. As he both presents his life and invites us to explore it through the poem, he quietly asserts his belief that the soul is immortal.

Wilbur renders the poem's autobiographical facts in vivid detail, often with references to photography and painting, artistic genres that can influence our memories by capturing them and lifting them from their contexts. In the first stanza, for instance, he evokes the chiaroscuro technique in Georges de La Tour's painting *The Nativity,* freezing his family (but only for a moment) in a serene but dramatically lit tableau—the dining room on an evening in the mid-1920s:

> In no time you are back where safety was,
> Spying upon the lambent table where
> Good family faces drink the candlelight

As in a manger scene by de La Tour.
Father has finished carving at the sideboard
And Mother's hand has touched a little bell,
So that, beside her chair, Roberta looms
With serving bowls of yams and succotash.
When will they speak, or stir? They wait for you
To recollect that, while it lived, the past
Was a rushed present, fretful and unsure.
The muffled clash of silverware begins,
With ghosts of gesture, with a laugh retrieved,
And the warm, edgy voices you would hear:
Rest for a moment in that resonance.
But see your small feet kicking under the table,
Fiercely impatient to be off and play.[1]

British Civility and Southern Manners

How the family came to be in that room—how Wilbur came to grow up in "a little British colony" in a small American town—involved a bit of serendipity.[2] In 1923, when he was two, his father, Lawrence Lazear Wilbur (1893–1976), met a British expatriate named Joshua Dickinson Armitage on a golf course in northern New Jersey. The men played their round with an Englishman named Stanley Pigeon, a mutual acquaintance. Pigeon, who spent time aboard a naval training ship with the British poet John Masefield when both were young and whose "extraordinary career doing this and that" included stints as a cowboy and an amateur violinist, had met Lawrence Wilbur while they were both enrolled at the Art Students League in New York.[3]

Armitage took a shine to Lawrence and offered him and his family, for minimal rent, residence in a handsome pre-Revolutionary-era stone house on Greenbrook Road, part of an otherwise British-style estate that Armitage was building for himself on 450 acres. As Wilbur explained in 2006, "My father and mother, who were always innocent people and willing to be influenced, took him up on it rather quickly."[4] Across the road, on property purchased from Armitage, lived Pigeon and his wife Helen.

Wilbur's father had left his hometown of Omaha, Nebraska, at age seventeen to study at the Art Students League, and he eventually became a freelance commercial artist. Though he never received the public recognition that J. C. Leyendecker, Norman Rockwell, and Howard Chandler Christy enjoyed, he was just as sought after by ad agencies and lithographic companies. His poster commemorating the fiftieth anniversary of the Red Cross brought fame to Marie Bard, his model for the nurse; her image appeared on a two-cent U.S. postage stamp in 1931.[5] By midcareer, Lawrence was receiving commissions for billboard-sized portraits of each year's "Miss Rheingold" pageant winner, and his illustrations were frequently featured on *Saturday Evening Post* and *Colliers* covers.[6] As technical advances in photography diminished the work available for magazine illustrators, he began focusing on portraits and landscape painting, glad to escape the four-color limitations of lithography to experiment with casein and watercolor.

Armitage was originally a Yorkshireman. Born circa 1866, he had immigrated to Boston's Beacon Hill from Manchester, England, bringing along his wife and a servant. On the 1890 U.S. Census he listed his occupation as a fabric designer. He held the patent for oilcloth and subsequently owned successful textile and paint-manufacturing operations in Newark, New Jersey, and in New England. By the early 1920s, Armitage, now a widower, was populating his North Caldwell "farm" with a community of British relatives, friends, and business associates, including the Nashes (his niece and her florist husband), a lawyer named Habberton, and other kindred spirits.

Armitage maintained that he had left England because of its landed gentry's disdain for men who made their fortunes "in trade." That may have been the only upper-class prejudice he rejected, for he retained the British aristocracy's Tory politics, which he naturalized into reflexive, anti-Roosevelt republicanism. Nonetheless, the people who lived in their various separate dwellings on the estate were, in Wilbur's words, "decent, attractive, civilized, kind, and gay," and living there suited his open-minded parents. Armitage, known as "Uncle," presided over his domain as if he had been born to the manor he had created, and young Dick Wilbur came to believe "that if the British did it, it was better."[7]

The Armitage estate was a multifaceted and instructive environment in which to grow up, and it offered Wilbur his first glimpse of adult society. The grown-ups organized cocktail parties and dinners, played bridge, lawn-bowled, and competed at tennis, although Uncle himself never appeared on the court. Wilbur describes that court, which was across the dirt road from the Wilbur house, as "rather strange."

> [Armitage had] laid it out in the wrong direction so that the sun was always in someone's eyes. It was surrounded by Japanese honeysuckle which flourished there and was very deep so that every ball that went over the fence took a lot of cussing to retrieve. I've never seen a surface like that

since. It was fine gravel, so that one had to drag and roll between sets; it became very dug up by people's sliding on it. But nevertheless it was not a bad court, and it was a very important center of the farm for everybody involved.[8]

On Sundays Wilbur attended church and, in season, played tennis. "The flavor of both was remarkably similar," he remembers. "The rules for behavior [on the court] were very strict, and it was a very high-minded sort of game." His early religious education, however, was somewhat less intense.

> We did say grace at dinnertime. I don't think we did for lunch, and it was never a long one, . . . probably a brisk saying of "For what we are about to receive let us be thankful." My father would never have been the one to say the grace. He'd been raised in a Presbyterian church, but not much raised. He didn't care for the piety. He'd go to an Episcopal church down in Montclair sometimes at my mother's insistence, and he'd come away saying, "Luke White [the pastor] seemed to talk sense this morning." He wanted people to talk sense and therefore had a resistance to a lot of religious talk. On some Sundays when my family was otherwise occupied I was taken by the head gardener of the farm to a nearby Baptist Sunday school, where we sang marvelous, rousing hymns and were given little tracts illustrated in terrible colors.[9]

The social spirit on the farm was cordial, inclusive, and respectful, though there were disruptions. One evening during the crisis that surrounded the abdication of King Edward VIII, Armitage declared that thrice-married Wallis Simpson was little better than a common whore. Fuming at his insult, Mrs. Habberton shot out of her chair. Declaring, "Uncle, I cannot stay at this table any longer," she abruptly left the room. The Nashes, who took a romantic view of Edward and Wallis, were distraught as well. The issue "caused a real division" and "broke up the universal admiration of England" held by most on the farm.[10]

But civility returned and prevailed, especially when Armitage's celebrity friends visited. Uncle arranged one afternoon for Wilbur's mother, Helen, to invite Sir Thomas Lipton, the tea-company and America's Cup magnate, to her home for some late afternoon refreshment. On bidding goodbye he complimented her, saying she was as charming as an English hostess. She replied, "And you, sir, have the manners of a southern gentleman."[11]

Helen Ruth Purdy Wilbur (1892–1981) was the daughter of a prominent Baltimore newspaperman, Clarence Melvyn Purdy, who worked for most of his career at the *Baltimore Sun,* moving through its ranks to become the city editor. Helen often spoke about her childhood memories of H. L. Mencken, one of the paper's eminent contributors. When he came to dinner, his laughter "began at the door and never stopped until he left."[12] Clarence Purdy, whom everyone at the paper fondly called "Pop," took his grandson Dick to the *Sun* offices to shake hands with Mencken and the columnist Frank Kent as well as with the cartoonists Edmund Duffy and Richard Q. Yardley. The experience influenced Wilbur's involvement with his school newspapers and led him to consider becoming a journalist.

Helen Wilbur was lively, literate but not learned, and a perfectionist. She was also an expert whistler who encouraged her eldest son's eclectic enthusiasms, from cartooning to shortwave radio. Nonetheless, her driven nature backfired periodically. When Dick and his brother Lawrie were very young, she was sidelined by exhaustion after a miscarriage. Wilbur's wife, Charlee, who got to know her in-laws intimately (she lived with them while her husband was in the army during World War II), described Helen as "strong of will but not of body . . . and it turned out later that she had blood sugar problems with attendant fatigue." Charlee also sensed that the cloistered ambience of the farm, where the Wilburs lived in the midst of people who had more money than they did, exacerbated Helen's aspiring social desires and compounded the stress of running the household.[13]

"Tears," a poem that Wilbur never included in any of his books, suggests that his own sense of the animosity among social classes remained acute at least into his late twenties. The poem begins with a sarcastic description of the rich, with all the "burdens" their possessions and privilege entail: "The straight old men with scalloped skulls who bear / The Atlas weight of eighty years of ease." In the last stanza, after categorizing them as ignorant, insatiable, and unappreciative, the poet can only hope they get to experience what they've missed:

> Pale porters of our wealth, who may not see
> The least magnificence with grateful eye,
> O takers of our ease, sad spenders whom
> The world can tease but never satisfy,
> I wish you other lives beyond the tomb,
> Of hunger, loss and sweet anxiety.[14]

Wilbur recalled reading "Tears" in North Caldwell at a lawn party hosted by Helen Pigeon in 1948, about a year after his first book drew critical acclaim. The poem failed to upset his parents' moneyed neighbors or the friends and Armitage family members who lived on the estate in various

Richard Wilbur and his mother, Helen Purdy Wilbur, winter 1922. *Courtesy of Richard Wilbur.*

rental or sale arrangements. They seemed to be telling themselves (with some truth, according to Wilbur) that they weren't "that kind" of rich while at the same time commenting to others, "Isn't that Wilbur boy a wonder?"[15]

The Wilbur's eighteenth-century stone house, venerable enough to be counted among those where George Washington had spent a night, had small rooms by 1920s standards. Before Uncle's tenure, in the days when the estate was primarily a farm, a large kitchen had been added in the rear to feed the hands. The Wilbur family employed live-in household servants during the boys' childhood but never more than one at a time, so the accommodations were ideal.

One black servant made a lasting impression on Wilbur. "Raymond was a pretty good cook, and when not cooking would whip on a cap and become chauffeur, and then appear in another rig as a butler. I remember him with delight," he said. "He had an amorous setback at one time. A new [child's model] typewriter had been given me and on it he typed, for the sake of a 'true confessions' magazine, I suppose, a story called 'My Stolen Love' [that] was never published. But he ruined my typewriter in the process."[16]

Helen's upbringing in Baltimore, a city with a strict black-white dividing line, complicated to some degree the Wilbur family's easy relationship with their black servants. Once, when Helen and Lawrence were away, the servants on the farm gave an unauthorized party. During the gathering someone showed Dick how to pare an apple so that the peel would fall away in an unbroken, spiraling strip. When he demonstrated this trick to his mother, she responded with suspicion about the circumstances rather than showing appreciation for her son's dexterity with a knife. Although she tried hard not to offend or show prejudice, and she genuinely liked the people whom she and Lawrence employed, she occasionally slipped into old southern ways. For instance, when calling attention to Dick's table manners, she once commanded him to "eat like a white man." As Wilbur recalled the scene, Roberta, the maid who looms over the table in "This Pleasing Anxious Being," was dishing out vegetables in that real-life moment. Everyone else winced, but Roberta, however she felt inside, remained outwardly cheerful.[17]

To express his views about social class difference, Wilbur wrote a number of poems based on observed or imagined scenes that were peopled by servants or the estate's hired hands rather than by its upper-class residents. In "A Summer Morning," for instance (from his 1961 collection *Advice to a Prophet*), he describes two servants relishing order and beauty both in the household and the natural world while their young "masters," who had partied too hard the previous night, sleep past breakfast. As the cook fries herself an egg and makes the coffee, she finds satisfaction in jelly jars lined up on the shelf, songs of the thrush and catbird in the terraced gardens, and the snip of the gardener's shears. The gardener, diligently at work before the heat of day, surveys the estate and "receives the morning." Making a distinction in the poem between what the servants satisfyingly *possess* and what the masters, in their oblivion, *own,* Wilbur echoes a judgment about the meaning of wealth similar to the one he made in "Tears."

"Thinking of happiness, I think of that"

Although Armitage's emigration from Manchester was driven by his resentment of the landed gentry, Wilbur surmised that Uncle "wanted to set up as a country squire. He had the money at least initially to do so . . . [but] less money as time went on. The scale of the farm was such that it can't ever have been profitable. The whole thing was charming, professional—he had good employees—but uneconomic, with saddle horses, milk cows, a bull, chickens, pigs, orchards, extensive vegetable and flower gardens, and hayfields."[18]

The crew of farmers and gardeners necessary to run the farm allowed young Dick and Lawrie to interfere in, or at least observe, all their operations. Wilbur recalled:

> I was involved in everything, tolerated as a child by the hands and allowed to participate in all sorts of exciting things like the spraying of the orchards and the killing of the pigs. I didn't kill a pig, but I was there when they were killed. They make an awful noise. I think if I was older I would have found some of this horrifying. But I found it fascinating as a child. Chopping off chickens' heads seemed the normal thing, and I thought it was funny when a chicken was decapitated and the body thrown out the window to run around for a while. . . . There was a lot of fun about it. I was allowed to ride in the hay wagon and bring the hay into the barn, and help shoot the silage up into the tower. Of course a farm like that is wonderful for playing games in, although Lawrie and I were repeatedly asked not to climb on the tiled roofs.[19]

Wilbur seemed to matter-of-factly accept death among the barnyard animals, but the loss of his beloved dog triggered childhood responses of fear, grief, and guilt. The collie, named Brownie, was struck by a car and dragged by the driver into a clump of pine trees and honeysuckle vine at the edge of the farm's tennis court. In "The Pardon," published in *Ceremony* (1950), the adult narrator recalls how the dog lay dead for five days, long enough for the odor of decay to mix with the heavy-sweet scent of the honeysuckle; the ten-year-old boy, transfixed, could only watch while his father dug a hole and buried the dog. This failure of nerve inspires a dream in which the speaker asks Brownie, alive and emerging from the grass in a haze of flies, for forgiveness. The moment, whether desired or real, as the narrator explains, provides closure combined with hope that the past is never past redeeming.

Exposure to the farm's flora and fauna grounded Wilbur's imagination in the natural world—not the often vague and distant landscape that Wordsworth spiritualizes but one precisely and intimately observed with a budding naturalist's informed eye and exact vocabulary. Wilbur's early enthusiasm for the world of the farm moved him to learn from books and observe in meadows, fields, orchards, and streams the life cycles of insects, creatures, and plants, which became the inspiration for the metaphoric structure of many of the poems we discuss in later chapters, notably "Water Walker" (1945), which uses the caddis fly as a trope, and "Mayflies" (1999).

Wilbur has been considered a religious poet (at least a third of his published poems are inflected by his Christian belief, an aspect of his work we will revisit) but almost never a visionary poet. When this visionary aspect does appear, it carries readers through a cycle from life to death and beyond. Six poems in Wilbur's 2004 *Collected Poems* are set (or open with a scene) on the farm. All of them qualify as visionary, and two warrant mention here: "He Was," first published in *Ceremony,* and "Running," from *Walking to Sleep* (1969).[20]

The title of "He Was" runs directly into the first of its eighteen lines, "a brown old man with a green thumb." The sounds that the speaker hears come not from the gardener's mouth but from his tools: the screak of his hoe and the "chug, choke, and high madrigal wheeze" of a spray cart soaking the orchard's trees. In the poem's last lines Wilbur shifts to language seen rather than heard: the "voice" that the old man expertly cultivated during his working life, with his hands buried in "livening clay," now rises among the leaves into the "sparrowy air" of the orchard.

In "He Was," Wilbur not only demonstrates his belief in a benign higher power at work in the world but also, by registering pleasure at seeing a man's labor come to fruition after his death, celebrates the gardener's connection to that power. For Wilbur, the gardener's legacy of flowering trees sends a message as meaningful as (and perhaps more profound than) any rendered by the spoken word. In evermore ambitious poems over the decades he has continued to explore the ways in which the natural and spiritual world reflect one other.

The first section of "Running," which is dated 1933 and set in North Caldwell, opens with a recollection of Wilbur's childhood fondness for games such as prisoner's base: he describes leaping into the air, bouncing off a hummock-side, and then sprinting across the flats, too young to tire or even to fear tiring. In the second section, set on Patriots' Day in Wellesley, the speaker is one among many spectators ("we fathers and our little sons") watching Boston Marathon runners sweep by as they ascend Heartbreak Hill. In the third and final section, we see the speaker, now pushing fifty, jogging out of the woods bordering his home in Cummington and then slowing "to a swagger," ribs aching, as the road turns and sinks toward a pasture in the west. The poem ends after he meets two boys who are throwing rocks and chasing a dog as it yaps and flushes out a pheasant from the tall grass. Imagery in all three sections evokes the movement of humans, flora, and fauna as they ascend toward and then descend from the heavens. (We return to the kinetic quality of Wilbur's verse in chapter 6.)

Such activity brings to mind Frost's poem "Birches," with its "going and coming back" to earth as well as its famous line, "One could do worse than be a swinger of birches." That poem, which opens as the speaker is observing saplings bent nearly to the ground, is often interpreted as a desire for a temporary escape, through the imaginings of childhood, from the adult world and its rationales. The speaker would prefer to think that the youngsters who swayed through the air on those pliant adolescent trees caused the trunks to bow so low, not "Truth . . . / With all her matter-of-fact about the ice-storm."[21]

But Wilbur has in mind a different aspiration in "Running" than Frost expresses in "Birches," with its longing to dip in and out of the pleasures of boyhood exuberance. In the third section Wilbur reflects on an intrinsic value of life that humans search for and want to cling to, first by acknowledging the near impossibility of possessing or even recognizing it:

> What is the thing which men will not surrender?
> It is what they have never had, I think,
> Or missed in its true season.

The speaker, who clearly identifies with such a metaphysical quest, is thus running, too, in pursuit of something he alone cannot overtake. His answer is to reclaim that joy from childhood—"Thinking of happiness, I think of that," as the North Caldwell section concludes—and bestow it as best he can on the future: "I make a clean gift of my young running / To the two boys who break into view," the speaker declares in the final Cummington section.

In both "Running" and "He Was," Wilbur's practice as a visionary poet is grounded not only in the idea of legacy—of spirit invested and reborn—but also in his connection to his surroundings in the natural world. In these poems and others like them, he has emerged on the page (much as he does in public) as a quiet, hopeful, and optimistic man. Compared to many twentieth-century poets who found the road to fame running through the valleys of despair and self-destruction—from Hart Crane and Delmore Schwartz to Lowell, Berryman, Anne Sexton, and Sylvia Plath—Wilbur may seem almost suspiciously normal.

"Be modest about any little thing"

Wilbur has described Joshua Armitage as "something of a Maecenas," a patron of the arts whose generous offer of housing had brought the Wilbur family to his estate in 1923.[22] In December 1928, perhaps as a Christmas gift to his patron, Lawrence Wilbur created a whimsical watercolor map of the property, which today hangs in Wilbur's Cummington home. Under a banner with the title "A portion of the estate of Mr. J. D. Armitage in North Caldwell, N.J.," he painted an unfurled scroll with a key to the map and a disclaimer: "A graphic design executed with an eye for depicting a few salient details and interesting truths rather than accurately conforming to the physical facts." The compass arrow points "somewhat North," and the main locations, labeled A, B, C, and D, are identified, respectively, as "The Orchard," "The Meadow," "The Deep Tangled Wildwood," and "The Old Oaken Bucket," the latter shown hanging from a rope underneath the covered well next to the Wilburs' stone house. In addition to homes, out-buildings, and farm structures such as a silo and a chicken coop, notable features include a tennis court, a pitch for lawn bowling, and a swimming pool.

Demonstrating a quirky sensibility (one that Dick Wilbur seemed to observe, internalize, and express in his own early sketches and cartoons), Lawrence left the court and the pool empty but, on a painted patch of lawn, added illustrations of figures serving a ball, doing the crawl stroke, and diving. Elsewhere on the map, scattered throughout the woods, meadows, and cultivated fields, he painted disembodied hands that point to figures engaged in activities such as hunting, bird watching, planting, and frolicking.

After living on the estate for several years, Lawrence and Helen bought the stone house. Although Armitage had built a north-lit portrait studio next to the house, Lawrence continued to commute to his studio on Twenty-third Street in Manhattan, which he still needed for his commercial work and contacts. For Dick, his father's urban workplace became a new base from which to investigate and explore. He haunted bookstores and magazine vendors, acquiring and reading much current fiction and a huge range of political journalism, including the *Daily Worker* and the *New Masses.* (Curiously, says Wilbur, his family never had a subscription to the *New Yorker,* but their modest house was filled with stacks of *Town and Country* and other magazines whose images would inspire scenes and settings for his father's commercial work.)

Lawrence was "utterly devoted to painting," and he found nothing more relaxing after a tiring day at his easel than to sit in a chair turning the pages of art books, all of which became part of Wilbur's own collection after his father's death. Art, in practice and as a subject of historical study, pervaded the North Caldwell household. In Wilbur's writing, its influence is palpable, not only in references to paintings (such the Georges de La Tour work mentioned in "This Pleasing Anxious Being") and in ekphrastic poems (such as "Wyeth's Milk Cans") but also in a remarkable essay that Wilbur wrote while he was a graduate student at Harvard, in which he distinguished Degas's approach to representation from that of his Impressionist contemporaries.

During one of our interviews with Wilbur in 2007, the subject of modesty crept in and out of the conversation. "I don't believe in a modesty gene," he exclaimed. He was talking about the fixed personality traits of the characters in Corneille's play *The Theatre of Illusion,* which he was translating at the time.[23] The discussion prompted him to reminisce about his upbringing and then about how his father, facing death, assessed the scope of his own achievement in comparison to his son's:

> I am sure I was encouraged by my parents to be modest about any little thing I'd done, and there were a lot of negative terms for those who were not. . . . I don't remember my father as saying a bragging thing, and he

was the sort of person who is good at everything he does. And he was never daunted on the croquet court or anywhere else. When he was dying my father . . . had a feeling which many dying men must have, that he was going to disappear without a trace. And he said to me during our last conversation, "All my paintings are scattered all over the place; you're lucky, all your stuff is in books." And I said to him, "But, Dad, a book can sit on the bookcase untouched for decades, whereas your paintings are up on the walls and people are looking at them and in many cases admiring them." And he agreed, tentatively, "Yes, I guess that's true."[24]

A seascape painted by Wilbur's father figures significantly in the second stanza of "This Pleasing Anxious Being," which is set on the Maine coast where the family vacationed when Wilbur was a child. He frames the scene within another picture—a photograph of a picnic in progress.

> The shadow of whoever took the picture
> Reaches like Azrael's across the sand
> Toward grown-ups blithe in black and white, encamped
> Where surf behind them floods a rocky cove.
> They turn with wincing smiles, shielding their eyes
> Against the sunlight and the future's glare,
> Which notes their bathing caps, their quaint maillots,
> The wicker picnic hamper then in style,
> And will convict them of mortality.
> Two boys, however, do not plead with time,
> Distracted as they are by what?—perhaps
> A whacking flash of gull-wings overhead—
> While off to one side, with his back to us,
> A painter, perched before his easel, seeing
> The marbled surges come to various ruin,
> Seeks out of all those waves to build a wave
> That shall in blue summation break forever.

By casting the photograph in the shadow of Azrael, the angel of death, Wilbur conveys an immediate sense of inexorability. He then exposes a strange, though mundane, aspect of our culture's affection for the family photo album, which over time exerts its power to both preserve and doom its human subjects. Note the grammatical economy with which he accomplishes this task. For instance, he pairs the "sunlight" of the picnic day with "future's glare." The word *glare* becomes an unusual personification—a vision of the future as a glowering prosecutor/judge who uses the photo as evidence to "convict" the people it captures "of mortality."

Present within the photo Wilbur describes is an image that transcends a photo's ability to freeze time: Wilbur's father painting a wave. The father sees, as his son interprets it, "the marbled surges [coming] to various ruin." Though the image of "marbled surges" nicely catches the white inlay of foam in the swelling darker water, it also involves us in real and historical time by connecting the wave to its imminent breaking (or "ruin"), as if the wave were an artifact (which it is becoming on the canvas).

One word in particular characterizes Wilbur's unflagging resourcefulness in critical moments of this poem: he calls the welling up of the water, just before it breaks, a "summation." Artist and ocean also come together in that word: the artist's imagination sums up many waves from reality's repertoire to paint and preserve the perfect one. Here is a beach scene, unlike the photo's, that has literally no downside, no mortal undertow.

In the third stanza of "This Pleasing Anxious Being," Wilbur makes swift cuts from one scene to the next. The word "flicker" in the last line invokes "moving pictures," which became the dominant medium of popular culture during his childhood:

> Wild, lashing snow, which thumps against the windshield
> Like earth tossed down upon a coffin-lid,
> Half clogs the wipers, and our Buick yaws
> On the black roads of 1928.
> Father is driving; Mother, leaning out,
> Tracks with her flashlight beam the pavement's edge,
> And we must weather hours more of storm
> To be in Baltimore for Christmastime.
> Of the two children in the backseat, safe
> Beneath a lap-robe, soothed by jingling chains
> And by their parents' pluck and gaiety,
> One is asleep. The other's half-closed eyes
> Make out at times the dark hood of the car
> Ploughing the eddied flakes, and might foresee
> The steady chugging of a landing craft
> Through morning mist to the bombarded shore,
> Or a deft prow that dances through the rocks
> In the white water of the Allagash,
> Or, in good time, the bedstead at whose foot
> The world will swim and flicker and be gone.

This cinematic focus seems to imply that what we see is all we know; the rest is inference. It suggests that our lives are films, which, like poems, flash forward and must always end. As the car plunges toward Baltimore through snow, its momentum into the dark gives the child a foretaste of riding through (and finally out of) time.

Wilbur disperses this thrust among three additional vehicles, all of them relevant because they, too, impart an awareness of danger and mortality to the person who once rode in them, whether they were real or metaphorical. The black hood of the yawing Buick morphs into the landing craft that carried the poet to an embattled French Riviera beach on August 15, 1944, and then into the "deft prow" riding over stomach-churning rapids in the Allagash. (Wilbur admitted that this river appears in the poem only because he liked the sound of its name and said that "stomach-churning" can characterize any number of his real-life experiences and adventures.) Finally, the family car becomes a ship of death crossing imagined waters over a lifetime and transporting Wilbur to the bed in which he will die.

Wilbur's construction of the stanza's last sentence demonstrates his mastery of precise and powerful implication. "The world will swim and flicker and be gone," while his own hovering "pleasing anxious being" remains the observer of his earthly life. In other words, the soul is immortal. He borrowed the poem's title from Thomas Gray's "Elegy Written in a Country Churchyard" (1751), which reflects on the lives of those buried in the cemetery by imagining a ghost who hovers over a grave and revisits scenes from the life he has just left.[25]

Wilbur's projection of his earlier self—as a boy with "half-closed eyes" who "might foresee" the dangers and death that lie ahead as snow "thumps against the windshield / Like earth tossed down upon a coffin-lid"—imbues the trip to Baltimore with a sense of life's inevitable end. The entire poem, like his father's breaking wave, is a summation of mortality as an invisible tidal force that shapes and darkens vivid childhood memories. Those memories evoke the most famous line that Gray ever wrote, also from his churchyard "Elegy," which may serve as the poem's implicit epigraph: "The paths of glory lead but to the grave."

"Adolescent necks stuck out for the yoke of adulthood"

Because Wilbur grew up in the Armitage farm's rural community, he rarely spent time with other children in his preschool years. Thus, self-reliance was not an optional virtue but inherent to his daily existence. He remembers only two boys who lived within walking distance, Rob Roy Tredennick

Lawrence Wilbur, Christmas-card portrait of his sons, Dick and Lawrie, circa 1930. *Courtesy of Richard Wilbur.*

and Medford Bach (pronounced *Batch*), not for the frequency with which they visited the farm but for their unusual names. His brother Lawrie, two and a half years younger, was his lone companion. The pair invented their own games, sometimes to indulge their mischievous spirits. For instance, when assigned to clear snow off the short front walk, they once shoveled a sinuous path several times longer than the actual walkway.[26]

Wilbur remembers that his parents had a talent for getting their sons into good schools: "I don't know how they wangled it. . . . It can't have been with money."[27] The first was Essex Fells Primary School, where Wilbur became a natural pied piper. Instead of joining his schoolmates in their playground games, he sometimes conscripted them into eccentric rites of his own devising. This trait often disturbed his teachers and the school's principal, Cathleen Tufts. During recess Wilbur once persuaded the entire student body to forgo the usual rope skipping, hopscotch, marble shooting, and ball games to assemble en bloc and parade around the school building, counting laps. Miss Tufts came outside and called a halt at lap 14.[28] His peers became increasingly intrigued by Wilbur and his quirks—for instance, his ability (in his words) to "turn his eyes inside out" so only the whites were visible—and Miss Tufts began to think of him, not in a positive way, as *capable of anything.*

One morning, as he was waiting for his fourth-grade teacher to arrive in the classroom, Wilbur drew a caricature of her on the blackboard. She was offended and took steps to identify the artist. Well aware of the boy's precocious draftsmanship, she asked him if he knew who had drawn the likeness. He answered, "I do, but I don't want to tell on him."[29] Flummoxed, and probably impressed, she eased up and complimented him for upholding the schoolboy honor code he had coolly ducked behind.

During seventh grade at Essex Fells, Wilbur organized something he called the Death Club. The club had no function other than to initiate new members (boys only). Though it involved a bit of harassing, its only relation to death was his "fascination with making jokes about morgues."[30] Nevertheless, the club's troubling name reached adult ears and gave Miss Tufts one more reason to watch him like a hawk.

Wilbur developed many "one-man interests" that helped him connect to the world beyond New Jersey. In eighth grade he took to the airwaves, constructing his own crystal set and learning to tap out Morse code. In ninth grade he assembled a shortwave radio with directional roof antennae so he could listen to voices from Europe and Asia and to broadcasts from Java's Progressive Liberal Party.[31] His childhood fascination with puzzles as well as his radio and code hobbies led him, as a teenager, to take a U.S. government course in elementary cryptography and acquire an expertise that facilitated his enlistment into the Army Signal Corps in 1942.

Despite his engagement in the larger world and his ability to enlist his schoolmates in his escapades, Wilbur told us that he was lonely during most of his high school years.

I felt like an odd bird when I was young, and I gradually became capable of the sort of ease and complacency it seems to me that some people are born with. Having had these thoughts about my feelings of oddity I thought maybe that's of no interest at all, maybe that's what everybody feels. Not everybody will own up to it, but I think of the teenagers I have known and it seems to me that most of them have had an awkwardness and inner agony going on. If there's anything interesting about me to tell [in that regard] it's mostly the struggle to find out to what uses I could put my verbalism. I enjoyed drawing pictures and using words and I've tried all kinds of ways of doing both.[32]

When Wilbur was eight years old, *John Martin's Book,* a children's magazine, accepted his poem "Nightingales," a precocious but otherwise unremarkable submission overshadowed by the second poem he sent to the editors. That eight-line verse, "Puppies," featured a set of poetic reflexes that has persisted throughout Wilbur's life. The word "opposite" will jump out at his fans:

> Said puppy one to puppy two,
> "I'm just the opposite from you.
> I always love a good hard scrub
> In a little wooden tub."
>
> Said puppy two to puppy one,
> "I was like that when I'd begun,
> But now I *hate* a good scrub
> In a little wooden tub."

Wilbur's fascination with opposites sparked an entire poetic genre drawn from the oddities of language, and his mastery of lexical mayhem has extended into a series of playful books: *Opposites* (1973), *More Opposites* (1991), and a collected volume of opposites called *A Few Differences* (2000), all self-illustrated in a style he began to develop with some notoriety in grammar school. In *The Pig in the Spigot* (2001) he delighted in exposing shorter words hidden in longer ones and then created silly verses to justify how and why they came to be that way. ("Moms weep when children don't do as they say. / That's why there's a *sob* in *disobey.*") In *The Disappearing Alphabet* (1998) he worked in an opposite way, imagining the absurd results if a particular letter were suddenly unavailable. ("No *N*? In such a state of things, / Birds would have WIGS instead of WINGS.")

Throughout childhood and adolescence Wilbur fed his early talent for developing surprising connections and comparisons by soaking up the work of the era's renowned humorists and cartoonists. In the process he honed his skills at teasing out implications and moral consequences through pictures and words. As a teenager, he amassed a collection of clippings that recounted bizarre incidents and absurdities deemed newsworthy. One from 1933 announced that a man registered at the Hotel Webster (on West Forty-fifth Street) as Frank Lynch of Fairfax, Virginia, had hanged himself in his room after writing six suicide notes, one of which bequeathed an autographed pack of cigarettes to the policeman who would discover his body.[33]

It is hard to read Wilbur's "Pity," published in *Ceremony*, without thinking he had been inspired by another such clipping, perhaps from the annals of *News of the Weird*. "Pity" reports the story of a murderer who leaves a canary trapped in its cage at the scene of the crime and then returns to set it free. In the unfolding narrative, Wilbur reveals a darkly ironic justification manifest in the damaged man's soul. As he likens the bird's escape to a bad thought fleeing a cracked brain, he suggests that, after taking a human life, it is possible to clutch at redemption by saving a bird's. Such sublimated irony and black humor appear in his grammar school musing and writings and certainly in the jaded voice of "puppy two."

Wilbur was actively involved in several youth publications, among them the *Nottingham News*, a mimeographed newsletter distributed to Boy Scout campers in 1933. His reporting for the newsletter ranged from the mundane (for instance, in an announcement that Mr. Bartlett, who had recently graduated from Springfield College with a bachelor's degree in physical education, would be returning the following summer to correct the boys' posture) to the whimsical, as in his short piece "The Difficulty of Getting Out a Newspaper (and what a paper)" ghostwritten under the name Buglestein P. Potts. Potts accused the editors of procrastination; "Neglecting [the news]," he opined, "is what they're good at."[34] Wilbur wrote for the *Scout Herald*, the *Tulip Leaf* (distributed to the Boy Scouts of Camp Glen Grey), and the YMCA's *Hi-Y*. He also published long, anticipatory articles in the daily *Montclair Times* about the upcoming Boy Scout National Jamboree scheduled for the summer of 1935 in Washington, D.C., an event that would be canceled because of an outbreak of polio near the site.[35]

Though he was physically active on the Armitage estate, Wilbur never joined a sports team. He did compete in and win a single interscholastic event, however, when Montclair High School's track team conscripted him into the high jump at a meet. His ability to leap over obstacles had been

honed on the farm and continued at Essex Fells, where he excelled at informal broad jump competitions. He usually ran the first leg of his seven-mile
high school commute, and he continued to run for most of his life. Helen
Pigeon, his godmother, a nationally ranked tennis star who had played at
Longwood, had taught him to play tennis at age eight. But Wilbur never
took to golf, the sport that had connected his father to Joshua Armitage.
In fact, as his poem "Lying" (1987) suggests (in the lines "Later, however,
talking with toxic zest / About golf, or taxes, or the rest of it"), he developed
an aversion to the game.

Wilbur's progressive politics and his attentive and respectful manners
sprang, in part, from the unusual circumstances in which he was raised.
Dick and Lawrie absorbed social graces from their neighbors on the estate,
where personal affection between the rich landowning industrialist and his
artistic tenants flourished. Although Helen and Lawrence were Republi-
cans, they did not share Armitage's extreme right-wing views or impose their
own politics on their eldest son. Nor did they discourage his fascination
with the entire political landscape and its global cast of characters (dozens
of whom he sketched in pencil, including Wendell Willkie, Groucho Marx,
and Adolf Hitler), his reading of radical publications, his support for Roosevelt's New Deal legislation, his investigation of socialism as an alternative
to capitalism, and his sympathy for the nation's suffering population during
the Depression.

Every issue of Montclair High's *Mountaineer* published during his term
as editor in 1937–38 includes a Wilbur cartoon that reveals his political sympathies and his capacity for indignation. One, responding to the
congressional debate on the Child Labor Law, shows the ghost of Lincoln
quietly calling Uncle Sam's attention to a young boy who staggers under
the weight of a sack labeled "Adult Load." Another shows a matron on her
way home from Christmas shopping. Laden with purchases, she snootily
ignores an unshaven and shivering homeless man huddling with a toddler
in the doorway of the "Cut-Rate" store.[36]

As Wilbur developed as a writer in high school, the performer's instinct
evident during his pied piper phase at Essex Fells surfaced in an increasingly
exuberant and sometimes reckless sense of humor. (A teacher named Mr.
Byrd, a cautious man who oversaw the school newspaper and didn't want
the editorials to be too violent, was always after Wilbur to read Wordsworth
as a calming influence.) When his sophomore English teacher assigned
the class to cover Shakespeare's *The Merchant of Venice* as if they were news

reporters, Wilbur handed in a detailed story with a series of headlines, including these two:

BASSANIO FAILS IN CASKET CHOICE AT BELMONT
Thereby forfeits right to marry

"POUND OF FLESH" TRIAL BEGINS TODAY
Shylock expresses his confidence in the outcome
Antonio seems concerned.[37]

Wilbur's *Mountaineer* editorials, similar to those he would write for Amherst College's *Student*, have almost nothing to do with high school issues but address either national controversies or a current idea that irritated or animated his sense of the ridiculous. He seemed not to have (as yet) internalized much inhibition or self-censorship. Usually gently, sometimes abrasively (as he would deride the upper class a decade later in "Tears"), but always with fearless glee, Wilbur chronicled the foibles and follies of whatever authority figure crossed his line of sight—a local Episcopal priest, his teachers, women bridge players, hometown or national politicians orating on Memorial Day, celebrity newspaper columnists.

During the nine months of his senior year Wilbur's varied *Mountaineer* articles demonstrated a consistent contrariness. The attitudes he displayed as a teenager are worth recording in some detail. Advocating pacifism, he assailed and then advised his readership: "You are the war makers. You, at the ringside watching bullmen batter each other, . . . peace is an individual effort. Peace is you saying 'I will not fight.' People laugh at you when you talk about turning the other cheek. Try it. It is the ultimate test of self-control."[38] He also used the forum to complain about a panoply of annoying topics: the dullness of editorials about "Christmas Spirit"; the pervasiveness of cynicism (in which he included a primer on how to make oneself a thoroughgoing cynic); the banality of suburban conversation; the insincere, automatic side of etiquette; spongers who cadge pens, cigarettes, and other handy items instead of buying their own.

On the other hand, Wilbur championed the unique nature of American humor and its brilliant contemporary practitioners, including Don Marquis, Robert Benchley, James Thurber, and E. B. White. He urged radicals and conservatives to engage in a rhythm of creation and stability that would allow the U.S. political system to do its work. He was an advocate of government support for the arts (but not governmental control or censorship of artists' works). He wrote about the characteristics of true thinking and how we mostly avoid it; the imminent decline and fall of the English language, with multiple examples cited from idle chat heard in northern New Jersey; the foibles of adults traveling down the path to self-improvement; and the wrong-headed idea that youth is the salvation of our nation. The following excerpt targeting adulthood appeared in the *Mountaineer* issue dated October 15, 1937:

> Stand next to a high school boy and you can almost hear him maturing. Hundreds of adolescent necks [are being] stuck out for the yoke of adulthood. . . . One of these years a younger generation is going to rebel. It is going to say: "The heck with becoming adult; we're immature and we love it. Go ahead and stay grown up if you want to—we're not interested." . . . The whole system of adulthood is all wrong, and has survived merely for the lack of an alternative. . . . Adulthood has degenerated into a mold. Dale Carnegie has just gotten out a book of exercises showing people [how] to be different from what they are. *Scribners* [magazine] and the psychologists have got the middle class half crazy wondering whether they are neurotics, escapists, psychotics, introverts, or just people. Think of the street of the future: throngs of people making friends and influencing people on every corner. Thousands of people who want to talk about YOUR problems. Eternally smiling, solicitous, engaging and thoroughly boresome. A frightening prospect.[39]

The seventeen-year-old who drove to Amherst College with his parents in September 1938—through Connecticut and Massachusetts up Routes 5 and 10, then called the College Highway—had graduated from high school demonstrating exceptional success as a writer and as an impromptu spellbinder. He was well grounded in the literary and intellectual habits he had been exposed to in his childhood and adolescence, was impelled to explore the larger world (physical, natural, and scientific), was impatient with convention and foolishness, and was attracted to the grotesque and the absurd. Unsurprisingly, however, he was less prepared for the social world of girls, parties, and proms. He was still uneasy about himself, despite his deep and assertive voice and his youthful but dashing appearance. Working against a seamless adjustment to Amherst's sophistication and mores was his awareness that he played roles in order to impress and possessed an overwhelming drive to succeed as a writer and editor. As the grandson of a highly respected newspaperman and the son of a commercial artist, the lure of journalism would defer his success as a student but not interfere with his matriculation as a scholar and intellectual.

2

Amherst College

"NOW THAT WE ARE IN IT"

The weekend at Amherst just past was so crowded with events and faces, so overlaid with much emotion that we are still both borne up and fatigued. To have one do anything with some degree of faith and effort is an accomplishment; that is for fifty years. Our class came back, 96 strong, and reaffirmed ties, knocked back booze like tars, danced half the night away to Dixieland strains, and we are in large part, lively and fit for over-seventy. It was heart-warming as well as great fun.

—CHARLEE WILBUR, letter to John Malcolm Brinnin, June 3, 1992

As freshmen, Wilbur and his fellow students in the Amherst College class of 1942 witnessed the ravages of nature; as seniors, they faced the hardship and dislocation of World War II. For the cover of the class's fiftieth reunion book, Wilbur wrote one of his signature opposite poems, looking back over half a century. The first eight lines introduced levity into memories of the turbulence that bookended their college years.

> The opposite of '42
> Would be some class that never blew
> With gusts and gusto into town,
> And brought the trees of Amherst down;
> Some class that did not celebrate
> Its happy graduation date
> By getting into planes and tanks
> And battleships and marching ranks,
> And making havoc and commotion
> In many lands and either ocean.

The gusts that blew into the town of Amherst on September 21, 1938, were from a hurricane whose winds reached 186 miles per hour as the storm roared up the nearby Connecticut River.[1] Wilbur's keenest memory of that day was of midafternoon, when he watched through a thick-paned door window in North Dorm as a soundless wind pulled "huge trees out of the quad by their roots." The hurricane toppled some five hundred trees at the college alone, and inevitably Amherst '42 became known as the Hurricane Class.

Over the course of their four years at the college, class members increasingly recognized that they were likely to play a central role in the war that was already engulfing Europe. Within weeks of arriving on campus Wilbur himself entered the acrimonious national debate as a pacifist, arguing that America should neither declare war against Nazi Germany nor provide military aid to the British Empire. His need to disconcert an audience, exercised during his editorship of Montclair High School's *Mountaineer,* found fresh scope at Amherst, where he seized the dual role of campus wit and political pundit. Attributing his early radical bent to an adolescent relish for asserting contrarian positions, Wilbur in retrospect has regarded his socialist and pacifist attitudes as more opportunistic than well considered. Nonetheless, the principles and logic with which he asserted those ideas in print remain impressive.

"We didn't pledge you to be an athlete"

Wilbur was exhilarated by the camaraderie and common interests he found among the students at Amherst. When normal campus activities resumed after the hurricane, fraternity pledging began in earnest, and he joined Chi Psi, the college's most athletic fraternity. The choice might have seemed odd for a boy who had never played a team sport, but his daily jogs across fields on his long high school commute had kept him fit, as had tennis— its physicality as well as its manners and genteel rituals. In 2006, Wilbur told us he believed that a poet who leads a life lacking in physical activity risks writing verse that lacks "vigorous rhythm." As a freshman, he discovered boxing in pickup matches to be a balanced mind-body exercise. "I've always liked boxing, not for its brutality but for its precision and quickness. At Amherst . . . in the ring there'd be some gloves lying there, and Tug Kennedy, who was the swimming coach, would show you a few things. He showed me what a left jab was by giving me one. He didn't knock my

Chi Psi fraternity brothers at Amherst College, circa 1941. Richard Wilbur is seated on the bench, second from the right; Frank Stockbridge, on the left, is lying on the ground. *Courtesy of Richard Wilbur.*

head off but I took notice." So did Wilbur's fraternity brother Gene Hubbard, the football team's center, after Wilbur appeared with a black eye and began occasionally complaining of headaches. "We didn't pledge you to be an athlete," he chided, "we took you into the house to raise our academic standing!"[2]

In high school Wilbur's grades had been excellent, and he brought a witty and mature prose style to Amherst. Yet his grades suffered throughout his freshman and sophomore years in college. He focused his writing efforts on the work he did for the *Amherst Student*, where, like all aspirants for the chairmanship, he began as a freshman reporter. He was also heavily involved with the *Touchstone*, Amherst's *New Yorker*–ish literary magazine. Writing in the *Student* about the *Touchstone's* October 1938 issue, a reviewer hailed Wilbur as the magazine's "white hope."[3] The byline to one of his *Touchstone* stories characterized him as "a pub-crawling, gambolling, cartooning humorist."

Late one night in their freshman year, Wilbur and his roommate Frank Stockbridge, having already downed a few beers at the Chi Psi Lodge, went out on the town. While heading north on South Pleasant Street, somewhere between the Alpha Delt house and Hastings stationery store, they began to walk like chimps, dragging their fists on the sidewalk. In later years Wilbur couldn't remember if they were trying to irritate the two cops sitting nearby in a patrol car or if they were innocently goofing around. In any case, the cops got out of the car and questioned them. Ignoring Wilbur's sidelong glance, Stockbridge informed the officer, "Sir, we shall function as we please." The officer immediately cuffed both offenders, locked them up for the rest of the night, and in the morning delivered them to police court in Northampton. Releasing them with a warning, the judge sentenced them to time served and lessons learned.[4]

"Wars are not fought in a spirit of pity"

Then as now, editors-in-chief of the *Amherst Student* oversee the competition among their would-be successors. During the fall of 1940 the job of overseer fell to Robert Morgenthau, a senior in the class of 1941, who assigned editorials and other tasks to the two juniors vying for the editorship, Wilbur and Miner D. McCrary, Jr.[5] In addition to his work on the *Student,* Morgenthau had founded the Amherst Political Union, which sponsored appearances by national figures such as Eleanor Roosevelt and Norman Thomas. The *Student* treated their speeches, as well as others by professors, politicians, pacifists, and interventionists, as front-page news.

In his *Student* editorials, Wilbur was vehemently anti-interventionist. For example, in a March 1941 editorial, he used the metaphor of a runaway toboggan to denounce what he saw as Franklin D. Roosevelt's maneuvers to drive the nation into war.[6] His editorial stance angered some students and many faculty members and alumni but especially Amherst's hawkish president, Stanley King. On occasion Wilbur satirized King as a warmonger—in print and by name.

Despite these controversies, Wilbur's boldness and pungency as an editorial writer made him the frontrunner for the editorship: he had condemned a favorable student body vote on fraternity hazing that "brought back the institution of paddling in all its medieval glory" and praised Smith College's president Herbert Davis (an obvious contrast to Amherst's King) for arguing that higher education's goal should be to "produce free spirits, and to let them work freely."[7] Morgenthau backed Wilbur to succeed him in January 1941.

During vacation that spring, Wilbur met in a Manhattan bar a U.S. sailor on leave from patrolling the North Atlantic. The sailor confirmed Wilbur's suspicions that Roosevelt had sought to provoke the Germans into attacking an American warship, thus committing a *casus belli* to which the United States could legitimately respond by declaring war. Wilbur quoted the eyewitness in the April 1941 *Touchstone:* "We've been hanging around in waters trying to create an incident. We've had orders to fire on anything that looks remotely like a German U-boat. The whole crew is nervous as hell; it's no fun just lying around hoping to be shot at."[8]

As a *Student* editorialist, Wilbur maintained not only his opposition to America's entering the war but also his composure, retaining within his scathing editorials his ability to startle, amuse, and enlighten. If Amherst's mission was to produce lucid and independent thinkers who couldn't be intimidated, then Wilbur exemplified its success. Yet the college president continued to disapprove of him, especially when stung by Wilbur's personalized barbs, such as this one in *Touchstone:* "I am told that most all authors [of letters in the *Student* protesting compulsory chapel attendance "during the current transatlantic unpleasantness"] have been hauled onto the Presidential mat. I also hear that schoolboy pranks of any sort will be punished with immediate expulsion. A little more of this and I shall feel guilty about smiling in public."[9] Wilbur resisted King's expectations that youth should defer to the wisdom of age and that Amherst undergraduates should become automatic patriots.

King wasn't the only Amherst figure whom Wilbur caricatured. In a cartoon that might have gotten him expelled had it been published, he depicted the history professor Laurence Packard (whose course was required of all freshman) as Don Quixote astride a reluctant donkey, armed with a long pen-tipped lance and about to charge a windmill whose four fan blades are configured as a swastika. Cooler heads (perhaps Wilbur's own) suppressed the cartoon, but it remains a white-hot flashpoint in his campaign against a war he believed the United States shouldn't fight.

With a typewriter as his weapon, Wilbur was a pacifist who took no prisoners. In a satirical skit, published in the February 1941 *Touchstone,* he invented an incident in which President King calls together an all-college

Wilbur's unpublished cartoon of Amherst College history professor Laurence Packard, circa 1940, at a time when many Americans did not anticipate the extent of Nazi savagery. *Richard P. Wilbur (AC 1942) Papers, Amherst College Archives and Special Collections, series 6, box 4, folder 42.*

assembly in Johnson Chapel to announce that, because Congress seemed reluctant to enter the war on Britain's side, Amherst will. King tells the gathering that he has hired a battleship and then leads the student body on a forced march to board the ship in Boston Harbor and sail her into battle.

The passion that drove Wilbur's antiwar stance reached a pitch in the last paragraph of a piece titled "The New Gloriousness," also published in the February 1941 *Touchstone:* "There is no such thing as Christian behavior between nations. . . . Wars are not fought in a spirit of pity; they are fought with canine viciousness. An American officer of the last war was quoted as saying: 'We've got to make these men dirty fighters. . . . In every respect they've got to be dirty. They've got to have the vicious look that shows a purpose to kill, kill, kill.' "[10] Given such displays of vehement pacifism, it is surprising that Wilbur expected King to offer dispassionate counsel when, in his final semester, he sought advice on his qualifications for military service.

The Declaration

Despite Wilbur's high-profile persona as an editor and eventually as an honor society member (of both Sphinx and Scarab, the latter comparable to Yale's Skull and Bones), his social life languished. He'd invited two high school girlfriends for prom weekends, but halfway through his junior year he still knew hardly any Mount Holyoke or Smith women to ask out. He turned his self-described awkwardness into humorous but practical pieces offering advice to prom goers. The first, called "Men's Rooms," appeared in a 1939 issue of the *Student*.

> When the collar hangs askew
> And the necktie drips awry,
> When the forehead glows with dew,
> And creeps a glaze upon the eye,
> Pause, my friend, and think upon
> The virtues of the simple john.
> 'Tis there the harassed male retreats
> To set his sorrowing soul aright,
> To still his heart's impassioned beats
> And turn with courage to the fight.
> Friend, who has not restored his soul
> Before the simple washing-bowl?

In the second piece he addresses potential dance partners.

> The thing that makes me
> Chew my nails
> Is girls who wear angora
> When I'm wearing tails.

On a blind date in March 1941, Wilbur met his future wife, Mary Charlotte Hayes Ward (known since girlhood as Charlee), the poetry editor

of Smith's literary magazine. Wilbur picked up Charlee on Elm Street at
Sessions House. Once a spacious pre-Revolutionary private home (with
its own secret chamber said to have sheltered runaway slaves), it became,
after 1921, a comfortable college residence in the heart of the Smith campus.
Gentlemen callers from as far away as Dartmouth, Harvard, and Yale waited
in the first-floor drawing room while the women upstairs were notified by
house phone that their dates had arrived. On that night in 1941 Wilbur rose
as Charlee entered, and they set out on foot. Within seconds she took his
hand.

In an era before dating depended on algorithms, housemates and fraternity brothers matched their college friends intuitively. In this case, Joan
Grose and Brooks Beck were optimistic that Dick and Charlee would click.
Since childhood Charlee had made her expectations clear: her ideal husband had to be both a prominent Amherst man (like both her father and
her grandfather) and a poet whose first name was Richard (as in Coeur de
Lion).[11]

In 2005 Charlee discussed her immediate awareness of Wilbur's talent,
choosing the word *combo* to describe the essential partnership and support
that sustained their long marriage. "I guess I wanted to free Dick to work,
which is one of the first things that entered my mind when I fell in love
with him. He had an extraordinary mind and sensibility; what he was going
to do with it I had no idea. I just knew when he went off he was going
to be a racehorse."[12] But although he was six feet, two inches tall with a
striking presence, many accomplishments, and an engaging manner, his
self-described oddness contributed to his shyness. Charlee's exuberance
drew him out.

The couple's histories and interests dovetailed. Charlee's grandfather,
William Hayes Ward (1835–1916), had graduated with distinction from
Amherst in 1856 and succeeded in several callings: in service to the Congregational Home Mission Society in Kansas; in science and archaeology and
as a linguist who contributed significantly to the eventual decipherment
of ancient Babylonian; as a preacher and a college professor; and, during
the last fifty years of his life, as the editor of an innovative New York–based
magazine, the *Independent*. That magazine, a liberal precursor of the *New
Yorker*, published the work of both Robert Frost and W. E. B. Du Bois.[13]

Charlee's father, Herbert Dickinson Ward (1861–1932), graduated from
Amherst in 1884 and went on to attend Andover Theological Seminary. But
at the end of his time there, Charlee said, "he defrocked himself in the

church where his father was ordained, simply saying 'I refuse,' and did not enter the ministry."[14] He then met and married Elizabeth Stuart Phelps, a highly regarded author of spiritualist novels, most famously *The Gates Ajar.*[15] Her tutelage and connections helped Herbert (who was seventeen years her junior) when he began to publish his own fiction, including a story in the *Saturday Evening Post.* He eventually became a familiar political figure in Boston, serving for a decade as the director of the Massachusetts prison system.

When Elizabeth died in 1911, Herbert was fifty years old. He met Edna Jeffries several years later, while both were vacationing in Biloxi. Edna, who had grown up outside St. Louis, was the first woman to graduate from Columbia University's law school. At the time of their meeting she was living with her parents and helping her father recover from reverses suffered in his law business. Herbert and Edna married in 1916; their only child, Mary Charlotte, born January 19, 1922, was conceived when Herbert was sixty and Edna forty.

When Charlee was two years old, Herbert moved the family to the island of Capri, thanks to the urging of Axel Munthe, a Swedish-born physician who had built his home, the Villa San Michelle, on the ruins of the Roman emperor Tiberius's villa. During their five years on Capri, Herbert tried, apparently unsuccessfully, to write a novel. Charlee's memory of those years was hazy, "and Mother's memory of it too seemed cloudy, even calculated, an amnesia of some sort. I never asked her questions because I felt something lurking under the surface that wasn't good. I was very fond of my father and found out a lot of things about him later, so that's difficult. He died when I was ten."[16] The family returned to Boston before his death, and Charlee and Edna continued to live there, summering on the Ward family estate in South Berwick, Maine.[17]

Charlee attended the Dana Hall School in Wellesley, Massachusetts:

> I was writing poetry of a horrible kind, but I was reading it all the time, and my best friend and I read poems aloud to each other all the time; that was what we did for pleasure. We collected volumes of poems from people in many states; we got lists of books from secondhand book dealers, that sort of thing. By the time I met Dick I was poetry editor of the Smith monthly magazine, and what came about with him and me was mysterious and immediate but understandable. It was a completely, and I'm not being corny, intuitive connection with us from the word "go." From the first night we were out together.[18]

On their first date Wilbur and Charlee headed to a college hangout called the Draper, an unpretentious, inexpensive hotel with a beer hall and a cafeteria on Northampton's wide main drag. During the next few weeks they saw each other frequently in Northampton, taking walks and sometimes going out for spaghetti at Joe's Restaurant on Market Street. They exchanged letters. Early in their relationship Wilbur wrote to Charlee:

> Incidentally, I have just one brother; a small muscular clown who is coming up to this other Eden next year. And I'm majoring in English. It is horribly true that we know next to nothing about each other. I am not going to pull any of this "seemed as if I'd always known you crap," but perhaps the good Lord construed us so fearfully alike that you seemed somewhat familiar from the first.
>
> Have you any sisters? . . .
>
> Mother writes me (I wrote to her about you) to say that—"don't make her walk too fast or too far, a girl can't keep up with those long legs of yours. She'd be a good sport about it, but she won't love you if you give her cramps. You really must cherish her."
>
> See you, Babe.[19]

One night they walked past Sessions and turned onto Round Hill Road, looking for a quiet place to stop and talk. They chose a dark house—the third on the left, Charlee said, which looked deserted or at least asleep—climbed its steep steps, and sat. Wilbur told her he "had been thinking" and then said that he loved her. She answered, "I've been thinking the same. I love you too."[20]

Caught up in the drama of what was in those days called "the Declaration," Charlee missed Smith's 10:30 p.m. curfew. As she and Wilbur lingered in an embrace at the back door of Sessions, two of her housemates called out from the upstairs window, "Charlee, you're late!" (A Smithie who broke curfew had to ring the housemother's private doorbell, often rousing her from sleep.) But Charlee came in radiant, saying that she didn't care about the damn curfew. She and Dick were in love. A few weeks later, in the grassy hollow between Amherst's Delta Upsilon house and the Lord Jeffery Inn, Charlee accepted his Chi Psi pin. Soon a delegation of his fraternity brothers called and serenaded her at Sessions.[21]

That spring Wilbur was invited to every fraternity's dance, a perk of both his *Student* chairmanship and his Scarab membership. Charlee thrived in the social whirl. Inspired by the girls in the local Polish community, she dressed her hair with a wreath of flowers, and she danced with everyone.

Much of the spirit of the 1920s survived intact on campus: big bands, jazz, mixed drinks, and lighthearted Hollywood-style musicals at the movie theater in town. But the festivities assumed an increasingly ominous exuberance as the semester drew to a close.

"The battleground of good and evil"

In June 1941, while most of his classmates looked eastward toward the war raging on the European continent, Wilbur and two Amherst friends, Tom Wilcox and George Shenk, decided to head west and reprise a trip that he had made during the previous summer. On that 1940 trip he had witnessed the Great Depression's effects firsthand: rather than driving or taking the train, he had hitchhiked and ridden in boxcars through forty-six states.

The three young men stopped off first in North Caldwell to see Helen and Lawrence Wilbur and then hopped a freight heading for points south. The drill was to catch a train coming slowly around a curve, grab a boxcar ladder rung, climb to the roof, and rejoin each other on top of a car. In the decades before the interstate highway system existed, freight hopping attracted huge numbers of the broke or adventurous who wanted to travel for free. One downside was the surveillance of rail hands and town police, followed by episodes of chase, flight, and escape.

On his return to Amherst, Shenk published an account of the trio's close call with a rail-yard worker and noted something even more discomfiting: "The biggest drawback to riding the rails in this posture was the thick, acrid blowback of smoke and soot, which could last for hours and hundreds of miles."[22] Wilcox suffered acutely from the engine's choking wake, so the three reverted to hitchhiking through the rural South and West.

In early July, Wilbur sent Professor Theodore Baird a postcard from New Orleans:

> I am writing primarily to apologize for a card which Shenk tells me he sent to you when intoxicated in Knoxville, Tennessee. I have not read it, but suspect its quality. An acquaintance informed me that it would be swifter, in securing cheap rooms, to introduce me as an artist. . . . We are rooming next to a whore in an airless attic, which endears us to all the bohemians and half-ass artists in town. New Orleans, and in particular, the Vieux Carré, is made up of grillwork, soldiers, tourists, antique dealers and every species of faker. But you can live on red beans and rice for $.30 a day, and talk to the shoe-shine boys, who are the most intelligent people in town.[23]

Wilbur's relationship with Baird began as student and mentor but developed into a lifelong friendship. Playful postcards from the road led to an overseas correspondence covering topics that ranged from Wilbur's wartime experience to the shared concerns of academia when he was later teaching at Harvard, Wellesley, and Wesleyan. Baird was one of three Amherst professors who recognized Wilbur's freshman and sophomore classroom performance as equal to his nonacademic or extracurricular achievements in journalism and cartooning.

In his junior and senior years, Wilbur took advanced English courses with Baird and Armour Craig and philosophy courses with Sterling Lamprecht. He began to produce original, often synoptic, accounts of literary and philosophical issues. All three professors rewarded Wilbur with admiring marginalia and, in his senior year, with straight *A*s. For Craig, Wilbur did something risky that was in fact a well-judged compliment to his teacher. He handed in none of the first few papers assigned. Then, halfway through the course, he submitted a long essay that detailed the logical development of eighteenth-century English philosophical prose, which he believed Craig had in mind when he chose the readings for the course. Lamprecht wrote, in response to Wilbur's historical critique of Protestantism from Luther through its American diaspora, "This is an astonishing performance. In more ways than one, you leave me with nothing to say."[24]

Another essay Wilbur wrote for Lamprecht in his senior year articulates the state of his religious beliefs before entering combat in January 1944 and summarizes what he saw in spring 1942 as the competing claims of religion and humanism:

> The battleground of good and evil is still the individual breast. In a democracy, the moral strength of the separate individual is an imperative necessity. If the Protestant and democratic idea of the worth of the individual, of freedom from imposed authority, is to be filled in at all by responsibility, and it must be, it will have to be a conscious, intellectual, habitual discipline such as Humanism offers. If we are to put our moral faith somewhere in an age of inquiry, it cannot be in inspiration, for inspiration in religion depends upon inherited Catholic dogma for its moral concepts, yet gives these concepts no support or refreshment, nor to Christian socialism, nor to Bibliolatry or Jesus-worship, since we no longer hold the Bible to be God's word or Jesus to be the Incarnation. Our hope, as I see it, lies in such education as exposes us to the classical tradition, with its truly practical estimate of men, its double requirement of balanced personal excellence and social participation. We must stop

believing that we can love everybody to the point of consistent virtuous action, and acquire thinking habits which will enable us to deal justly with men out of intellectual conviction, internal discipline and a clear view of the glorious possibilities of our democratic society. That, of course, is a matter for another paper.

Lamprecht underlined "another paper" and wrote above it: "Which paper has already been written, c.f. Spinoza, *Ethics,* Part IV."[25]

"How about the infantry, sir?"

By autumn 1941 the war had been devastating Europe for eighteen months, and it was becoming clear that the United States would enter it sooner rather than later. In the 1930s isolationist America had watched Japan invade Manchuria and China, then watched the Wehrmacht drive the British army off the European continent in three weeks and defeat the French in six. The nation possessed a powerful Pacific fleet, but its air force and land army had been neglected since World War I. Vacillating, Roosevelt declared a national emergency in the face of Axis aggression but backed off when politicians failed to rally behind him. He promised British prime minister Neville Chamberlain that America would fight Hitler to save Britain but never made the promise public. He agreed with his advisers that Hitler was a global menace who must be defeated at any cost. But before joining the fight he needed to convince the American public. According to pollsters of the time, Americans were evenly divided on whether or not to oppose fascism with force. The president waited—for his courage to hold firm, for the public to elect a pro-interventionist Congress, or for his hand to be forced. In purely political terms, his caution seemed justified. The military draft remained highly controversial: it was renewed in August 1941 by a single-vote margin in the House of Representatives.

Wilbur still opposed American involvement. He and others who argued against entering the conflict or even materially aiding our allies believed that choosing not to fight would spare the nation and the world unimaginable horror and death. For the nation's policymakers it was no simple matter to distinguish allies from enemies because American banks and corporations had invested far more money in Nazi Germany than they had, for instance, in the United Kingdom. Preserving neutrality and continuing overseas business as usual were priorities for a huge coalition of isolationists, pacifists, America First advocates, international investors, and American corporations as well as for millions of farmers who raised crops for export. Adults had raw memories of the last war's toll, and youth of military age dreaded the toll of the next one.

In his "toboggan ride" editorial Wilbur had warned that Roosevelt's newly passed lend-lease legislation, which allowed the nation to supply arms and warships to Britain, would provoke Germany to torpedo American shipping and plunge the United States into a cataclysmic world war. But few foresaw Pearl Harbor.

On December 7, 1941, as they drove back from a trip to Connecticut with two other Smith-Amherst couples, Dick and Charlee heard the news on the radio. When their friends dropped them off in Northampton, they headed for Joe's Restaurant. After the waitress brought spaghetti they sat numb, not eating, barely talking. Eventually giving up on their cold dinners, Wilbur walked Charlee to Sessions and then thumbed the eight miles, over the Connecticut River and along Route 9 through rich Hadley farmland, back to Amherst.

Once in the Chi Psi Lodge, he wrote the editorial that would appear in the December 8, 1941, issue of the *Student*. On the front page, in its own box, the article's all-caps headline read, "NOW THAT WE ARE IN IT." With these resolute but dispassionate words, Wilbur abandoned the antiwar stance he had advocated since his freshman year. He believed he spoke for his generation, the first in history, as he had earlier written, "inoculated from birth with a dislike and mistrust of war." In his December 8 editorial he addressed the crisis and the college in a chastened tone and faced, with ironic exactitude, the enormity of what lay ahead:

> We all knew that we'd be in it soon enough, and it's just as well that it started this week, as next. We are now relieved of the scholar's obligation to hunt a few plain issues in the war, and can commence to act, which is simpler. . . . We needn't rhapsodize over our intervention like the editor of the *Williams Record,* but we should suppress our obstructing doubts . . . confining our thoughts to the job before us, and to the post-war world, which it will be our great pleasure to put together. Now that we are fighting, what is needed is unanimity and determined action. . . . If we feel any allegiance to the race in general, we will strive to make the post-war world more hopeful and less combustive than the world of the past twenty years, to which we are now bidding a noisy farewell.[26]

Wilbur didn't disown his prior doubts about the wisdom of intervention; rather, he recognized their irrelevance. He focused on actions that he and his generation must immediately take and then turned his attention to the distant but inescapable problem of reordering the postwar world so it would be "less combustive."

Stanley King addressed the college that morning in Johnson Chapel, which, as the *Student* reported, was "packed to capacity and almost electrically charged by the excitement of the Pacific situation." King predicted a long war against "wily adversaries" but had no doubt that the "United States will mobilize at once the whole force of the nation—military, naval, air, industrial, financial." He also warned: "The country will have no use for slackers, slackers in the service, slackers on the industrial front, slackers in the routine of daily living." He charged the sea of faces before him to "do your work here until you are called up for service, and do it well."[27]

Life on campus militarized overnight. Wilbur continued to publish critiques of both national policy and King. Yet on several occasions during the spring semester of his senior year, he visited King's office, hoping the president's experience during the Wilson administration (as an adviser at Versailles and an envoy to Russia) might help him choose his branch of service and specialty. To be able to choose, he would need to enlist before his draft notice came. In 2006 Wilbur reconstructed the pattern of dialogue in these exchanges with King:

> Do you think me well qualified to join army intelligence, sir?
> You may have problems there.
>
> How about the infantry, sir?
> Too much grit needed for that, lad.
>
> Perhaps the navy?
> The gentleman's service? That might not be a comfortable fit.

It seemed that King thought him unqualified for any military employment whatsoever. But the president's skepticism stung less than this pointed rebuke did: "Mr. Wilbur, there are, in wartime, men willing to follow orders even when they know that doing so might cause them to be killed. I don't believe you're that kind of person."[28]

As graduation approached, Dick and Charlee weighed two options: should she finish her degree at Smith or marry Dick before he went to war? Smith discouraged its students from marrying and in fact expelled women, even those who were of age, who married without their parents' consent. Therefore, Charlee chose not to complete her senior year, even though

Dick and Charlee Wilbur set out for their honeymoon to Boothbay Harbor, Maine, June 20, 1942. *Courtesy of Richard Wilbur.*

Edna Ward did not object to the marriage: "When my mother came up to get me for Christmas vacation I said to her in the car, 'You're going to be shocked but Dick and I have decided that we must be married.' And much to my astonishment she didn't launch any protest whatsoever. In the light of what had happened in the world, she understood it."[29]

Edna also understood the futility of arguing with her daughter. "She had wanted me to come out, have my debut in Boston, because my father had wanted that, and I absolutely flatly refused," Charlee said. "One morning at Smith I opened the Boston paper, and there was my picture, with a notation that I was making my debut. I had a horrible blowup with her; told her under no circumstances was I going to do that, and she'd have to call the paper. And I'd have nothing to do with her until that was settled."[30]

Dick and Charlee married on June 20, 1942, at the Ward family's summer home, Hayes House, in South Berwick. She wore, according to a local newspaper, "a very becoming princess basque gown of Mousseline de soie with long train, a veil of tulle, [and] a cap of rose point lace trimmed with orange blossoms."[31] A matron and a maid of honor as well as four bridesmaids attended the bride. Wilbur chose Frank Stockbridge as his best man. Lawrie Wilbur, as well as Dick's rail-riding buddies, Tom Wilcox and George Shenk, and Richard Head, a friend from Montclair, served as ushers. Wedding guests drank champagne and danced in the barn to records played on a Victrola.

The newlyweds honeymooned in Boothbay, Maine, for a few days—practicing Morse code, according to Wilbur—before his mother called to tell them that the envelope from Wilbur's draft board had arrived in North Caldwell. They immediately boarded a Pullman for Manhattan. When the train arrived, they headed downtown to the induction center on Whitehall Street.

Wilbur weighed his enlistment options. As a college graduate, he was eligible for Officer Candidate School if he scored at least 90 on the army intelligence test. The prospect of joining his Amherst classmates in the commissioned ranks was at first appealing. But he learned of a more attractive option for a couple who had been married for less than a week: if he enlisted as a common soldier in the Signal Corps Reserve, he and Charlee could be together for six months while he studied radio transmission and repair. So he enlisted in the reserve, and they rented an apartment in the Village on Christopher Street.

Charlee found a management-trainee position at Macy's. Her primary qualification may have been an assertive and sympathetic personality, but her practical experience didn't hurt: she had worked during the summer of 1940, between her freshman and sophomore years, in Filene's "College Center" as a fashion consultant, part of a team of seven young women representing New England colleges. The Macy's job required her to work in many different roles—on the floor in the fine china department, for instance, and in human resources, where she was able to hire Wilbur part time to sell miniature radios on Thursday mornings and on Saturdays. As the holiday season approached, she got him a stint as a "helper" who herded children and parents into line to see Santa.[32]

Wilbur's Signal Corps training took place uptown in a vacant school. He and Charlee settled into a daily routine. Charlee's hours at Macy's were 9 a.m. to 5 p.m. whereas Wilbur's classes met from 3 to 11 p.m., an accommodation for reservists who still held civilian jobs. Charlee would meet him uptown after his last class, and they'd take the bus or subway back to the

Village, sometimes stopping for a drink or a late-night snack. On weekends they visited with Lawrence and Helen in North Caldwell or with Wilbur's best friend from Amherst, Tom Wilcox, who had enlisted in the navy and was training in Mansfield, Connecticut.

Wilbur aced the demanding and highly technical Signal Corps course, but in December he still didn't know where he'd be sent for basic training. On New Year's Eve, as Charlee recalled, she attempted to lessen one uncertainty in their future by abandoning birth control, hoping to conceive a child before Dick was put on active duty. On January 22, 1943, he took his oath on Whitehall Street and was immediately bused across the river to Fort Dix, New Jersey, to begin basic training. By then, Charlee was pregnant.

3

World War II, Stateside and in Italy

"War poetry shd. deal with the one and the many"

All's hugger-mugger here, but one thing is perfectly plain, that we are going overseas in the next few months, which I look forward to with frank excitement & pleasure. And relief; it will probably be much more restful overseas.

—RICHARD WILBUR, letter to Armour Craig, October 4, 1943

In April 1943, while training at Camp Edison to become a cryptographer in the U.S. Army, Richard Wilbur read a poem published by Allen Tate in the *Partisan Review* that celebrated "our young pro-consuls of the air."[1] Provoked, perhaps, by an aversion to Tate's praise of an empire on the march, Wilbur quoted a few lines from the poem in a letter to his Amherst College mentor, Theodore Baird. Reacting to Tate's poem, Wilbur implied that World War II poets should not repeat themes of the Great War's poets—Rupert Brooke's sentimental patriotism or Wilfred Owen's and Siegfried Sassoon's disillusion and fury at Britain's ruling class. This generation's war poets ought to look beyond the fighting and their own hardships to include afflicted civilians: "War poetry shd. deal with the one and the many, is my guess."[2] This statement foreshadows the ways in which Wilbur's war poems would reflect, both directly and obliquely, the suffering that war caused and yet say nothing polemical about war's futility or the stupidity of commanding officers.

"A real old impasse"

For Wilbur, the *Amherst Student* and *Touchstone* had remained free-speech zones even after the nation entered the war. But at Camp Edison, in Sea Girt, New Jersey, his leftist expressions and his willingness to criticize both army policies and Roosevelt's management of the war began to strain the tolerance of his commanding officers. Even though Wilbur was immersed in secret code training and privy to highly sensitive information, he continued to speak his mind, conducting himself as if the army were just another educational institution willing to respect his exuberant free speech. He soon discovered, however, that the army had made a preemptive assumption: freely expressed radical opinions could lead to acts of treason.

An informant relayed Wilbur's conversations with barracks mates to an intelligence officer, and his subscriptions to "subversive publications" such as the *Daily Worker* (and perhaps the FBI's perusal of his prewar *Student* editorials) triggered a clandestine search of his footlocker. After officials discovered a copy of *Das Kapital,* he was expelled from the Signal Corps. On or about July 22, 1943, army officials removed him from his training classes without explanation. Writing to Baird on August 5, Wilbur expressed frustration about his now-uncertain work as a code expert:

> When an impasse occurs in the Army, it's a real old impasse. I have been out of training for two weeks now, and the War Department cannot decide what to do with me. A week ago the first Sergeant told me that I was going to Washington with a "hot assignment." The orders were cancelled at the last moment. Shortly afterward I was ordered to Colorado, but that was also revoked. I keep adjusting myself to the idea of working in that unimaginable Pentagon building, then to the idea of scrambling letters in Boulder, and then to every blasted idea that rumor brings along. And rumor is our daily bread.
>
> The army has the "keep 'em busy so they won't brood" theory, as you'd expect. So I have been lackeying around camp these two weeks, cleaning grease pits at first and mowing lawns; but finally I found myself a white-collar job preparing G.I. lectures. I sit in a lieutenant's office in dress uniform with many books about me, and write the notes which a hundred unfortunate lecturers must adhere to.
>
> I don't like this "keep 'em busy" program because I don't brood and am able to keep myself busy. Some people brood. One chap down here found the Army pretty uncongenial, & thought it all out & decided to see what would happen if he shit in his foot-locker for 10 days. On the 10th

day there was a foot-locker inspection, and the inspecting officer with no hesitation declared that he had a disorderly foot-locker. The chap got a mental discharge, which I think he had richly deserved. Other people have less imagination, like the one who fired an M-17 on the range the other day with the muzzle in his mouth. But by and large my colleagues are either contented or stoical, and don't brood much.

The irritating thing about hanging around is that I go home on weekends & say I am bound to ship next week, & the neighbors shake my hand and clap my collarbone and say they're sure I'll come back a hero, as a descendent of Light Horse Harry Lee should, and put extra rum in my tea & give me advice like pissing on a sock if my gas mask goes bum etc., and then I say goodbye to my wife and my family. Then back I come next weekend without even so much as a wound, & feeling very disappointing indeed.[3]

Wilbur remained with his unit when it moved on August 8 from Camp Edison to a secret training facility at Vint Hill Farms Station, a rustic wilderness camp in western Virginia. Yet despite the August 7 notations his commanding officer had made to his service record at Camp Edison—he was rated "Excellent" for both "character" and "military efficiency"—he was still kept out of the code classroom.[4] For a while he received martial arts training in judo as well as tumbling lessons and instruction in the use of grenades and bayonets, in preparation for a possible transfer to a commando unit, but that assignment never materialized.

Politically based dismissals from the Signal Corps were common. In May, some six weeks before his removal from code training, Wilbur had written to Baird about his "red friend" Leslie Schwadron, whose Marxist principles and skill at union organizing Wilbur admired, but not uncritically.

[Schwadron's] imperatives are very few—trust the humanitarian emotions, honor the individual; it seems to me the activity of Marxists is in inverse proportion to their concern with the dialectic. He has been very active. In the school at Sea Girt an hour per day is given to current events, & after the 2nd day he simply took over and lectured for an hour each day. An FBI spy posing as a private in his barrack turned his name in, & half the Regiment has been called to H.Q. for secret interviews concerning him. He will probably be given an S.D. [Suspected of Disloyalty] on his Service Record. These are easy to get—a Chapel Hill Prof. at Sea Girt got one because he used to have Negroes like Richard Wright to dinner (in North Carolina) & belonged to the Teachers' Union. The FBI would rather have you a Ku Kluxer than a Union man.[5]

Wilbur was still at Vint Hill on October 1, 1943, when Charlee gave birth to their daughter Ellen. The army granted him an immediate three-day compassionate leave. Writing as if he were still a humorist for *Touchstone*, Wilbur explained to Armour Craig what had happened when Charlee went into labor at his parents' home in North Caldwell:

> At 4:30 AM Charlee . . . rousted out Mother. They sat around staring at the Ingersoll and counting pains. Dad got up at 7:30 and decided to have breakfast. Lawrie, home on furlough, got up at 7:45 and started to pack his luggage for the return. At this pt. Mother and Charlee decided that they damned well better hurry, so Mother got the car and they were all ready to roar off when Dad appeared on the lawn clutching a napkin. . . . "You're crazy to be going off without any breakfast," he said. "Don't you want some fruit or milk?" "You don't understand," said Mother, trying to be calm and succeeding too well. "Don't be silly," said Dad. "Don't you want something, Charlee? Milk? Toast?" Charlee said that she wasn't very hungry. . . . Lawrie then flung up the bathroom window and shouted, "I can't find my shampoo or my gas mask!" Mother said his gas mask was on the hall table and that he could have Dad's shampoo. "What color is the bottle?" yelled Lawrie. Mother lost her calmness and cried, "Lawrie, you and Dad don't understand that Charlee is having a baby *any second!*" Dad, walking back into the house, called over his shoulder that they could have had breakfast while they were standing around yelling.[6]

Less than a week after Wilbur returned to Vint Hill, the army consigned him to Camp Shenango, a giant replacement depot in western Pennsylvania. Wilbur described it as housing criminals (petty or worse), shirkers no outfit wanted, and other undesirables, like himself, who were awaiting shipment overseas. Sporadic violence had occurred at Shenango before Wilbur's arrival, including a race riot in mid-July 1943 that began at the PX when a white soldier and a black soldier exchanged racial slurs. In the ensuing brawl other soldiers took sides.[7] The army's official history of the camp summarized the outcome: "The depot commander separated the two groups, but the blacks reportedly returned armed with rifles and ammunition and started firing on the whites. Military policemen returned the fire, killing one black soldier and wounding seven others."[8]

In the summer and fall of 1943 the American military suffered heavy casualties in its North African campaign and its invasions of Sicily. Commanders called for an infusion of fresh troops, however ill trained or potentially troublesome, to bolster Lieutenant General Mark Clark's Fifth Army in Italy. The army began to transfer replacements from Shenango to Hampton

Roads, Virginia, where they boarded troopships for North Africa. Wilbur was aboard one that sailed on November 13.

On December 8 Wilbur arrived at Bizerte, Tunisia. Three days later he wrote to his Amherst friend Tom Wilcox, lamenting the "ripping good time" he'd be having if not "encumbered with an army." The long sea voyage, Wilbur said, had proved to him that "ontological thinking on the ocean is dangerous and timeless."

> It is a splendid country . . . littered with anomalies. The whole city is Dada and makes a peace-born American wonder greatly what is the norm of *la condition humaine.* A bathtub leans on a road sign, an Arab slips along in G.I. pants and a turban, children go to school in the parlor of a brothel, a breach in a nunnery wall gives on barbed wire and sacred statues. Our place and location is secret, to *you.* We eat much and well. My only complaint is that this is artichoke country—and our cooks don't boil us any. We drink something, which laughing up our turnovers we call cognac. This is an anti-freeze called vino.
>
> The other night we went out looking for firewater and one of my friends addressed an Arab as follows. "Hey Charley, where the hell do you get liquor around here." The Arab gasped and did not speak and we trundled away. "These brethren," said my friend, "can't answer a fucking civil question."[9]

"The strangeness of battle noises"

After ten days in Africa, Wilbur boarded a troopship in Bizerte and, on December 21, arrived in Naples. The Fifth Army had seized the city on October 1, pushing the Germans back thirty-five miles north, to the Gustav Line in the Apennines. Since then, as Wilbur discovered, the infield of the Hippodrome in the suburb of Aniano had been converted into a vast and picturesque replacement depot, essentially a military job fair where soldiers queued up in front of desks manned by officers looking to match their units' needs with the qualifications of available men.

At first Wilbur was assigned to guard one of the Hippodrome's many entrances, primarily to prevent curious or famished Italians from crashing the picnic—which is what the depot's field kitchens and campfires resembled. Although he disregarded orders and allowed the throngs to enter, nobody seemed to mind. When his stint at the gate ended, he joined a roving group of rejected trainees and disreputables from Camp Shenango who were yet to be assigned. None had been trained to use the standard-issue

Garand rifle—a major downside, they agreed, when applying to join an infantry unit. Wilbur's own training had qualified him to fire only the 1917 Enfield, a weapon no longer in use.

When they learned that a paratroop division, the 82nd Airborne, was signing up infantrymen and promising to train them to jump, use the lighter airborne carbines, and execute behind-the-lines combat tactics, Wilbur and a friend headed toward its tent. As they crossed the infield, a voice reverberated from the loudspeakers: "*Richard P. Wilbur!* Report to the 36th Texas Division's headquarters immediately."[10] Wilbur changed course and headed toward the 36th's tent, where he met, at the division's Signal Company table, its commanding officer, Captain Charles "Foxhole Charlie" Wingo.

Wingo's interrogation of Wilbur demonstrated the sharp difference between stateside army officers, who defended themselves against worst-case scenarios for which they might be blamed, and frontline officers, who were replacing battle casualties and cared only about finding men trained to do specific jobs. The 36th Texas Division had lost more than a thousand men during its invasion of the Italian mainland at Paestum. Thus, it needed hundreds of infantrymen and scores of officers, particularly second lieutenants. But the division also needed one highly trained individual who could work a SIGABA code machine; one of its three code technicians had gone mad during the fiercely contested and precariously secured Paestum landings.[11]

Captain Wingo read aloud from Wilbur's service record, a small, narrow book rubber-stamped with dates and covered with ink scrawls.

> "I see you're fully qualified in cryptography and radio operation."
> "Yes, sir."
> "It also says here that you want to overthrow the government. Well, do you want to overthrow the government, Private Wilbur?"
> "No, sir."
> "Then I want you to join our message center. But if we catch you overthrowing the government, out you go."[12]

Late one night in early January 1944, as the 36th Texans deployed near Monte Rotondo, a Jeep delivered Wilbur to a farmhouse where the soldiers of the message center had requisitioned sleeping quarters. The next morning, he wandered outside to inspect the grounds and found the artichokes he'd been longing for in Tunisia. Here, in the kitchen garden, they were growing like weeds in the Mediterranean climate. He harvested a few

Richard Wilbur mans the command center's phone at the 36th Signal Company headquarters, Italy, 1943. *Courtesy of Richard Wilbur.*

ripe ones, brought them to a boil over a campfire, improvised a sauce from G.I.-issue butter, and carried this breakfast to the mess table. When a Texan asked what the hell he was eating, Wilbur characterized himself as a Yankee improviser living off the land. He did not want to seem like an effete East Coast elitist within a cohort homesick for hog cracklings.[13]

Most of the men in Wilbur's new unit were native Texans who had joined the division when it was a reserve unit operating out of Fort Mabry in Austin. Because the Signal Company had suffered fewer casualties than the 36th's infantry regiments had, it had received fewer replacement troops from other parts of the United States and thus retained throughout the war its Texas accent and attitudes. Like its counterparts in other divisions, the Signal Company was a small unit (in Italy it had about 220 men) and was charged with keeping information flowing from army headquarters to division commanders and from the commanders to the troops on the ground. Its means varied: shortwave coded messages (Wilbur's assignment), local radio transmissions, telephone landlines radiating from division headquarters to the regiments in the field, message-carrying Jeeps and motorcycles, ultralight airplanes, and, briefly and unsuccessfully, carrier pigeons.

Less than three weeks after Wilbur's transfer into the 36th, the division was ordered to prepare to cross the Rapido River. Camped on the river's eastern side, the men were soon under constant mortar and airburst fire, and Wilbur became a connoisseur of ordnance noise. He sent the following descriptions to Charlee, meaning to be funny but instead causing alarm at home:

> You cannot conceive the strangeness of battle noises, however vividly the movies may present them. For one thing no movie can convey their incessancy and the continual jar of them. It is possible to learn the sounds of outgoing [Allied] artillery and gun-fire, so that you've no apprehension when they go off, but the blighters make you jump just the same. You never get used to them. We'll be lying in our tent at night, reading by a candle under a pierced can, then suddenly there will be a crump, crump, and the ground will quiver. "What the hell is that?" one will ask. "Bombs, I think." "Ours, or Jerry's?" "That's mortar fire, incoming." "The devil it is; you hear that boiler-factory sound?" "I think that's B-2 bombing." "What do you mean, B-2 bombing?" "Be too god damn bad if we were under it." "Shut up; listen to that." "That one's ack-ack." "The devil . . ." and so on.

> It makes for rather silly conversation, but explosives force themselves on your attention. Some of them have most peculiar sounds. Some machine guns sound like rural telephones, then some like goats. Some shells coming in are like someone dropping a laundry bag on the floor above, and others sound like the last 10 4ths of July. There is a sound like a croup cough, and one like a braying horse. Shells coming over have an unsympathetic rush and scream. And some blooming thing sounds like a whip in the air, to the 10th power, followed by a pound on a timpanum [*sic*]. The echoes of the out-going artillery are long and rambling, and sound like a runaway freight. Now, that should be enough homely similes for you; but I do think they're fairly accurate.[14]

In mid-January, as the men were building up for the Rapido crossing, Wilbur's code duties were limited to eight hours a day. During his off-hours he aided the division's efforts to alleviate the war's impact on civilians. Because the retreating Germans had stolen the locals' harvests and slaughtered their livestock, villagers were starving in the countryside around the Texans' encampment. Italians of all ages gathered daily at prearranged sites to meet the U.S. troops who had been sent to distribute their uneaten rations. Serving leftovers to famished Italians led Wilbur to write the first poem he'd attempted since joining the 36th. For this poem, and for several others that date from his first weeks at the front, he chose unrhymed free verse. On each draft he noted the town nearest to the scene that had inspired him. In the case of "Hand-Dance," the village was Maddaloni:

> When our tents were staked in the dry vineyard,
> (blanched olive-leaves, and the tree-bark
> bitten with shrapnel)
> Women came daily up the path from the village,
> One who cried always, white as Lazarus risen,
> I remember her hands.
> They made a dance of hunger.
>
> First the thin fingers, fine as bird-bones, reached,
> Quickly bent back from hope. Their little lances
> Stung, but her fear stung more.
> She shot her hands
> Downward to flee her voice, closed on her pride
> And I might read the proud white bones,
> (the skin was like old ivory, and transparent).
>
> Then her head fell down
> The hands rose full and open, and the palms
> Held silken shadows.
> Art can so abstract,
> Though it rise out of hunger, I could forget
> To bring her body bread, watching her little
> Hand-dance.[15]

This somber and observant poem conveys a time-honored theme: art rising out of pain and suffering. In this poem Wilbur suggests that the power of art lies in not only its ability to evoke feeling in response to suffering but also its potential to distract the beholder from the root of the suffering.

In "Two Statements," also written in Maddaloni, Wilbur presents a pair of very different scenes. First, he watches an Italian man transplant roses with a care that reminds him of his mother gardening in North Caldwell, especially in how he cradled the roses, "As if they didn't entirely belong to him; / It was his having a kind of respect for roses."[16] These lines echo two others from the "The Beautiful Changes," the title poem of Wilbur's first book: "Your hands hold roses always in a way that says / They are not only yours . . ." They also reiterate the idea of gardening as a legacy that appears in "He Was," a poem from *Ceremony*, which (as we discussed in chapter 1) describes how an orchard bears fruit long after the death of "a brown old man with a green thumb."

In the second scene of "Two Statements" Wilbur switches to first-person plural, a composite voice that combines the stories of several village women:

> When the war passed here, we went and lived in a cave,
> Up on the hill. We had a terrace there,
> There was not much food, my husband is weak since Africa.
> Many days, we boiled dandelions.
> Down in the town they fought in between the houses.
> The boy went down once, I told him not to go down;
> There was a dead man lying outside in the orchard
> And some in the well.
> All of the buildings went down, at night there were fires,
> It was like watching the face of a dear one insane.
> Now we are back in the house. The hole in the roof,
> It will be all-right while it is summer, the soldiers
> Came and took out the grenades,
> I like to hear
> The stonecutters' hammers down at the street;
> They are mending the statues. After such things
> It is not good to rest, it is not like resting.
> It is much better
> To wake in the morning hearing the sound of hammers.[17]

Wilbur never published any of the poems written during his first few months of combat. But in Maddaloni he began to act on his conviction that war poetry should include "the one and the many."

"Completely surrounded by Texans"

In late January 1944, the Texans' immediate objective was to establish a beachhead on the western side of the Rapido, toward Rome. Meanwhile, across the river the 15th Panzer Division and its machine gun nests and artillery calmly waited in carefully prepared positions to prevent them. At the time Fred Walker, the general in charge of planning and leading the attack, was the oldest division commander in the U.S. Army. During World War I he had watched the Germans attempt to make a river crossing during the Second Battle of the Marne that was as foolhardy as the one Lieutenant General Clark was ordering him to execute now.

The Rapido was only about forty feet wide, but it was deep and had a current as swift as its name. The river was a major component of the German defenses across the ten-mile mouth of the Liri Valley. The Germans had dug in their machine gun and mortar positions so they were immune to all but direct shell bursts. Clark's plan for the 36th involved cumbersome four hundred–pound canvas boats that Walker's men would have to portage for more than a mile to the crossing points—and the German artillery possessed the exact coordinates of those points. When the division's engineers tried to span the torrent with rickety footbridges during the night attack, all but one of the structures were quickly destroyed. The troops who did make it across the river were pinned down, picked off by concentrated German fire, or captured. Very few made it back across the Rapido when Walker ordered the inevitable retreat.[18]

As Walker detailed in his postwar memoir, he had serious misgivings about the wisdom of sending two regiments across the river in one night. Nonetheless, he followed Clark's orders to attack, hoping for a miracle. When the worst happened, Walker persuaded Clark not to throw more lives after those he'd already lost, requesting a truce so that both sides could retrieve their dead and wounded. The Germans agreed, and the war was suspended on this horrific stretch of ground for six hours. Wilbur, new to his job, had been stationed well behind the lines during the Rapido attack but heard nauseating stories of the huge number of dead underfoot (and under wheels) as the trucks brought the bodies back from the river and its mudflats. Reflecting on the attack in 1997, Wilbur said,

> I never heard anyone say at the time that a *difficult* crossing had been ill-planned by the divisional command, or that an *impossible* crossing had been ordered by Mark Clark in deference to higher-ups who felt that there would be psychological advantages to taking Rome before such and such a date. Those conflicting views were never heard by me until after the war. I suspect that ordinary soldiers don't usually know, in a broad strategic sense, what the hell is going on, and so don't do a lot of informed criticizing.[19]

The 36th was no longer capable of engaging the enemy after its heavy losses, and in late January it returned to a bivouac above Naples to absorb and train thousands of urgently needed officers and troops. Blaming the disaster on the division's tactical leadership rather than on his own strategic hubris, Clark immediately replaced most of Walker's headquarters staff and his regimental commanders, though he left Walker himself in command.[20]

When the 36th rejoined the fighting in the Liri Valley early in February 1944, it was stationed near the town of Cevaro, directly beneath Monte Cassino and the ancient Benedictine abbey, once the home of Saint Gregory the Great, on its heights. In the valley the Signal Company's message center was within easy range of the German artillery, which was never silent for long and whose shells burst frequently within the company's perimeter. A truck in which Wilbur worked his eight-hour shifts on the code machine was parked in a garage at the edge of Cevaro, on the side closest to the mountainside town of Cassino. Close to the code truck, Wilbur and his fellow signalman, Bobby Parent, dug a deep two-man foxhole, where they spent most of their time when not working.

Eventually a British reconnaissance unit camped and dug in nearby. Daily at 4 p.m., one of the Brits would build a smoky fire to boil tea water, which every day attracted the attention of the German artillery crews, with predictable results. After a couple days of near misses, Wilbur walked down to chat. He politely explained that when the Germans saw the rising smoke, they fired their guns toward it. The tea brewer responded, "Were you in Africa, soldier?"

Wilbur said, "Briefly, but I didn't fight there."

"Well," said the Brit, "I did, and came to realize that we get a few of them and they get a few of us. But in the end it evens out."[21]

Both aerial reconnaissance crews and ground observers in the 36th suspected that the Germans had been directing artillery strikes from within the abbey. Although the German field commanders insisted that they were not occupying or using the structure for any military purpose (the Geneva Convention forbade them from doing so), they did admit to visiting it from time to time to dine with the monks.[22] Whether or not the abbey was actually used as an observation post, Field Marshal Harold Alexander, the Allied commander in the Mediterranean, was swayed by its looming presence and its adverse effect on troop morale. He decided to send in scores of B-17s and Lancasters to bomb it into rubble.

Wilbur was on duty in his 6 x 6 (a six-wheel-drive army cargo truck) when he decoded the message: the abbey (which had already been destroyed twice by sacking, once by an earthquake, and rebuilt three times since its founding in 529) would be hit at 9:45 on the morning of February 15. In an effort to spare the hoards of refugees who had sought shelter in the building, Allied planes had dropped leaflets warning them to evacuate immediately.

But hundreds did not, and were killed in the daylong bombing. Wilbur's short story "The Day After the War" (1946) describes what he saw that day from below: "The mountain went all dirty crimson and green smoke like a bonfire bursting into burning, [while you were] waiting with your flesh afraid [and] your bones eaten out with ennui."[23] Other observers in the valley said the mountaintop suddenly resembled an erupting volcano.

Shortly after the abbey was destroyed the 36th pulled out of the battle line and moved south to Caserta for rest and further training in cold-weather mountain combat; the Texans needed both, having failed in their two previous missions. The message center staff was skilled at improvising celebrations during such respites, as an account Wilbur sent home makes clear:

> We gave a party for some of our allies [from New Zealand] last night. 10 of us threw in two dollars apiece, which got us 2 5-gallon cans of white wine. We built a bar in the corner of our stable, and set ration-boxes about for chairs. We set candles in the stalls, which gave out a dim irreligious light. In our partitioned meat-plates we put cigarettes and rolls of lifesavers. From somewhere we dug up a set of three glasses of various shapes, and from the rafters we hung Scott tissue, in swirling semicircles. It was a pleasant bit of idiocy, & quite a success, though connoisseurs might have grimaced a bit over our choice of swill.[24]

When training in the field resumed, Wilbur's bunkmates named their abode "Harmony Tent" to reflect the peace that ensued after a daily release of aggression they called "Animosity Hour." Wilbur described the routine to his mother: "We may all be horrid & rotten to each other."[25] But protocols that encouraged amiability were prudent within tents that mixed Texans with a few New Englanders, as Wilbur reassured her:

> I think you shd know that I am completely surrounded by Texans. They have a violent defensive provincialism. Once while the unit was in the States & having a party, a Northerner was very badly beaten-up for refusing to stand while they played "Deep in the Heart of Texas." I really think Texans are abashed by the East; their reaction is physical, & they are particularly proud of having "ripped that old Massachusetts apart while we was there."[26]

Still, several Texans were capable of spoofing their state's bellicosity. Sergeant Sidney Bruton from Houston once stood up in a bar full of message center comrades and after only one drink shouted, "God damn it, I can lick any gawd damn man in the place. Get the hell out, all of you. I'm tough as nails and I'm going to clean out the joint." Then he breathed a loud "pooooufff" and sat down smiling.[27]

"A great index of human possibilities"

Despite its battered condition and deprivations, Naples, the only large liberated city in Europe in March 1944, had reverted to its timeless role as a tourist destination; its entertainment and prostitution industries mobilized to receive on-leave G.I.s. On March 18, a group from the message center, including Wilbur, piled into a 6 x 6 for a day in nearby Pompeii. After arriving they went off in different directions—some to bars, some to whores, some to cultural pursuits. Wilbur and a few others took the opportunity to tour the partially excavated ruins of the ancient city. A Greek refugee guided them: she deciphered Latin inscriptions and graffiti and explained the mythical subjects of the wall paintings, the uses of each building, the sophisticated water systems, the courtyard architecture—everything that sustained daily life until Vesuvius spewed hot volcanic ash and mud on August 24 in the year 79.

Vesuvius erupted again during Wilbur's visit. As black flakes began to fill the air, the Greek guide panicked and fled. The message center group walked through the ancient cobbled streets and retreated to a bar just outside the ruins. While ash fell thickly and evenly on Pompeii, both ancient and modern, they drank a bottle of brandy and joked about improving their slouching postures at the bar; if the ash kept falling, they might be committed to those positions for centuries. One of the drinkers remarked that he'd never felt closer to Pliny the Elder, the prolific scholar who died in the great eruption.

Most of the men in the group had never heard of Pliny the Elder. Wilbur later compared this man's sudden identification with him to a remark he'd heard from a drunken soldier, who, on the ride back to camp, showed off his souvenir, a replica of the ancient sculpture that depicts a she-wolf suckling Romulus and Remus: " 'How about that,' he said. 'Man, ain't that the dirtiest god-damn statue you ever saw?' " The train of thought inspired one of Wilbur's finest essays, "Round About a Poem of Housman's." It begins by describing the Vesuvius eruption he experienced and states that historical and cultural references play a powerful but potentially audience-diminishing role in poetry.[28] Modern readers, Wilbur wrote, are likely to miss the point of allusions to people such as Pliny and mythological characters such as Romulus and Remus. Should poets restrict themselves to familiar and contemporary references, or connect their own time to the past with allusions that might confuse or put off less sophisticated readers? The essay argues for the value of historical parallels: "The past . . . both temporal and timeless . . . is, above all, a great index of human possibilities. It is a dimension in which we behold, and are beheld by, all those forms of excellence and depravity that men have assumed and may assume again."[29]

The form of depravity on Wilbur's mind was one that A. E. Housman had lamented in "Epitaph on an Army of Mercenaries" (1922), his poem about common British soldiers who were sacrificed during nineteenth-century colonial wars in India and Africa, not for a noble cause but to benefit a callous aristocracy trying to preserve its empire. In contrast, Americans in World War II were fighting a just war to save Europe from Nazi subjugation, and Wilbur's reference to Housman's poem helped him define that justness. Like the soldier who sympathized with the doomed Pliny, Wilbur saw history as a powerful means to magnify the scope and authority of a poem that takes off from a present moment or concern: "For every poet, whatever he may say as critic or polemicist, Pompeii is still a busy quarter of the City of Imagination."[30] Six months later Pompeii was still in Wilbur's mind as he wrote "First Snow in Alsace" (later published in *The Beautiful Changes*), in which flakes of snow reverse the menace of Vesuvian ash by blanketing and healing a war-punished landscape.

In mid-May the 36th was shipped to Anzio and held in reserve until it was needed for the Fifth Army's breakout offensive. The entire beachhead was under relentless German shelling, including monster blasts from Anzio Annie, the railroad cannon with a twenty-five-mile range that its gunners kept in an impregnable mountain tunnel. The entire 36th Division dug foxholes and slept inside them, and Wilbur inventoried his in a V-mail to his parents.[31]

> I have dug myself another marvel of primitive architecture: 6 x 3 x 3. Reading from the clay floor upward; evergreen boughs, oak leaves, a sprinkling of insecticide, mattress cover, two blankets, mosquito netting, pup tent. I am to be found between the two halves of the first blankets, my hands, face and hair smeared with GI Insect repellent. (Time Magazine remarks: citronella repels bugs abt 15 minutes. Whereas GI repellent keeps you happily ostracized for 3 to 4 hours. Of course it feels like pure acid, but it does the job.)[32]

Action resumed when the Seventh Army's VI Corps (150,000 men commanded by Lieutenant General Lucien Truscott), preceded by a thousand-gun artillery barrage, launched its massive drive north from the Anzio beachhead at 6:30 a.m. on May 23. The 36th Division, with Wilbur and the other signal corpsmen, advanced behind it. German field marshal Albert Kesselring's battle-savvy defenders had already dug in south of Rome across a forty-mile front. After five days of a determined but tactically predictable attack on what the Germans called the Adolf Hitler Line, the Allies were stalled.

On May 29 Truscott called a meeting of his division commanders at Fred Walker's headquarters, a huge dairy barn near Velletri, a strategic walled town two miles west of Monte Artemisio and about twelve miles south of the front lines. Truscott informed Walker that on May 30 his 36th Division would take over the attack on the German line west of Velletri from the spent 34th. Walker was dismayed. He had just spent a sleepless night devising a way to exploit a situation that his patrols had discovered: on the steep, four-mile-long slopes of Artemisio (running northeast from Velletri and Highway 7), small German units armed only with rifles and bazookas defended a two-mile-wide gap atop the mountain. A junior officer had also found an overgrown logging track on Artemisio's south slope.

The division's chief engineer, Colonel Oran Stovall, had warned Walker back in January that the Rapido crossing was doomed. So on May 29 Walker, Stovall, and a scouting party explored the mountainside to check the accuracy of their relief maps. Stovall, whom many historians see as the war's most skilled combat engineer, now saw that a passable track for heavy armored vehicles could be bulldozed up the mountain during the dark of night and into the following day.

Walker immediately ordered his staff to prepare two distinct sets of plans and marching orders, determined to confront Truscott with a forceful proposal for his alternative attack route. The two generals met at 9 a.m. on May 30, and Walker laid out the detailed plans for his alternative: a classic infiltration and flanking maneuver. Truscott was impressed, asked for an hour to consider, and, despite his own chief engineer's scornful opposition, gave Walker the green light before noon.

Immediately, the 36th began to truck its forces from its bivouac, ten miles south of Velletri. It embarked on a sixteen-mile loop toward the east, intending to confuse German forward observers, then circled back to the west and debouched the 142nd and 143rd regiments (a total of 9,000 men) at the foot of Artemisio. Meanwhile, the 141st prepared to launch at dawn a diversionary attack on Velletri.

Just beyond the crest of Artemisio lay a volcanic depression. Beyond the depression were the Roman hills, the lakes Nemi and Albano, and back roads stretching over rugged terrain for ten miles toward the last mountain village, Rocca di Papa. Beyond and below Rocca lay the wide-open Roman plain. At nightfall on May 30, Walker put his plan into action. He ordered the men of the 142nd and 143rd regiments to remove the ammunition clips from their weapons. They were to refrain from shooting, smoking, or talking and would follow the white tape his engineers had laid up the ancient logging track and around the extinct volcano. The sergeants passed the word through the ranks: any soldier who fired his weapon would be court-martialed.

In the wake of the two regiments, who advanced up the mountain on foot, came thirty-six bulldozers, each biting off and pushing aside foot-wide chunks of volcanic soil. Engineering troops with spades, explosive charges, and huge two-man saws (to fell and remove the larger trees) followed to clear and shape the road. As the slope steepened, Stovall reduced the number of bulldozers to fifteen. Behind the vanguard, Sherman tanks, tank destroyers, artillery caissons, and ammunition trucks edged uphill, heading for the heart of Rome.

The 36th's advance parties surprised and captured a few German forward observers, one while bathing naked in a chilly brook. Some light German resistance slowed their progress through the hills south of Rome. But by dawn on May 31, advance units had made headway through the hill towns, and the infiltrators on the Highway 7 side had swarmed in behind the German lines and were attacking Velletri. When tanks and motorized artillery arrived on the western ridge of Artemisio, they began to lob shells into the now-exposed German garrison hunkered behind Velletri's medieval walls. Within a few hours the surviving Germans decamped through a rear portal. The 141st moved into the city, and the 142nd and 143rd fought past Rocca di Papa. On June 4 they broke through the last organized German defenders south of Rome.

"Yesterday was all madness"

On June 3, Private Wilbur and several other signal corpsmen were detailed from the rear to help lay wire to the 36th's advance command post, now established underneath a railroad underpass on Highway 7, just north of Velletri. A Jeep dropped off Wilbur and the other men at the worksite; then the driver, Corporal Lloyd Tywater, circled back, returning a few minutes later with Lieutenant Colonel David Barton, the division's new intelligence officer. General Walker had ordered Barton to bring a field telephone forward along Highway 7 for his personal use. To indicate where the telephone should be left, Walker had parked his own Jeep at the underpass, with its two major general's stars visible to northbound traffic. But Barton and Tywater apparently missed or ignored the Jeep and raced through the American lines into a German machine gunner's sights. Wilbur looked up, aghast, as the Jeep whizzed past his wire-laying team: What the hell was Tywater up to? Minutes later, both Barton and Tywater were killed by German machine gunners, a thousand yards down the road from where Wilbur was working. Their Jeep remained skewed across the roadway for several hours.

The report of Captain Paul Wells, the commanding officer of the Signal Company, conflicts with both Wilbur's eyewitness account and Walker's journal entry. According to Wells, "LTC Barton and T-5 Lloyd E. Tywater were killed by enemy small arms fire as they rode along Highway 7 north of Velletri. . . . From all available information, they were en route to recon the village of 'Rocca di Papa' . . . for possible use as a relocation of the 36th Division Command Post." Wells, who wrote this account many years later in his memoir, was almost certainly misinformed or mistaken.[33] The village of Rocca di Papa, the highest point in the Colli Laziali, the hilly region northeast of Anzio, was more than twelve miles away from Walker's forward command post, located along a side road that veered northeast into the hills. On the afternoon of June 3, Highway 7 beyond Artemisio was still contested ground, infested with German tanks, snipers, rear-guard machine guns, and bazookas, and Rocca was still in German hands. Would Walker have ordered or permitted Colonel Barton to undertake such a suicidal mission? His journal states explicitly that he ordered Barton only to stop and deliver the field telephone to his Jeep. He gave no instructions for a reconnaissance, and his journal expresses his puzzlement and regret.

Later that day, Wilbur and a small convoy of other message center troops piled into Jeeps and 4 x 4s (four-wheel-drive trucks) and followed the freshly bulldozed track up the slopes of Monte Artemisio. They pulled off the track in the dim moonlight to rest until dawn—the officers in a roadside cave, Wilbur and the other non-coms outside it. A German sniper fired occasional shots in Wilbur's direction until, for the first and only time during the war, he returned fire. The sniping ceased.

The next morning Wilbur and his friend Jack Yore waited for transport in the glassed-in lower story of a hillside house that overlooked the road through the Roman hills. Their conversation turned to Hollywood films. They agreed that Westerns were modern counterparts of the ancient European war epics; they approved of the modern genre's dramatization of moral virtue and the courage needed to assert it. Suddenly a German shell, just missing the house, exploded the window glass around them.

A Jeep arrived to pick them up, and the soldiers proceeded down through the hill towns onto the flat plain where many roads converged toward Rome.[34] Wilbur later recalled glimpsing the wide, fixed eyes of a dead German, who seemed to be staring up at him from the roadside. The Jeep skidded sideways, and a wheel grazed the soldier's head—a moment Wilbur alluded to in his 2008 poem "Terza Rima."

By 10 p.m. on June 5, the 36th Texans, in trucks and Jeeps and on mobile artillery, had followed the tanks of the 1st Armored Division into the southern outskirts of Rome. They paused, expecting to camp in the spacious back lots of Cinecittà, home of Italy's movie industry. At about midnight, however, Walker received an order from Truscott: rouse the 36th, move it through the Roman streets before dawn, past the Vatican and up the Gianicolo hill, and prepare to chase the retreating Germans along the northwestern coast toward the mountain town of Tarquinia.

The Signal Company was apparently excused from the general's order, for its men stayed behind at Cinecittà and slept through the early hours of June 6. Later that morning they crossed Rome to bivouac as guests inside the Vatican walls, where Wilbur took the opportunity to write to Charlee:

> I took off my underwear—with a chisel—and showered under a cascade of water gushing from the wall of a bombed factory. . . . I have been kissed on both cheeks, fed tumblers of Vino, hand-shook, pickpocketed, mobbed by candy-mad urchins, had grown men tell me they love me, been called "Liberator," pounded on the back and so on. With a few draughts of wine in me I lost my Northern restraint and commenced tossing children in the air. . . . My worst scare was having the roof shelled off the second floor of a house, on the first floor of which I was unhappily lying. I should like to shake the hand of the man who made that ceiling; I just ducked broken glass and sweat like a nigger at election-time. All's well now.[35]

Charlee immediately copied the letter and sent it to Helen and Lawrence with the following note: "I was so excited reading this that I could hardly hold the V-Mail in my hand and had to sit down as my knees were shaking so violently."[36]

The 36th moved out of Rome on June 8 along the Via Aurelia and its network of roads to pursue the Germans retreating into Tuscany (where the enemy's resourceful engineers would build another lethal defensive line). The Signal Corps followed. On June 10, the third day of the pursuit, a truck carrying Wilbur and four other message center men veered off the main track of the division's advancing tanks and infantry, an error they didn't realize until Italians on the roadside began shouting at them. Wilbur described the upshot to Charlee:

> Yesterday was all madness. There were five of us—four Pvts and a Cpl., in the back of a 2½ ton truck full of military secrets, and we got lost. Went by a few farmhouses in an otherwise deserted stretch of country. The people ran out of the houses waving their arms like mad. "I don't like the way they wave," said one of the boys. "They act as if we are the first Americans they've seen." Finally, we stopped the truck and crawled out to quiz the civilians: They'd seen only two other U.S. vehicles (presumably recon cars). There were Germans in a house 200 feet away. There was fighting "about 5 km back there where you came from." "Maybe we ought to get our carbines," said somebody. "They're in the truck under the chairs, tables, sofas, and bedrolls," said another. We dug them out and turned the truck around and headed back for our lines. We didn't see any Germans. We didn't see any GIs either, no blown-up vehicles, no dead horses, no craters, no bodies, no noise—absolute pastoral tranquility and yet we were kidding around a couple of miles behind the wrong front lines, and it all seemed so perfectly asinine that we commenced laughing like idiots, and I broke out your box of Cadwell's candy-bars, and we had our back-to-our-side party as we rolled along.[37]

By June 29 the 36th had fought its way past Grosetto and Venturino and had halted just south of the coastal town of Cecina, about seventy miles from Florence. There the 34th relieved the division, and a less-than-appreciative Lieutenant General Clark relieved Walker of his command, despite the fact that his brilliant maneuver had hastened Rome's liberation and saved many Allied lives.[38] For the next six weeks Wilbur's letters home brimmed with simple pleasures and a blissful release from tension. He wrote from Paestum: "Today I had two steaks with a mountain of French fries. Things are looking up. ⅛ mile from here is a fast clear river. . . . The flow is so swift you have to swim your hardest to stay in one place, but this has the advantage of leaving you where you went in, when you get tired. It's very cool water, + vital on days of sapping heat like this."[39] In June, as the Roman festivities were dying down, Wilbur had told Charlee that his "taste for history [was] quickly satisfied." Rather than remain awed by what the Fifth Army had just accomplished, he now wanted to "indulge [his] recurring appetite for the personal and supposedly trivial."[40]

During this rest period at Paestum Wilbur completed "Tywater," his elegy for the Jeep-driving corporal killed by German gunners, which follows in its entirety. The poem focuses on the flamboyant Tywater, once a rodeo rider in Texas and possessed of unsettling skills and a penchant for violence. Writing about the thrills and danger inherent in Tywater's virtuosity seemed to intensify Wilbur's own poetic craft, for he abandoned his recent unrhymed iambics for brief terse stanzas with resounding rhymes. He also left behind the present-day war, alluding only to wars fought long ago.

> Death of Sir Nihil, book the *nth,*
> Upon the charred and clotted sward,
> Lacking the lily of our Lord.
> Alases of the hyacinth.
>
> Could flicker from behind his ear
> A whistling silver throwing knife
> And with a holler punch the life
> Out of a swallow in the air.
>
> Behind the lariat's butterfly
> Shuttled his white and gritted grin,
> And cuts of sky would roll within
> The noose-hole, when he spun it high.
>
> The violent, neat and practiced skill
> Was all he loved and all he learned;
> When he was hit, his body turned
> To clumsy dirt before it fell.
>
> And what to say of him, God knows.
> Such violence. And such repose.

The tone, unusual for an elegy, is at first cool, distant, and jarring. In the first line Wilbur played sardonically on ancient British titles and names—Nihil echoes both Niles and Nigel—to convey that Tywater is in thrall to the need to destroy (in the second stanza, for instance, he takes dead aim at a sparrow) and, given how he dies, perhaps to his own destruction. Yet the poem's grinning hero exhibits adroit and admirable prowess: he throws knives, shoots guns, ropes calves, and tosses lariats. Everywhere the poet's artistry is present, and the suddenness with which the poem extends and emboldens Wilbur's range of reference is notable: it offers a classical allusion to "ai," the bitter cry of pain that Apollo etches with his tears on the newly formed petals of the hyacinth; it uses adjectives evocative of battle, such as "charred" and "clotted," to modify pastoral words such as "sward." Wilbur's lifelong ability to rhyme naturally conversational phrases, a practice Robert Frost urged poets to follow instead of constructing lines around handy end rhymes, is evident in every stanza.

On October 1, 1987, Polly Tywater Burton, Corporal Tywater's sister, discovered the poem in a national magazine and wrote to Wilbur, describing the "eerie feeling" of suddenly reading about her brother "forty-three years and four months" after his death. She asked Wilbur to send her an autographed copy of "Tywater" so she could frame it with a photograph of her brother. In the note she wrote in thanks, she explained, "I alone know how you captured the true spirit of Lloyd, because I suffered a lot of rope burns from being lassoed so often."[41] Tywater, who himself may have wearied of the daredevil figure he cut, once confided to Wilbur: "I just want this motherfucking war to end. I just want to go home to Texas and screw my ole lady."[42]

When dead, the reckless Tywater of Wilbur's poem leaves no legacy except for puzzlement on the part of narrator, who in the final two lines defers to divine judgment: "And what to say of him, God knows. / Such violence. And such repose." Inexplicable as the real Tywater's death seemed at the time, Wilbur *did* know what to say, and how to say it, as he encountered the greater violence to come in France, Austria, Dresden, Berlin, Kufstein, and Hiroshima.

On August 10, 1944, Wilbur and the 36th Signal Company sailed from the port of Naples toward the southern coast of France, part of an armada of 885 warships carrying the Seventh Army (with Truscott in command) and 1,375 smaller landing craft. Five days later, at dawn, American troops invaded the Riviera at eight locations from Nice to Cape Nègre. Wilbur's detachment came ashore at midmorning on a secured beach a mile east of Fréjus. The fifty-five soldiers of his message center unit were among the roughly 220 members of the Signal Company who provided the communications equipment and expertise needed to connect Major General John E. Dahlquist's 36th Division command headquarters to its 15,000 troops.

German artillerymen stationed inland had already blown up several ships, including one LST full of ammunition.[43] But the Texans' landings near Fréjus had caught the Germans at a time when they had shifted most of their forces toward the north and west. The enemy's best available unit, the 11th Panzer, could not arrive from eastern France in time to oppose the four Free French divisions that came ashore after the three American divisions (the 3rd, the 36th, and the 46th) and liberated the ports of Toulon and Marseilles. Though shelling and small-arms fire from coastal and inland strong points lasted into the night and delayed the progress of the Allied forces, the 36th suffered few casualties, and the Seventh Army's VI Corps (under Truscott) quickly established and extended the beachhead.

Wilbur's narrative of the message center's progress through France and Germany, written in postwar Germany as a semi-official history for the unit's members, referred to the Fréjus landings as "a peaceful arrival."[44] In a letter to his parents he described the mood on his LST as it approached the beach, some hours after the arrival of the 36th Division's first wave:

> We sailed to a point 10 miles or so off the coast . . . [and] came [in] riding a snubby bouncing job [an LST] . . . smoking lots of cigarettes, & keeping up . . . a strenuous line of banter [and] . . . you can't help feeling an exhilaration. The guy in front of me prayed incessantly. When we skipped up onto the sand I ran out anticipating all hell, but it wasn't there. I didn't fire at anything and nothing fired at me, except for a three-minute session of rather shabby shellfire, which I sat out in the gully. I can report that I am altogether in good repair. My pores are gently pouring, my respirations are deep, with happy little whistles on the ends, my eyes are clear nearly to the point of vacancy. I've got a nice stretch of light-olive parachute silk, which I'll get some madam or mademoiselle to make into a scarf.[45]

Once ashore, Wilbur waited for transport to the message center that was being assembled in the village of Boularis, a mile west along the coast road. Always curious, he opened the unlocked gate of an impressive waterside villa, the sort with a name such as "La Mimosa" or "Villa de Hier" spelled in wrought-iron script on its stucco façade. Inside the deserted mansion he found a well-stocked library and began to explore its contents. This tropism toward books and quiet was characteristic of Wilbur and shows how readily he could be distracted by literature, even under fire. He pulled a slender book from a shelf, sat down in a comfortable chair, and began reading it. The book was *Helmbrecht le Fermiêr,* a French translation of the long medieval German poem; other than a Wehrmacht helmet and a Colt revolver confiscated from its Austrian owner, it was the only war spoil he took home. It would prove unexpectedly invaluable to his career.

4

World War II in France, Germany, and England

"OBOE VICTOR EASY ROGER"

Let's realize that the [atom] bomb cannot be relinquished as a military weapon. Let's realize that another war would slaughter all creatures indiscriminately, and reduce our great cities to cinder. And let's therefore set out in a practical way to make a peace that will stick. Until we do we are all under sentence of death.

—RICHARD WILBUR, editorial, *T-Patch*, October 28, 1945

From Boularis along the coast, Wilbur's detachment moved rapidly north with the Seventh Army under Truscott—a headlong advance through the Alpes Maritimes on the vertiginous Route Napoleon that required frequent dismantling and repacking of heavy electronic gear into 6 x 6 trucks. A message center advance party, arriving in recently secured towns, would locate and requisition suitable working space and sleeping quarters in abandoned barracks, hotels, schools, large residences, farms, and garages; when no permanent structures were available, the men would pitch a capacious command tent. Then the race would begin to get radios and code machines operational.

When Wilbur arrived in Boularis, he took on the responsibility of writing a semi-official account of his unit, later compiled as the *History of the 36th Signal Company, Message Center Section* and covering the period between August 15, 1944, and May 8, 1945. His intention was to enable the men in his unit to recall both the immediate and the larger contexts of their experiences in France, Germany, and Austria. He addressed them directly

71

in the preface: "This isn't a diary, and it isn't a history. It does not pretend to be literary. The purpose of it is to help you remember the places you've been, the things you've seen and sweated out, and the guys you shared the time with. Just about everybody is mentioned, but of course I couldn't tell you everything about everything."[1] Wilbur was not an eyewitness to everything that happened; his accounts of the division's activities from mid-April to early May, while he was on leave in England, were reported secondhand. Thus, the voice in Wilbur's *History* is often more objective than the one in his letters home or in the poetry he was beginning to compose. But the *History* was not his only forum for addressing his peers in the service. After V-E Day, he wrote numerous columns and opinion pieces for the army newspapers *T-Patch* and *Robert Reveille,* where he began to address the consequential issues his generation needed to face in the postwar era.

"Bouquets and 20-odd kisses"

In town after town the festive, affectionate French of the Midi welcomed Wilbur's detachment during the earliest days of its march north. Accommodations in private homes were usually comfortable; the food was hearty and often splendid; and the soft mattresses and plentiful access to baths and showers evoked prewar memories. A French couple once relinquished their own feather bed to Wilbur and slept in the hallway instead; one woman laundered his trousers overnight. Members of the unit developed an active social life with these French civilians, and some soldiers conducted brief romantic affairs.

When Lieutenant John Mercaldo fell passionately in love with a young Frenchwoman from Duxelles, he judged his French skills adequate for coping with townspeople and shopkeepers but not eloquent enough to express affection in private. He asked Wilbur to ghostwrite a *billet-doux.* Being more fluent than most of his unit, Wilbur was frequently called upon to translate in both official and social situations. "My French works pretty well," Wilbur wrote to his parents. "Sometimes I don't even have to think before I gabble, but I haven't managed to coordinate my face and my words. I speak always with a worried look, & suspect the answer is to forget the damn syntax and just talk."[2]

Early entries in Wilbur's *History* convey the high spirits that prevailed during the days after the invasion. Between August 17 and August 20 the message center staff stayed at a communal farm in Collet Redon, just north of Fréjus. Wilbur noted that one farmer's ample wine supply "made our duties far lighter," and that "everybody ate a good deal of grapes on the house."[3] Nonetheless, even though the unit was not often exposed to close-range German fire, artillery barrages left more than a dozen men dead or wounded by the war's end. As the designated chronicler, Wilbur often adopted a tone of Anglo-American understatement when recounting exposure to enemy fire. Explosions that failed to kill anyone were noted as momentary inconveniences. Describing one work space in a "frowsy type of barn" with a "thick atmosphere of onions," he wrote that the "personnel kept up an endless game of poker" interrupted only by a shell fragment that came "tickling over the tiles of the barn roof."[4]

A few days after the landings at Fréjus, the German divisions that had been caught out of position near Marseille began to surge north up the Rhone Valley, intent on returning intact to their homeland. Wilbur was part of the detachment handling communications for the motorized Task Force Butler, assembled and named by Truscott after its commander, Brigadier General Fred Butler. Originally intended as a reconnaissance force, it was quickly ordered to block German infantry, tanks, trucks, horse-drawn wagons, and heavy equipment heading north along the two-lane Route 7 that parallels the Rhone.

The 36th Division, now divided into smaller units, fanned out east and west across a 125-mile expanse between the Swiss border and the Rhone, stretching the message center's personnel and equipment thin. Wilbur's detachment had set up its machines on the north edge of Marsanne near Route 7 when the city came under heavy German bombardment. Having wandered alone into the city center before the barrage began, he experienced a moment of real fear. He took shelter in a giant warehouse, where he lay on his stomach, his "blood yelling" but his "marrow cold as the marble floor." During a lull he ventured outside and found another lone soldier, who turned out to be Wilbur's division commander, Major General John Dahlquist. Radio communications with Dahlquist's three regimental combat teams had broken down. Now, after a sleepless all-night Jeep ride to Marsanne, the general was disoriented. Wilbur explained he was himself looking for the message center. Dahlquist responded, "You're lost, Corporal Wilbur? Well, I don't know where most of my division is. Somewhere downriver blocking the highway, I hope."[5]

Task Force Butler had retreated. Regrouping after the first German attack, it then moved north by heading inland and blocked Route 7 further upriver, enabling air strikes and artillery to destroy and disable hundreds of stalled enemy trucks, guns, and tanks and to kill, wound, and eventually capture more than 20,000 Germans from their three retreating divisions. One was the still-formidable 11th Panzer. Ultimately, half of the 250,000 men of the German army in southern France were killed, wounded, or captured by the Seventh Army.

On September 4, corporals Tucker and Wilbur were operating a courier service between the temporary command post in Bourg and the signal agency in the Bois des Seillons. In the course of their shuttle trips, as Wilbur wrote in the *History,* they collected "a back seat full of bouquets and 20-odd kisses."[6] Two days later their unit arrived in the old and beautiful town of Arbois and set up camp in a school building once used as a German barracks. In a letter to his parents posted on September 9 from Arbois, Wilbur described what he had learned from a pharmacist who had confided in him:

> He was a young guy with a pretty wife and three handsome kids, extremely intelligent and gay people. They'd been well-to-do people before the war, but there was a munitions plant in the northern town they lived in, & the Americans bombed the whole town flat. [The pharmacist told me,] "Nobody was angry, though we had lost everything. After the bombing we came out of the cellars crying Vive l'Amerique!" He thought, as even the most informed Europeans do, that all Americans are filthy rich. I told him that we had many poor who lived in greater poverty than could be found in France. He replied, "But you are all rich in liberty." He pointed out the window at the public square, where a gray stone fountain played. "On the steps of that fountain I saw [German soldiers] take five young men and kick them in the genitals, beat them in their faces with gun butts, and then shoot [them] dead. I had a friend, the best surgeon in this department. He took care of one partisan who was wounded: the Germans dug out his eyes with a fork and with little knives cut off his arms and legs." I have never seen such hatred as these people have.[7]

On the afternoon of September 16 the unit entered Luxeuil, where they found "the citizenry . . . assembled before the City Hall to celebrate the liberation of the town by shaving the heads of *collaboratrices.*" The following day Wilbur wrote to his parents about these public humiliations, which occurred all across France when towns and cities were liberated:

On this fine evening I . . . had my hair cut and Lucky-Tigered by a barber named Schmitz, and was plied with homemade kirsch (made from native cherries) by another barber. Kirsch tastes about like Lucky Tiger. The barber was called away in the midst of a toast to clip the heads of several married women of the town who'd slept with the Germans—this is done in public with much spitting, dousing, & slapping of faces. In one town we passed through, they had a list of 84 such women but didn't dare make a start on it, as it included the mayor's wife. (I spent an evening drinking with that mayor, & wondered why he seemed so dolorous.)[8]

During the first day of the 36th's stay in Éloyes, Wilbur watched a haycart move slowly along the main street while German prisoners followed, picking up their own dead and hoisting them, in tarpaulins, onto the cart floor. He later described this corpse-retrieval cortege in "Fingers." The poem, darker in tone than "Tywater" and never published, reflects the French citizens' hatred for the German invaders. Wilbur personified the Germans' defeated and powerless state by focusing on the uniformed sleeve of a dead soldier whose now unthreatening hand—which remained, in Wilbur's eyes, an individual human being's, right down to its fingerprints—salutes an audience that is glad to see it dead.

> Under shocked walls the antique haycart goes,
> Loading at door and gutter tarpaulined dead.
> Heaved to the dusty planks, and laid in rows,
> Loosely they roll, discovering heel and head.
>
> Thrust from tenebrous windows, heads of crones
> Follow with strengthless gloat and jagged smile
> The young men dead, above the hopping stones
> Carelessly riding the bitter staring mile.
>
> Rigor of death has raised one greensleeved wrist.
> The hand appears to wave.
> The fingers, curled,
> Waggle and point, and cannot make a fist:
> There are no two alike in all the world.[9]

In October, as the 36th Texans crossed the Moselle and advanced into Duxelles, they moved into a new phase of the war: "No more quick, long jumps, and no more 'champagne war.' The enemy had now assembled his forces and prepared his positions, winter was coming on, and the terrain

had become mountainous. The division's command post remained in Duxelles for twenty-one days, and at no time was the fighting out of earshot." In
the *History* Wilbur noted how the attitude of the civilian population began
to change: they had less tolerance for the "circus parade" aspect of war in
which enemies and allies marched alternately by, shelling and destroying
their homes. "These people had been severely rationed as the southern
French had not, and they had no wine, nor fruit, nor bread with which to
greet the American troops. They welcomed us gravely but without question
sincerely."[10]

The VI Corps made little progress through most of October and November, and for many weeks during the winter of 1944–45 the 36th was either
withdrawn from combat or in defensive positions to counter a resurgent
and reinforced Wehrmacht defending its fatherland. Until late April the
division's advance would be incremental, and sometimes it was hurled back
by German counterattacks. For the message center staff this period in their
operations was the most perilous and thus the most dramatic. The Germans
almost overran the center several times, forcing Wilbur's detachment to
retreat to a town it had just left. The Germans now frequently shelled and
sometimes strafed the center's installations and billets. If an enemy attack
seemed likely to overrun their operations, the signalmen became infantry.
Jeep and truck drivers armed themselves to fight while the cryptographers
prepared to destroy their radios, SIGABAs, and codebooks with incendiary
bombs and thermite explosives.

During the Battle of the Bulge, which began on December 16 across the
Allies' northern front, the 36th remained stalled in Alsace, far south of the
northern plains and forests where the Germans aimed the brunt of their
Ardennes counterattack. But the division nevertheless experienced several
battering setbacks. Wilbur described one such incident, which occurred on
the evening of December 12 after Captain Paul Wells ordered the company
to prepare to take defensive positions. A quickly assembled infantry pla-
toon, made up mostly of drivers, arrived at the message center's installation.
"Pfc. 'Commando' Stapp was laden with two bandoliers of ammo and
festooned with grenades." German short-range rockets and 120-millimeter
mortars burst around their encampment throughout the night. Although
reinforcements soon halted the German advance, signal company personnel
remained vigilant. In each residence of the town where they were billeted,
guards were on full alert every night. During mid-December the enemy

tossed various types of projectiles into the town with increasing frequency. Wilbur favored understatement to describe his unit's reaction:

> Sgt. Virgil White arrived at the Message Center on the morning of the 14th looking a bit shaken, and reported that the house next to his had inexplicably blown sky high during the night. The most annoying feature of the enemy artillery action was that it seemed to favor the kitchen at meal times; on several occasions, numbers of shells tore up the crossroads next to the kitchen, and knocked corners off all adjoining buildings. On the morning of 18 December at approximately 0600, an enemy rocket blew up three of the section's messenger Jeeps, which left us rather short on vehicles.[11]

For the *History* Wilbur kept track of battle wounds, close calls, and civilian casualties. In Ribeauville, for instance, a mortar fragment struck and wrecked the carbine of Corporal Jesse L. Adcock, who was unhurt, although his Jeep suffered a flat. A passing fragment lightly scratched the temple of Lieutenant Mercaldo. "Sergeant Virgil White and the company first-aid man carried a wounded French child to the medics in the Message Center Jeep; the child died on the way. The advanced detail made no installation, and got back to Ste. Marie in time for lunch."[12]

On February 15, a massive bombardment from a long-range siege gun, dubbed "Alsace Alice" by Wilbur's unit, hit the town of Brumath. This frontline storm, raining down at fifteen-minute intervals from the high-velocity railroad gun situated in a tunnel across the Rhine, "inclined everyone to take to the cellars." An Alice shell, Wilbur wrote, "was hardly inferior to that of a blockbuster; it made buildings look like Shredded Wheat. The annoying thing about high-velocity guns is that their projectiles do not whistle; the pleasant thing about high-velocity guns is that it takes so long to load them that the bursts may be anticipated with some accuracy."[13]

His unit's long stay in Brumath, however, had "its good side," as Wilbur went on to explain: motion pictures in the evenings, pubs filled with amiable civilians, and a barbershop for the "vainer members of the section . . . where two beautiful girls gave shampoos and massages." When the company began issuing passes and furloughs to Bains-les-Bains, Nancy, Brussels, Paris, and the United Kingdom, "the lucky ones who got them left Brumath spic & span, toting musette bags full of cigarettes and chocolate and returned filthy & weary, but contented, with empty musette bags." Several soldiers returning from leave were busted for inebriation while operating an army vehicle, including Emmet "Boogie" Wood and Joe Larussa, who returned "from Strasbourg in a state of delighted incapacity. 'Wood,' said Lieutenant Hicks, 'you are in no condition to drive. And you, Larussa—you're not even in a condition to ride.' "[14]

"The line of goodth that ties us irrevocably together"

During the first three weeks of April 1945, the 36th had been ordered to halt near Erlenbach across the Rhine and await orders to advance. "Now that we had ample free time, for the first time in Germany," Wilbur reflected, "many of the men felt the pinch of the non-fraternization rule, particularly as there were at least 10 attractive enemy females within 50 yards of our dwellings."[15] There were also attractive Allied females in Paris, London, and other distant cities that were recovering their peacetime atmosphere now that the Siegfried Line had been breached. Wilbur was able to visit his brother, Lawrie, who was working in England as a weatherman for the Office of Strategic Services, in mid-April. On his return to join his division, he stopped off in Paris.

Wilbur's poem "Place Pigalle" takes place in Paris on an evening toward the end of the war when, as he imagines, tradesmen are heading home to supper and the hope of "improved conditions." The city quiets except in the red-light district, where a G.I. meets his "ancient friend" in a doorway, marking a territory that is "boldly out of bounds." Wilbur universalizes the couple's timeless erotic gestures via allusions to classical Greek art and poetry—in which the act of intercourse is as natural and immemorial to war as death in battle—and begins the final stanza with Shakespearean phrasing ("Girl, if I love thee not, then let me die"), characterizing the quick sexual encounter as destructive, subject to an ineluctable force of war. By using the verb "wring" to describe how the prostitute embraces her client, as his "desperate soldier's hands which kill all things" gently seize her "muchtouched flesh," he evokes not only the physical act of killing an animal (by twisting and breaking its neck) but also taking advantage of or extracting something from someone (in this case, the G.I.'s francs).

Wilbur has never been one to sensationalize his personal life. If a poem takes off from or seems to refer to something personal, he has invariably, as here, merged his own experiences with universal ones that he's confident his readers will recognize and possibly share: "Place Pigalle" speaks of what's been common to all wars in which women have been seen as the prizes and comforters of warriors. Wilbur's love poems are very likely the most monogamous of any major American poet. "Place Pigalle" is an exception.

In March 2006, Charlee recalled the war years and the difficulties of a protracted separation. While her husband was in Europe, she, a gregarious, free-spirited twenty-one-year-old, lived with her newborn daughter and Wilbur's parents in North Caldwell. In order to remain as independent as possible, she offered to pay room and board from Dick's army service allowance and to arrange for her own babysitters when she went out with male and female friends in suburban New Jersey and Manhattan. To his mother and father, Charlee had even explained honestly (although euphemistically, and leaving her own desires unmentioned) that she understood her husband's need for "comfort and companionship" and "hoped he [was] having it."[16]

A careless mistake provoked Charlee to apply, in real life, this commonsense approach to love in times of war. A message center officer, Lieutenant Jack Weiner, mailed her some photos of Wilbur taken in France. The packet included one he might have done better to omit: it showed her husband with a pretty French girl. Wilbur warned Charlee about the photo by letter and then had a bottle of her favorite perfume, L'imperatrice, mailed to her from New Orleans. Weiner, in another effort at damage control, asked his wife, Sylvia, to phone Charlee to prepare her for what was coming. Charlee immediately wrote to Dick:

> You're a dolt! Did you really think you had to "forewarn" me about that picture of you and that sexy-looking French Frail? Even if I saw a picture of you actually in bed with such a babe, I shouldn't think any other thought than—"god, I'd like to be in her shoes!" (Or out of them, as the case might be.) You must remember that I have tremendous respect for your essential *taste*. And I also have great faith in and dependence upon our common love so that whatever you did couldn't possibly touch the line of goodth that ties us irrevocably together.[17]

In 2006, when Charlee recalled her own and her generation's fears concerning a couple torn apart by war, she never mentioned receiving the photo from France or the perfume from New Orleans. Our interview with her took place a year before her death, and the letter just excerpted was recovered several years later, when her daughter Ellen Wilbur found it in the basement of Wilbur's Cummington home among a large cache of letters that Charlee had written to Wilbur while he was overseas. But whenever Charlee spoke of their separation, she was adamant about relationships formed during the war to which Wilbur was also irrevocably tied. They were not with women he befriended or may have had sex with—they involved men with whom he *lived* and *fought* the war. To Charlee, these were relationships she would never be able (or need) to compete with, bonds that had a profound impact on him and ran deeper than those with non-wartime but lifelong friends.

"Finie, la guerre"

While Wilbur was on leave, the 36th had resumed the offensive, finally crossing the Rhine and driving swiftly due south, covering more than 150 miles through Alpine forests and mountains to the Austrian border. The message center unit's final spell of action began on April 23 as the company moved after the infantry. Basing his reports on accounts of others in his unit, Wilbur wrote in the *History* that "seldom was there time to size up any town before an advance was alerted to move out for another one." On April 30 the company advanced toward a castle near Weilheim, where Admiral Miklós Horthy, the Fascist puppet dictator of Hungary, was being held under German protection. On May 2 Wilbur recorded an anecdote about Horthy's capture:

> A buck slip was passed about, forbidding the confiscation of Admiral Horthy's liquor supplies from the castle cellar. This narrowed the liberation down to a few staff officers in headquarters. SS troops were converted into palace guards for Admiral Horthy, [along with] a personal staff retained by the former regent. Lt. Mercaldo once called and demanded of one of Horthy's flunkies to see the Admiral. "I will see if his Majesty will receive you," replied the flunky. "His Majesty, hell," replied the lieutenant. "Tell that bum to get down here."[18]

Wilbur's own encounters with the German SS concentrated his intense hatred of the enemy and provided chilling images for his poem "On the Eyes of an SS Officer," later included in *The Beautiful Changes*. The first stanza invokes the polar explorer Roald Amundsen, the second "a Bombay saint asquat in the market place, / Eyes gone from staring the sun over the sky." Neither can resist what destroys him—for the explorer, the arctic cold; for the saint, the blinding glare. In describing the SS officer, the subject of the third and final stanza, Wilbur focused on how his "iced or ashen eyes devise / Foul purities." The destructive attraction for the officer is the doctrine of transcendent Aryan superiority that "devised" the Holocaust and incinerated the living flesh of European Jewry. Wilbur released his fury and revulsion by shifting to a first-person voice in the last two lines, not settling this time, as he did in "Tywater," for sardonic irony. Rather, he declared, "I ask my makeshift God of this / My opulent bric-a-brac earth to damn his eyes."

The final secondhand report in Wilbur's *History* began on May 5 with the advance to Kufstein, where the men occupied a German barracks and enjoyed a respite and the first inklings of the end of the war.

By now all roads were full of surrendering Germans. At 1630 the radio section received a flash message, announcing the surrender of all German troops on the Seventh Army front, and Message Center men began here and there to celebrate. On 7 May, the German barracks occupied by signalmen were requisitioned for use as a displaced persons center, and the company removed to a resort hotel, high on a hill above Kufstein. Message Center men, who had accumulated quantities of pistols, cameras and other desirable articles in the course of the drive into Germany and Austria, had also managed to gather together several cases of champagne, white wine and schnapps. On the eve of V-E day, with the war in Europe over at last and small prospect of any 36th Signalman going to the Pacific, there was scarcely a sober man to be found in the section.

On the 8th, we all moved off in convoy for Kitzbuhl, to occupy for a while, and savor the peace. The town of Kitzbuhl had been, in quieter days, a favorite resort of the international smart set. Set deep in a sunny valley, amid mountains covered with snow, it was an excellent winter-sports spot. Our first Message Center was in a home in mid-town but later we moved up to the famous Grand Hotel, above Kitzbuhl at the foot of the mountainside. The Grand Hotel bar served free drinks for two days, which did not improve our efficiency but made the work more pleasant by far. Our living quarters were a block of homes from which the civilians had been persuaded to depart. Air Marshal Goering was wheeled into town following his capture, for interrogation and a chicken dinner. It was easy to tell that the war was over; sunbathing signalmen on the Kitzbuhl porches could look down into the streets and see German MPs directing our military traffic. *Finie, la guerre.*[19]

"Look how them bastards jumped"

On his way to rejoin his unit in Kitzbuhl, Wilbur met his friend Jack Weiner, either in Paris or Strasburg. They drove in Weiner's Jeep along back roads through France, Germany, and Austria, and on May 7 began to traverse a vast forest. Rumor had it that SS storm troopers were preparing a last stand in the mountains around Hitler's Berchtesgaden, and Weiner and Wilbur were on edge as the Jeep sped through terrain still rife with armed German soldiers. Would they be an easy target for frustrated Jerries eager to kill a few last Yanks? Apparently, however, most of the German soldiers were just as ready as the Americans to leave behind the privations and animosities of war, and Weiner's Jeep emerged safely into open country.

In "The Day After the War," a short story published in *Forefront* magazine in the spring of 1946, Wilbur described what he had witnessed in Austria and southern Germany as the imperatives of war dissolved overnight. In the story, a truck carries American infantrymen over the back roads through southern Germany toward Kitzbuhl. The mood is one of liberation and recovered life surging up through the scars and damage of war. Wilbur's story displays intense and unqualified emotion, a quality that critics have not always seen in his writing. The cumulative effect is to communicate a release of tension palpable among the wayfarers, soldiers, and other living creatures that are filling the Austrian roads.

> The tires rolled and rolled with the steady easy kiss and ripple on the roads, and the men in the back of the truck were lying every which way among their packs and rifles, with the sunshine jumping in on them now and then on the turns and sprinkling down on them through holes in the tarp. . . . Now it was the blown up cars, carts dragged in some panic to smash, tanks tipping here and there with burnt guts, that looked adrift on the landscape, the haste, danger, use all gone out of them. All the ditches were full of charred, stomped, torn, broken things. Scraps. Ammo. Photos. Rag. Stool. Grenade case. Stock. Shoe. Housing. Ammo. Field wire. Cap. Clip. Rags. Dead dog. . . .
>
> When there is no home left to go to, when you have outgrown your life, when all you loved is dead or changed, when your body is prematurely old, when you have not hoped for three years, five years, seven years, when all within you and without you has long lost meaning . . . [then] it's over. OBOE VICTOR EASY ROGER. . . .
>
> Three German soldiers came lugging their loads along the side of the road, and twenty feet in front of the truck they threw everything down and sat on their packs exhausted. We sat in the truck and ate, tossing cellophane and clattery cans out onto the pavement, and looking at their indistinct crunched figures. Finally one of the enemy stood up and came over to the truck. His face was without expression, filmed over with the dust of the road, and grey dirt was in all the crevices and folds of his flesh. He said something in a noncommittal voice, and I recognized "essen" and

Richard Wilbur standing next to the Signal Company's 6 x 6 truck in Germany, May 1945. *Courtesy of Richard Wilbur.*

gave him three K rations. He made a slight inclination of the head and
said, "Danke." At first I felt a sadness because of the uneasy pride of the
man, and because one of the boys said we shouldn't feed the stinkers, let
them starve. And then I suddenly got angry at everything and wanted
to scare the Krauts. So I reached down between the seats and took up
a German rat-gun and let fly at a tree on the slope; the fast loud sound
shocked us all, and the bullets tore up the tree-trunk, unseaming the
bark. Emmett laughed harshly, "Look how them bastards jumped," and
the three Germans were hurrying wide of the truck, stumbling in their
clumsy grey coats, looking at us with their vague faces, afraid we would
shoot if they ran but walking as fast as they could short of running.

"You try to start the god damned war all over again?" said somebody,
and I was ashamed, close to crying.

"The Day After the War" ends as the truck, continuing on for miles and
miles in the dark, approaches a horse that is standing stock-still in the middle of the road, its legs "trammeled in golden wire. . . . Poor stalwart fool."
Wilbur wrote, "He's lost in this war, his heart is for Agincourt and Marston
Moor, and the battles of the splendid pounding charges. . . . Easy, baby, you
won't kick me in my silly metal head, will you? Easy now, Rosinante, I'll set
you free."[20]

"It scares me more than somewhat"

As the people in his story do, Wilbur carried an exhausted relief into his
immediate postwar years. His narrator's pity for the war's displaced survivors is keen and detailed; but as his alter ego's spontaneous burst of Mauser
fire conveys, accumulated rage and a continuing mistrust of the German
people still gripped him. They kept Wilbur from freely mixing with the
civilian populations of Germany and Austria while he was stationed among
them.

Though he remained a code technician and still worked regular stints
at the SIGABA, the war's end liberated him to pursue various outlets for
his creativity and curiosity, many of which hearkened back to his prewar
focus on journalism. Shortly after V-E Day he began to publish opinion
columns—first, in the divisional newspaper *T-Patch* and later also in a
four-page daily put out by the division's headquarters, *Robert Reveille*. On
July 30, 1945, Wilbur wrote to Theodore Baird about the satisfaction and
recognition that such writing was giving him:

Although throughout hostilities I kept to my project of being solely a soldier, shortly after the surrender & the commencement of this Great Wait I agreed to write a short daily column for our Divisional newspaper. Result: instant Division-wide-fame. Grand Persons dropped around to my code room to "meet" me. Captains had me step in for a shot of their second-best cognac. Majors said hello. The Colonel denounced me. The Brigadier said I was clearheaded & responsible. The Major-Gen habitually read me over his morning eggs. And my friends considered me a prose Mauldin—steam valve—though not one column in five was anti-officer, & I had made no effort to please. The whole thing depressed me, because it was so easy. The atmosphere of a resting Army is as unstrenuous as that of Amherst, & disproportionate recognition makes you angry & ashamed, if you're the sort of person who can't support lassitude yet needs competition. I'd have given an arm to be called a good soldier.[21]

Wilbur's "instant Division-wide-fame," coupled with his message center *History,* were partly responsible for an opportunity that influenced both his immediate and his long-term futures. The U.S. Army's postwar planners had been thinking ahead about how to channel the free time and the desire for self-improvement of its suddenly underemployed and millions-strong European force. Well before the fighting ended, they had set in motion multiple study opportunities and constructive diversions. Now they awarded Wilbur a place in a new university in Shrivenham, England. When he learned of the offer, he wryly noted that perhaps the 36th Division brass wanted a respite from his frequently stinging "Mock Turtle" columns. In his letter to Baird, he had referred to "the Colonel [who] denounced me." This officer, who was now dispatching him to England for seven weeks to study English literature, was the same one he had satirized in the press for maintaining his riding-booted, whip-wielding, pistol-toting affectations without either horses or enemies in the vicinity.

While he was at Shrivenham, Wilbur was also free to spend time with his brother in London. Like Dick, Lawrie had attended Amherst College, where he had won the Armstrong Prize for freshman composition before enlisting in the OSS in 1943—what Wilbur called "the operational side" of the war. In 2006 Wilbur recalled seeing some evidence of his brother's psychological distress when they met in London to go the theater:

We didn't talk about what he was working on. And truly I don't know what sort of work he did. I do know that at the time I saw him [in London] there was a plan for some OSS people, of whom he would be one, to be parachuted into Scandinavia somewhere. So he was looking forward to that. . . . My brother was incipiently strange at that time. He was beginning to lose it a little. Lawrie had a theory that great men, people like Napoleon, had gotten along on very little sleep. And he, too, was trying to get along on very little sleep. . . . Lawrie and I went to see a George Bernard Shaw play. I think it was *Getting Married.* And I recall that he slept through the second act.

When I tried to figure out why he was cracking up I thought the pressure of that [parachuting] prospect might be considerable for him. But that was just an amateur's guess. I didn't at that time know that he'd really had a history of incipient schizophrenia all his young life.[22]

In an interview not long before Lawrie's death, Wilbur would put these impressions into context with what he called his brother's "growing troubles."

He was such a sweet guy. Everybody loved him, and it seemed quite enough for him just to be himself. But early in his grammar school years he began to be a little slow, to have things a little hard for him. . . . He was always starting over. The thing with the piano—I never played the piano worth a damn—but Lawrie had a few more lessons than I, was technically very good. The problem was that he kept stopping and starting. But this is all seen in retrospect; at the time they were lovable oddities.[23]

Although Lawrie would later go to Yale on the G.I. Bill, his symptoms increased; and some years later he was diagnosed with what doctors today call bipolar disorder. After spending a number of years in halfway houses for the mentally disabled, Lawrie entered the VA hospital in Northampton, Massachusetts, not far from the Wilburs' home in Cummington. Wilbur spoke in 2008, shortly after Lawrie's death, about the history of mental illness in his family.

Everybody today talks glibly about bipolar mental problems but there was no genteel vocabulary for mental problems when I was a kid. One of my relatives, my father's brother Ray, ended up in an asylum. Dad would not talk about it. He'd evidently been in the theater out there in the Omaha area and he'd done a bit of drinking and then he seemed to become unhinged. I'm sure this is not very accurate but that's the way Dad described it: "Ray got in with the wrong crowd." I imagine it came up only because Dad was slowly made to recognize that his second son was a mental case, was schizophrenic. Bless him, he just didn't believe in such things, in madness. There came a time when I had to go down to

North Caldwell and intervene to get Lawrie to the VA hospital, which required some persuasion. . . . What it was [for Lawrie] was a helpless slowing down, and I remember he said once that in the third grade they were given something to write out, a test of some kind, and he said [to himself], "If I don't finish this I'm going to have a different sort of life than the people around me." So he finished it, with strain. There was strain always, but not enough joy in him, alas.[24]

For Dick, however, there was much exhilaration in postwar London culture, even if Lawrie didn't fully share it. The Arts Theatre was staging Henrik Ibsen's *A Doll's House* (in which "Nora's ignorance of syphilis got a musical-comedy laugh" from the Yanks in the audience) as well as plays by Shakespeare, George Bernard Shaw, and Luigi Pirandello. London bookshops were full of Hindu translations and writings by Saint Teresa, Jakob Boehme, Rainer Maria Rilke, and Søren Kierkegaard, although, as he wrote to Baird, he couldn't find any "magazines called Protest, Blast, Eructation, or Damn-Your-Eyes." He identified with the English intellectuals he met who were "considering extreme experimental lives," and, he admitted, "I must say I note the same seismograph behavior in my own little head."[25]

Wilbur anticipated the pleasure of studying at Shrivenham without the protocols of army routine. As he explained to Baird:

> We are allowed 3 courses, held daily, & there are no rules governing election. . . . There's to be reveille at 0600, but otherwise, so long as we make our beds prettily, there will be little of what is called Chickenshit. It no longer requires thought to tuck the necktie under the second button & over the third, & these 2 months should have only academic harassments. No chapter of DKE has yet appeared, & I do not think there will be competitions for Prom Chairman or Glee Club Manager until the ivy is up.[26]

A trip to Oxford prompted Wilbur's acerbic appraisal of the intellectual scene there, and he knew Baird would be a receptive audience:

> I met a man named [John] Betjeman [later a popular architectural critic and eventually Britain's poet laureate] who is in favor of beauty & against the suburbs. I asked him how people study English Lit. there, & he got off a spittley drawl to the effect that it's *Anglosaxon & so many dead languages, and Caedmon, Chaucer & all those old bores, & stops altogether at Wordsworth, rally you shouldn't care for it, Sergeant.* I got sore at his patronizing, & didn't like his clerical odor anyway, so I went & found a woman named Dorothy Whitehead who didn't feel violated by the presence of an American Sgt., & curled up on a sofa & told me all abt. English education.[27]

In the meantime, he outlined a campaign to get himself demobilized and sent back home to his family. The army's procedure for assigning an individual's demobilization priority was based on a point system with four components: service time, overseas time, combat time, and number of dependents. Wilbur scored 91, well beyond the 80 points that normally assured a soldier's prompt return to civilian life. But for reasons he never understood, the army kept him in Europe until early November 1945.

Wilbur's "Mock Turtle" columns, which ridiculed various military pretensions and presumptions, may have offended his superiors and thus been part of the explanation for his delayed demobilization. In the July 14, 1945, issue of *Robert Reveille* he criticized the army's gaudy penchant for what he considered the unseemly festooning of its uniforms with medals and campaign insignia, in contrast to the ostentation-free chests of the Brits: "Solomon in all his glory never looked like a headquarters master sergeant stepping out for an evening."[28]

Yet despite his longing for home, Wilbur was conflicted about leaving the military. Writing to Baird on September 17, he expressed his fears:

> Most soldiers I have talked with view return to civilian life with a feeling of exhaustion. Many will publicly deny any ambivalence of feeling abt it, because for so long "going back" has been the end-all in their minds. A man who signs on for another hitch is regarded as queer. But most will admit privately that they fear leaving this world of regular meals, fixed relationships, and no necessity for making choices. It scares me more than somewhat.[29]

Fear seemed briefly to overcome his eagerness for a return to civilian life. Wilbur took and passed a test for promotion from staff sergeant to warrant officer. But the end of the war against Japan lessened the chance he would remain essential to the war effort, so he declined the promotion and reenlistment in favor of going home and going to graduate school on the G.I. Bill.

"Let's not have to do this again"

With the end of the war in sight, editorials and news stories in the 36th Division's newspapers shared a common theme: the conviction that G.I.s would return to their civilian lives saying, "Let's not have to do this again." As an editorial in the June 27, 1945, *Robert Reveille* declared, "*C'est la guerre* must remain forever a form of jest—words of derision for the loser of a parlor skirmish."[30]

During the first weeks of the occupation, films, photos, and testimony from both the skeletal survivors of Auschwitz and their liberators forced the Allied victors to confront the fact that the German people had largely acquiesced to and participated in the murder of 6 million of their fellow citizens. Their first reactions were to ban Nazi officials and party members from political life and to try the Nazi leaders at Nuremburg. Yet few Allied commanders and civilian administrators connected the Nazi savagery with what the Allies had done to Hamburg, Dresden, Hiroshima, and Nagasaki. Wilbur confronted these evasions in several of his most scathing and thoughtful columns. In one, he noted that even though the Allied high command had forbidden former Nazis to hold any civilian leadership positions, many Germans still deferred to their Nazi masters in the workplace. Wilbur asserted that the German character, as he had observed it during the occupation, had retained the racial prejudices and totalitarian reflexes that the Nazis had inculcated. As evidence, he focused on the discovery that, in Kaufburen, where the 36th had been stationed for a month after V-E Day, Holocaust atrocities had continued after the war was over. On July 10, 1945, he wrote in *Robert Reveille:*

> We are informed by yesterday's *Stars & Stripes* that while we were bivouacked in the sunny, pleasant and hygienic Bavarian town of Kaufburen, a Nazi institution for the extermination of the idiot children continued serenely to operate in our midst. It is probable that each of us strolled by the place more than once. Conceivably, we nodded and smiled at some of the doctors, nurses and holy sisters employed there in the purification of the race—it is a chilling thought. It is a chilling thought because it strikes home to the common suckerhood of American soldiers—our easy-going reluctance to imagine evil behind the enemy's amiable morning smile, our refusal to believe in the devilishness of the Nazi mind.[31]

Wilbur had been in London during the bombings of Hiroshima and Nagasaki and the subsequent end of the Pacific war. On the day the bomb annihilated Hiroshima, an acquaintance in a London pub challenged Wilbur to write a good poem about the prospect that the new weapon had opened for wiping out the human race. He offered Wilbur ten dollars if he could bring it off and did not specify a time limit. It took Wilbur decades to win the bet, but in 1961 he did finally manage to produce the title poem of his collection *Advice to a Prophet.* By then he had lost contact with his wartime bettor.

Wilbur's final secular sermon, published in an October 28, 1945, column for the dwindling audience of T-Patchers remaining in Germany, shows how deeply and specifically he had thought about the bomb:

> Christian ethics do not condemn the atomic bomb any more than any other weapon. According to the Decalogue, David's slingshot was evil because it took life. An M-1 takes life more efficiently but its evilness is not correspondingly greater. It breaks the same law. The evil of the atomic bomb is the evil of all scientific weapons intensified, and this evil can only be described in terms of a pagan ethic wherein evil is *ignorance and pain.*
>
> The atomic bomb makes war a matter of nation against nation, rather than army against army; it increases and generalizes the suffering of war. And it further dehumanizes the experience of war. Already many soldiers are peculiarly insulated from the people they kill: the artillerist sends his projectile slithering through the air to scatter a man into bits 20 miles away. The radar man plots the approach of unseen Messerschmitts, and telephones the ack-ack to be ready; the ack-ack gunner sees a silver shadow through a hole in a cloud, and blisters the sky with his flack; the plane crashes five miles away.
>
> These soldiers of scientific war are good technicians, but they have a strange irresponsibility of feeling, a strange ignorance [that] they are adjuncts to machines. They don't see the damage they do, they don't come face-to-face with the enemy; they perform certain memorized processes under pressure, and have no time nor occasion to react to war as a complex, moving and terrible type of human experience. Science has de-dramatized warfare, and strangled pity and a sense of guilt in routine; and that is why the atom bomb is evil.
>
> But, gentlemen you can't turn back the clock. In any age, you must work within the materials of that age. If we aren't aghast before the atom bomb, . . . if clerics are reduced to an unconstructive railing against the Times, it is only that much more important that we strive to comprehend the meaning of atomic power to our lives. Let's realize that the bomb cannot be relinquished as a military weapon. Let's realize that another war would slaughter all creatures indiscriminately, and reduce our great cities to cinder. And let's therefore set out in a practical way to make a peace that will stick. Until we do we are all under sentence of death.[32]

Another war would slaughter all creatures indiscriminately. There, in one sentence, was the core fear that Wilbur would elaborate on years later in "Advice to a Prophet":

> . . . What should we be without
> The dolphin's arc, the dove's return,

These things in which we have seen ourselves and spoken?
Ask us, prophet, how we shall call
Our natures forth when that live tongue is all
Dispelled, that glass obscured or broken.

In late October Wilbur was transferred, without logic or explanation, to an anti-aircraft artillery battery; the rest of the division had been sent back to the States in mid-October. He received final clearance to leave the European theater in November and finally shipped home on November 13 from Marseilles to Newport News, Virginia, where he was honorably discharged on November 29.

Harvard had already accepted Wilbur for January 1946 admission. Shrivenham had given him insight into the kind of writer he would like to become: one who immersed himself in his own time and was unrestricted by any academic discipline; who could strive for excellence unimpaired, and be able to write frequently, for money, on anything that interested him. As he had told Baird in August,

I am reviewing the XVIII century with a Dr. Moore, of Indiana University. . . . I *have* got out of [his course] a great admiration for [Daniel] Defoe. [Defoe's] energy is what appalls me. It isn't enough to say that the great age of curiosity is gone, or that men in other times had better-ordered minds and therefore more retention and centrality. It doesn't even apply to Defoe, this last, because his interests were scattered, as they say in Texas, like a mad woman's shit. Where do swallows go in winter, shouldn't there be a Royal Academy of Music, what to do abt the Negro & the insane, a plan for a League of Nations & for the occupation of a defeated nation, etc. And he cared abt these things enough to be right on a lot of them. Maybe to be a great man like him you must first be unashamed about being a good hack.[33]

Or you might become, as Wilbur would, a poet who welcomed into his verse a continually enlarging range of earthly experience, perhaps not as eclectic as Defoe's but rich with pleasure, grief, curiosity, felicity, monstrosity, as well as the astounding and exemplary creatures that nature thoughtfully provides.

5

Religion and Wilbur's War Poems
"I weary of the confidence of God"

I'm afraid that I'm not very catechistic. Sometimes I happily think and feel within the terms of Anglican liturgy; at other times I remember what Gilbert Murray said about the Olympians: "the gods were not the gods, but a way of conceiving the gods."

—RICHARD WILBUR, interview by Paul Mariani, 1995

Wilbur's wartime poems fulfill the conviction he expressed to Theodore Baird: his generation's war poems should reflect the experiences of the "one and the many."[1] Yet in more than half of the ten war poems Wilbur published in *The Beautiful Changes* (1947), he aspired to another goal he never articulated: to reconcile his doubts and convictions about the existence of God. On a more universal scale these poems aim to reconcile paradoxes in the world—for instance, by intertwining fear and hope or chaos and coherence.[2] With his wartime religious poems Wilbur began a spiritual and intellectual investigation he would continue throughout his life.

"The whole world's wild"

In August 1997 Wilbur began to correspond with Joe Cox, a teacher at Haverford College who later published an interview with Wilbur, based on their letters, in the journal *War, Literature, and the Arts.* Cox asked him to clarify a remark he'd once made to Stanley Kunitz, that the wartime world had gotten "out of hand."[3] As Wilbur explained:

No doubt war is disturbing and disorienting for everyone, civilians included; it cancels one's plans and alters the playing field; it calls for sacrifice and for degrees of discipline and physical courage less required in peacetime. It also puts the future of one's country and civilization at doubt. Some people, however, come into their own in times of war, and I was not one of those. To find myself in the Army was a shock to my anti-war youth, my anti-militarism, my dislike of regimentation; and once I was in a combat unit, the war challenged my sanguine suppositions about human nature and the goodness of God's world. On the positive side, I learned a lot about loyalty, mutual dependence and (something I had never expected to experience), esprit de corps.[4]

War requires "new and risky words," Wilbur wrote, in which to express one's confusion and attempt to make sense of it. When writing poetry—"a serious game" requiring one to be fully articulate about oneself and the world—the old vocabulary will not suffice. Over the years he has used the term "versifying in earnest" to refer to both the seriousness and concentration of writing in the vicinity of combat. No other art, he has said, is so portable: "you can't set up an easel in a foxhole."[5]

Wilbur has repeatedly dismissed any notion that a so-called foxhole conversion, the kind exacted from agnostics and atheists by fear of imminent death, deepened his religious beliefs. Similarly, during a 1995 interview with Paul Mariani published in the journal *Image,* he denied any link between his postwar fascination with Edgar Allan Poe's "self-dwelling, self-immolating, and self-transcending imagination" (as Mariani called it), and the fact that Wilbur was reading Poe's stories in an Armed Services edition while holed up for a week under the monastery (and the Germans' mortars and artillery) at Monte Cassino.

> I could only have wished for such an esemplastic feat as that. I don't remember feeling an expressible relation or contrast between the bombings . . . and my detection of symbolic meaning in Poe. But of course one can't confidently recall the consciousness one had in combat circumstances. I've noticed that when men are swapping war stories, the fear, horror, and incredulity have long been edited out, and the talk is mostly of tactics and black-comedy anecdotes.[6]

In his review of Wilbur's *Collected Poems, 1943–2004,* the critic Adam Kirsch notes that Wilbur's earliest war poems exhibit "a style so elaborately formal that the most awful subjects are sublimated into irony, or even black comedy. There is something deliberately, monstrously cartoonish about 'Mined Country,' where 'Cows in mid-munch go splattered over the sky.'"[7] Cartoonish imagery, black comedy, and irony are indeed deliberate techniques that Wilbur had used in formal prose and light verse since high school. His intent was not to sublimate or dilute, as Kirsch suggests, but to dramatize and accentuate—and in the case of "Mined Country," set in the French countryside around Ban-de-Lavelines in northern France, he focused on the very things that caused fear, horror, and incredulity among not only his fellow soldiers but also civilians.

"Mined Country" conveys Wilbur's awareness of how war disrupts its victims' relation to reality, each other, and ultimately divinity. (A phrase in the fourth stanza, "some scheme's gone awry," refers to God's plan.) The poem pictures war imposing itself violently on the landscape and the people, with the most phantasmagoric depiction of mayhem being the cows that explode into the sky. Soldiers swing their mine detectors from side to side ("like playing pendulum"). As the poem unfolds, its irony crystallizes. Landmines hide beneath an attractive camouflage of flowers and undermine trust in the familiar rural countryside:

> Danger is sunk in the pastures, the woods are sly,
> Ingenuity's covered with flowers!
> We thought woods were wise but never
> Implicated, never involved.

As the poem's narrator explains, "Shepherds must learn a new language; this / Isn't going to be quickly solved."

> Sunshiny field grass, the woods floor, are so mixed up
> With earliest trusts, you have to pick back
> Far past all you have learned, to go
> Disinherit the dumb child,
>
> Tell him to trust things alike and never to stop
> Emptying things, but not let them lack
> Love in some manner restored; to be
> Sure the whole world's wild.

These final two stanzas display a composure derived from not only Wilbur's technical skill but also his spiritual faith; in them the poet suggests that elders must perpetually instill new ways to express both love and fear in the next generation's children, who must learn to mistrust before they can trust again.

Paradoxical Peacefulness

Wilbur was raised in the Episcopal Church and is still a communicant. Today he does not accept all of the church's thirty-nine Articles of Religion, but he does remain a man of Christian faith. When Mariani asked him to describe his "religious temper" and "philosophic bent" in an arc—with "the *ecstasis* of a Hopkins or a Dickinson" at one end and "the controlled indirections of an Eliot" at the other—Wilbur said that he leans toward Gerard Manley Hopkins. "I'm the sort of Christian animal for whom celebration is the most important thing of all. When I go to church, what doesn't particularly interest me is the Creed, although I find that I can say it. The Creed strikes me as very much like a political platform of some sort, and I believe that's what it was. What I respond to is, 'Lift up your hearts!' " Such lines in the Mass, he said, belong to his kind of religious experience.[8]

In Mariani's view, a paralyzing terror exists just below the surface of the "light and the comfort and the wit" of Wilbur's poems. Yet beyond, he says, is "something more, a belief in God, a trust in the underlying goodness of the world, in an Other who sustains and informs our world." According to Wilbur, the scariness in these poems is less tangible than the "feeling that the order of things is in peril or in doubt, that there are holes in things through which one might drop for a long distance. The terror is there and it's countered continually by trust and by hope, by an impulse to praise."[9]

In late 1944, Wilbur was stationed in the Alsace region of northeastern France, which extends to the borders of Germany and Switzerland. While there he wrote two poems that show his increasing ability to draw on descriptions of local scenes and ingrained customs of a particular place as a way to reflect what was on his mind. These poems are imbued with an appreciation of the war-torn countryside's paradoxical peacefulness; church bells or churches figure in both, and God appears climactically in one. Both suggest that he was experiencing a religious inwardness that was deeper than the one he recalled when he spoke with Mariani, an inwardness that transcended study of the Catholic missal given to him by an army chaplain. Both poems are "ways of conceiving" God.

For "First Snow in Alsace" Wilbur used Dante's stanza form, terza rima, to record an expedition into the realms and mind of divinity.[10] At the start of the second stanza, he chose the adjective "absolute" to describe snow that will sooner or later disappear. With this seemingly incongruous choice he invoked a variant of the word as it is used in a religious context: snow is an *absolution* granted to the landscape and for a time heals the violence done to it and its inhabitants. The third and fourth stanzas establish the snow's benign blanketing of rooflines and ration stacks in the war zone. In the fifth stanza Wilbur extended its power of concealment further as snow covers the open eyes of dead soldiers. In the seventh stanza snow transports residents—citizens and soldiers alike—back to a more innocent time when frost made "marvelous designs" on windowpanes. In the eighth stanza, and the single concluding line of the poem, Wilbur shifted the reader's perspective to a sentinel who is leaving his watch:

> The night guard coming from his post,
> Ten first-snows back in thought, walks slow
> And warms him with a boyish boast:
>
> He was the first to see the snow.

In "A Dubious Night" Wilbur found an image that captured his immediate religious doubts and perplexities and again chose the terza rima pattern. In the first six lines, a bell rings in a nearby village.

> A bell diphthonging in an atmosphere
> Of shying night air summons some to prayer
> Down in the town, two deep lone miles from here,
>
> Yet wallows faint or sudden everywhere,
> In every ear, as if the twist wind wrung
> Some ten years' tangled echoes from the air.

So many bell tollings for so many war deaths interfere and mingle with each other. These confusing, uncertain ("dubious") sounds call the villagers, with their wavering, much-tested faith, to prayer.

The word "diphthonging" in the first line alludes to the process by which two vowels in a single syllable combine, often with one sound melding into the other (as the "oy" sound in the word "oil"). Wilbur's internal rhymes— "night air summons some to prayer" and "down . . . town . . . deep lone miles from here"—allow his readers to hear the beckoning bell sounds as they carry over two miles to Wilbur's Alsatian billet. Another echo effect, "everywhere, / In every ear" carries across a line break.

The remaining lines of "A Dubious Night," seven through thirteen, follow:

> What kyries it says are mauled among
> The queer elisions of the mist and murk,
> Of lights and shapes; the senses were unstrung,

Except that one star's synecdochic smirk
Burns steadily to me, that nothing's odd
And firm as ever is the masterwork.

I weary of the confidence of God.

In the seventh and eighth lines, Wilbur engaged in religion-inflected wordplay by echoing the kyrie eleison, a Greek prayer used in Christian liturgies, which begins, "Lord have mercy." The word "kyries," (pronounced roughly as *keer-ee-ays*) repeats the diphthonging bell's pitch change in an altered tone, suggesting how bell sounds themselves waver over a distance. The unwritten word *eleison* is recalled in "elisions."

In the last four lines Wilbur switched to a first-person voice. A "synecdochic smirk," a single flickering star, is itself "diphthonged" with a doubled significance: Wilbur saw it shining both physically and metaphysically above him in "the masterwork," the word he used to refer to the heavens. God's flickering message is *I'm still here, despite what's happening down there.* That divine smirk can be read as God's assurance that all would finally be well in what the poet saw as a godforsaken place and time.

"Da capo da capo returns"

Though Wilbur agrees with Hopkins's statement, "the world is charged with the grandeur of God," he prefers to express it as he did in "A Wedding Toast" (from *The Mind-Reader*, 1976): "the world's fullness is not made but found." In other words, the world brims with possibility and fullness that must be perceived before it can be cherished.[11] "Cicadas" (from *The Beautiful Changes*), a poem Wilbur probably wrote at Vint Hill Farms in Warrenton, Virginia, reflects the constant and distinguishing presence of sensory awareness in his personal faith.[12]

The father of entomology, Jean-Henri Fabre, made the curious discovery that cicadas are not merely tone deaf but also acoustically deaf. That information, which Wilbur read in a book he borrowed from the Armed Services library in the fall of 1943, gave him a scientific basis for rejecting the myth that cicadas possess a prophetic insight and periodically attempt to communicate it to humans. "Cicadas" is striking for its aural effects— the mimicking of the drowsy, humid evenings in which short-lived cicadas pulse a massive mating call in unison; as the poem's narrator asserts, cicadas are much too busy with their love life to pay attention to our troubles; and

because they can't hear us anyway, they have no basis upon which to proph-
esy. The poem introduced a practice that has recurred in Wilbur's work: the
use of an analogy from the insect world to bolster or illuminate a religious
idea. In "Water Walker" (from *The Beautiful Changes*) caddis flies became a
trope for religious conversion; in the much later "Mayflies" (2000) the brief
life of these insects and their resemblance to the distant flickering stars gave
him a synecdoche for creation and his own role as poet in praising it.

"Water Walker," the longest and most ambitious poem Wilbur wrote
in Europe, demonstrates the power and versatility of his secular and frequently scientific parallels as well as their drawbacks. The poem uses the
life cycle of the caddis fly to convey the self-transformations and the courageous forays into hostile cultures that characterized Saint Paul's ministry.
Wilbur became fascinated with Paul after reading an Armed Services edition of *The Apostle,* Sholem Asch's historical novel about the saint. "Water
Walker" develops analogies between Paul's mission to the Gentiles, the
caddis fly's life cycle, and the poet's secular progress toward self-knowledge
and enlightenment.

Because the poem is formidably allusive and circular in its design, it
requires *slow reading,* a technique that Armour Craig introduced to Wilbur
at Amherst. Popularized by I. A. Richards at Harvard in the 1930s, it involves
working through a poem or a novel's imagery and its text's multitudinous
implications to arrive at a unifying reading that might seem farfetched to
casual readers but is convincing once explained. "Water Walker," a poem
that can only be fully comprehended if closely read multiple times, was a
departure from the more immediately understandable poems that Wilbur
was writing while he was moving through France with the message center.
Its intricacies and complexity suggest that he wanted to create something
worthy of the penetrating attention his mentors at Amherst were giving to
John Donne's and George Herbert's religious lyrics.

Although "Water Walker" deserves an essay in its own right, analysis of a
few passages can broaden an understanding of Wilbur's maturing style and
themes. In it he employed for the first time a highly allusive strategy, perhaps encouraged by the Hopkins poems he had begun to study in France.
An initial understanding of the poem depends on taking the caddis fly's life
cycle, a succession of astonishing transformations, as a Christian parable.
Dying, the fly lays its eggs on a river in late summer or autumn. They sink
and become pupae that enclose themselves in tent-like cocoons of silk and
grit. After clinging over the winter to underwater stones, the pupae shed

their cocoons and hatch in late spring or summer as winged creatures that float to the surface, dry their wings, and then rise into the air, where they remain airborne for a fortnight before themselves laying eggs on the river and dying.

In the poem this series of metamorphoses becomes a metaphor for Saint Paul's conversion from Judaism to Christianity. (The poem first introduces him as "Paulsaul the Jew born in Tarshish [Tarsus]"; Saul was his name before his conversion.) Paul's poised position among cultures gives him a powerful advantage as he proselytizes among Jews, Romans, and Greeks.

Like the caddis fly, Wilbur's Paul is a self-transformer. In the eighth of the poem's ten stanzas he discovers the essential difference between Judaism and Christianity in a passage of striking verbal ambiguity:

> Still pearled with water, to be
>
> Ravished by air makes him grow
> Stranger to both, and discover
> Heaven and hell in the poise
> Betwixt "inhabit" and "know."

Wilbur here plays on the Greek verb *gignosko,* which can mean both "I know" and "I become," and thus interprets Paul's intent: a Christian does not merely *understand* Christ's meaning, he *inhabits* and *becomes* Jesus, as Jesus inhabits his followers when they take communion. To know Christianity's creed or its narrative does not suffice. The believer must transform his infidel or Jewish self to become one with God the father, through the agency of his son.

"Water Walker" may also be a parable for viewing human understanding as a never-ending loop or cycle, as seen through the poem's sequence of interrelated vignettes: a newly minted atheist walks sobbing past churches and rituals he once cherished; caddis flies drop their "heirs" on bodies of water; Saint Paul commutes between his Jewish and Christian heritages. The speaker himself ponders shedding his New Jersey identity for life on a Virginia plantation but quickly goes back to view the caddis larvae awaiting rebirth on a river bottom. The poem returns to the wayfaring speaker on an Illinois porch watching a moonlit suburbanscape. He imagines "an old man stitching a tent," like Saul, a tentmaker by trade who, forsaking Tarsus for his mission to the Gentiles, formulated the essential difference between Christianity and all other religions. Next, the speaker resurfaces as a soldier contemplating a metastasizing America:

Can I rest and observe unfold

The imminent singletax state,
The Negro rebellion, the rise
Of the nudist cult, the return
Of the Habsburgs, watch and wait
And praise
The spirit and not the cause, and neatly precipitate
What is not doctrine, what is not bound
To enclosured ground; what stays?

"Water Walker" ends with Saul trapped between conflicting beliefs, the Old Testament and the New, but he finds in this dilemma a tension to cherish.

Wilbur followed each eight-line stanza with a single, stand-alone, three-beat line. Several of these single lines connect syntactically to the lines above and below. A single line concludes the poem: "Da capo da capo returns." *Da capo* is a musician's phrase meaning "take it from the top"; thus, Wilbur invited the reader to reread the poem until its diverse components cohered.

"Water Walker" is clearly awkward in places—difficulty verging on obscurity is also one of the poem's drawbacks—and it stretched Wilbur's poetic technique beyond its current comfort zone. But its vision of the kinship linking the natural, the spiritual, and the historical realms will stay with a reader who stays with the poem. For such a reader "Water Walker" remains an invigorating, if vertiginous, spiritual exercise. Because its meanings and beauties must be painstakingly liberated from its foreshortened phrases, intricate sentences, screeching halts, and zigzagging cross-references, it does not assert its achievement with the confident and steady accumulation of insight and sound effects that readers have come to expect from Wilbur's mature poems. "Water Walker" presents religious life as an engagement, a process—a pilgrimage that materializes and de-materializes within a person's total being. Yet considering Wilbur's own metamorphosis during the war years—from a young man who interpreted war and civilized life in largely political terms, to one who, after two years of combat, saw how both the personal and the religious were crucial to his understanding—the poem is a testament to the maturity he had achieved by his mid-twenties.

When Jewel Spears Brooker interviewed Wilbur in 1992, she suggested to him that his poetry is neither blatantly Christian nor, in a technical or defiant way, theological; and yet, she said, "the doctrine of the Incarnation as understood by Christians has made a difference in [his] grasp of the spiritual" within ordinary things. Wilbur agreed. When Brooker asked him if Saint Paul's command to rejoice in the Lord had been one of the specific doctrines of belief that had nourished his work, he answered yes, telling her, "I think it is probably a strange thing to feel commanded to rejoice, because we associate joy with spontaneity, but I do think of making a joyful noise as an obligation which it would be distressing to fail. I think that one thing poetry needs to be, whatever it's talking about, one thing it needs to be is celebratory."[13]

6

The Cambridge Years

"A young poet of promise"

The real themes of literature, the ageless endless ones, are the ones you never learn. Joy you never learn, death you never learn, renewal is always unexpected, love is a perpetual rediscovery.

—RICHARD WILBUR, unpublished notebook, circa 1948

On November 30, 1945, Charlee Wilbur spotted her husband among a throng of G.I.s who had just arrived in Manhattan by troopship or train. Talking about that day more than sixty years later, Wilbur recalled that she was standing in front of the Plaza Hotel, next to Central Park, where she had booked a room for their reunion. But Charlee insisted (and Wilbur conceded) that, in a city swamped with returning soldiers, the only available room she could find was near Times Square, in an establishment that charged by the hour. Not surprisingly, she said, her husband looked pale and thin. Still, he weighed more than he had when reporting for active duty in 1943.[1]

When the Wilburs arrived at his parents' home in North Caldwell, two-year-old Ellen was in the front yard, playing in the snow. Wilbur bent down and introduced himself to his daughter, whom he hadn't seen since the army granted him compassionate leave for a few days after her birth. During December and early January, surrounded by family, he regained his energy and composure as he prepared to begin his classes at Harvard.

Many veterans studying at Harvard had written poems at the front, and in Cambridge, Massachusetts, they found an attentive literary public, on and off campus. John Ciardi was on the Harvard faculty, and by the late

Richard Wilbur greets his two-year-old daughter, Ellen, as he arrives home from the war, December 1945. *Courtesy of Richard Wilbur.*

1940s Donald Hall, John Ashbery, Robert Bly, Frank O'Hara, Kenneth Koch, and Adrienne Rich (at Radcliffe) had all arrived as undergraduates. Nonetheless, although Wilbur had taken his poetry seriously while serving as a cryptographer, he was reluctant to make the transition from a poet at war to a poet at Harvard. He accepted Robert Frost's caution that you weren't a poet until others declared that you were.

"The Wilbur years had begun"

In mid-January 1946, Wilbur, Charlee, and Ellen moved to 22 Plympton Street in Cambridge. They had found the first-floor apartment through

Wilbur's Amherst friend Tom Wilcox and Tom's wife, Darlene, who had rented the second-floor apartment a few weeks earlier. Wilbur and Charlee scraped and painted walls, reupholstered chairs, bought additional furniture, and declared themselves lucky to have the place, even though the Wilcoxes' toilet had backed up into their laundry tub and dead mice were decaying pungently in the walls.

A few doors up from 22 Plympton toward Massachusetts Avenue, then as now a lively street of shops, bookstores, bistros, and restaurants, was Grolier Poetry Book Shop. Gordon Cairnie had founded the Grolier in 1927 to bring the world's poetry to Cambridge's considerable community of poets and poetry readers. Almost daily during his Harvard years Wilbur spent quiet and congenial moments chatting with Cairnie, and there was plenty going on in the literary world to discuss. Just after the European war had begun, W. H. Auden and Stephen Spender had moved to America, much to the disgust of their blitzed countrymen. Robert Lowell was living in his native Boston and about to publish *Lord Weary's Castle,* which would win him a Pulitzer Prize at age twenty-eight; and rumors were circulating that Dylan Thomas was coming from Wales to read his poems to an already impressed American audience.[2]

Plympton Street was a few minutes' walk from Harvard's Widener Library and the university's squash courts, where, as Wilbur reported to Armour Craig, "Wilcox beats me 3 or 4 times a week."[3] Wilcox and Wilbur had both entered graduate school intent on earning doctorates in English. Wilbur kept in reserve his plan to switch to a journalistic career if neither he nor Harvard lived up to his expectations, but there was no need to fall back on that choice: he took to Harvard like the racehorse Charlee believed she had married. He displayed his mastery across seven centuries of British and American poetic tradition, correctly identifying every spot passage on his first exam. During his first three semesters he completed all the coursework required for a PhD; in two summer sessions in 1946 he took back-to-back German courses and passed one foreign-language exam of the three required. Had he chosen to continue toward his doctorate, he would have easily been able to pass the exams in both French and Latin.

Wilbur and Wilcox were soon alerted to the perils of Harvard's doctoral exam system, thanks to the lessons they learned from Craig, who was not only their teacher at Amherst but also a 1937 graduate of the college. He had been teaching at Amherst since 1940, where he had rapidly earned a reputation for his learning and his analytical rigor. During the war Craig had studied at Harvard, working toward a PhD in English; but in early February 1946 he failed his orals. The examiners had apparently not given him a chance to impress them with his critical and pedagogical abilities but had peppered him with philological and bibliographical questions that had stumped him. Visiting the Wilburs' apartment immediately afterward, he was both devastated and angry. He told his two former students that he blamed political bias for his failure.

Although Craig did pass the oral exam and receive his PhD from Harvard in 1947, he remained curious about the academic protocol and postwar atmosphere on campus. He repeatedly asked Wilbur to describe his teachers and generalize about the Harvard professoriate. Wilbur eventually sent Craig and his wife, Peggy, the requested assessment, with the disclaimer: "Since your awful experience here, we have not written you, on the theory that anything would offend."

> At present we [Wilcox and I] are taking the same courses, under [Hyder] Rollins, [Geoffrey] Bush, a Jr. Fellow named [Walter Jackson] Bate, & [Frederick] Deknatel. . . . The nearest [Rollins] has come to textual criticism or enthusiasm, was last Wednesday, when he developed a glottal catch over a bathetic 3-lines of "Marmion"—whether it was emotion or phlegm I cannot say for sure. Bush we like; but he is patently miserable teaching a "conference group" of 65 persons, & his lectures are unprofitable. Bate, a young man with a dewey-decimalled mind, is very enlightening to talk to, & is concerned with philosophic ideas & their relation to literature in much the same way Armour is. However, he gives his lectures by means of a grand heap of papers, from which he reads full sentences at top speed & with a Rabbinical absorption. . . . There is no time to weigh or condense. . . . We were saying yesterday that Amherst classrooms really spoiled us, & made us expect something of the lecture system.[4]

Wilbur's dissatisfaction hints at the Amherst English department's competitive attitude toward Harvard's during the immediate postwar years. Many Amherst faculty members held Harvard degrees, and one Amherst graduate, Reuben Brower, returned to Harvard to accept a tenured position there. Amherst routinely sent many of its best English majors to Harvard, including such important figures as William Pritchard, Thomas Whitbread, David Ferry, and Richard Poirier. But the literary cultures of the two institutions differed. Harvard sought to appoint only the most distinguished scholars in each research specialty, regardless of their interest in or aptitude for teaching. In contrast, Amherst chose committed teachers who were expected to instill in students the ability to close-read a text and a sophisticated awareness of the practical relations among experience, reality, and verbal or artistic expression, regardless of their field of study.

Many of Wilbur's fellow students in Harvard's graduate English program shared his complaints; and between 1943 and 1948 members of the English department, perhaps aware of its deficiencies, had asked graduate students to respond to an extensive questionnaire about the quality of the program.[5] When asked if their training at Harvard had been less good than expected, 70 percent of them had answered yes. Their written comments were blunter, if less graphic, than the one that Wilbur had shared with Craig. One respondent wrote, "Too impersonal; designed to turn out research men and editors, not teachers. Too divorced from real life or student needs." Another said, "Gross waste of time in classes. Insufficient supervision of individual scholarship." A third noted, "Not enough professor-student relations either professionally or socially. Complete lack of interest in students."[6]

Though many students resented the endemic indifference of the faculty, Wilbur thrived at Harvard and, despite the reservations he expressed to Craig, remained engaged and professional in the classroom. In a matter of months he began to receive the respect that made his life in Cambridge absorbing, pleasurable, and privileged. As he and Charlee received invitations to social events, his prewar sense of himself as awkward and shy vanished, and he developed a striking public persona: handsome, deep-voiced, convivial, well mannered, and broadly gifted. Among his friends and in his letters he developed and refined the self-deprecating, fun-loving tone characteristic of his youth. Charlee, who radiated confidence and charm, was skilled at finessing pro forma social rituals and discovering what really mattered to the person she was talking to. As the poet Henry Taylor recalled after Charlee's death in 2007, "She lifted my spirits just by crossing my mind."[7] In early September 1947, just twenty months after the Wilburs' arrival at Harvard, the young poet John Malcolm Brinnin, who became a lifelong friend, summed up their aura in his journal with a single sentence: "The Wilbur years had begun."[8]

"Fidelity to Nature . . . directed by intelligence and taste"

Shortly after moving to Plympton Street, the Wilburs met the poet and Amherst graduate André du Bouchet. His presence both exhilarated and shook up their circle:

An informal gathering at the Wilburs' apartment in Cambridge, Massachusetts, early 1946. Richard Wilbur is seated at the far left, next to Tom Wilcox and André du Bouchet. *Courtesy of Richard Wilbur.*

> André . . . has been a regular visitor, & we enjoy him a great deal. . . . Charlee is now taking a course of reading under him, beginning with Gide's *Les Caves du Vatican.* André's attitudes are so opposite to mine, or at any rate so absolute, that we have the most animated disputes. His own criticism I can only define as writing a poem to criticize a poem. It comes, very often, to "How wonderful!" but quite as often to something creative in itself. As an Existentialist, he upbraids me for justifying Empsonian Criticism as a fine teaching method—I am not to think of myself as a potential teacher but as an individual. At any rate, André's mordant attacks & personal energy have given us a pleasant shaking, & set us to dreaming, over late beer, of a year at the Sorbonne.[9]

While visiting the Wilburs one afternoon in February 1946, du Bouchet leafed through the purloined copy of *Helmbrecht le Fermiêr* that Wilbur had brought home from the war. Inside he found a copy of "Tywater." At about the same time, Charlee gathered a sheaf of Wilbur's poetry and asked du Bouchet to read through it. He took the typescripts away for an hour or so, returned to their apartment, kissed Wilbur on both cheeks, and pronounced him a poet.[10]

Writing about du Bouchet's immediate enthusiasm for his poetry, Wilbur told Craig: "André's taste I cannot afford to doubt, since he is about to print 6 of my poems in *Foreground,* where he is poetry editor; he has been most hyperbolic abt. my poetry, & thinks it wd be best for Wilcox & me to go to France, where intellectuals can be 'properly arrogant.'"[11] Arrogance was an indulgence Wilbur would eschew, however, in France or anywhere else, as he established himself in an ever-widening circle of writers and academics.

Before the war, Wilbur had almost no luck placing his prose or poems in publications that weren't associated with his school or the army, in part because he seldom tried. After graduating from high school in 1938 he sent a short prose piece to the *New Yorker,* which the editors pleasantly declined with an invitation to submit again. During his first semester at Amherst he sent the *New Yorker* another article, which they brusquely rejected. Charlee tried to place a few of the poems he sent her during the war, but she succeeded with only one, "Italy: Maine." It appeared in the *Saturday Evening Post* on September 23, 1944, thanks to the influence of Betsy List, a friend who worked at the magazine.

Du Bouchet's pronouncement changed everything. Wilbur began to submit and publish poems in local and national journals as well as the newly launched literary magazine *Foreground,* which attracted some world-class contributors to its earliest issues. A piece by Jean-Paul Sartre, for instance, appeared adjacent to Wilbur's short story "The Day After the War" in the magazine's second issue. A New York publisher, Reynal and Hitchcock, had engaged du Bouchet to scout for literary talent among the veterans now flocking to Harvard and Cambridge, and he persuaded the editors to ask Wilbur to send them a selection of his poems. In March 1946 Monroe Engel, then a Reynal editor, wrote that the editorial department was reading the poems with great interest.[12] Confident of a favorable final verdict, Engel offered to send around Wilbur's unpublished poems to magazines that might want to feature them. By the time *The Beautiful Changes* was released, well-established journals, including the *Harvard Advocate, Accent, Poetry,* and *New Directions,* were accepting his work.

Wilbur added new poems to his manuscript, and Reynal welcomed them, until the delivery deadline of June 1, 1947. Proof pages contained only two red-penciled corrections: Wilbur insisted that "the proper &" be used instead of the title "And" for a poem about the ampersand, and the editors changed the placement of the Hopkins epitaph in the poem "Grace."[13] Early on, Wilbur had suggested "Water Walker," the collection's longest poem, as its title. Although Engel was no longer responsible for the book, he joshed Wilbur about the idea; the first pick for the jacket photo showed Wilbur standing next to a rustic building that looked like an outhouse, and Engel thought it had the potential to impose an unfortunate double entendre on the title. The issue resolved itself when Wilbur wrote a poem whose second stanza began with the line, "The beautiful changes as a forest is changed." The first three words became the title of both the poem and the book. As the book title, it provided an elegant dual meaning: without the context of the full line, the word *changes* can be read as a verb or a noun.

To mark the fiftieth anniversary of the book's publication, Brinnin sent Wilbur a reminiscence of the original book launch party in November 1947, where "no one . . . went hungry or, in chinos & dirndls, resisted the jukebox to which, for nickels, you could dance to the 'Beer Barrel Polka.'"

> *The Beautiful Changes* was celebrated at birth, with . . . a surprise party inspirited by the illusion that either you were really flabbergasted or couldn't, in your charity, let us down.
>
> The conspirators, each of us tapped by Charlee well in advance, were ten or twelve. Those I recall with certainty were the Stones, . . . the Wilcoxes, Bill [Read] and me. To maintain our cover we assembled secretly at Bill's Charles St. apartment . . . around six & somehow got, en masse, to Ida's Italian Restaurant in the North End by seven. A cheer went up upon your arrival after which, of course, we totally ignored you—mostly to prove our sophistication in the teeth of such childish delight. . . . The general euphoria carried us all the way to your place . . . and into the early morning. Bless us all.[14]

For some months after publication, *The Beautiful Changes* received admiring reviews from Louise Bogan, Robert Fitzgerald, Babette Deutsch, M. L. Rosenthal, Richard Eberhart, David Daiches, and Francis Golffing, all of whose reputations as accomplished poets or critics immediately burnished Wilbur's own. A phrase from Bogan's review soon became a watchword of low-key critical perspicuity: "Let us watch Richard Wilbur. He is composed of valid ingredients." Her word *ingredients* was apt, for she identified several poetic capabilities in the space of a single paragraph:

He has a remarkable variety of interest and mood, and he can contemplate his subjects without nervousness, explore them with care, and then let them drop at the exact moment that the organization of the poem is complete. . . . Wilbur's gift of fitting the poetic pattern to the material involves all sorts of delicate adjustments of the outward senses to the inner ear. Fidelity to Nature (that old fashioned virtue) underlies every word, and this fidelity is directed by intelligence and taste.[15]

Golffing called the book "remarkable" but, citing "The Regatta" and "Superiorities," wrote that Wilbur "too often spoils his chances by concessions to modishness" and "attempts at genres that lie outside his range." While Bogan had sought to spur Wilbur on, Golffing cautioned him to "secure . . . serious attention" by "staying within his proper competence." Golffing might have felt that his strictures were too grudging; he concluded the review by stating that two poems, "Grace" and "The Beautiful Changes," were "as good as any poetry written in English today, save Eliot and Stevens at their best."[16]

Though only 351 copies of *The Beautiful Changes* were sold by December 31, 1948 (not counting the books sent to reviewers, literary figures, and Wilbur's friends), it immediately raised Wilbur's visibility. More journals and anthologists sought his work. Newspapers and magazines asked him to review new books of poetry, which he did, expressing his dislikes and reservations freely, as was common practice during the era. But he was never a self-aggrandizing or combative reviewer, and in time he restricted his reviews to books he admired.

"You run to rhyme"

During his early days in Cambridge, Wilbur began to fill a large notebook with accounts of nonacademic experiences and the meditations they prompted. As the following four excerpts demonstrate, his topics ranged from postwar self-analysis, to ecstasy in the natural world, to social and literary commentary. The first entry reveals his thoughts during a time of transition and confusion, when he was torn between writing poems and focusing on scholarship. His fascination with the self as actor is a theme that surfaces in other passages throughout the notebook. In retrospect it offers a curious connection to comments by James Dickey and others, who faulted Wilbur's early poems for their reliance on formal technique and a cleverness that masked his hesitancy or inability to reveal, express, and feel deep emotion.

> Nostalgia for war is primarily a sense of the loss, through the acquisition of property, security and the future, of the sense of the self. In Italy and France . . . the self of which I was aware was so isolate, so disjoined from what it wore or did, so much a thing of the present moment, so little a career, that at any instant its possibilities seemed infinite. . . . The soldier is theatrical—my dealings with all but two or three persons overseas were consciously thespian—a way of defending the critical lump of being called the self. As Tom [Wilcox] says, "When I appeared in Piccadilly as a young bomber pilot. . . ." I now regret the loss of interval between myself and my role—I have caught myself thinking of myself as "a young man preparing for the teaching profession," as "a young poet of promise"; I let the praise and blame of people strike past my persona to myself. This is a great moral failing and vanity. If you admit no rational moral code existing without, the only hope is that you keep your self unconfounded with the aspects under which your self appears; that you don't believe that photograph of yourself, in which your hair is so well parted, your eye so acetylene, your brow so inadequate a retaining wall to the world of wonders behind. Once in southern France I went three weeks without looking into a mirror.[17]

The second passage looks back to 1945 and the week Wilbur spent in the village of Etretât on the French coast, awaiting transport to England. Not only does it dispel any doubts about his capacity to register and express deep emotion, but it also shows his tendency to analyze and stand apart from such emotion—here, by imagining how a poet might examine the relation between love (and sensuality) and objects of that love in the natural world, a meditation that foreshadows the title and focus of Wilbur's third book, *Things of This World*.

> My own feelings of release, coupled with the fresh plenitude of the place, then full of the Spring leaves and always cruised by sea winds, combined to bring about an unprecedented intoxication in me. One evening I actually kissed the leaves of a tree, with tears pouring from my eyes. All natural things, and even the walls of the houses, I approached with a free sexual adoration. I touched everything. In writing poetry, one tries to approximate this universal libidinousness: I think of Robert Frost, Gerard Hopkins. . . . When it is achieved, I wonder what manner of love it has been? The infant affects only his unknown self, or rather his belly and his

skin, milk, softness, warmth. In manhood love is more and more objectified: yet is concurrently channeled and solidified. Is the investment of multitudinous outward things with sexual love a growth beyond the adult canalization and departmentalization of desire, or is it a drawing of all things back into the penumbra of infancy?[18]

Wilbur cited Frost and Hopkins because both captured the spontaneous immersion in nature (not to be confused with Wordsworth's "emotion recollected in tranquility") that had so surprised him at Etretât. Frost, for instance, displayed a similar surge of sexual feeling for the natural world in his poem "Putting in the Seed."[19]

The third excerpt recalls Wilbur's indignant high school columnist voice, now tempered by matured sensitivity and perception.

As I returned from an insurance office medical examination today, coming along from Milk Street toward the subway, a broker had just jumped from a very high window into the street. He hit slightly to the far side of the street, so that traffic could still get by. A policeman stood by the body directing vehicles around it. Eyewitnesses were pointing at the windows to another policeman. I couldn't see which window: just a dismal mountain of windows, and every reason to get out of it. But not by jumping. I have no patience with suicides who risk other people's lives by jumping into crowded streets and turning themselves into a beastly blot on the pavement. Crowds were standing around waiting to see how they would get "it" off the street and into some conveyance. Most faces blank and wholly unreceptive. Someone whistling "I'm looking over a four-leaf clover that I overlooked before." No one crying, sick, disgusted. A certain silence, but the silence of waiting. No hats off for the presence of death. One bystander broke his trance as I passed by and said to no one in particular, as he began to walk away, in a tone of emotional uncertainty containing some elation of having been in on something. "Well, we'll read about it in the papers." (A reason for not waiting, and an anticipation: a very subtle line for an actor to try to speak.)[20]

The fourth passage displays how Wilbur's characteristic conversational eloquence reached beyond the academic formulations he was hearing and reading in his coursework. Here, he explained his interest in the mysteries, the unspoken realities, and the unrealized dreams of characters in the work of Henry James, contrasting those novels with "our [current] debased habits of imagination."

The real themes of literature, the ageless endless ones, are the ones you never learn. Joy you never learn, death you never learn, renewal is always unexpected, love is a perpetual rediscovery. One reads Nashe and nods; yes brightness falls from the air. That all passes and nothing stays is a thing admitted, agreed to; on the other hand we always pretend of some things that they are changeless—a spiritual legerdemain—and so keep calm. But calling at a house and finding all the people gone, or seeing a woman terribly beautiful, or the tall coffins of strong men who have died—"strength stoops to the grave"—teaches you mutability again. And you run to rhyme to heal the horror of it.[21]

The phrase "you run to rhyme" captures a poem's power, physiological as well as emotional, to heal both the person who writes it and the person who reads it. The phrase counters the accusations of critics who have said that Wilbur doesn't have a sense of the tragic; in fact, he understood, at least as soon as he wrote his first serious poems, the inadequacy of human reaction to loss. Several of his war poems, particularly "Tywater," "On the Eyes of an SS Officer," and "Mined Country" as well as the unpublished "Fingers" and "Two Statements," were early attempts to come to terms with (or find relief from) violent wartime experiences. The idea of mutability, much on his mind in this notebook, is inherent in the texture of *The Beautiful Changes*.

At Harvard, however, the mutations of fortune that Wilbur continued to encounter were almost all auspicious. In fact, both his academic performance and his sudden poetic success affected the trajectory of his career: the faculty were so impressed with his achievements that he was invited to apply for a Junior Fellowship, the highest accolade the university could bestow on a student. As a junior fellow, Wilbur could remain at Harvard, take courses (and even teach one) outside the PhD structure and requirements, and become an employable academic without earning a doctorate. The award, which he received in April 1947 (the fellowship officially started the following semester), also allowed him to travel to Europe and devote as much time as he wished to writing poetry.

Harvard had initiated the Society of Fellows to reward originality and nonconformity among its own and the nation's graduate students—and, with what some might call self-awareness, to protect its best students from its own institutional timidity. The society was founded in the 1930s by several Harvard professors who had admired the Prize Fellows program at Cambridge University's Trinity College.[22] Both Wilbur and Tom Wilcox were nominees for membership when the senior fellows voted that spring, but the results led to an incident that deeply distressed both friends. When Wilcox picked up the mail that had been delivered to 22 Plympton and left on the hall table, he spied the society's return address on an envelope, looked cursorily at the first three letters of the addressee's name, and tore open the letter. His heart leaped at the phrase "pleased to inform you." He then realized that the letter was addressed to Wilbur.

Wilcox's expectations had been high. He had received excellent grades during his first semesters at Harvard. At Amherst his critically prescient senior honors essay on American proletarian novelists, combined with his grades, had earned him a degree magna cum laude, whereas Wilbur, though he received four *A*s and a *B* in his senior year, got no honors. Yet Wilbur's reputation since his arrival at Harvard, where he was seen as not only an accomplished poet but also a serious and original scholar in both literature and art history, better suited the senior fellows. In their adoption of Trinity criteria, they sought to identify and appoint applicants who possessed brilliance in their disciplines as well as enough imagination and impatience to extend the reach or revolutionize the assumptions of those disciplines. The letters supporting Wilbur's candidacy are sealed until 2027, but it is likely that F. O. Matthiessen, I. A. Richards, and Frederick Deknatel wrote on his behalf.[23]

Degas and the Dandy

Wilbur believes that his essay "Degas and the Subject," written for Deknatel's course in nineteenth-century European painting, helped convince the senior fellows to vote in his favor. In the essay he expertly employed and extended the vocabulary of art history, and his facility suggests that he could easily have shifted his graduate work to that field. Nonetheless, the piece remains unpublished.

Wilbur's objective was to establish Edgar Degas's precise relation to the subjects he painted and to differentiate his approach from those of his fellow artists in France. (Degas was clearly not an Impressionist, though he had exhibited with the Impressionists in at least one of their annual shows.) The Impressionists adopt attitudes toward their subjects, Wilbur claimed, whereas Degas dramatizes the inherent action in his models' poses and in his ballet, theatrical, and racetrack scenes. In this following passage from the essay Wilbur accepted the classification of Degas's subjects—the dance, the café concert, the races, modistes (hat and dress designers), laundresses, and nudes—formulated by Paul Lafond, an art critic and the first Degas biographer:

In all of [the canvases] there is some element of characteristic physical movement: the formal gestures of the danseuse and the chanteuse, the immemorial nervous grace of the thoroughbred horse, the stylized movements of the modiste and the woman of fashion, the ironing-woman's *coup appuyé* and *coup circulaire* [pressure stroke and circular stroke], the habitual actions of the toilette. What is to be deduced from this? . . . Degas was primarily fascinated by the problem of arresting fugitive and typical movement; . . . his art is one of acute perception of the momentary dispositions of bodies in exertion.[24]

Later critics reached similar conclusions, but no earlier critic, either French or English, had anticipated the approach that Wilbur formulated in 1946. In the latter part of the essay he cited literary analogues to Degas's artistry in Zola and Joyce. He ended with this summation: "Degas is unique among the artists of his time because his paintings are psychological or dramatic interpretations of his subject; his portraits are epiphanies of character, and his paintings of contemporary life are dramatizations of a metaphysic."[25]

While studying Degas, Wilbur noted that the English literary critic Cyril Connolly defined Degas as a dandy. Deknatel provided further context for dandyism's origins. It began in Regency England, was snuffed out by Victorian stodginess, but lived on in Paris. Then it reappeared in England in the 1890s, embodied in the personalities and works of Oscar Wilde, Aubrey Beardsley, and Max Beerbohm. The dandy was a social and cultural phenomenon, a source of bemusement, and a spark to energize intellectuals and poets.

Wilbur read various accounts of the dandy, including Captain William Jesse's biography of Beau Brummell and Jules Barbey d'Aurevilly's slim, hyperbolic, and at times insufferable 1833 volume *Dandyisme*. He enhanced his essay's argument by pointing out an affinity between the aesthetic of Degas and the principles of *dandyisme* that Charles Baudelaire had epitomized: "Le Dandy doit aspirer à être sublime sans interruption, il doit vivre et dormir devant un miroir."[26] Wilbur elaborated on Baudelaire's conception of dandyism and attributed it to Degas as "a species of perfectionism, of sacramental behavior; it is also a mode of self-defense, of safeguarding the personality, it requires a life of extreme order and discipline." In addition, he distinguished between two categories of dandy, literary and social:

The dandy in literature and art is firstly a formalist. He strives for an impeccable style which will bear no trace of the great labor and anguish it has cost him. He knows that elegance lies in simplicity and spareness, and he hates superfluity. He does not openly express his feelings, but conceals them in paradox, [in] ambiguity and in consequence. Just as the social dandy strives to impress his society with his perfection, but cannot bear to give the impression of striving, the dandy artist desires to produce emotion and thought without being boldly emotional or thoughty. He deals with the moment, the transient impression, the brief perception, and so his art [has] subtle hints of sacramental significance. The dandy artist despises the public and commercialism. He does not belong to any literary or artistic movement. He is essentially religious in a mystical fashion; politically and socially he is an absolute conservative.[27]

Wilbur's portrait of the Baudelaire-Degas incarnation of the dandy, while not intended as a poetic or a personal manifesto, does foreshadow some of his later convictions and attitudes, particularly the high standards he set for himself in literary and personal life, his reserve when expressing emotion, and his search for religious illumination in the everyday world, all of which became permanent aspects of his professional and poetic character. On the other hand, his social life was fairly freewheeling, and he was never a prig or (in modern political terms) a conservative. Yet Baudelaire's version of dandyism, which condemned bourgeois taste while insisting on rigorous elegance and integrity, became for Wilbur a permanent touchstone. It helps explain his later refusal to participate in the confessional, the Beat, or the agitprop antiwar movements that began to dominate American poetry in the late 1950s. The nature of the dandy (and certainly Beau Brummell's success) derived entirely from sartorial style and affect, which, very much like Wilbur's own, attracted notice not for its bravura or ostentation but for its understated finesse and its sensible restraint.[28]

Had Wilbur pursued dandyism as a possible dissertation subject, he would have begun with Brummell's rise, reign, and disgrace. He'd already written a poem in 1946 about Brummell's last years in Caen, the safe haven to which he had absconded to avoid the debts he'd incurred during his years of unparalleled social success and influence. (Wilbur had visited the city while still a soldier, in July 1945.) But after several trusted editors rejected "Brummell in Caen," including André du Bouchet, Wilbur accepted its lack of distinction and put the poem aside. He did the same for dandyism as a topic of research.

A constant pattern of Wilbur's studies, noticeable at Amherst but intensified at Harvard, was to apply knowledge and energy from his coursework to his other pursuits, especially poetry. The required courses he took in Anglo-Saxon and English Renaissance literature, for example, later provoked him to write three memorable poems: "Beowulf," "A World without Objects Is a Sensible Emptiness," and "Merlin Enthralled." Now, after studying Degas's style so intensely, he began to write poetry as Degas painted: he incorporated into his own art the drama and physical exertion that Degas's brushstrokes evoked in horses, bathers, and nudes. In the poems of *Ceremony* the language pulses and shimmers, from New England's churning surfscapes to marvels of human dexterity, as seen in these lines from "Juggler": "It takes a sky-blue juggler with five red balls / To shake our gravity up." He turned verbs to nouns and vice versa—for example, in the following passage from "Part of a Letter":

> Easy as cove-water rustles its pebbles and shells
> In the slosh, spread, seethe, and the backsliding
> Wallop and tuck of the wave . . .

He also plucked verbs from their usual contexts and placed them where they would build new energy and nuance, as in these lines referring to fallen leaves in "In the Elegy Season": "Haze, char, and the weather of All Souls': / A giant absence mopes upon the trees."

Cambridge Lionizers and the *New Yorker* Brass Ring

Poetry held a central place in American postwar culture, but other differences between that era and our own arouse less nostalgia. The literary world recognized several women poets as major among the company of men, yet women were still in most respects second-class citizens, not only in the workplace but also in academia. Adrienne Rich, a Radcliffe student in the late 1940s, who published her first book of poems with the Yale Younger Poets series when she was twenty-two years old, was not allowed to enter the Poetry Room in Harvard's Lamont Library when it opened in 1949. Its namesake donor had designated it for Harvard undergraduates, and thus for men only.[29]

Likewise, there was still a strong barrier to public acknowledgment or acceptance of homosexuality. Matthiessen, for instance, who was one of the most distinguished members of the English faculty when Wilbur arrived at Harvard, lived off and on for twenty years with the painter Russell Cheney. Although he revealed his relationship with Cheney to his closest Harvard friends, Matthiessen often played the role of the single "extra man" at the dinner party table.

Communism had become anathema in both the public and private spheres, though many people, especially academics and union workers, thought its socialist core made more sense than cutthroat capitalism did. (At least one of Wilbur's close Cambridge friends was an active member of the Communist Party and tried, unsuccessfully, to recruit him.) Even those professing only a theoretical respect for Marxism could be summarily expelled from government, university, and public-sector jobs. People who were members of party cells were often prosecuted for advocating the "overthrow of the government," a phrase that Wilbur recalled all too clearly from his own experiences during the war. A person's political beliefs and activism were serious matters when they became public or were exposed by FBI informants. All of these circumstances directly affected the Wilburs, were constant topics of discussion, and caused both alliances and breaches among friends.[30]

During the Wilburs' years in Cambridge the House Committee on Un-American Activities (known as HUAC) was busily pursuing suspected Communists. The issue hit close to home when Dirk Struik, a mathematics professor at the Massachusetts Institute of Technology, was indicted in 1950 for plotting to overthrow the government. He and other suspected Communists had been identified by an undercover FBI informant named Herbert Philbrick, who had, for close to a decade, been active in progressive organizations in the area. The indictments generated by Philbrick's accusations created a national uproar.

When Wilbur joined a committee to raise funds on behalf of Struik, the FBI took note. Decades later, an Amherst fraternity brother, Stansfield Turner, who was appointed director of the Central Intelligence Agency in 1977, told him that the FBI had been aware of his political activities and sympathies during the 1940s and 1950s. This news did not surprise Wilbur, given the "Suspected Disloyal" designation he had received after enlistment and his subsequent removal from army code training.

In the postwar years, American academic institutions were infused with undergraduate and graduate students who were also well-traveled war veterans. This growing cosmopolitanism paralleled an intellectual openness to influences such as Jean-Paul Sartre's existentialism and European-style communism. As a result, American novelists and poets were turning to new and more adventurous literary journals to get their works into the world.

Du Bouchet had helped to launch *Foreground,* sponsored in part by James Laughlin, a Harvard graduate who later founded New Directions publishing company. In addition to Ciardi, Lowell, and Wilbur, its Cambridge-area contributors included Brinnin, who did his graduate work at Harvard and taught for a time at Vassar College; Howard Moss, who became fiction editor of the *New Yorker* in 1948 and poetry editor in 1950; and Jackie Steiner, who, in her senior year, had been chosen by the Vassar faculty to represent the school in the Irene Glascock poetry competition at Mount Holyoke College.[31] All became the Wilburs' close friends.

Throughout each academic year visiting literary celebrities performed on campus. In the notebook Wilbur began to keep in 1946, he reflected on the competitiveness such visits unleashed among Harvard's literati: "The person most resented is he who acts with precisely our own motives, but openly: we feel a vicarious exposure, and that is painful." Nor did celebrity worship escape his comment:

> Now everybody knows that all Cambridge is full of lionizers, & that when the Sitwells, for example, come to town there is the beastliest sort of scramble to meet them, and much sour grapes from those who fail to. And anyone knows that—except at such a Sitwell "meeting" as we had at the Eberharts, with only 8 people and much quiet talk—meeting in Cambridge is much like a break-up in pool. One merely collides en masse with the visitor.[32]

Dame Edith Sitwell (1897–1964) had been publishing her poetry since 1913, but the poems she wrote during World War II were bringing her back into the public eye. Her 1949 tour of America garnered considerable attention, even in publications such as *Life* magazine, where there was as much focus on her costumes and jewelry as there was on her often obscure poems, many of which were set to music. During her public reading at Harvard in March of that year, her voice, according to the *Harvard Crimson,* was nearly inaudible and her poems difficult to grasp.[33] Yet Wilbur was impressed enough by what he knew of her work to want her to think well of his own. When she expressed interest in reading his poems, Jack Sweeney, the astute and benevolent curator of the Lamont Library's Poetry Room, presented her with a copy of *The Beautiful Changes.* In his notebook Wilbur imagined watching her read the book, apprehensively second-guessed her choices, and wrote of wishing he could tear out many of its pages.

Although many of the era's poets lived in Boston and its environs, New York was still the center of the publishing world. Likewise, the *New Yorker* was the brass ring for poets who were submitting individual poems to journals, even though the magazine had only recently begun to publish more serious poetry in addition to the scintillating light verse of Dorothy Parker, Phyllis McGinley, Walker Gibson, and others. Bogan's brisk and favorable review of *The Beautiful Changes* in the *New Yorker* had encouraged Wilbur to submit "Museum Piece," a poem inspired by an anecdote he had come across while researching Degas's life and work. The novelist Peter De Vries, who was the magazine's poetry editor at the time, recommended its publication to Katherine White. She raised no initial objections. But when she passed on the poem to the fact checkers, the magazine's last line of defense against inaccuracy and infelicity, they raised red flags.

To create a rhyme for "shoes," Wilbur had shortened the painter Henri Toulouse-Lautrec's full name to "Toulouse." The fact checkers, unsympathetic to the resulting emphatic rhyme, insisted that "Lautrec" was the preferred short form for the artist's name. They were confident that Wilbur could find an alternative rhyme that clicked with it.[34] Still, the rhyme scheme was the least of their problems. They also indicted the final image of "Museum Piece," which explains how Degas, undressing for bed, hung a pair of pants over an El Greco painting that he had propped against the wall. De Vries framed the issue for Wilbur: "we like to be sure of our facts before we publish a poem, and the affect of this one hinges so completely on a crucial detail that we'd like to be especially certain."[35]

Wilbur dropped everything else he was doing and focused on establishing that his image was indeed solidly factual. He bolstered his answer to De Vries by acknowledging that none of the several Degas experts he consulted could cite a source to prove the story's basis in fact; nonetheless, he said, all thought it highly probable and characteristic of the artist. He told De Vries, "Lafond's *Degas* (I, P. 94, P. 118) gives some circumstantial evidence: Degas owned two Grecos, did have pictures against his bedroom wall, and used to fling his clothes at the servant Zoe, which argues he didn't hang them up in a closet from a seated position in bed." Resting his case, he cited another Degas expert who was puzzled that the editors would not allow "poetic license" to poetry.[36]

Any defense that invoked poetic license was unlikely to carry weight at the *New Yorker*. Its editors proposed a way to keep the story in the realm of hearsay or to admit that it might be apocryphal: they suggested changing the line "Edgar Degas purchased once" to "it's said that Degas once possessed."[37] Wilbur stood his ground: "I have, of course, no interest in perpetrating a minor anecdotal fraud; but I think this use of a highly probable anecdote entirely justifiable poetically." After somewhat recklessly implying that anyone who disagreed that poetic truth trumped literal fact was mad, he ended his brief with the hope that he did not seem unreasonable.[38] De Vries repeated that the magazine would not waver on points of fact, neither for prose nor for poetry, so Wilbur withdrew the poem. *Poetry* magazine, however, was happy to publish "Museum Piece" immediately, along with six others that Wilbur submitted. Eventually, he found documentation in Randall Jarrell's library supporting the fact that Degas hung his trousers every night on one of his two El Grecos.

Paris and the Artist's Engagement with the World

Few at Harvard doubted that poetry was Wilbur's calling and deserved his primary attention. The historian Crane Brinton, who presided over the Society of Fellows, took him aside to reassure him that he need not feel obligated to justify election to the society by a focus on scholarship. He should live the life of a poet; he should write. Thus encouraged, Wilbur sought and received permission from the senior fellows to travel to France for three months during the spring semester of 1948.

Du Bouchet had predicted that the Wilburs would thrive in Paris. So did Stanley and Eileen Geist, friends who had left Cambridge in August 1947 to tour Europe but found postwar Paris so stimulating and inexpensive that they settled there. When Wilbur and Charlee arrived on the *Mauritania* in March 1948, the Geists introduced them to the city's easygoing lifestyle. Charlee, pregnant but not due until July, intended to enjoy herself. (Four-year-old Ellen was in North Caldwell with her grandparents.) After a night at Le Bal Nègre she wrote, "It is a truly fantastic place where the music is hot Negro jazz with a Martinique twist and causes immediate madness in all who listen. . . . We stayed until 3 AM and I danced myself silly with no one latching to the fact that I was pregnant: a triumph that I am being a perfect shit about."[39]

What impressed the Wilburs most was not the city's artistic avant-garde—though they met many of its major figures—but the peaceful and dedicated atmosphere in which its poets, novelists, and visual artists seemed to live and work. They did not find, or engage in, the political and philosophical conflict that cultural historians associate with postwar Paris. Through the Geists, the Wilburs soon met the sculptor Alberto Giacometti and the artist Jean Hélion, who lent Wilbur his guitar. At parties Wilbur was easily persuaded to strum and sing. He favored the blues, a genre he had heard often during his two rail-riding summers during the Depression. Du Bouchet and Pierre Schneider, an art historian who was also inducted as a Harvard junior fellow in 1947, provided contacts to not only other American expatriates but also practicing French poets and artists. One of those new contacts, the editor of an avant-garde magazine called *transition*, commissioned Wilbur to translate two French poems by Henri Pichette: "Apoéme 1" and "Apoéme 2."

The productions of Molière's plays that Wilbur saw at the Comédie-Française proved to be an invaluable influence when he reconsidered his plan to write his own verse drama during a Guggenheim fellowship in 1951. In the meantime, whenever he stepped outside his lodgings at the Hôtel d'Isly on Rue Jacob, he saw potential subjects for poems in every direction. For instance, the famous outdoor bird market on Ile de la Cité inspired the poem "Marché aux Oiseaux," whose last quatrain unleashes full-throated scorn on the sellers and prospective buyers who imprison these exotic, melodious creatures:

> We love the small, said Burke. And if the small
> Be not yet small enough, why then by Hell
> We'll cramp it till it knows but how to feed,
> And we'll provide the water and the seed.[40]

In "Giacometti," written after he visited the sculptor in his studio, Wilbur conveyed his belief that Giacometti intended to contrast the attenuated, scarified, and suffering figures he sculpted with the hulking statues of rock-ribbed, clenched-faced French military heroes and politicians stationed around Paris. Giacometti's iconic representation of the human form, "Towering like a thin / Coral, out of a reef of plaster chalk," soon went striding into the modern consciousness. Wilbur explicated Giacometti's vision of contemporary, alienated humanity in the post-Auschwitz, post-Hiroshima era and spoke of the result via a collective "we." Yet it is unlikely that Wilbur thought of himself or Charlee as alienated from his or her own life experiences. In fact, while the couple was relaxing in Grasse, visiting their new artist friends Marcelle and Ferdinand Springer, a moment of clarity changed Wilbur's approach to artistic creation. He explained the shift in his thinking in a series of long exuberant letters to Tom Wilcox. Wilcox, however, read Wilbur's thoughts as a betrayal of art's serious moral purpose.

He was particularly offended by this passage in the first letter: "I find that the most salutary effect of Europe is instant dissipation of ambition. One does only what one enjoys, and as a consequence everything done is done better. We go on reading and writing things like regular Cambridge people, but there is no moral stress involved in deciding not to do a damned thing for a while."[41]

The debate between Wilbur and Wilcox involved their essentially different ideologies. Wilcox believed that intellectuals, writers, and artists should concentrate their energies on a political shift toward socialist principles and the election of socialist office holders. He suspected that a too-focused pursuit of one's own concerns would lead to narcissism. In contrast, Wilbur thought writers and intellectuals, and especially poets and painters, should work to perfect their talents. "No need to point out that this is not so in America," he wrote. "The American intellectual is always worrying about whether teaching is 'action' or painting abstractions is 'social involvement.'" The endemic suspicion of the intellectual in America leads "him to self-suspicion."[42]

In each letter to Wilcox, Wilbur recapped what he interpreted as Tom's side of their ongoing disagreement. "Tom wonders," for instance, "whether he had not better balance his existence between masturbation and sexual forays by forcibly estranging himself from his work in the direction of political engagement or what-not." To that summary he attached a strong defense of his own point of view:

> A painter said to us yesterday that it took a hell of a lot more willpower to be a painter than to be a soldier or a dictator. Clearly he was not thinking of art as a soft indulgence, but as the *most manly* of callings. I think he was right. . . . In my last letter I said with approval that artists here go quietly and work in the country: if art is self-abuse, this is contemptible, but if art is the most willful human activity this is admirable: it means cutting yourself off from all possible escapes from the confrontation of the difficulties of your art. If you were failing to paint what you wanted to paint, would the arrival of a summons to go picket the Rumanian embassy be a blessing, an invitation to life, or a temptation to cowardice? It is harder to paint a picture than to picket, and an artist who does too much picketing is a weak man or he is merely a dabbler in art and is no artist at all.[43]

A few months before leaving for France and beginning this debate with Wilcox, Wilbur had written "Tears," in which he assessed the burden of the rich, who bear the "Atlas weight of eighty years of ease."[44] He sent the poem to the *New Yorker* after receiving an encouraging note from De Vries, who wrote that he and Mrs. White had read *The Beautiful Changes* with a good deal of pleasure. They would be delighted to hear from him, De Vries said, if the skirmish caused by the editorial sticklers in the office over "Museum Piece" could be forgotten.[45] Wilbur explained that "Tears" was the only poem he had on hand. He and Charlee were soon off to Paris, he said, and he hoped the city would stimulate him to write more.

De Vries declined to publish "Tears" and on May 19, 1948, also passed on the chance to take "Marché aux Oiseaux." He did, however, accept Wilbur's new airmail offering, "Grasse: The Olive Trees."[46] In a subsequent letter he shared some quibbles and queries about the placement and omission of commas and pointed out a "which" where the editors preferred a "that." The letter did not reach Wilbur before he left Europe in June and was forwarded to his parents' home. After reading it, Helen Wilbur wrote to De Vries to say that if the suggestions couldn't await her son's approval, she advised against acting on them. "You will find in his other works," she said, "just such combinations as *heavy jammed, slow complete,* and *faint disheveled* without the customary comma inserted . . . and therefore they [and a few other queried items] might be assumed to be intentional." The word combinations remained comma-less, and the "which" stayed.[47]

Bards at Bard

On November 5, 1948, Wilbur headed to a poetry conference at Bard College in Annandale-on-Hudson, New York. Not only was this the first event outside Cambridge at which he was publicly recognized as a rising talent among his generation, but it also brought together a number of younger poets, most of them still at early stages in their careers. Immediately, these poets recognized that they had a lot in common. Invitees included William Carlos Williams, Richard Eberhart, Kenneth Rexroth, Elizabeth Bishop, Lloyd Frankenberg, Jean Garrigue, and Robert Lowell. Also present were James Merrill and Joseph Summers, who were teaching at Bard, and Elizabeth Hardwick.

Several of the attendees wrote brief recollections of the conference's most memorable moments. In them we learn that Rexroth was the odd man out; he wore a red shirt and yellow suspenders, picked fights with as many poets as possible, and insisted that every poet present (except for Williams) was an effete East Coast snob. On Friday night he granted the "snobs" some

peace by persuading three of the prettiest undergraduates to spend the evening with him in a cemetery. Wilbur recalled eating breakfast on Saturday
morning with Bishop and a couple of the others. Everyone was accounting
for what they'd done during the previous evening. When Bishop wondered
about Rexroth, Wilbur answered, "Oh, he was out in the graveyard being a
natural force."[48]

The keynote speaker was Williams, who talked about free verse, according to Bishop, in a "completely scatterbrained way."[49] Once the formal
presentations and discussions ended, however, the poets gathered together
without an audience and gradually coaxed each other to read their poems.
Now theory vanished and live poetry took over. Only Bishop demurred
when asked to read, but Lowell gallantly stepped in and read her poem
"The Fish," one of her best.

Over the course of two days the participants reached a general agree-
ment: that most of the invited poets, who had begun to call themselves
"new formalists," were giving the genre new energy; that they appreciated
one another's poetry and thought it was mostly terrific; and that most of
them drank too much. This last realization had been tested and confirmed
by their enthusiastic consumption of a brutal concoction called glügg—a
mixture of wine and whiskey, whose potency was camouflaged with herbs,
berries, and spices. Bishop remembered that she and Hardwick had to help
an unsteady Lowell from the punchbowl to his room. She also remembered
that after Lowell loosened his tie and shirt, Hardwick commented, "Why,
he's an Adonis!"[50] Writing to Wilbur a few weeks later, Bishop acknowledged that the intensity and pace of the conference never let up, and that
she was anxious to get away to Key West.[51]

The legacy of the Bard conference lived on, beyond its anecdotes of conflict and intoxication, through the kind of enhanced self-confidence that
members of a group can confer on each other. In the late 1940s Wilbur,
Ciardi, May Sarton, Richard Eberhart, and John Holmes formed a group to
read and critique their own new work, meeting monthly for three winters
at each other's houses. In 1962, just three months before his death, Holmes
sent Wilbur a ten-page narrative poem in twelve parts celebrating the poets
of his generation. Part 1, "The Five," focuses on their group:

> Good God bless all such big long bickering nights
> Among the cheeses and bottles, coffee and carbon copies,
> In Medford or Cambridge—or Nashville or Chicago!
> The fact is everything we read is in our books,

Our best poems. If those confrontations were painful,
Rowdy, sometimes the fire of bloom and absolute,
We couldn't hear a clank of armor some of us wore.
Or see which came naked or afraid, but it was so.
. . .
No bruising Wilbur. Whatever he read he stunned us,
In that clear clipped rhythmic our youngers imitate.
His poems were his polished pleasure, and ours,
And literally they brought the world up from dark.[52]

Just as Wilbur's poems were "polished pleasure," his prose was consistently arresting, pleasing, and insightful. But until the late 1940s its chief virtues were wit, irony, and understatement. During his time in the Society of Fellows—when he was permitted to relinquish scholarly publication and oversight—his critical prose became more combative. It showed that he was, on occasion, keen to demolish his opponents' arguments while continuing to acknowledge their accomplishments. This honing of his tone and prose style was a natural result of his desire to articulate what good poetry demanded and how to write it.

The Bard poetry conference's clash of convictions gave him a chance to assert his own views at a moment when Williams, a poet he revered, was disparaging them. The conference opened with sessions in which each poet laid out his or her poetic principles. Louise Bogan began by making a somewhat defensive case for formalism. Williams came next, insisting (in an unconvincing way, the new formalists thought) that free verse was the only truly American way of writing poetry. Lowell, Eberhart, Bishop, Bogan, Garrigue, and Wilbur felt that they were under attack.

There followed throughout the weekend, Wilbur recalled, a "knockdown discussion of poetic form." He himself picked up Williams's gauntlet when Theodore Weiss asked him to argue for the formalist position in his reaction to Bogan's and Williams's talks. Wilbur's riposte was privately circulated at first, but Weiss eventually published it in an issue of the *Quarterly Review of Literature,* a journal he had founded in 1943 and brought with him to Bard in 1948. Wilbur sassily titled the published essay "The Bottles Become New, Too," wording that played on Bogan's remark about what happens when poets put new wine in old bottles.[53]

Wilbur began his response to Williams by likening his talk to the letters Cezanne had written to his artist friend Emile Bernard about his own artistic methods: "Both are unsatisfactory in an inspiring way. In each case you hear the voice of a practicing master too deep in his own work to talk like a critic." Wilbur didn't think that Williams was incoherent, but he did think he was eccentric. And, he wrote, just because Williams had found a successful strategy for writing his own poems, "this does not mean that his critical theories are right." Wilbur acknowledged that writing good poetry in one's own era involves "rejecting other ways of writing, past and present." One of the great and frequent failings of poets, he said, is to write in "The Tradition" and thus constrain their originality by replicating earlier forms, themes, subjects, and attitudes. But Williams's critical solution—to abandon all form and rhyme—seemed, to Wilbur, just plain wrong.[54]

Asserting the advantages of formal verse, he insisted that iambic pentameter is superior to free verse as a way to render human speech because it can absorb the full range of speech rhythms. Free verse has no equivalent way to accent that flow. After noting the early origins of the sonnet and terza rima forms, he concluded, "I have seen sonnets, villanelles, inversions, and all that Dr. Williams reprehends do great services in the last few years, and when this is so, one cannot say that the poets have surrendered to traditional forms. They have taken them over, rather."[55]

Likeminded formalists embraced this rhetorical knockout of Williams. Yet as Wilbur told Craig Lambert in an interview for *Harvard Magazine* in 2008, he has little interest in form per se or poetic craft for its own sake: "The kind of poetry I like best, and try to write, uses the whole instrument. Meter, rhyme, musical expression—everything is done for the sake of what's being said, not for the sake of prettiness." He does believe, however, that "for anyone who knows how to use these forms powerfully, they make for a stronger kind of poetry than free verse can ever be."[56]

Critics who think Wilbur has overburdened his poems with rhymes, pentameters, intricate stanzas, and allegiance to tradition may be surprised to read the essays that delineate his process of writing them. *Spontaneous* is a word that often appears in these discussions. One unpublished meditation begins: "Rhyme works as words work in dreams."[57] To find vivid rhyming phrases that advance a poem, Wilbur argues, poets need to troll their subconscious selves to bring to the surface hidden connections and realities. This reliance on associative powers has reinforced how Wilbur has thought and written about poetic inspiration. His essays affirm that the writing of a poem always involves various stages of uncertainty and struggle. If a poet begins with a conviction or in full possession of an argument, the poem will not have much surprise or original insight.

"If you explain it I won't like it anymore"

Harvard's influence on Wilbur's academic and creative future took many forms, some of them fortuitous and many quite complex. I. A. Richards, Robert Frost, and F. O. Matthiessen stand out as examples of the people who helped shape Wilbur's experience there. For instance, by studying with and later assisting Richards, one of the most formidable of the mid-twentieth-century critics and intellectuals, Wilbur became familiar with the close analysis of a work's organization and texture and applied what he learned to the essay he wrote for Deknatel on Degas's paintings and drawings.

Richards's methodology also helped shape Wilbur's later thinking about Edgar Allan Poe, whose stories he had first read in February 1944 while in a foxhole beneath Monte Cassino. (Wilbur never studied Poe at Harvard, though in the fall of 1949 he taught a graduate seminar on him that attracted eight students.) Over the course of several years Wilbur devoted himself to a study of Poe's life and works, developing an interpretation of the writer that he related in a series of essays. Poe's stories engaged him more than the verse did; except for a few poems Wilbur thought his poems were overwrought and overrated. Nonetheless, in the following passage, which Wilbur contributed to an introduction of Poe in *Major Writers of America* (1962), he encapsulated the extreme nature of Poe's cosmic vision and its fusion with the role of a poet:

> The universe, as Poe conceives it, is a poetic or artistic creation, a "plot of God." It has come about through God's breaking up of His original unity and His self-radiation into space. . . . Since God, in creating the universe, fragmented Himself into his creatures, and now exists only in those "infinite individualizations" of Himself, it is they who must by some counter-impulse, restore the original sense of things.[58]

Only poetic imagination, Poe assumed, can accomplish this mighty task; and Wilbur's insight, original and persuasive, has become widely accepted among Poe scholars.

Theodore Baird had been pressing Wilbur since his first semester at Harvard to write down his impressions of Richards. Baird's interest was keen; he had learned of Richards's methodology while he himself was a student at Harvard and had incorporated it into his own courses in composition and criticism at Amherst. Wilbur, however, did not weigh in on Richards until several years after he had both taken a course with him and served as a teaching assistant in his influential introductory course, General Education A. He began his analysis of Richards by looking at him from the viewpoint of a dispirited subordinate, creating a pastiche based on a famous passage from T. S. Eliot's "The Love Song of J. Alfred Prufrock":

> No! I am not Prof. Richards, nor was meant to be;
> Am an assistant prof, one that will do
> To mark the papers, take a class or two,
> Advise the Prof; a useful tool, I hope,
> Politic, cautious, fearful of derision,
> Absorbative of the things my betters say,
> A novice of the grand synthetic vision
> Who feels, at times, decidedly *borné*—
> Almost, at times, a dope.[59]

Wilbur delayed in assessing Richards—and, when he did, resorted to an oblique parody—because he was "much puzzled by him," even though he had watched him teach class twice a week for at least two semesters. Richards's "detachment" and his preference for being alone were additional complications.[60] Moreover, despite the admirable coherence of his lectures on Western intellectual history, Wilbur had "to strain [his] brains to remain on Richards's level of abstraction." Only then was he "aware of immense jellings." Richards's "freshmen are much of the time entirely baffled," Wilbur continued, "and R does not perceive this."[61]

Wilbur's negative critique of a man he otherwise thought "wondrous" and "fascinating to work with" (when not teaching freshmen) helped him to identify, by implication, some of the positive characteristics he was adopting in his own teaching and writing: "What bothers me about Richards is that he too seldom speaks in instances and examples, but rather presents his hearers with the abstract end-products of his thought, and connections between those products: a proceeding which contradicts his own theory of education."[62] Wilbur's poems, starting with those he wrote when he was seven years old, attest to his way of accumulating "instances" on the way to arriving at universals. Also implicit in this critique is Wilbur's attachment to the "things of this world," part of a phrase he borrowed from Saint Augustine for the poem "Love Calls Us to the Things of This World," which has become identified with his entire poetic oeuvre. During the years he was at Harvard, Wilbur was also strongly (though temporarily) attracted to a platonic metaphysics that claimed superiority over the unstable world outside his mind. In the poem "A World without Objects Is a Sensible Emptiness," he rejected this view decisively as a mental desert, declaring that the visible world glows with spiritual satisfaction.[63]

Wilbur never studied with Robert Frost, who resigned from his teaching post at Amherst just before Wilbur arrived as a freshman in the fall of 1938, but Frost lived nearby when the Wilburs arrived in Cambridge in 1946. The couple developed a lasting friendship with him that had its origins not only in Wilbur's early promise as a poet but also in the role that William Hayes Ward and Susan Hayes Ward (Charlee's grandfather and great-aunt) had played in furthering Frost's literary career. The national magazine they had edited, the New York–based *Independent,* was the first to publish his poetry. Frost so admired Susan Ward that he had written "Wild Grapes" at her insistence, after she had persuaded him that he should "remember the ladies" by writing a female counterpart to "Birches."[64]

Having memorized a prodigious amount of Frost's poetry, Wilbur would recite the poet's work back to him when he visited him at his home. As the Wilburs became regular guests, they ceased to sit on the carpet (literally) and continued the friendship on an equal footing. Frost, out of interest or an instinctive competitiveness, kept abreast of current poetry. One day in 1947 he praised Wilbur's somewhat mysterious poem "The Puritans," which had just appeared in the *Advocate.* Because the poem is a parable with an unstated subject, Wilbur began to explain that it was about religious zealots who commit the very sins they excoriate. Frost cut him off, saying, "If you explain it I won't like it any more."[65]

There were other subjects that Frost was disinclined to pursue, as Wilbur discovered. The younger poet was reading widely from the poetry of earlier eras, often finding lesser-known poets he liked well enough to study and bring to the attention of others. He found himself suddenly drawn to the early-nineteenth-century poet of gloom, Thomas Lovell Beddoes—in particular, a section of his poem "The Phantom Wooer," in which the speaker is a ghost who is attempting to persuade a woman to join him in death:

> Young soul, put off your flesh, and come
> With me into the quiet tomb;
> Our bed is lovely, dark, and sweet;
> The earth will swing us, as she goes,
> Beneath our coverlid of snows,
> And the warm leaden sheet.[66]

Wilbur immediately saw that Frost had borrowed Beddoes's phrasing and rhythm ("Our bed is lovely, dark, and sweet") for a line in the famous last stanza of "Stopping by Woods on a Snowy Evening": "The woods are lovely, dark and deep."[67]

Years later Wilbur wrote about this Beddoes echo in his essay "Poetry's Debt to Poetry." He noted that Frost's poem never mentions cold; rather, "the characterizing words are 'easy,' 'downy,' 'lovely,' 'dark' and 'deep,' words that evoke just such a snowy coverlet and featherbed as were offered" by Beddoes's ghostly seducer, "and which twice over oblige Frost to put away the thought of sleep." During a conversation in the late 1940s Wilbur off-handedly asked Frost if he were fond of Beddoes. Frost said that, yes, he had read the poet. But, Wilbur recalled, "he said so with a warning glitter in his eye, and I did not pursue the subject."[68]

In his Harvard-era notebook Wilbur began an extended account of Frost with a harsh judgment and then qualified it: "Robert Frost's conversation is full of malice, & he's a very aggressive man. His demonstrated integrity balances this, however, and of course the humor, so that he is delightful to listen to."[69] There was a humorous side to Frost's literary jibes and anecdotes, Wilbur recalled, but most of it involved exposing the shortcomings of rival poets. For instance, Frost faulted both Ezra Pound and William Butler Yeats for their lack of linguistic expertise. Pound's translations were "eclectic," he claimed, because he has "six trots before him on the table; Ezra didn't know a conjugation from a declension." Of Yeats, Frost said, "he simply couldn't learn a language."[70]

F. O. Matthiessen was another important influence during the Harvard years. He was an Americanist, whose most famous work, *American Renaissance,* was a study of Ralph Waldo Emerson, Henry David Thoreau, Nathaniel Hawthorne, Walt Whitman, and Herman Melville, all of whom published their major works during the early 1850s. The book triggered the establishment of American literature and later American studies as independent disciplines, departments, and undergraduate majors in institutions around the nation. Wilbur took two courses from Matty (a nickname Matthiessen himself used) and also worked as a teaching assistant for him. More than any other Harvard professor, Matthiessen had an explicit impact on Wilbur's work and thinking. In turn, Wilbur impressed the professor as both a poet and a literary scholar. Matthiessen's backing, Wilbur believes, was decisive in his election to the Society of Fellows.

Within Wilbur's circle, and within many other circles beyond Harvard,

Matty was both revered and seen as controversial. His membership in leftist groups, which he may or may not have known were communist fronts, made him a target of anti-communists. Moreover, although he was universally respected in academia and his semi-closeted homosexuality never affected that respect, the social climate of the late 1940s was decades away from open acceptance of gays.[71] When his partner Cheney died in 1945, Matthiessen was deeply lonely, and Brinnin, among others, knew he'd been diagnosed as clinically depressed. Friends tried and failed to help him find another partner; and a few months after one such introduction, he jumped to his death. Brinnin described his reaction to the news in his journal:

> April 1, 1950. Westport. 7 a.m. Flip on the bedside radio. Matty a suicide in Boston. A fall from 10th floor of a fourth rate hotel. On windowsill his Phi Beta Kappa key . . . wristwatch, Skull & Bones insignia.
> Phone V. in Poughkeepsie, his first thought mine: grief unassuagable. Says reporters will play with "contributing factors" . . . anything but truth. Man died of broken heart. Period.[72]

Matthiessen had accepted an invitation to the Wilburs for the evening of April 1. In a telegram sent at six o'clock that morning, he informed them that he'd been taken sick and was very sorry he'd be unable to have dinner.[73]

Politics were central to Matty's sense of himself as an intellectual. His activism was calibrated, but it was both public and outspoken. Although he was not a Marxist, he, like Tom Wilcox, believed that American values demanded a socialist governance that would work toward a more equitable distribution of goods and services and that critics and artists must actively concern themselves with the major political and social issues of the day. Given Wilbur's personal disagreement with Wilcox, it's not surprising that he gradually backed away from the outspoken socialism that Matthiessen was advocating. Yet he remained grateful for his support and dedicated his second book of poems, *Ceremony,* published in 1950, after Matty's death, to "F.O.M."

Critical reaction to *Ceremony's* publication was generally favorable. Nonetheless, many reviewers expressed reservations in the form of three basic appeals: they wanted Wilbur to include fewer poems that were merely technically impressive, they wanted him to deal with the grittier and more universal aspects of experience, and they wanted him to take more chances. In the November–December 1951 issue of the *Partisan Review,* Randall Jarrell brought up all three perceived weaknesses. Yet his review (which we will discuss in detail in chapter 10) paradoxically became a touchstone for Wilbur's fans as well as for his detractors. As they were writing retrospective commentaries on Wilbur's first few books, other reviewers—notably Clive James and Robert F. Sayre—implicitly responded to Jarrell, plumbing the depths of Wilbur's lyric and narrative poems to cite specific examples that Jarrell had not. The original 1951 challenge stung, however, and in his later books Wilbur included longer and more defiantly ambitious poems than he had in *Ceremony*.

Although Wilbur was appointed in 1950 to a five-year term as Harvard's Briggs-Copeland Assistant Professor of Creative Writing, he taught there for only three years. After he was awarded a Guggenheim in 1952–53, he was able to spend a full academic year translating Molière in Corrales, New Mexico, while still receiving a semester's pay; and when he received a Prix de Rome for 1954–55, he went to Rome for the final year of his Harvard appointment. On October 28, 1954, while in Rome, Wilbur received a letter from Herschel Baker, the chair of the English department, formally announcing that he would not be considered for a permanent position. Baker emphasized that this refusal implied no adverse judgment on Wilbur's teaching performance or his ability to get tenure, and he made it clear that Harvard had greatly appreciated and admired Wilbur's service.[74] The letter confirmed what Wilbur had already understood when he was appointed: at the end of his contract there would be no tenure-track openings in the department.

7

Claiming Molière for His Own Native Tongue

"In short, trust the words"

I have always done some translating, for good reasons and bad. The worst reason for translating is that it makes possible an escape from the painful origination of one's own poems into the exercise of technical dexterity. The best of the good reasons is that one has fallen in love with something, and wishes to do it honor and claim it for one's own tongue.

—RICHARD WILBUR, letter to Donald Carne-Ross, February 14, 1968

In the fall of 1950 a group of Cambridge poets came together at the initial urging of Violet R. Lang (known as "Bunny") to form the Poets' Theatre. Richard Wilbur, Richard Eberhart, and John Ciardi were senior members of this loosely affiliated group, whose goal it was to revive verse drama for the American stage.[1] Members wanted complete control over what they wrote and planned to run the theater themselves: acting, administrating, directing, and selling tickets. Although consensus on what made good, contemporary poetic drama was hard to achieve, so was the members' willingness to acknowledge having joined a group to advance it. According to Nora Sayre, a Poets' Theatre intern in the mid-1950s, "Wilbur said that the Poets' Theatre was like the Communist Party: everyone belonged to it, but nobody wanted to admit it."[2]

The time seemed right to launch a theater group devoted to verse plays; audiences and critics had already shown that they were receptive to the dramatic work of several poets whose plays had been produced in London in the 1940s and were later exported to Broadway. In 1950 Christopher Fry's

The Lady's Not for Burning won a New York Drama Critics Circle award for best foreign play, and T. S. Eliot's *The Cocktail Party* won a Tony for best play. On November 21 of that year Eliot delivered the first lecture in the Spencer Memorial Series at Harvard (named for the poet Theodore Spencer), choosing a topic he thought would have interested Spencer as much as it did himself: "the problems of poetic drama." He opened by explaining his "intentions, failures, and partial successes" in writing *The Cocktail Party* and two other poetic dramas, *Murder in the Cathedral* and *The Family Reunion*.[3] He hoped to be of use, he said, to those who might follow his experimentation and perhaps go further. Wilbur was in the audience that day and later attended the party that Dorothea and I. A. Richards gave in Eliot's honor.

Eliot's debate—with himself as much as with the audience—began with an assumption: "If poetry is merely decoration, an added embellishment, if it merely gives people of literary taste the pleasure of listening to poetry at the same time they are witnessing a play, then it is superfluous. It must justify itself dramatically, and not just be fine poetry shaped into a dramatic form." He declared that dramatic action and the emotion generated by the characters should hold the audience's attention, keeping them so intent upon the play that they remain unaware of the style and rhythm of the characters' dramatic speech. That is, the audience should be unconscious of the medium, whether it be prose or verse. Elizabethan audiences were accustomed to hearing both prose and verse and "liked highfalutin and low comedy in the same play." But, Eliot warned, modern audiences were less amenable to mixing the mediums. Instead, they expected humble or rustic characters to speak in a homely language and those of exalted rank to declaim in verse.[4]

With verse drama living and breathing in the Cambridge air, and with Eliot and the Poets' Theatre championing its cause, Wilbur decided to try his hand at writing one. He proposed the project to the Guggenheim Foundation and won a fellowship in 1952. Because the award placed no restriction on where he could do the work, the Wilburs were free to leave Cambridge; in September, with Ellen (age ten), Christopher (age three), and Nathan (fourteen months old), they moved for the academic year to Corrales, a village in Sandoval County, New Mexico. Ed Hoenig, a Harvard friend, had praised the area's cultural wealth (both Spanish and Native American) and its role in inspiring artists such as D. H. Lawrence and Georgia O'Keeffe. That, plus the climate and a desire to devote his energies to writing without academic distraction, reinforced Wilbur's decision to go.

On Old Church Road the Wilburs rented spacious living quarters in a rambling, single-story adobe complex that looked outward onto an apple and pear orchard (and a pump house full of black widow spiders) and inward onto a courtyard with a small outbuilding that Wilbur appropriated as a study. Casa Gutiérrez, as it is still known, takes its name from the family who built the original structure, probably before 1800. After the flood of 1868 washed away the old San Ysidro church, Francisco Gutiérrez, the patriarch at that time, donated a piece of land abutting the house, where a new church was built.[5] While the Wilburs were in residence at Casa Gutiérrez, Bruna Sandoval, Francisco's granddaughter, lived with her son in a separate portion of the complex. She shared with them her memories of growing up on the property—including a recollection of digging in the yard and finding bell shards, left over from when Mexican artisans had cast the bell for the church next door. As of 1952, she had been the caretaker of that church for seventeen years.

In early September Wilbur wrote to Brinnin with the news that he, Charlee, and the children would be making a "mad dash for it in the Mercedes," hoping to get to Sandoval County in five days. (The "Mercedes" was really a Ford sedan; Wilbur was teasing Brinnin, who had a penchant for flashy cars.) "We will have room at all times for the right sort of person. . . . If at any time you feel you have *changed completely*," he joked, "we wish you would come & visit at length." Since 1949, Brinnin had been the director of the YMHA Poetry Center (today known as the 92nd Street Y), which was earning nationwide prominence on his watch. With that in mind Wilbur asked for a favor:

> My main business is to repeat in deepest gravity that I wd. love to have a series of readings arranged by the Poetry Center for, say, January. Preferably not more than 2 weeks on the road, at places not too far apart, & at terribly high rates. What could I ask? And could I ask for something-plus-travelling expenses? I should like to raise something between $500–$1,000, to put an end to the sort of demonstration now taking place on my lawn, where a jostling group of *commerçants* in ugly paneled neckties are jumping up & down tirelessly & shouting "Moolah! Dinero!" and other vulgarities. I cannot hold them off forever with paper aeroplanes, though some of them have weakened since I began using paper clips on the noses.[6]

This subject remained a subtheme of the letters that Wilbur sent from Corrales to Brinnin, who was traveling in locales ranging from Nassau to Venice. No reading materialized, however, not even one that Richard Eberhart tried to arrange independently at the University of Washington. Nevertheless, "solvency has set in somewhat," Wilbur wrote to Brinnin in April 1953; he had sold the short story "A Game of Catch" to the *New Yorker* and the poem "Voice from under the Table" to *Inventario*.[7]

In late May he admitted that "the West may not have gotten a fit of Disbursement Fever at the mere mention of my name." No one, not even the summer programs in Arkansas and Utah, had offered a possible date for a reading, never mind a stipend. Anticipating the family's departure from Corrales, Wilbur sent a note to Brinnin in Cambridge:

> You're extremely decent to write apologetically about the mild demand for me, considering that I was just sitting here on my great bay horse while you were wasting time & postage on me & never getting a fee for yourself. I'd love to read at the Poetry Center again, provided I can have music like Roethke: my preference is for Merle Evans' Circus Band. Or even better, I would like Billy Roses' Aquacade: I could be underwater in a diving suit, reading to myself, & every now & then one of the girls would bring me to the surface to say a really good line. I've just done a draft of Act I of Molière's *Misanthrope* in rhymed couplets, and I *think* it's good. We leave here 18 June; will stop over at . . . my family's place in NJ—then back to Lincoln, where the "lawn" will be up to the eaves. If you have any free moments during June, would you run out and cut our lawn? Thanks ever so much.[8]

Several years after the sabbatical in Corrales had ended, those translated rhymed couplets finally made their impact on the theatrical world, and the royalties Wilbur began generating from his translations of Molière (and later Racine) alleviated his money worries for good.

"Ellen enraptured"

Before Wilbur arrived in Corrales, he had characterized it to Brinnin as "largely Spanish, with a slight arty-farty fringe."[9] After living there for nearly a month, he sent a more nuanced description to Rab Brooks, a friend (and also a former junior fellow) who was then a classics professor at Harvard.

> We are established about 10 miles from Albuquerque, now supposed to be the fastest growing city in the state. There is considerable ocular evidence to support this contention; I have never seen any urbs which looked so little urban or urbane. It sits in what we Easterners would call

desert, and amounts at first sight to a great wash of neon on either side of
Route 66. Utterly planless; miles of motels, Laundrettes, Kwik-Kleaners,
Ozone Heights developments. The two bits of the city which seem to
reflect some taste & leisured planning are the University, beautifully done
in southwestern style, and the old Plaza, a single square of the old town
which the speculators have not been permitted to raze. Fortunately, however, a five-minute drive out of town brings one to beautiful country; in
most directions to undulant grazing land, mesas and mountains; in our
direction, which is north, to Spanish American farming country. We live
in Sandoval, more generally called Corrales (because it used to be a mess
of corrals).[10]

Wilbur kept a notebook, as he had done in Cambridge, during his first
five weeks in Corrales. Entries in early October show that politics in Massachusetts occupied his mind, even on a day when he and his family were
taking a long excursion away from the "urbs" to explore the terrain and the
pueblos to the north.

> Mrs. Stout, a local notary, witnessed our marking of absentee ballots,
> both of us voting for Stevenson, I voting otherwise for Massachusetts
> Republicans. This was not wholly sensible, I was aware, since the exec-
> utive requires a favorable congress, etc., yet I could not bring myself to
> support Governor [Paul] Dever [the incumbent Democratic candidate],
> a . . . crook and a desolating orator. Henry Cabot Lodge, though not
> clever, is a gentleman, and we must hold on to gentlemen even when the
> gentleness is merely hereditary.
> Then we drove along the Rio Grande, taking the children, and saw the
> *bosque* almost in full gold. Cottonwoods exclusively, none of the New
> England mosaic of fall colors. Forty miles north we came to Jemez pueblo,
> lying either side of the highway amid the mountains, the dwellings adobe
> and the corrals of desert wood, crazily constituted but solid. . . . One asso-
> ciates the color gold with weight and excess, which is why it is so exciting
> in light cottonwood-leaves in this spare country. The sun hot and dry, the
> shade cool, the water cold.[11]

The cottonwoods impressed Wilbur as much as any other feature of the
southwestern landscape. "The cottonwoods are spending gold like water,"
a line from the poem "Fall in Corrales" (in his 1961 collection *Advice to a
Prophet*), reflects the ironic beauty of a natural world depleted by human
desire, activity, and consumption, all of which have left the land parched
and the human spirit wanting—yet, because this is a Wilbur poem, not
bereft of rejuvenation or hope.

At the Jemez pueblo a middle-aged woman invited the family into her shop, where Charlee purchased three brightly colored ashtrays. George Manierre, a retired industrialist from the East who lived near Corrales, had recommended a picnic spot overhung by cottonwoods along the sandy flat shore of the Jemez River, which was shallower than the Rio Grande in the fall. The Wilburs ate lunch there and happily waded and skipped stones with the children.

Traveling further north in their Ford, they came to the Zia pueblo. It sat "atop a high mesa rising out of a valley and beside a river, over which we crossed on a board bridge of some length." Naked Zia children ran and kicked in the water while three women on the bank washed wheat in baskets, preparing it for milling, as a man looked on. Charlee went down to the river to talk to the women. They told her how pleasant it was "to be spoken to rather than goggled at" and invited the Wilburs to take a guided tour on another day. In 2006 Charlee remembered that time in the Southwest as "exhilarating" but made it sound as if she were the woman who drew the stares. Growing up in New England, "I thought I'd lived in the cradle of the country. When I went to New Mexico it felt like I'd dropped in from the moon."[12]

Wilbur responded to the otherness of the native culture, especially its spiritual quality, as he made clear in a letter to Brooks about a ceremonial dance at the Jemez pueblo:

> I had expected to see something quite alien and merely curious, but found it an experience more overpowering than any high mass could be. Two squads of dancers, each with its chorus of old men, the first squad being the "Summer People" & stained squash-flower color, the second the blue "Winter People." Behind each male dancer a woman in dark clothing: the men dance with a pounding step, alternating feet with the double hop on either; the women, since they represent the earth-principle, never raise their feet from the ground, but shuffle. Men and women are decked with fir balsam boughs; the women wave such boughs in either hand, the men have rattles.[13]

After dinner on the day of the Zia pueblo trip, Wilbur wrote in his notebook that he had finished a poem, "Merlin Enthralled," inspired by Heinrich Zimmer's *The King and the Corpse,* a collection of stories that draw from Western and Eastern traditions to explore our eternal conflict with evil in the world. In Wilbur's poem King Arthur and his knights ride in search of the sorcerer Merlin, "leaving their drained cups on the table

round." Wilbur created a dreamily eerie mood of passing time and dimin-
ishing potential, perhaps influenced by the long days he spent in his studio,
looking out onto a vast expanse of mesas and mountains as he tried without
much success to draft his play. Although only Merlin's disembodied spirit
is present in the first stanzas, he is fully possessed of his powers over nature
and humankind. Bewitched by the "Siren's daughter" of his own imaginings, he sleeps and dreams in his high bed, eluding the searching men and
their horses.

> History died; he gathered in its forces;
> The mists of time condensed in the still head
>
> Until his mind, as clear as mountain water,
> Went raveling toward the deep transparent dream
> Who bade him sleep. And then the Siren's daughter
> Received him as the sea receives a stream.
>
> Fate would be fated; dreams desire to sleep.
> This the forsaken will not understand.
> Arthur upon the road began to weep
> And said to Gawen *Remember when this hand*
>
> *Once haled a sword from stone; now no less strong*
> *It cannot dream of such a thing to do.*
> Their mail grew quainter as they clopped along.
> The sky became a still and woven blue.

The adjective "woven" reminds us of how fully Wilbur was able to incorporate the legend of Sir Gawain and King Arthur into his own lyric and
at the same time succeed in providing his readers with the kind of "waking dream" that Keats constructed in "Ode to a Nightingale."[14] Emotion
in these lines is palpable, as if Arthur's parting words express the poet's
own fears: although exhilarated by the expansive skies and hale in bodily
strength, he is concerned he might fail to enact his own legendary feats if he
cannot seize his moment to create.

"Merlin Enthralled" appeared in *Things of This World* (1956) on the page
facing "A Plain Song for Comadre," a poem that Wilbur wrote in Corrales
about Bruna Sandoval. Every Sunday, the speaker explains, she took care of
the church of San Ysidro: "From the clay porch to the white altar. / For love
and in all weathers, / This is what she has done." The poem is one of the
very few that Wilbur wrote before going to Rome in which, from otherwise
mundane images, he evoked a surge of Christian feeling—flowing as the

dirty scrubwater does, spilling from Bruna's bucket, and catching the rays of early morning sun.

In both "Merlin Enthralled" and "A Plain Song for Comadre" Wilbur explored themes and achieved tonalities new to his poetry, but focusing on the project for which he'd been awarded a Guggenheim required a different kind of creative energy and skill set. Although he was able to devise a plausible plot for his original play, the essential dramatic momentum, along with palpable foreshadowing of conflict and character, stalled when he began to write dialogue. Biding his time in hope of a breakthrough, he kept busy writing poems and documenting the events of family life.

On October 26 Wilbur jotted in his notebook, "Mrs. Sargent brought us the horse Copper for a one-week trial." After two trips back and forth to borrow a halter and return the saddle and bridle, "Copper [is] tethered in our orchard & looks quite a 50-dollar horse, which is high for this region. Ellen enraptured." Three days later, he noted that $67 in royalties from Harcourt had made it conceivable for him to buy the horse, who was "tractable" but lively:

> Only one mishap so far: Ellen was leading Copper on a rope, with Christopher sitting on her bareback, & Ellen unwittingly led them under a very low branch. I stepped around the corner of the study-building just in time to see Christopher removed from his mount. Instinctively he held on to the branch, and hung minutely very high in the air, then dropped to his feet in the grass. He had done reflexively as well as any stunt-man could have done deliberately. He stood there a moment utterly mute, then grasped the enormity and indignity of the experience, and yelled bloody murder; but was quickly calmed by my amusement and flattery.[15]

Politics and Poetry, Artifice and Reality

The 1952 election, now just a week away, continued to occupy Wilbur's mind. On October 29 he copied into his notebook two pages of excerpts from a letter he had drafted to Arthur Schlesinger, who had been helping Adlai Stevenson (then governor of Illinois and the Democratic presidential candidate) with his campaign speeches.[16] "Perhaps it might amuse you to hear what one lay-mind who has just absentee voted for your candidate might find perplexing and paradoxical in this election," he wrote. He then launched into a general critique of American democracy, elaborating on his uneasiness with Stevenson's advocacy of "government with a heart." Wilbur much preferred Abraham Lincoln's "of, by, and for the people."

He did acknowledge, however, his respect for several aspects of Stevenson's campaign conduct: "the governor's willingness to treat the electorate as themselves reasonable and responsible," the way in which Stevenson had "not oversimplified budget balancing and Korea," and the candidate's willingness to suggest that "Alger Hiss is an historically explicable phenomenon." He admired Stevenson's ability to recognize "the complexity of things in the midst of a political campaign, when one is prepared for the most abandoned simplicities."[17]

Meanwhile, Wilbur's work on his verse drama came to a halt. In 2014, as he tried to describe the play's concept (it was meant to be a political comedy about the Mexican government, with a plot that involved Americans' being arrested and tried in Mexico), he admitted he had abandoned the idea so early that he couldn't remember much about it.[18] Charlee recalled in 2006 that she was reading the pages of the play as Wilbur was drafting them and she knew he was having a problem with dramatic momentum: "He found he couldn't bisect himself, he could not manage to get out of the single lyric voice. He couldn't manage characters; he had just the voice of a lyric poet."[19] Faced with a cast of doppelgängers, he was finding it difficult, if not impossible, to generate the palpable conflict essential to a play.

In his Spencer lecture at Harvard two years earlier T. S. Eliot had spoken about undergoing a similar dilemma. Now those words were resonating with Wilbur. "A writer who has worked for years, and achieved some success, in writing other kinds of verse, has to approach the writing of a verse play in a different frame of mind from that to which he has been accustomed in his previous work." Whereas a writer can test his own verse in terms of his own voice, communication in the theater poses a different problem: writing verse in other voices. And those other voices will not show any indulgence to a poet's previous successes; every line will be "judged by a new law, that of dramatic relevance."[20] Eliot's dictum turned Wilbur's thoughts back to the lively postwar Parisian theater scene, particularly to the memory of a Comédie-Française revival of a mid-seventeenth-century Molière masterpiece. As Charlee told the story in 2006, one night in Corrales, Wilbur approached her with an idea. "Remember that marvelous production of the *Misanthrope* we saw? I'd like to translate that, just for use in colleges as a text. That may be the way I can break into theater, by the back door."[21]

In 1952 French theatergoers were still receptive to the plays of Molière (born Jean-Baptiste Poquelin in 1622). They knew what to expect and were more than prepared, as Eliot had said, "to put up with verse from the lips of personages dressed up in the fashions of some distant age."[22] Given that Molière's verse comedies and satires had been written in rhymed couplets and Wilbur had great facility with rhyme, his decision to attempt a translation seemed appropriate. To fulfill his Guggenheim commitment, he would abandon work on his stalled drama and instead claim a comedy he loved for his own native tongue.

Wilbur has said that he sees *The Misanthrope* as different from comedies in which society's laughter is part of a ritual to address individual extravagance. "In this play, society itself is indicted. . . . Falseness and intrigue are everywhere on view; the conventions enforce a routine dishonesty, justice is subverted by influence, love is overwhelmed by calculation, and these things are accepted, even by the best, as 'natural.'"[23] Alceste, the central character in a cast of variously vain, egotistical, cold, and insincere aristocrats (the exception is the honest Éliante), is quick to criticize others for their hypocrisy but denies his own. In other words, Alceste may be a critic of his society, but he is a critic whose motives are impure.

Wilbur grasped and reproduced in an American idiom the daring technique that Molière used in the play's first act: the shock elicited by a hypocrite's full disclosure of his nature and motives. Even as the playwright introduced his characters without pretense or subterfuge, he also dramatized their inability to change: the audience cannot help but recognize their inflexible mentalities. In fact, Molière's original audiences were so upset about seeing their own hypocrisy reflected in his characters that they attacked him for exposing it.

For Wilbur *The Misanthrope*'s thematic appeal aligned with a poetic vision he had begun to develop during the war, sharpened in his defense of formalism at the Bard conference, and further refined in the essay "The Bottles Become New, Too." In that essay he argued, "It is the province of poems to make some order in the world, but poets can't afford to forget that there is a reality of things which survives all orders great and small. Things *are*. . . . No poetry can have strength unless it continually bashes itself against the reality of things."[24] The essay goes on to connect his praise of Molière's "aesthetic daring" to his own poetic theory:

> [This] is why the first act of *Le Misanthrope* is so splendid. The vain and effeminate courtier reads to Alceste a competent, brittle and conventional cavalier poem, and demands his opinion. Although it is a poem well done of its kind, Alceste can't bear it because it is so neat and chilly, because it is

a loveless poem. Because it is mere autonomous artifice. He strides to the footlights—almost out of the play itself—and declaims with great gusto and with tears in his eyes, a popular song in celebration of love, gay, genuine, and having blood in it. The thirst for the genuine, which elsewhere makes a fool of Alceste, here shows him a hero. This is a damnation of self-existent artifice, spoken within a play—and a play is artifice. This is a gesture toward life from the midst of art, and it takes the art of a Molière to contain such a thing.[25]

Toward the end of the essay Wilbur returned to what he called the "oblique" idea of a relationship between the artist and reality: "If you respect the reality of the world, you know that you can approach that reality only by indirect means. . . . So that paradoxically it is respect for reality that makes a necessity of artifice."[26]

"A *happy* free-thinker"

By election night 1952 Wilbur seemed to have lost patience, not only with America's political situation but also with the social banter it generated. He and Charlee began the evening with dinner at the Old Town Chili Parlor with their friends the Manierres, enjoying an "excellent enchilada with egg." Afterward they headed to the home of another couple to watch the election results on television. Their hostess had gone to great lengths to support Stevenson, even sewing a pro-Stevenson banner that she had draped across the patio wall. Although Wilbur acknowledged that the campaign was "her first real engagement with politics," he was not particularly pleased by her "endless reprobation" of the voting public as the election returns came in.[27]

On November 5 Wilbur summed up the election fervor with a single statement: "Eisenhower has won by six million votes: may he not die in office and leave us to the mercies of Richard Nixon, a man with the voice and soul of a radio announcer." The rest of the long entry describes the day's events: he had struggled that morning with three final lines of a draft poem "Death by Exposure," whose final version never materialized, and then turned to a copy of Yeats's poems sent to him by Gordon Cairnie, the owner of the Grolier in Cambridge:

> I am reading for the first time his *Last Poems.* They are powerful as to style, very cranky & personal, & the effect of them is to convince me that this style is what he was after—that it was for style he dabbled so deeply in occultism, and not for the sake of 'the truth' or intellectual order. Having

built the style by means of his occultism, he writes in his *Last Poems* what amounts to a confession that he used phony theosophic means to a good stylistic end.[28]

Three lines from Yeats's "The Circus Animals' Desertion" contain a probable reference to the building of that brusque vernacular style: "Those masterful images because complete / Grew in pure mind but out of what began? / A mound of refuse or the sweepings of a street."[29]

Some months later Wilbur was still thinking about Yeats. But this time, as he wrote to Brinnin, he was focusing on his father, John.

> I've been reading the letters of J. B. Yeats, Willie's father: he was a fine if incomplete painter, and a personality far more engaging than his son. Whereas in WB's grandest verses I often feel a bloated hollowness, there is none of that in the old boy. He lived planlessly, & died in New York out of a constitutional inability to arrange passage back to Ireland; he outlived most of his friends & the whole world he had grown up in; he sat reading Charles Lamb in New York of 1920—and yet at 75 he was saying that he had just got going, & that he hoped to live indefinitely. No *death* in him as in WBY; he never felt homeless. He subscribes to the notion that the nightingale sings with a thorn against his breast, but the thorns which made him an artist were not those of Willie and most everyone else since: the pain of social alienation, spiritual confusion, emotional insulation.[30]

Wilbur described J. B. Yeats as "a *happy* free-thinker" and quoted several more snippets from the "old boy's" philosophy—including the notion that "rhetoric expresses other people's realities, poetry one's own"—to convince Brinnin to read the letters if he hadn't already.[31]

As critics compared Wilbur to "most everyone else" writing in the 1950s, 1960s, and even later, many perceived an absence of social, spiritual, and emotional pain in his poetry and saw this lack as a flaw.[32] *Perceived* is a necessary and cautionary word when discussing such an assessment, just as it is when discussing Wilbur's so-called normality or the sense that his personal life was blessed with boundless good fortune. Such assumptions can cut two ways when evaluating the man and his work.

One reason for perceiving Wilbur as "too normal" has come from judging him to be "too happy." For instance, in his *New Yorker* review of *Collected Poems, 1943–2004*, "Get Happy," Adam Kirsch raised the subject of the poet's hopefulness, which he defined in part by quoting Wilbur's 1977 *Paris Review* interview: "[seeing the world as] comely and good . . . in the teeth of all sorts of contrary evidence is based partly on temperament and partly on faith." According to Kirsch, this has left Wilbur "ill-equipped for certain kinds of moral inquiry." While the review argues that the poems in which he attempts "to do justice to the horror of the modern world" are his "least convincing," it does acknowledge that Wilbur's hopeful temperament and "the poetic fruit of his own metaphysics . . . [are] also the source of his enormous poetic gifts."[33]

As one more example of a poem that shies away from evil and horror (see his assessment of "Mined Country" in chapter 5), Kirsch chose "On the Marginal Way," from the 1969 collection *Walking to Sleep*. In the poem's first and second stanzas the narrator describes his impression of a beach that has been shaped by the natural force of erosion, with a rock formation whose "rondure, crease, and orifice" suggest a "hundred women basking in the raw." The scene changes in the third stanza:

> Has the light altered now?
> The rocks flush rose and have the melting shape
>   Of bodies fallen anyhow.
> It is a Géricault of blood and rape,
> Some desert town despoiled, some caravan
> Pillaged, its people murdered to a man.

By the fifth stanza the images have changed again, not unlike clouds moving swiftly in the sky, to invoke a more recent historical massacre, the Holocaust:

> If these are bodies still,
> Theirs is a death too dead to look asleep,
>   Like that of Auschwitz' final kill,
> Poor slaty flesh abandoned in a heap
> And then, like sea-rocks buried by a wave,
> Bulldozed at last into a common grave.

According to Kirsch, who faulted "Mined Country" for its cartoonish images, "It is typical of Wilbur that this murderous vision should be, precisely, a vision, a mirage":

> Indeed, what Wilbur sees is twice removed from reality: the rocks remind him not of "blood and rape" themselves but of "a Géricault," an already aestheticized violence. And while Wilbur goes on to invoke "Auschwitz' final kill," the poem does not take account of that evil in such a way that the memory of evil would affect the imagination of good. Instead, in its last stanzas, "On the Marginal Way" turns away from evil altogether, in order to receive an unaccountable consolation.[34]

Kirsch contends that the mention of Théodore Géricault's painting "The Raft of the Medusa" softens for the reader the image of violence. Wilbur's intent, however, was not to show how our minds seek to alter and prettify our attitudes and perceptions. Kirsch may be unaware of Wilbur's belief that respect for reality makes a necessity of artifice, a "gesture toward life from the midst of art."[35] Here, as he has done in other poems, Wilbur chose to refer to a specific work of art so that it supports and enhances a powerful literary experience; Kirsch seems to forget that words and pictures both exist at a remove from reality.[36]

To fully understand "On the Marginal Way," we need to look at how the poem progresses scene by scene. In the sixth through ninth stanzas the narrator describes still more mirage and artifice ("tricks of sense," as he calls them) that fuse scientific and biblical visions of creation (God as the ultimate artist). He remembers that seismic violence created the rocks before him as well as the cliffs that stand behind him: "Weathered until the sixth and human day / By sanding winds and water, scuffed and brayed." But then, in the tenth stanza, the narrator comes into the present moment to see airborne pages of newspaper "flap / The tidings of some dirty war" over the porch of a nearby home. (Wilbur wrote the poem against the backdrop of the Vietnam War; those tricks of sense the narrator acknowledged earlier were actually triggered by "the time's fright within" him.) And yet, he admits, "It is a perfect day."

> And like a breaking thought
> Joy for a moment floods into the mind,
>   Blurting that all things shall be brought
> To the full state and stature of their kind,
> By what has found the manhood of this stone.
> May that vast motive wash and wash our own.

In the stanza above, "what has found the manhood of this stone" is human imagination. Joy fuses with imagination—and the power of imagination, not the human accountability for evil, is the true subject of the poem. The joyous moment of certainty is fleeting, the narrator asserts, because the natural order of things (which in the poet's view has been created by a divinity) includes not only the violence in our world but also the potential to cleanse and re-cleanse our dealings with our fellow humans.

Kirsch claims that Wilbur's attempts to make comprehensive moral statements that "aim to do justice to the modern world . . . are among the least convincing." Yet when Wilbur read "On the Marginal Way" at the

Town Hall in New York City, where he joined seventeen prominent writers for a reading to promote peace, a *New York Times* reporter commented that it elicited the warmest response from the audience. The poem, with its images of the New England coastline and the cleansing air and water that might rid the world of "some dirty war," was not typical of the tone of the other readings. The general mood, the reporter noted, was one of sorrow and despair for the bloodshed and slaughter of innocents.[37] The occasion seemed to exemplify how Wilbur's calming persona could preside with dignity and grace on a painful occasion and how a poem's allusive and suggestive images, which Kirsch criticizes for softening the aftermath of war, could nonetheless provoke a powerful reaction among men and women who wanted their leaders to be in every way accountable.

"Translating, for good reasons and bad"

On the last page of his Corrales notebook Wilbur transcribed a metaphysical question-and-answer session that he conducted one evening with his young son Christopher, just "to see what he would say":

> Q. What is the moon?
> A. The moon is when you stay in the house at night and have to go to bed.
> Q. What is the moon made of?
> A. The moon is what it is.
> Q. What is the difference between jumping and falling?
> A. Jumping's good and falling's bad.

The morning after this bedtime interview with Chris, Wilbur drove to the University of New Mexico library in nearby Albuquerque and checked out a French copy of *The Misanthrope*. He read the play several times, mostly steering clear of commentary and interpretation until he felt comfortable with the characters and the milieu. As he set to work, he discovered he had both an aptitude for translating and an immediate pleasure in doing the task.[38] His rhymes had always been pitch-perfect in his own poems, but his facility for finding unpredictable and thus highly satisfying rhymes as he translated was a moment of self-discovery. At the time he might have justified his new focus on translation as "an escape . . . into the exercise of technical dexterity," a shortened version of the "worst reason" for translating that he later formulated for Donald Carne-Ross in 1968.[39] Nonetheless, theatergoers and lovers of Molière would hardly worry about whether his motivation was good or bad. His rhyming ability, as it carried over from original poems to translations, set him apart from his contemporaries. To find poets with comparable skills, one would need to look back to John Keats and before him to Alexander Pope and John Dryden.

At Montclair High and Amherst, Wilbur had studied French for a total of five years, with a focus on grammar, not literature. During the war his conversations with French citizens had honed his idiomatic conversational skills, but Charlee had a more literate and formal fluency in the language. She was a sounding board as he refined the basic syntax and the crucial nuances of *The Misanthrope,* and she remained his collaborator for many translations over the years. The task came to exemplify the partnership she had envisioned early in their relationship.

Wilbur once remarked, "Perhaps God didn't mean for me to write my own lines of dialogue," but he brought to his French translations a pre-ternatural facility for capturing dramatic points in lines of dialogue.[40] His method was to use colloquial speech patterns—that is, he did not invert the natural flow of dialogue to secure a rhyme. Thus, the conversations in his translations please because his rhymes coincide with the normal emphases of English speech. In one passage from *The Misanthrope,* for instance, Alceste is speaking to Celimene, a lady with many suitors. As a way of denouncing a particular man whom he sees as a dangerous rival for her affections, he pays him a snide compliment: "Is it that your admiring glances linger / On the splendidly long nail of his little finger?"[41] According to a seasoned stage actor who has performed numerous roles in Wilbur's Molière translations, the difficulties of delivering a character's lines vanish because "some of the rhymes in Mr. Wilbur's script come out sounding conversational all by themselves."[42]

In his introduction to *The Misanthrope* Wilbur noted that Molière's dia-logue possesses two pervasive attributes (redundancy and logic) and one striking absence (metaphor). If a character repeats essentially the same thought in three successive couplets, the repetition is not for dramatic emphasis. Molière's intention, Wilbur wrote, was always to stabilize "the idea against the movement of the verse" and give specific rhetorical pleasure. In a prose translation such effects are lost. Logic and the complex grammar that articulates it are crucial to *The Misanthrope*'s stylistic convention; and because Molière's dramatic verse is almost metaphor-free, much of its rich-ness comes from this argumentative virtuosity.[43] Without the combination of surprise and felicity in Wilbur's rhyming practice, the playwright's logic in English would sound legalistic and stodgy.

According to Wilbur, the "best diction" for translating plays written centuries ago mediates between then and now. Thus, his translation retains Molière's use of mid-seventeenth-century terms such as "spleen" and "phlegm," terms deriving from ancient Greek medicine and philosophy, but avoids archaic expletives such as "zounds" (short for "God's wounds").[44] The characters use occasional vulgarities, he noted, because they are aristocrats and therefore not genteel. He also wrote that their names should be pronounced in a *roughly* French fashion but without nasal and uvular agonies.[45]

Wilbur's slow, painstaking method involved translating the French rhymed hexameters couplet by couplet into English rhymed pentameters, all the while "aiming for maximum fidelity to sense, form, and tone." "My chief virtue as a translator," he told the poet Dana Gioia in 2009, "is stubbornness: I will spend a whole spring day, a perfect day for tennis, getting one or two lines right."[46] Getting all of *The Misanthrope*'s lines right prevented Wilbur from finishing the translation until his Prix de Rome year of 1954–55.

The Misanthrope premiered in Cambridge at the Poets' Theatre on October 25, 1955. The theater space at 24 Palmer Street was a tiny attic, so cramped that after two nights the production was moved to an auditorium at MIT. On November 2 the *Harvard Crimson* reviewer, John Popk, praised the theater's "discrimination" in choosing Wilbur's "lively and facile" translation, its "well-conceived and well-executed" settings and costumes, and the director Edward Thommen's "wit and polish in matters of pacing, blocking, and maneuvering."[47] The poet Peter Davison starred in the role of Alceste. From the stage Davison felt Thommen's engagement, noting during an early rehearsal that he seemed to be "galvanized by what our voices were saying."[48] According to Popk, the principal actors ranged from "captivatingly acidulous" (Eustacia Grandin as Celimene) and goodheartedly cynical (Robert Beaty as Philinte) to confidently pompous (William Morris Hunt as Oronte). Davison was credited for handling Wilbur's verse translation with "easy authority" and earned praise for portraying the misanthrope's "comic and tragic elements" with a sympathetic dose "of frustration and courage."[49]

Popk also noted the play's "irresolution," writing that Alceste was "a figure who condemns the false standards of his society" yet nevertheless adheres to them—a situation he saw as "mildly troubling" but not distracting.[50] This assessment alluded to an aspect that had not only attracted Wilbur to *The*

Misanthrope but also motivated him to translate more of Molière's work. Wilbur's own keen moral sense comported with the playwright's, which allowed for a wider, more cynical, and more accurate accounting of human conduct than he had as yet been willing to admit into his poems.

The Poets' Theatre production of *The Misanthrope* launched Wilbur's career as translator of verse drama. A little more than a year after its Cambridge premiere the play was staged off Broadway, opening at Theatre East on East Sixtieth Street, on November 12, 1956.[51] Over the decades Wilbur would translate nine more Molière comedies: *Tartuffe* (1963), *The School for Wives* (1971), *The Learned Ladies* (1978), *The School for Husbands* (1991), *The Imaginary Cuckold, or Sganarelle* (1993), *Amphitryon* (1995), *Don Juan* (1998), *The Bungler* (2000), and *Lovers' Quarrel* (2005). They have been performed in New York, regional, and university theaters as well as on television and radio.

Perhaps the greatest fan of Wilbur's Molière translations was Brian Bedford (1935–2016), a Tony Award–winning actor who played a range of Molière characters (not only the title roles) at numerous venues in New York—from Orgon in *Tartuffe* at the Roundabout (2010) and Arnolphe in *School for Wives* at the Lyceum (1971) to Alceste in *The Misanthrope* at Circle in the Square (1983). By 1983 Bedford had developed a better grasp of Alceste's character than he had possessed in his first performance of the role in 1981 at the Stratford Festival in Ontario. As he told a *New York Times* reporter, "I think I was misled by the director, who thought Alceste was a saint. . . . And of course, he's the absolute opposite of that. This man is to a great extent a monster. Some of what he says is justified and even heroic, but some is monstrously egocentric." He garnered critical praise for the role in 1983 by "railing at hypocrisy with searing wit," in part due to the guidance of the director, Stephen Porter, in part due to Wilbur's translation, which allowed Alceste to sound, Bedford said, "crazier and more extreme . . . actually . . . funnier."[52] Porter, who later brought *School for Wives* to the Phoenix Theatre in New York City, had an understanding of both Molière and Wilbur that fostered greater harmony than most directors were able to achieve.

In a *Playbill* interview in 2003 Bedford agreed with the prominent literary, film, and theater critic John Simon, who assessed Wilbur's accomplishments in translation as equal to those of the original dramatist in his own language and culture. Bedford elaborated on Simon's analogy: Wilbur did with Molière what Julia Child did with French cuisine. "Her influence has changed all our lives with regard to our appreciation of food. I wish other classical playwrights had their Wilbur. I wish Chekhov had. Occasionally we get a decent Chekhov translation, but usually we don't. Ibsen? Ibsen needs a Wilbur."[53]

"Moe Leary" and French Connections

As a private joke, Wilbur and Charlee began to refer to Molière as "Moe Leary," as if the playwright were a Mafia don for whom Wilbur occasionally did a job. Such jobs reaped considerable theater-generated royalties, and Wilbur found himself now earning more money than most poets did, even those lucky enough to teach at Ivy League schools. Nonetheless, there were tensions. He sometimes clashed with directors or producers who "showed no respect" for traditional staging, lines in verse, or characters who belonged to the mid-seventeenth-century "world of real and intelligible power and order."[54] In Wilbur's mind the best of the stage productions demonstrated what radio productions relied on: the verbal élan of Molière's serious comedies.[55] Because these comedies were so "thoroughly written," he advised directors and actors to trust the words to convey the point and allow the language to be sufficiently entertaining. He likewise urged them to avoid farcical stage business and especially modern updating, costuming, and props.

In the fall of 1972 Wilbur wrote a set of stage notes to Paul Weidener, the director of a Hartford Stage production of *The Misanthrope*, after seeing an early performance. He mentioned that he found "the losses" resulting from modern-day costuming "greater than the gains" and expressed "a few bitches and reservations" about clothes and props, especially those intended to evoke "the distaste for hypocrisy amongst the Greeners of America." When Alceste talked to his valet, Wilbur complained, he was "like a boy begging to use the family car." The production felt as if the play were "kidding itself. . . . Nothing in Molière's world corresponds to a lounging and a pot-smoking Acaste. . . . Molière's Alceste would not make hitch-hiker gestures with his thumb."[56] Worst of all, he said:

> *The actors do not know their lines.* To know a line of a verse play is to remember and speak it exactly as written, so that the meter and its variations are preserved. One can't, therefore, substitute "I've" for "I have," one can't forget the first half of a line and substitute the approximate sense of it, and one can't toss in those extra "Ahs" and "Yes Buts" and "I means"

which do small harm in prose drama, and above all one cannot leave out "thats" and "whiches." . . . In a prose play little is lost if such a speech as "I said that I would meet her" is shortened to "I said I'd meet her," but in a verse play such omission and contraction can spoil the movement of a whole passage.[57]

A run of *Tartuffe* in 1965 demonstrated the type of disharmony likely to occur when the director neglected to follow Wilbur's simple but important rule: "in short, trust the words."[58] The play opened at Lincoln Center on January 14, in an American National Theatre and Academy production directed by William Ball. As Wilbur's notes on his translation warn, "fussy anxiety on the part of the director, whereby the dialogue is hurried, cut, or swamped in farcical language, is the commonest cause of failure in productions of Molière."[59] But Wilbur did not remain true to his own conviction—and later regretted it. He made concessions to Ball, allowing a song to be added and several lines to be altered in the final scene. Although a professional relationship continued between the two men, the conflict between them simmered, escalating into a canceled production a decade later.

Molière's original *Tartuffe* was first performed at Versailles on May 12, 1664, and was instantly controversial.[60] Either Louis XIV or the Catholic secret society known as the Compagnie du Saint-Sacrement intervened to prevent the play from being produced in Paris, and those directives prevailed until 1669, when the character Tartuffe was portrayed as a man of the cloth. In Molière's time France was engulfed in religious turmoil, caused in part by resistance to the Jansenist focus on human depravity, original sin, and predestination. By releasing a play that clearly favored heretics and free thinkers and condemned the new repressive theology, the playwright may have intentionally courted wrath. Immediately after the Versailles performance, a pamphlet denounced him as "a demon made flesh" and declared that the play was "a discredit to the church and its curacy of souls." However, in the "polemical preface" to his 1669 edition of *Tartuffe,* which appeared after the five-year production ban had been lifted, Molière argued that the play was a satire on religious hypocrisy, not on religion per se.[61]

Wilbur has described the character Tartuffe as "a versatile parasite or confidence man with a very long criminal record, for whom the posture of a holy man is only one of his *modi operandi*." In his view the satire in the play is incidental. Likewise, several contemporary critics have argued that

Tartuffe is a deep comedy in which events cannot be controlled by a knave's chicanery (on Tartuffe's part) or a fool's unconscious imposition of moral values (on Orgon's).[62]

F. W. Dupee, a Columbia University professor and literary critic, reviewed Ball's Lincoln Center production for the *New York Review of Books*. His article quickly establishes the pains Molière took while revising the play to remove any element that his original censors saw as equivocal. One strategic solution, Dupee noted, was an example of "art's triumph over caution." It involved allowing the audience to experience "the awful, and ludicrous, devastation wrought on [Orgon's] innocent family" for two long, increasingly tense acts without seeing Tartuffe himself; Molière does not bring that "criminal impostor" on stage until the third act.[63]

Although Dupee praised Ball for using Wilbur's eloquent translation in lieu of a "radical modernization of the play's soul," he did not share the director's implicit judgment that "*Tartuffe* as written was not a sufficiently well-made play for New York audiences." If Ball's staging was not entirely disloyal to the play's soul, Dupee wrote, it was "nevertheless odd enough" to warrant criticism. "For one thing, Ball softened the famous *coup de théâtre* of Tartuffe's delayed entrance" by having "the scoundrel . . . take part in a dumb show at the start of the play," thus alerting the audience to his presence in the wings. As Dupee suggested, Ball's directing did not trust the words, and his "art" did not triumph over his "caution."[64]

Both Wilbur and Charlee let Ball know that his additional tampering with the production had upset them. On March 22, 1965, Ball sent Wilbur an apology that blamed everything under the sun (and the theatrical spotlight) for the problems at Lincoln Center: panic due to the loss of the show's producer, a bellicose designer who abandoned ship, a frightened cast. He encouraged Wilbur to visit the production in a month or so, when he would find the grace of the verse restored and the words given room to breathe.[65]

By June 1965 Ball had been appointed director of the American Conservatory Theatre and was preparing to rehearse *Tartuffe* in Pittsburgh. He requested Wilbur's help in revising a short welcoming speech that an actor would deliver at each performance to reflect on a new season in a new venue. This prologue also had to inform the audience that smoking in the theater was banned.[66] A handwritten verse draft of the new prologue, with its numerous revisions, excisions, and marginal notes, reveals Wilbur's cooperative spirit and good humor, despite the pair's disagreements:

Ladies & Gentlemen, if you'll kindly harken
For just a moment, before the house lights darken,
I'd like to tell you just how pleased we feel
To be in this ~~town~~ place of smoke and steel
Where, in the weeks to follow, we propose
To bring you ~~all a splendid set~~ a delightful batch of shows . . .
Remember therefore: wait until you get
To the outer lobby; then light your cigarette![67]

Wilbur's patience with Ball may have been tested by the director's inclination "on the one hand to ornament the play with unsuitable and distracting 'business,' such as the throwing about of holy water, and on the other hand to transform it into bourgeois melodrama."[68] But their tense professional association ended when the American Conservatory Theatre replaced the *Tartuffe* production, scheduled to open at San Francisco's Geary Theater on April 3, 1973, with Arthur Miller's *The Crucible*. An article in the *San Francisco Chronicle* chalked up the change in plans to a conflict between the ACT's performance style and the translator's "academic attitude" and quoted Ball at length: "I think Wilbur was eager for a Broadway hit, so was ready to compromise. Since that time, many other companies have used his translation, as has John Gielgud at the Old Vic, but none have worked. I believe that Wilbur doesn't understand the function of a translator, but he has the copyright for his verse. . . . In a sense he wants to direct the play." Ball concluded this inaccurate explanation by hyperbolically defending his desire to stage an "imaginative and energetic production of the play" rather than yield to Wilbur's insistence on preserving a classic.[69]

In his response to the *Chronicle* editor, Wilbur demonstrated grace, logic, calm, and a tinge of regret. He corrected numerous errors in reportage and in Ball's statements. While he admitted to squabbling with the director over his "attempted interpolations and tamperings," he also offered several examples of "splendidly done" productions of his translations that had obviously "worked." In the final paragraph he wrote:

San Francisco is very fortunate in having William Ball's ACT around, and I regard Mr. Ball as a lively and imaginative director. But as for "Tartuffe" and how to present it, we simply disagree; and I will not grant his assumption that to disagree with him is to be drearily "academic." I see "Tartuffe" as a highly verbal, clearly written comedy, which does not stand in need of surprising reinterpretation by him. . . . I wish, that since Mr. Ball's abilities are great, that he and I should see eye to eye, but since we are both very stubborn, there seems small chance of it.[70]

Wilbur has not mellowed with age in response to seeing his translations updated, at least not much. In December 2007 he attended a Yale Repertory production of *Tartuffe* and was unhappy to see TV monitors broadcasting "off-stage" close-ups of characters who had no part in that particular scene. About other stage business—for example, the young son smoking and threatening Tartuffe with a cap gun—he was more puzzled than perturbed. He was quick to note that there were many "good speakers of verse" among the student cast but was surprised that the director, fascinated by Wilbur's "left-field" rhyme of *jail if* and *bailiff,* had the actor pause to, literally, spell it out.[71]

No degree of spelling out could save face for another *Tartuffe* rhyme, which didn't translate well across the Atlantic. In 1967 reviewers panned a Tyrone Guthrie production at London's National Theatre because John Gielgud appeared not to know his lines. More egregiously, they called the lines "doggerel" and chided Wilbur for relying on his American ear when he rhymed *fossil* with *docile.* Writing to Robert Lowell about the reviewers' harsh words, he ended the letter with two of his own: "Fucking Limeys."[72] It was not the last expletive he used when reacting to theater culture.

Over the years Moe Leary and his "French connections" gave Wilbur more than royalties. He received, for instance, a 1983 PEN translation award for *Four Comedies: The Misanthrope, Tartuffe, The Learned Ladies,* and *The School for Wives.* With each new translation published, the list of staged productions grew. He and Charlee traveled frequently to openings and galas, in big cities and small ones. Wilbur became a celebrity in the theater world. As Wilbur told Carne-Ross, translating Molière (and later Racine and Corneille) was welcome work, for good reasons and bad. Although it required painstaking technical concentration that had the potential to compete with his creativity, it did coexist with his need to write poems, appear in public for readings and symposia, fulfill academic responsibilities, and adjust to challenges in his personal life.

8

Prix de Rome

"The morning air is all awash with angels"

I am amused by Dick and myself as we approach the city by two entirely different roads. He reads Augustus Hare's Walks in Rome, *decides in the morning that he is going to the Campidoglio and then goes there with book in hand and comes back with every date at hand. I get on a bus and deliberately get lost and haven't read anything yet. But we seem to fill in for one another.*

—CHARLEE WILBUR, letter to John Malcolm Brinnin, fall 1954

When the American Academy of Arts and Letters awarded Wilbur a Prix de Rome for the academic year 1954–55, he was filled with anticipation. The city overflowed with art that drew upon Christian and pagan traditions, in forms ranging from early paintings, frescoes, and statuary to baroque architecture and music. All of these elements, plus Rome's *dolce vita* moment— its street life, thriving cinema, and postwar building boom—would find a place in the poems he wrote that year.

For Charlee, crossing the Atlantic on the *Cristoforo Columbo* was just the beginning of a trip "never to be duplicated": shining calm days by the pool, gala champagne dinners served on confetti-covered table linens, dancing to music from a five-piece hootchy-kootchy band. "I have no notion of time," she wrote, in lieu of a date, at the top of a letter to John Brinnin describing her first weeks in Rome.[1] The Wilburs traveled tourist class; but because there were only three first-class children on board, Ellen, Christopher, and Nathan Wilbur (now eleven, six, and three years old) could spend their mornings and late afternoons with the ship's governess and their evenings after supper watching puppet shows and movies. At noon they joined their mother at the pool. Charlee sunned and swam three times a day, boasting to Brinnin that she'd acquired "the most becoming tan of my life . . . displayed fetchingly each night on the polished [dance] floor." The Wilburs found good company among the mix of tourist-class passengers. Among the Italians returning home, they met Dino Rotundi, a young Roman water engineer. Once in Rome, he became their friend and devoted *cicerone,* showing them historic views, out-of-the-way fountains, and neighborhood cafés.[2]

One day, at the end of a four-hour tour of architectural marvels, the trio stopped at the Sagrestia, a trattoria across the cobblestone square from the Pantheon, where Dino introduced them to another of Rome's wonders—a clairvoyant (*veggente,* in Italian) so formidable that he read Charlee's mind "like a book" and "narrowed in on Dick so accurately that he still hasn't returned to normal."[3] The clairvoyant told him, "The job you need to undertake in Rome is not well defined, since it will be useful tomorrow, not today. In any case, you are in Rome for your erudition and you will complete your mission well."[4] For twenty years the memory of this charming, chain-smoking, inwardly tormented veggente would haunt Wilbur, until he finished and published "The Mind-Reader," one of his finest and most ambitious poems.

"Pressing to devour the city in great heady gulps"

The academy did not offer living quarters for the fellows' families, so the Wilburs rented a furnished fourth-floor apartment at 17 Via Sprovieri in Monteverde, a pleasant hilltop neighborhood with a large outdoor market. The academy was only a few minutes away, and the most direct route cut between an enormous cage filled with exotic birds and an ivy-covered wall fountain in the park called Villa Sciarra.

For the first week or so the Wilburs ate dinner in the academy's high-ceilinged dining room or outdoors in the courtyard. Between cocktail hour and after-dinner billiards time, both spaces buzzed with conversation. Charlee grouped the "mélange" of residents into categories of her own devising: very young scholars, "bearded and predictable"; artists, especially sculptors, whose conversations she found stimulating; prima donnas wary of being upstaged; and cat haters, a reference to the fellows who were not charmed by the ubiquitous *gatti de Roma* that haunted the city.[5]

Liz Young, the wife of the British journalist and writer Wayland Young, who was covering Rome for the *Observer,* first met the Wilburs at a November 6 dinner party hosted by academy residents Robert and Claire White. She had the impression that Wilbur was "a neat gangling, college, tidy young man who is to be a resident poet at a women's college somewhere" and was taken aback by what she assumed was his naïveté: "He believed two things I told him and that shocked me rather, because people ought to look at what you say carefully, they ought to accept it as examinable, neither as gospel nor anathema. He sang nice American songs very charmingly."[6] A snapshot from her photo album shows him in a jaunty beret, still looking as young as an Amherst student and standing shoulder to shoulder with Charlee, who has a Burberry plaid scarf wrapped around her neck. The Youngs and the Wilburs became friends, and Wilbur credits their outings to churches around the city for helping him distinguish baroque style from the gilt-edged mirrors and moldings of the rococo period.[7]

The architectural historian William H. Macdonald (Bill), who received a 1954–1956 academy fellowship, had met the Wilburs in October, when he and his wife, Dale, moved into their quarters in the main villa. Writing to a friend about the academy's ambience, Bill included Dick and Charlee in a group he described as congenial and pleasant: "This atmosphere of intelligent people will spoil me completely should we end up sometime in an average neighborhood—that sounds very snobbish but these people have, most of them, a genuine curiosity in knowing what the world's about, and a number of them have a few of the answers."[8] Others in that group included the poet Anthony Hecht, who was spending a post-fellowship year in Rome with his wife, Pat; Adja Yunkers, an abstract painter who was spending a Guggenheim year in the city with his wife, the art critic Dore Ashton; Robert White, a sculptor (and the grandson of Stanford White, whose architectural firm had designed the academy), and his wife, Claire; Jack Zajac, a Hungarian-born sculptor from California, whose work greatly impressed Charlee; and Charles Singleton, a Dante scholar from Harvard, and his wife, Eula.

Nonetheless, by November Charlee noticed that the group's initial excited intimacy had worn thin, a reaction that was rather similar, she thought, to what generally happened among the writers at Bread Loaf after the first week. Everyone seemed embarrassed by knowing too much about everyone else. Charlee especially sympathized with Hecht, because his marital problems were attracting gossip and unsolicited advice.[9] She and Dick decided to dine at home for most of the week, where they could spend time with the children before bedtime. A woman named Franca was serving as the family's housekeeper and nanny, and she cooked them simple but sumptuous local fare, sometimes alongside Charlee. Franca made a ritual of serving the family at an ornately carved wooden table in the dining room, bringing grapes and cheese, as well as coffee and grappa, at the end of each evening meal.[10]

Wilbur spent alternate eight-hour days working in a little brick studio set at the edge of the academy property against part of the Aurelian Wall, a third-century fortification that had defined the city limits until the nineteenth century. His studio had begun life as a potter's shed; its forsaken wheel and kiln still stood outside the door. On its garden side, windows looked down onto rows of artichokes, cabbages, fig trees, onions, and every conceivable variety of lettuce. Burlap covered its back wall, to which Wilbur pinned verbal "artifacts" inscribed in his best italic hand—for instance, the words *reticulum* (from the Latin) and *areté* (from the Greek), which would appear in "A Baroque Wall-Fountain in the Villa Sciarra," the great fountain poem he was about to draft. Every day a noontime cannon boomed from Piazza Garibaldi, a few hundred yards away, announcing lunch and a siesta to follow; and he could hear the nuns singing in a nearby convent.

On non-writing days Wilbur took walking excursions around the city. During his first months in residence his guide was Augustus Hare's *Walks in Rome,* a late-nineteenth-century book that focused on the city's ancient *centro.* Charlee, however, took off by herself, seeking not destinations but experience—getting deliberately lost, chatting with the locals at espresso bars and cafés, and recovering the Italian she had learned as a child on Capri.[11]

One night, when Wilbur was suffering from a sinus infection, Charlee and Dino walked for ten miles through the city, drinking from fifteen fountains along the way. With the twin bell towers of Trinità dei Monti at their backs, they headed down the long, wide marble stairway (known as the Spanish Steps) and into the Piazza di Spagna, where water spills from a fountain shaped like a sinking ship. They wound along narrow byways toward the Tiber and sat on Tiber Island dangling their feet in the water. At three in the morning they found an open bar and dined on mussels. Afterward they rode till dawn in a *carrozza.*[12]

The details of his wife's Fellini-esque romp though the city prompted Wilbur to write "Piazza di Spagna, Early Morning," his first Roman poem.

In the final two stanzas a cinematic focus tracks Charlee as she pirouettes down the Spanish Steps, poised at a pivotal moment in her life and caught unawares:

> Nothing upon her face
> But some impersonal loneliness,—not then a girl,
> But as it were a reverie of the place,
> A called-for falling glide and whirl;
>
> As when a leaf, petal, or thin chip
> Is drawn to the falls of a pool and, circling a moment above it,
> Rides on over the lip—
> Perfectly beautiful, perfectly ignorant of it.

In a November letter to Brinnin, Charlee alluded to the mood that the poem captured: "It is a distinct relief to begin the business of living here rather than pressing to devour the city in great heady gulps. I feel . . . satiated, languorous, and ever so slightly drowsy. I want now to be taken unawares by things, to move softly and slowly for a while, and to be surprised by tastes."[13]

Still in this frame of mind, she described an autumn trip to Frascati as a feast for the senses. She, Wilbur, and a few academy acquaintances arrived mid-afternoon on a "blazing blue and gold day with that sky, that sky which brings the unbelieving eyes to actual pain." Wine barrels were everywhere, and on almost every corner stood a "weather-beaten cart breaking with ripe grapes" for the first press. "Within five minutes of entering the town, I was dizzy drunk from the fumes," she told Brinnin. The group chose a cantina with cavernous rooms below street level and ordered a liter of Frascati drawn straight "from the mother barrel into a cool flask." Someone mentioned that drinking one tumbler of it was the same as downing two good-sized martinis. "Naturally," Charlee wrote, "I laughed and drained it off. With the residue of wine in my nostrils, I was easily levitated after the first glass." From their table they could see the workers outside on the street. Wearing breechcloths, they were totally soaked and stained in wine, and Charlee was struck by their smiles and their jovial spirits. As she said to Brinnin, the scene seemed to bring to life *The Kermess,* a painting by Brueghel the Elder that portrays peasants dancing merrily at a village feast.[14]

The academy party went down three flights of stairs into the cantina's lowest cavern, where many years' worth of barreled and bottled wine sat under the hanging stalactites. Someone in the party purchased a bottle of old champagne made from the proprietor's prized grapes. As they prepared to leave, Charlee recalled, "The *padrone* all but cried at the notion of the wine traveling back to Rome in the car. The motion would ruin it, he said, so there was nothing left but to drink it on the spot. My God, what an elixir from Heaven. Home very late, and Dick and I, needless to say, spent the rest of the night with Frascati, Frascati, Frascati."[15]

The Wilburs went on a number of day trips organized by resident archaeologists and historians. Bill Macdonald introduced them to the ancient Italian countryside and to the now land-locked harbor at Ostia Antica, with its small, perfectly preserved theater and its ancient wine bars on every corner. He showed them the Etruscan tombs near Tarquinia, whose colorful wall paintings celebrating the inhabitants' carousing and copulating had once charmed D. H. Lawrence. Macdonald also brought the Wilburs to the necropolis at Cerveteri, a hive of mounded, igloo-like tombs; to the many-fountained garden of the Villa d'Este at Tivoli; and to Hadrian's vast countryside villa. Everywhere Macdonald gave impromptu lectures to explain the original purpose of a ruin or to verbally reconstruct a library or a temple from a bit of rubble and a few column drums.

Wilbur had certainly read earlier poets' meditations on Rome's grandeur. He knew that Johann Wolfgang von Goethe's experience in Rome had liberated him from his bureaucratic duties in Weimar, and that living in Rome had freed Percy Bysshe Shelley from persecution for his atheism and adultery. In Wilbur's case the city sparked a need to write poems that probed deeply into the religious beliefs he possessed but had yet to express. What Hecht characterized as Wilbur's "philosophical bent" and "religious temper, which are by no means the same thing," began to "consort comfortably together" in Rome.[16]

One morning, after waking to the screech of a clothesline pulley and the sight of billowing white laundry, Wilbur was inspired to write "Love Calls Us to the Things of This World," which itself inspired the title of his third book, *Things of This World* (1956).[17] The first stanza of the poem ends with these lines: "Outside the open window / The morning air is all awash with angels." This angel motif also figures in "A Plain Song for Comadre" (written in Corrales and also published in *Things of This World*), a poem in which Wilbur imagined stained suds flashing like angel feathers on sunlit church steps as he described how a woman's steadfast service to her church attests to her faith. In "Love Calls Us," however, he looked more intensely at how ordinary people, as they go about their mundane rounds of work and pleasure, seek and find evidence of a divinity in their lives.

Wilbur chose his Roman subjects with care. Two spectacular fountains; shirts flapping in the wind; the inner dome of a great cathedral; a clairvoyant mind; a railway station's jagged roofline: all became arenas in which divine and human awareness engaged. His most ambitious Roman poems aim not for Frost's "momentary stay[s] against confusion" but for clarities that remain when the book is closed. In contrast to his pre-Rome work, Christian belief is central in five of the six poems he wrote or conceived in 1954, providing structure, imagery, and passion.[18]

The Veggente

Many academy fellows and visitors consulted the clairvoyant who had astonished the Wilburs on their first night in Vecchia Roma. One was Charles Singleton, who accompanied Wilbur to the Sagrestia several times. (Wilbur dedicated his poem "The Mind-Reader" to Singleton and his wife.) Another was the American classicist and Amherst professor John Moore, also a fellow in the mid-1950s, who included a verbal portrait of the clairvoyant in a letter to his sister Betty, dated January 22, 1956:

> The Sagrestia. A well-known pizza joint, not notable for its food but for its mind-reader and fortuneteller. He's a slender, sweet-natured, dignified old gentleman: he's also part of the music and plays the violin. You write your question on a piece of paper, in Italian, and fold it up, all the while thinking very hard about the question you want to have answered. He takes the paper for a moment in his hands and gives it back again (he claims it's important for him to touch the paper—I'm sure it is!) and then he goes into a trance, from which presently emerging he writes down the answer to the question on a piece of paper. He then asks (I forget on what pretext) to hold the question again, after which he restores to the client both question and answer. The question I asked was: "Where is my brother Dan?" The answer: "I can't see where your brother Dan is right now; but do not be anxious, you will hear from him within the year"! I was taken to that place by Berthe Marti, one of the people at the Academy (there are several in all) who patronize this fortuneteller, some just for the game, others half or more than half convinced. According to their accounts he sometimes doesn't ask to hold the question but only to touch it in the clenched hand of the client. But it seemed perfectly plain that the

routine he used with me gave him opportunities for sleight of hand which any good magician should have found sufficient. But the odd part of it was that I didn't want to believe that I was being imposed upon, because I liked him so much.[19]

In "The Mind-Reader" Wilbur speaks in the voice of a clairvoyant possessed of an uncanny gift that turns out to be an intolerable burden. The poem, which was not published until 1976, shares certain qualities with Robert Browning's dramatic monologues and Frost's *North of Boston* poems, especially "Home Burial" and "Death of the Hired Man." Like them, "The Mind-Reader" projects waves of implication from a highly charged but realistic encounter between two people.

In a 1995 interview with Paul Mariani, Wilbur divulged an important detail reported to him by "a friend," probably Singleton, who heard the clairvoyant say, "It's no fun to be a mind reader, you know. It's no fun to have a mind like a common latrine." Wilbur told Mariani:

> The invadedness of the mind-reader's mind was what appalled me and made it necessary to write the poem. Thinking about what it must be like to have a mind so vulnerable led me to seek, in vain of course, to imagine what the mind of God must be like, continually besieged by all of us, by all that we have to say, all that we have to confess. That's at the center of the poem, really: a kind of amazement at the thought of what a mind must be like that can put up with all of us and still be inviolate.[20]

The paranormal aspect may have first attracted Wilbur to this savant of the pizzeria, but the religious implications led him to shape the clairvoyant's life story into a metaphysical parable.[21]

As the poem begins, the mind reader is sitting in his neighborhood trattoria and telling a professor how his vocation found him. The routine recounted in the poem is virtually identical to John Moore's description of the real clairvoyant. Speaking in oblique, well-chosen metaphors, the mind reader muses on the mysteries of objects "truly lost"—a hat dropped from a rampart into a forest, a pipe wrench "catapulted" from the back of a truck, a book blown out to sea. He traces the origin of his calling to a childhood gift for discovering the whereabouts of lost things and goes on to explain how he "got from that to this." But he notes that his ability to penetrate another's thoughts is not infallible; about 10 percent of the time he must cheat in order to access an answer to an invisible or puzzling question. His gift, he tells us, impairs his emotional health: invasion of another's privacy

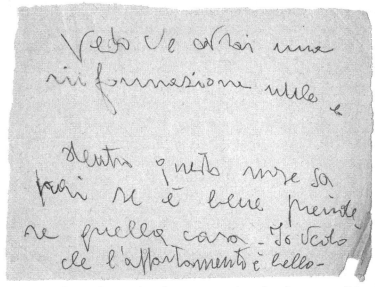

In a second note the mind reader commented on the pleasant condition of Wilbur's apartment in Rome. *Courtesy of Richard Wilbur.*

is a cheerless experience, a limited version of divine omniscience, and thus a source of immense distress. It removes all barriers between him and the pain felt and uttered by the people he entertains and serves.

So summarized, the narrator's predicament seems unenviable, though hardly godlike. But Wilbur's own sleight of hand gradually transformed the mind reader's clairvoyance into a divinity's ability to access the conscience of every mortal. Wilbur seeded his character's ruminations with thoughts, images, and unspoken abysses that demand we take the portrait of this rueful clairvoyant as more than a sympathetic look at a man who unhappily knows too much. The poem invites its readers to pursue more deeply what it might involve to become an all-knowing divinity.

Wilbur took pains to define exactly what his character—and, by extension, his God—can and cannot do. Does God truly possesses total access to our minds, of the kind asserted in 1 Samuel and Matthew, highlighted in the Anglican communion service (in which Wilbur participated for years as a lay reader), and alluded to in the last act of Shakespeare's *Hamlet*? If the answer is yes, then why doesn't he intervene more often to keep us out of sin's way? Wilbur explained that God prefers to forgive and heal the sinner rather than prevent the sin. His forbearance demands a moral discipline that both he and the mind reader find lacking among their respective flocks. But unlike God, the mind reader has no healing or forgiving power; and his clients, he says, are content only to be heard. This comforting aspect provides a potent metaphoric vehicle for Wilbur's mighty tenor.[22] Like the mind reader's clients, believers in an all-knowing God are more reassured than terrified to imagine that their hearts are open to divine inspection.

As Wilbur detailed his clairvoyant's abilities, miseries, and limitations, he himself received a glimpse of what it might feel like to enter the mind of God. Was God troubled, as the mind reader is, by the human squalor and sinfulness he couldn't escape? Did his excruciating attention sometimes flag?

So it seems. At one point the mind reader wonders if he might miss something that would reveal a hidden goodness in his trespassing "communicants." Does God himself worry that he might miss something redeeming? Do the guilty and defenseless worry that he'll miss something exculpatory? In the climactic riff of the poem Wilbur, through his Anglicized seer, imagined how God experiences us:

> Faith, justice, valor
> All those reputed rarities of soul
> Confirmed in marble by our public statues—
> You may be sure they are rare indeed
> Where the soul mopes in private, and I listen.
> Sometimes I wonder if the blame is mine,
> If through a sullen fault of the mind's ear
> I miss a resonance in all their fretting.
> Is there some huge *attention,* do you think,
> Which *suffers* us and is inviolate,
> To which all hearts are open, which remarks
> The sparrow's weighty fall, and overhears
> In the worst rancor a deflected sweetness?
> I should be glad to know it.[23]

Wilbur seemed to imply that the infinite attention of God's mind as an alternative grace differs from the redeeming sacrifice of Christ: "Is there some huge *attention,* do you think, / Which *suffers* us and is inviolate?" Here the word *suffers* recalls the Greek verb *pathein* ("to suffer"), the New Testament term for the passion of Christ. God "passions" humankind through the enormity of Christ's sacrifice on the cross. A creator who imagines and endures universally sinning minds is a far less extreme but perhaps more comprehensible deity. This father now joins his son, according to the parable that "The Mind-Reader" works out, so that both "suffer" the entirety of human sin through total access to human consciousness. But however godlike the mind reader feels—whatever peace he lacks because he cannot escape the constant assault of human suffering he hears—he, unlike God, can escape into oblivion, especially in the form of *vino rosso* or *bianco,* which he cadges from his customers.

In this punctilious, musical, drunken, part-charlatan, Wilbur found an analogy for the openness of all minds to God and joined the existential unhappiness of God to humankind's own. In sympathizing with the gentle *veggente,* he invited the reader to sympathize with God. To some, this trope may seem presumptuous, even blasphemous, but its insight is immense and unique in America's mostly secular poetry.

Human-Divine Collaboration

Like "The Mind-Reader," Wilbur's other Roman poems suggest that a believer's relation to God is an inescapably collaborative enterprise: Christ's hand didn't write the gospels; his believers' hands did. Wilbur's rendering of human-divine collaboration raises the stakes of every one of these poems but especially "For the New Railway Station in Rome" and "A Baroque Wall-Fountain in the Villa Sciarra." "For the New Railway Station" makes effective use of fugue form as the God invoked in its first stanza returns to preside over humankind's heavenly destination in its last. The eight-stanza poem begins by arguing that pilgrims to the holy city shouldn't gloat at the triumph of Christianity over its pagan predecessors, whose imperial might lies in ruins. It denies that "God is praised / By hurt pillars" or that the leveling of man's ambitious structures is God's way of reminding us of his preeminence and our limitations and insignificance. The poem finds proof that something divine exists in purely secular architectural grandeur, using as its example the Stazione di Termini, Rome's post–World War II railway station, which replaced the one Allied bombers destroyed. It celebrates the station's startling jaggedness and the rightness of its placement next to the ruin of an ancient wall, and the poem's inclusive, outreaching lines visually convey the physical form and structure of such inspired human creativity. The poem's final five stanzas follow:

> See, from the travertine
> Face of the office block, the roof of the booking-hall
> Sails out into the air beside the ruined
> Servian Wall,

> Echoing in its light
> And cantilevered swoop of reinforced concrete
> The broken profile of these stones, defeating
> That defeat
>
> And straying the strummed mind,
> By such a sudden chord as raised the town of Troy,
> To where the least shard of the world sings out
> In stubborn joy,
>
> "What city is eternal
> But that which prints itself within the groping head
> Out of the blue unbroken reveries
> Of the building dead?
>
> "What is our praise or pride
> But to imagine excellence, and try to make it?
> What does it say over the door of Heaven
> But *homo fecit*?"

Wilbur has been criticized for exalting such a "pedestrian" venue as a "booking hall" and for using what seems, to at least one classicist, to be excessively clever wordplay. In the seventh stanza, for instance, the verb "prints" and the adjective "blue" in two successive lines evoke *blueprints,* the architect's plan for incorporating an ancient Roman wall into his modern creation. Then, in the eighth stanza, the English-Latin pun embedded in the rhyme sounds of "make it" and "fake it" invokes the literal meaning of *homo fecit,* or "manmade."[24] To some that pun is unfortunate because it burdens an otherwise dignified classical Latin phrase with a homophonic, atheistic undercutting that suggests, in a superficial reading, that we deny our mortality by imagining an afterlife. Yet according to Wilbur, the pun was an unintended and unfortunate lexical irony.[25]

The link between human creative power and an imagined heaven is supported by two facts of historical and metaphysical life. First, humans have made heaven as they understand it, just as they have written gospels that assert a world-transforming religious dispensation. Second, because humankind is not divine, its imagined heaven, in all its splendor, is made of hopeful guesswork. Nonbelievers may respond, *pace* Wilbur, that our efforts are chimerical, even fake, but surely they are never intentionally so.

As the poem leads readers toward its final two stanzas, the narrator invokes the "building dead"—artists (such as the architect Bramante, who first imagined the vast dome of Saint Peter's as a way to create an earthly echo of the vaster one above it) and religious visionaries (such as Dante, who mapped the afterlife in burning, penitential, and glorious detail using the Aristotelian and Aquinian master plans). For these artists "pride" in their work fuses with their "praise" of God. The stanzas form Wilbur's most explicit and memorable aria in celebration of human and godly collaboration. Here, human beings have not only imagined an excellent heaven and prescribed the conduct for attaining it but have also created and populated that heaven by means of the sincerity of their belief and by living honorable and generous earthly lives, even as they are beset by temptations to which they sometimes yield.

"No one knows, at sight a masterpiece"

Since 1950, Howard Moss had been the poetry editor of the *New Yorker,* and he and his colleagues were receptive to Wilbur's work, accepting a few poems every year. Though Moss was personally impressed by almost every Roman poem Wilbur sent to him in the autumn of 1954, he failed to persuade the magazine's poetry committee to accept any of them. In addition to Moss, the committee included Harold Ross, the magazine's founder and editor-in-chief; Katherine White, who maintained stylistic and grammatical control over the contents; the novelist William Maxwell; and Rachel Mackenzie, an assistant poetry editor. Moss may have been the chief poetry editor, but acceptance was by consensus or democratic vote. He could be, and often was, overruled by Ross, who strictly enforced an *obiter dictum:* nothing would be in the magazine that he didn't understand.[26]

Throughout the 1950s and 1960s many first-rate poets were at work in the English-speaking world, and the *New Yorker* committee had its pick of distinguished and enjoyable poems even as it exhibited a wariness toward extravagance, emotional or otherwise. During this fecund era, many accomplished poets primarily wrote formal verse, and a certain version of this style came to be known as a "*New Yorker* poem." The term was used mostly by those who had yet to write one, but even poets who published regularly in the magazine invoked it to separate their more adventurous poems from those crafted specifically for publication in the prestigious and well-paying magazine. A "*New Yorker* poem" generally fulfilled the following minimum requirements: it struck a fresh or pleasantly nostalgic note, displayed evident skill, contained no nonfactual statements, and neither unsettled nor

embarrassed the magazine's audience. It had to peacefully coexist alongside
ads for luxury items from Chanel, Cadillac, and Tiffany.[27] Nonetheless,
despite the limitations inherent in these parameters, the magazine, during
Moss's tenure as editor (1950–1987), published a significant number of the
era's best American poems.

It seems likely that Wilbur's Roman style clashed not only with the magazine's sophisticated self-image but also with its sense that religious belief
should be a private and unspoken concern. The *New Yorker's* rejection
of these poems brings to mind the famous line from Ezra Pound's poem
"Mr. Nixon" (1920): "And no one knows, at sight a masterpiece."[28] In the
autumn of 1954 Wilbur began to send Moss what Charlee referred to as his
"glistening" new poems, work that revealed "his best singing quality."[29] But
for months "Piazza di Spagna" and "For the New Railway Station in Rome"
languished in foggy and chilly Manhattan, and Wilbur heard nothing from
Moss. On November 27, the poet forwarded "Love Calls Us to the Things
of This World," accompanying the submission with a brief, self-effacing
note. He implied that the quantity of poems he'd turned out had prevented
him from taking time to assess their quality. He hoped Moss's silence meant
that at least one poem had found an advocate in the editorial office.[30]

In a November 30 letter that crossed Wilbur's in the mail, Moss rejected
all the poems Wilbur had sent him from Rome but accepted "All These
Birds," which he had submitted to the magazine before sailing to Italy. In
some respects the editors' objections, as Moss summarized them, anticipated later critical reservations about Wilbur's poetry. "Piazza di Spagna"
seemed too sentimental, Moss told him. Thanks to its enormously skillful
execution, "For the New Railway Station" had almost made the cut, but
Moss said that it had too many adjectives, and he disliked its exalted tone.[31]
In a December 10 letter he rejected "Love Calls Us." He expressed his personal regret, telling Wilbur that the committee had liked it but thought it
was "a little too special" for their magazine.[32]

Wilbur and Charlee both knew that he was writing well and in a new
vein, so these rejections did not depress or discourage him. In any case,
Botteghe Oscure, an acclaimed multilingual literary review based in Rome,
soon accepted "Love Calls Us."[33] The journal had been founded in 1948
by Principessa Marguerite Caetani, a Connecticut-born heiress, who had
established her literary credentials in the 1920s as the editor of the French-
language journal *Commerce. Botteghe Oscure* had previously published
Wilbur's "Looking into History."[34] Now the principessa drew the Wilburs

into her literary circle, inviting them to lunches at her home (which also housed the journal's editorial office) in a Roman neighborhood that had been fashionable since the Renaissance.

In January the Wilburs went on a day trip to Ninfa, where Caetani hosted a gathering at her summer palazzo. The party topped off a two-week whirlwind of academy-related events. The composer Paul Hindemith had conducted an ensemble at the church of Santa Cecilia, the Belgian embassy had hosted a concert of Franz Joseph Haydn's music, and the pianists Arthur Gold and Robert Fizdale had performed at the Villa Aurelia. There had been a "smoky, babbling" cocktail party for the novelist Katherine Anne Porter at the Irish embassy and a stuffy reception at the French embassy; and the academy's director, Laurance Roberts, and his wife, Isabel, had hosted two "state dinners" (as Charlee called them) at the Villa Aurelia.[35]

Wilbur made one last attempt in the spring of 1955 to send the *New Yorker* a poem that revealed his new visionary scope. "Altitudes" describes two domes: a majestic one in a Roman cathedral, whose gleaming white wainscoting is edged with gold rosettes; and a lantern-shaped cupola on the Amherst, Massachusetts, home of Emily Dickinson. In that year critics were responding to a newly released volume of Dickinson's complete works. Allen Tate, for instance, had noted how her imagination engaged religious ideas and abstractions, a focus that Wilbur certainly shared as he explored his own spiritual awakening in Rome. In "Altitudes" he portrayed the two domes, one sumptuous and one spare, as equally suitable places for religious contemplation. The poem reveals a deepening affinity not only for Dickinson as a poet—one who insists "on discovering the facts of her inner experience" and "describing and distinguishing the states and motions of her soul"—but also for her next-door neighbor who is "lost in thought." The neighbor is, as Wilbur explained years later, "a kind of generic New Englander making up his religion for himself."[36]

But when "Altitudes" reached the *New Yorker,* it, too, was rejected. Not until August 1955 did a poem conceived in Rome (but finished in Wellesley, Massachusetts) break through. Moss called "A Baroque Wall-Fountain in the Villa Sciarra" "a beauty" and was "glad to have it."[37] Although committee members thought that the poem was wonderfully worked out from start to finish, they still had the usual editorial queries and corrections. Most of their concerns were on target, and their suggestions sharpened the final draft of the poem.

"A Baroque Wall-Fountain" begins with a playfully detailed verbal sketch

of the Villa Sciarra fountain that Wilbur passed daily on the way to his studio. The endlessly replenished water falling over three scalloped levels of the
fountain creates a transparent tent for its mythical stone tenants—a male
and female faun and their pet goose. The naïve happiness of this family
wrapped in an eternal "saecular ecstasy" and the ease with which a "stocky
god" holds the bottom level aloft seem too simple to represent life as human
beings live it. So the narrator finds an alternative model across town among
the plain fountains that Carlo Maderno designed for Saint Peter's Square.[38]
He asks, "Are we not / More intricately expressed" by its main jet,

> Struggling aloft until it seems at rest
>
> In the act of rising, until
> The very wish of water is reversed,
>   That heaviness borne up to burst
> In a clear, high, cavorting head, to fill
>
>   With blaze, and then in gauze
> Delays, in a gnatlike shimmering, in a fine
>   Illumined version of itself, decline,
> And patter on the stones its own applause?

The quietly magical lines condense the hunger for spiritual life into a
brilliant, exuberant testing of itself against the law of gravity. *We are the
water* is what the narrator seems to be saying here. So are those drenched
fauns and their uninterrupted pleasures nothing more than a sentimental
myth? He invites us to take a second look. This time we see their "humble
insatiety" and are led to consider Saint Francis of Assisi, who saw God's
hand in the natural, physical phenomena of our world—from birds and
animals to water and stones—and interpreted them to be as much God's
children as we are:

> Francis, perhaps, who lay in sister snow
>
>   Before the wealthy gate
> Freezing and praising, might have seen in this
>   No trifle, but a shade of bliss—
> That land of tolerable flowers, that state
>
>   As near and far as grass
> Where eyes become the sunlight, and the hand
>   Is worthy of water: the dreamt land
> Toward which all hungers leap, all pleasures pass.

Early eighteenth-century fountain in the garden of the Villa Sciarra, which inspired Wilbur's poem "A Baroque Wall-Fountain in the Villa Sciarra." *Courtesy of Richard Wilbur.*

"A Baroque Wall-Fountain" suggests the existence of a bliss as truly humble as the one Saint Francis imagined: a level in which human beings accept kinship with the blameless but God-created things of our world—the water and grass and sunlight that might be undervalued as inanimate. Analogous use of this saint's sense of kinship also animates "For the New Railway Station," where the "least shard of the world sings out / In stubborn joy" at the astonishing rebuilding project that culminates in the construction of heaven from human imagination and earthly materials. Both endings move quietly through well-prepared and well-argued revelations toward final resolutions in which seemingly discordant ways of living reconcile. Wilbur imagined his paradise, but the materials with which he built it are, as his poems insist, things of a world he shares, not imposes.

Frailty and Fulfillment in the Roman Spring

Spring blossomed as Wilbur's fellowship year drew to a close. The Rome he was experiencing now had little in common with the place he'd entered with the 36th Texans more than ten years earlier, when the American Fifth Army liberated the city. Yet the academy's location on the Gianicolo, where his division had rested overnight before chasing the retreating Germans northward, and its proximity to the Via Aurelia, the dangerous route he had traveled with the Signal Company, were surely constant reminders, even subliminally, of the war.

From his studio nestled against the Aurelian Wall Wilbur could look across to the tennis courts on the lawn of the southern side of the main academy building. Tennis, which he had played all his life, was a reliable, blood-pumping stress reliever and a welcome distraction from his daily routine. But one evening at home, after he had played too many sets on a sweltering spring afternoon, he suddenly staggered and fell, feeling sick and dizzy and suffering severe heart palpitations. Franca, the housekeeper, witnessed his collapse and ran into the children's bedroom, exclaiming, "Tua Papa e morto!"[39] Wilbur was in fact conscious but obviously stricken. Charlee immediately suspected a post-exertion heart attack and phoned their doctor at the nearby Salvatore Mundi Hospital. He was on duty and unable to leave, but Wilbur seemed to be rallying. So Charlee sat with him until the doctor could make a house call.

The doctor diagnosed Wilbur's condition as anginaloid syndrome—not a true heart attack but a heart spasm caused by "extreme fatigue and tension."[40] He suggested that the tension, exacerbated by the intensity of writing and working, had been building ever since World War II. Charlee concurred; she was fully aware that her racehorse had been driving himself in the belief that his body was indestructible. Finally, it seemed, the stress of so much exertion and accomplishment had caught up with him.

For five days Wilbur recuperated in hospital. An electrocardiogram found no damage to his heart. His doctor's recommendations for avoiding a more serious episode were strict. No smoking. No tennis for a while. Limit writing time. Take it easy and stop often when climbing back up the 424 steps that led from the Gianicolo and the Wilbur's apartment down to Trastevere and Rome's center. "He did allow me," Wilbur remembered with rueful humor, "to continue having sexual relations with my wife."[41]

Though he did not follow the doctor's advice for long, the incident had a profound effect on Wilbur. First came the shock of having, for the first time, been really afraid for his life. As Charlee later explained to Brinnin, the episode pushed him to think of himself as newly susceptible to frailties of the body. He was now beginning "to look at other people more closely," she said. At the same time she felt sure he knew now how much he really needed her. She was glad the episode had happened, she told Brinnin, and hoped that Dick would begin "to live naturally closer to the ground"—that is, more connected to the people he would need and to those who would need him.[42]

That spring, the evidence that Wilbur's wartime traumas were occupying his mind had surfaced in a moment of disorientation when he and Charlee were visiting the novelist Elizabeth Spencer in her apartment on Via Flaminia.[43] Writing about the evening in his journal a few years later, he remembered:

> I elected to drink Martinis and was taken drunk, babbling so foolishly that I never returned to retrieve the pipe which I mislaid there. For several minutes at least, as I recall, I entertained my hostess by dilating on my own character; then, noticing that her eyes had widened, I realized I had informed her both that I was timorous and that I was intrepid. "Elizabeth," I exclaimed, "I'm lying!" But perhaps I was not. It's true that in 1952, picking apples in Corrales with George Manierre, I suddenly lost my nerve and simply could not crawl out onto a high branch to harvest it, though a fall would scarcely have killed me. On the other hand, as our landing-craft moved towards the San Raphael beach where we *might* have met resistance, and many were ducking and shaking and praying round about us, Jim Kenney and I chatted and cracked jokes, feeling perfectly capable and calm. It's enough to make one think in terms of the Greek gods' dealings with man—now empowering, now forsaking. Still, in a rough way one averages out to be predictable in many things, and in a few things, for all practical purposes, absolute: I am absolutely unimaginative in mathematics; I am frightened of speaking impromptu, on most subjects, to any large body; I do not consciously lie; I am heterosexual; I am punctual; I believe in God; I am behind in my correspondence.[44]

In his journal he noted that the strange evening had jarred him to speculate on the treacherousness of human nature and the possibility that "all statements about characteristics are lies." He wondered if the Harvard psychologist Henry Murray's theory of apperception was correct—that subjective processes shape human behavior. The theory had led Murray to believe, as Wilbur wrote, that "we may soon dispense with the concept of personality."[45]

By early June the doctor thought that Wilbur had recovered enough from his anginaloid episode to travel. At the time Wayland Young had been assigned to do a piece for the *Observer* about Padre Pio (1887–1968), a Catholic priest with an immense popular following, who even in the 1950s was a betting man's candidate for early sainthood.[46] Young and his wife suggested that Dick and Charlee might like to accompany them to Apulia, south of Rome, to see the priest in action. In 2006 Wilbur recalled the trip in a letter to his old friend from Rome, Bill Macdonald:

> We stayed at a hotel called Santa Marie delle Grazie, where a bell rang in every room at 4 a.m. to turn people out for the Mass at which the Padre would officiate. There were many pilgrims, and attendees at the Mass overflowed the chapel. Monks admonished an excited pilgrim for climbing up on the holy-water font. An old woman shimmied up my back and cried "Eccolo! Eccolo!" One thing that impressed both Charlee and me was that in the midst of all that sweat and fervor the air was fresh and sweet.[47]

Pio's qualifications for sainthood were numerous—among them, his stigmata, his miraculous healings, and, as Wilbur described it, "a capacity for bilocation." At the close of his next letter to Macdonald, he joked about striving to top the saint's achievement: "As for me, I am sometimes in two places at once but shall not settle for less than ubiquity."[48]

On another occasion the Wilburs drove south to Positano on the Amalfi coast, where they enjoyed ten days of sun, sea, and companionable isolation without the children. Charlee compared Dick's happiness and exhilaration in Amalfi to his behavior when the family first arrived in Rome, at a moment when he was exulting in his freedom from academic duties and his ability to write with abandon. Now he was doubly relieved, to have produced poems brilliant enough to justify his fellowship and to have finished translating *The Misanthrope*.[49] The release of those pressures allowed them to enjoy their last weeks in Italy. In 2005, as she recalled their Rome year, Charlee spoke with some regret as she alluded to the different "roads" by which she and Dick had approached the experience: "Looking back on that year I think he shortchanged himself terribly. He concentrated as he always does on the fellowship year of work, on discharging the obligations he set for himself that year." Yet she knew it was "hopelessly impossible" to change his conscientious and industrious nature.[50]

On June 9 the Macdonalds hosted a farewell party for the Wilburs and several other friends who were leaving Rome. On June 13 Dick, Charlee, and the children boarded the *Cristoforo Colombo* in Naples, and the family arrived in New York City on June 21. They stayed briefly with Helen and Lawrence in North Caldwell and by July were settled in their house in Wellesley, where Wilbur would start a new teaching job at the college in September. During his time in Rome Wilbur had lifted his poetry to a new place—one where the world's resilience and bounty were not suspect but manifest; where his poems could establish bonds of pleasure and exhilaration with his readers; where squalor, failure, pain, and misery occurred within a cosmic order and thus reminded his readers they were not alone.

9

Candide *and Other Broadway Misadventures*

"Glitter and be gay"

Working with Lenny [Bernstein] on Candide, *I sometimes felt a certain territorial anxiety. I couldn't read or write music, but he could read books, played a mean game of anagrams, and was exceedingly clever with words. I feared that I couldn't afford a writer's block, lest this very literate composer grow impatient and write my lyrics for me.*

—RICHARD WILBUR, "Apropos *Candide*," 1993

In December 1955 Wilbur joined the composer Leonard Bernstein and the playwright Lillian Hellman in their collaboration, already underway, to adapt Voltaire's satirical novella *Candide, ou l'Optimisme* (1759) as a Broadway musical comedy. Hellman would write the book, Bernstein the score, and Wilbur the lyrics. The events in the novella take place during the height of the Spanish Inquisition, a period of religious hysteria that reached its height in the fifteenth century, when representatives of the Catholic Church tortured and killed many suspected heretics. As the hero Candide travels from one exotic locale to another in search of adventure, he encounters successive examples of human evil. Nevertheless, he remains convinced, like his mentor Dr. Pangloss, that "all's for the best" in the "best of all possible worlds."[1]

Throughout the book Voltaire mocked his character's denial of evil and his "brave new world" optimism. This scornful satire appealed to Hellman, who herself was dealing with a contemporary version of an inquisition: Senator Joseph McCarthy's House Un-American Activities Committee

(HUAC), which was instigating the communist witch hunts of the 1950s. When called before the committee and asked to reveal the names of suspected Marxist or Stalinist sympathizers, she had refused to testify against her friends, colleagues, or acquaintances. Her May 1952 letter to the HUAC chairman included a statement that became a rallying cry against the McCarthyites: "I cannot and will not cut my conscience to fit the political cloth of the times."[2] To Hellman, the similarities between HUAC and the inquisition were impossible to ignore.

A Musical to Shake Up America

By 1953, when Hellman was first beginning to think seriously about adapting *Candide* for the stage, she was famed for her tightly constructed three-act dramas and her acid wit, but she had never written a comedy. She approached her friend Leonard Bernstein about writing incidental music for this potential "French project," a task he had already undertaken for her upcoming production of *The Lark,* an adaptation of Jean Anouilh's 1952 play about Joan of Arc. At first he declined, but he soon changed his mind.[3] Creating a *Candide* production that would shake up the "complacent America" of the Eisenhower era appealed to them: Bernstein soon started envisioning it as "a big three-act opera with chorus and ballet."[4] Hellman, full of misgivings about creating a musical, tried to put her doubts aside.

Work on *Candide* got off to a slow start in 1954. Bernstein was juggling other projects, including the symphonic suite that became the film score for *On the Waterfront* and a commission by Isaac Stern for *Serenade,* while Hellman was struggling through the many revisions of her script. Harry Levin, a professor of comparative literature at Harvard who had already assisted her with the Anouilh adaptation, agreed to read her early drafts. He also suggested that she contact his friend Richard Wilbur to see if he would be willing to write the lyrics for Bernstein's songs. As Wilbur recalled, Levin suggested that she take a look at his translation of *The Misanthrope* because "I did fairly well with one clever Frenchman, and I might do well by Voltaire."[5]

In the spring of 1954 Hellman asked Wilbur if he would be interested in the *Candide* collaboration but had to rescind the offer because Bernstein had already committed to the lyricist John Latouche.[6] Bernstein, Hellman, and Latouche spent the summer on Martha's Vineyard working intently to pull a show into shape, and during the autumn they continued to meet in

New York three or four times a week. Yet by December only one act was complete, so Bernstein and Hellman decided to drop Latouche.[7] They tried out other lyricists, including James Agee and Dorothy Parker, and thought about the possibility of writing the lyrics themselves.

At the end of March 1955, Bernstein approached Hellman with two substantial problems. The first was practical. *Candide*'s producer, Ethel Linder Reiner, had yet to find a director, and without one in place it seemed unreasonable to book a theater for their projected fall 1956 opening. He wondered what Hellman thought of asking Garson Kanin, or possibly Bobby Lewis, to direct.[8] The second problem concerned their conception of the show. Should they take the easy route and opt for pure entertainment, or go for a stylish operetta with limited commercial appeal? Or could they combine elements of both?[9] In April 1955 Hellman wrote twice to Bernstein while he was on a concert tour in Italy. Each letter mentioned a longer one she'd drafted that detailed the pros and cons of these contrasting approaches, but apparently she never ended up sending it.[10]

In the meantime the lyric problem remained unresolved. Agee's involvement with the project had been fleeting. By June 1955, when Bernstein had begun to write music for *West Side Story*, he and Parker had settled on the lyrics for only one *Candide* song. According to her biographer Marion Meade, Parker assessed the experience this way: "There were too many geniuses in the room."[11] Meade wrote, "Some years later she was still shaking her head over [Bernstein's] mania 'to do everything and do it better than anybody,'" which Parker agreed he did manage to do—"'except for lyrics.'"[12]

At least *Candide* had found its director: Tyrone Guthrie, a British citizen who had recently founded a Shakespeare festival in Stratford, Ontario, signed on in July 1955.[13] In early December of that year, Hellman renewed her offer to Wilbur, this time with Bernstein's backing. They sent him music for two songs, and on December 9 he submitted two lyrics. He prefaced his drafts with a short disclaimer: "My uncertainties are vast, my inexperience is borne in upon me, and Bernstein's music has got mixed up in my head with some tune from another show. Could you glance at this third draft of an attempt at Candide's 'Lament' and tell me if I'm slogging in the right direction?" The song's first quatrain followed:

> Is that warm heart
> grown so cold,
> When its love was

> scarcely told, love?
> Could our young joys
> just begun,
> Not outlast the
> dying sun?[14]

Hellman responded immediately. Both she and Bernstein, whom she said had called the lyric "a charmer," were very pleased.[15]

On December 21 Wilbur wrote to ask if he should produce something else to convince them he was qualified.[16] In January he sent several drafts (including lyrics he'd written on New Year's Day because Hellman wanted them quickly) to replace dialogue at the start of act 1, scene 3. A week or so later, after meeting with his potential collaborators for two hours at Hellman's New York City apartment, he waited at the Algonquin Hotel while Bernstein, Hellman, and Reiner discussed whether or not to hire him. Impressed by his intelligence and his fluency as a versifier, they agreed he was their man. Hellman brought the good news to Wilbur later that evening.

By March 1956 Wilbur had completed more drafts of lyrics, sending them to Hellman, who passed them on to Bernstein. Their collaboration seemed to be the best of all possible theatrical worlds. Within hours of receiving the drafts Hellman wrote back to Wilbur, praising his work and assuring him they were going to be happy working together. Jokingly, she told him to warn Charlee that she was already deeply in love with him.[17] Before long Hellman was calling him "sweetie-pie," an endearment she regularly used as a salutation in letters to her friends. As time went on, Bernstein became "Lennie pie" and Wilbur "Dickie pie" or, when things were going especially well, "Dearest of pies."

Given their other commitments, however, the partners could not resume work on the music and lyrics until summer. Bernstein had conducting commitments in Europe and with the New York Philharmonic; Wilbur was teaching at Wellesley. They reconvened in June on Martha's Vineyard, Hellman established in her newly purchased home on the island, Bernstein (with his wife Felicia and their children) in the Lambert's Cove house he'd rented to work with Latouche, and Wilbur (with Charlee and their children) in a rented house near the shore. Although the three adhered to an arduous schedule, the script remained in flux. Realizing that his work was not likely to end by September, Wilbur took a leave without pay during Wellesley's fall 1956 semester.

Although he has often spoken fondly of the collaboration with Hellman and Bernstein—"we all seemed to hit it off"—Wilbur has also acknowledged its stressful side. The work "was exactly as intense as show writing is always said to be, or shown to be in horror movies about such experiences."[18]

> At one point, there was enough discord amongst the collaborators that it was seen as a happy thing that Tyrone Guthrie had arrived on Martha's Vineyard. Lillian said, *He looks like Charles de Gaulle and I think that perhaps he can get us all into line.* Actually, [Guthrie] was not particularly dictatorial, though I have one fond memory of him. I had written what I guess was the best lyric I wrote for the show, one called "Dear Boy," also called "Pangloss's Song," and given it to Lenny for setting. He spent a couple of days trying to set it and said to me with a face full of misery that he simply could not get inspired, at which point Tyrone Guthrie said to him, *Lenny, we all know that you were water-skiing at Peggy Warburg's yesterday. Now you sit down and write a nice piece of music for Mr. Wilbur's song.* Which he did; he wrote a perfectly wonderful tune once Guthrie had given him the De Gaulle treatment.[19]

"Dear Boy" appears in the musical when Candide, after believing that Pangloss is dead, discovers he is still alive but suffering from syphilis.[20] Candide asks his teacher to justify how his condition could be "for the best," and Pangloss responds with what Wilbur has called a "fuzzy professorial song of rationalization." Here is an early draft of this lyric, from March 24, 1956:

> Dear boy, you will not hear me speak
> With sorrow or with rancor
> Of what has paled my cheek
> And blasted it with canker;
> 'Twas Love, great Love, that did the deed,
> Through Nature's gentle laws,
> And how shall ill effects proceed
> From so divine a cause?[21]

Guthrie cut "Dear Boy" before the New York opening because he worried it would be offensive. Exercising similar caution before the show's Boston opening, he cut all satirical allusions to HUAC from the dialogue in the inquisition scene—the moment when Candide and Dr. Pangloss arrive in Lisbon, are condemned as evil heretics, and sentenced to an auto-da-fe.[22] Yet, recalled Wilbur, "If there's anything tasteless or raunchy about 'Dear Boy,' it can be blamed on Voltaire. Of all the lyrics I wrote for *Candide*, this is the one which is most simply a versification [of what he wrote]."[23] "Dear Boy" was eventually reinstated in much later productions of the show, but the HUAC references returned only once, in a revival of *Candide* in 1966.

In early autumn 1956, despite distractions and discord among the strong egos working on *Candide,* rehearsals were set to begin at the Colonial The-atre in Boston, where the play was scheduled to run for a three-week tryout. Guthrie had invited Boston critics to attend the dress rehearsal, which would double as a charity benefit. The show at this stage consisted of a series of songs and musical interludes interspersed with the characters' dialogue. No one had bothered to calculate its exact length or do a complete run-through until it was about to open. Now the collaborators realized that its running time was nearly five hours, an unheard-of length for a musical. Before the show started, Guthrie conveyed his chagrin and apologized to the audience. He then asked the critics not to review that night's performance, promising to give them a shorter, more concentrated show in a few days.

The reviews of the trimmed version were favorable but not as enthusi-astic as its authors or producer had hoped. The *Variety* critic, for instance, warned that the public's ignorance of Voltaire's original was a substantial hurdle to overcome.[24] Even Wilbur's close friend John Brinnin offered a stinging (though unpublished) assessment of the show's Boston run. On October 29, 1956, he wrote in his journal:

> Boston: *Candide,* the opening night. Undigested, over-produced, it has settings as grand as Thebes & as costly. No style, no charm, no point Voltaire hasn't made better. Bernstein's score might have saved it. But the book weighs a ton, revived at moments by Wilbur's lyrics but, in the end, a drag. At intermission, Cal & Elizabeth [Robert Lowell and his wife Elizabeth Hardwick]. She mentions Brecht. These days a code word for something awful pretending to be mythical.[25]

During a one-week tryout run in New Haven in November, backstage tension reached crisis proportions. Lester Osterman, the associate producer, had stayed in New York, assuming that Reiner could handle any problems that might arise. But Reiner was holed up in her hotel room, so the show's stage manager, Thomas Hammond, pleaded with Osterman to come to New Haven to save it from "going down the drain." Osterman arrived in time for the last fifteen minutes of one performance, only to be "almost knocked down by people hurrying to leave." He called an emergency meet-ing in his hotel suite, and Hellman and Bernstein rapidly made cuts and adjustments to deal with complaints that the book was hard to follow and the scenes repetitive.[26]

When *Candide* finally opened on Broadway on December 1 at the Martin Beck on West Forty-fifth Street, four of the seven newspaper reviews were positive.[27] Brooks Atkinson of the *New York Times* was full of praise: "Since Voltaire was a brilliant writer, it is only right that his *Candide* should turn out to be a brilliant musical satire. Voltaire's cynical acceptance of war, greed, treachery, venery, snobbishness, and mendacity as staples of civilization provokes no disbelief in the middle of the 20th century."[28] The negative reviews, however, lingered in the collaborators' minds. Walter Kerr of the *New York Herald Tribune* had nothing good to say:

> Three of the most talented people our theater possesses—Lillian Hellman, Leonard Bernstein, Tyrone Guthrie—have joined hands to transform Voltaire's *Candide* into a really spectacular disaster. Who was mostly responsible for the great ghostly wreck that sails like a Flying Dutchman across the fog-bound stage of the Martin Beck? That would be hard to say, the honors are so evenly distributed. . . . Once the air has cleared a bit, I imagine Mr. Bernstein will come off best, if there is a best to be salvaged from the singularly ill-conceived venture.[29]

In the *New Republic* Mary McCarthy went on the attack as if she were defending Western civilization against the barbarians: "Was it a good idea to try to turn *Candide* into a musical operetta? Many people thought so. I confess I did myself. The materials seemed to be there: a gay, quite dirty story with exotic settings and a sufficiently improbable plot." She pointed out that "a satire on optimism . . . could be expected to have a certain topicality," an allusion to contemporary tendencies to gloss over unpleasant realities.

> What went wrong then, with the musical *Candide*? Four authors, all of them prominent, worked for a year with a prominent composer and a prominent scene designer to translate to the stage a tale that Voltaire wrote in three days, and the result is a sad fizzle which is more like a high school pageant than a social satire. The gaiety is gone; the dirt is gone; the negativism is gone. This is an uplift *Candide,* with a ringing message at the end.[30]

McCarthy chided the collaborators for failing to see "that *Candide* is a dangerous work. It is really and truly subversive. A fuse burns in it; that is why it is exciting." She found many faults with the production but said that "failure of nerve" was its greatest flaw: "A *Candide* without the deviltry, without that element of risk that makes the spectator catch his breath, is not worth doing."[31]

After the opening reviews Bernstein fled to Nassau to lick his wounds.[32] He talked to no one for three days, except when he was ordering meals. For the moment Hellman remained in New York, but she, too, planned to go to the Bahamas between late December and early January. Charlee and Dick went home to Wellesley and looked forward to a quiet holiday with Ellen, Christopher, and Nathan.

Despite several good quotable reviews and a publicity campaign touting the imminent release of the cast recording, ticket sales remained lackluster. Bernstein's reputation as a musical magician was not powerful enough to lift *Candide*'s dead weight. Box office receipts dropped sharply less than a month after opening night, even after (or perhaps because) the marketing team began to promote the show, more accurately, as a comic operetta rather than a musical.[33] But when the theater announced that *Candide* might close by mid-January, box office sales rose dramatically. The show grossed more than $44,000 in each of the two weeks after the announcement, double the take of the previous two weeks.[34] Osterman, more so than the others, remained optimistic about *Candide*'s future.

Through it all Hellman and Charlee had become close friends and confidantes. Hellman had offered the Wilburs the use of her place on the Vineyard while she was in the Bahamas, and on December 27 Charlee accepted, hoping it would speed her recovery from a high fever and the worst sinus headaches she had experienced in years.[35] On January 10, when the Wilburs were back in Wellesley, Charlee wrote Hellman (her "Dearest Pie") a four-page letter full of details, mundane and intimate, about the visit to what she dubbed "Pie house." She and Dick had settled in, making a huge pot of tea and drinking it by the fire and then walking to Cronig's to buy groceries. The evening, as Charlee described it, began with good food, drink, and slow talk, and it ended with "slow love." On this four-day vacation, she wrote, she and Dick were able to reclaim their senses after the dull emotional separation that had characterized their marriage during the entire *Candide* collaboration. Charlee admitted to borrowing Hellman's bath soap and drinking some of her liquor but said she had left other things in the pantry to compensate.[36]

Before ending the letter she brought up *Candide*. She was frustrated by not only the production's financial loss but also Bernstein's outsized ego. She mentioned a trip to New York that she and Dick were planning for

January 25. Wilbur would receive a prize from the Poetry Society of America, then meet with Harcourt to discuss a contract to make a recording to accompany a tenth-grade literature textbook. They planned to see *Candide* one more time, she told Hellman. As for the show's latest publicity:

> There was a grand big ad on Sunday in the TIMES for the album, a quarter page. The show ad of the moment is that small and rather goofy cartoon. I think it is completely lost on the page and rather a lousy idea, myself. Most of the publicity I have seen of late comes by way of Lennie who spreads all over the American cultural scene like a skunky mulch . . . [as in the] LIFE spread . . . complete with a shot of the Beautiful Torso being massaged with cologne by Felicia during intermission at Carnegie. The music shop in Wellesley has two or three bigger-than-life posters of Lennie around, advertising the new Bernstein multiple album. I feel creepy every time I go in that place now. His hour and a half Omnibus show was on last night, and at about nine exactly when it was scheduled to begin, John [Brinnin] looked at his watch and said, "Isn't it restful *not* to be watching Lennie." I sound bitter, don't I?[37]

Backstage Drama

Candide provoked a number of postmortems that attempted to answer the basic question McCarthy asked in her *New Republic* review: "What went wrong?" As Bernstein's biographer explained, the set designer, Oliver Smith, believed "it was an unnecessary failure, that Mrs. Reiner 'arbitrarily closed'" the show on February 2, 1957, despite the recent surge in tickets sales, "because she was mad at Lillian Hellman. The two women had a tremendous row at his house, Smith recalled; 'Hellman could be very cruel, screaming and yelling at her, and Mrs. Reiner had just had it and said the heck with it.'"[38]

Osterman, the show's associate producer, had had no previous theater experience, but he possessed plenty of people skills acquired from his successful Wall Street and real estate dealings, and was a calming and rational presence, especially during the early backstage drama in New Haven. According to Hellman's biographer William Wright, he was also involved in a strange situation on the last night of the Broadway run. On that Saturday, a mysterious phone call raised hopes that the show might go on: "A man with the voice of a New Jersey thug phoned Osterman to say that his boss, 'a Joisy businessman with a lotta dough,' wanted to use some of it to keep *Candide* running. The caller would not give his boss's name, but said that the man would be at the theater that night with a good-looking blonde and would make himself known to Osterman."[39]

Noir scenes ensued, beginning with the sharp eyes that were cast on every blonde who entered the theater. Osterman eventually made contact with the caller and went off with this mysterious "angel" to Reiner's apartment. Along with Osterman's wife Marjorie, Hellman and Guthrie waited for news at a nearby restaurant. Every half hour Marjorie called from a phone booth for an update. Instructed to sit tight, they did, passing the time by polishing off a bottle of scotch. By the time Osterman could let them know that the terms of the offer were reasonable, they were too drunk to care that Reiner had agreed to them. But on Sunday morning the benefactor added one stipulation: that he be repaid before any of the other backers were. Reiner flat-out refused. Hellman wrote to the Wilburs, then in Wellesley, about the benefactor's last-ditch efforts to compromise.

> Ethel, for no reason that anybody can figure out, refused and came back later in the day with a ridiculous counter offer. On Monday night, also for no reason that anybody can figure out, she carted away the scenery, thus adding another possible ten thousand to anyone who might want to bring it in again. I [had] stayed there [at the Martin Beck] all day Sunday, all Sunday night and well into Monday night making desperate efforts to get people to bring her into line. Along the way I lost my temper so badly that I began to cry on the phone and to tremble afterwards in what felt like a high-fever chill. I have never been through anything like those few days. . . . Somewhere Tennyson said half-lies were more damaging than complete lies, and indeed he was right. I have told her lawyer—a silly old pussy man—that I feel vindictive about her, and I will live to play it out. I would even pay to play it out. Lester [Osterman] was darling and kind and generous and all the nice things, and we are all in his debt for the fight he made for us. Unfortunately he doesn't know much about the theatre and was victim to Ethel's double-talk figures.[40]

Yet despite her disappointment, Hellman was relieved: "All is over now and, beginning with Boston, it seems to me as if I had been in [a] coma."[41]

Reiner's misrepresentations weren't the only ones that haunted Hellman in the course of the *Candide* collaboration. She, too, had problems with Bernstein. In a letter written to Wilbur in Wellesley several days after the New York opening, she reacted to a feedback session.

> If you live, and hang on tight, I guess nothing is as bad as you thought it would be. . . . You will see there is work for you to do, but not too much.

But I feel more cheerful about the show than I ever have felt before. . . . There were tough times, however. The Master [that is, Bernstein] was the Master. I didn't snap as often as I used to, but I did take to loud sighing. It is remarkable how he forgives all of us—we need forgiving since he was always in the right. I made what I thought was an excellent suggestion—you will see it in the notes, it concerns the overture—only to find that he had tried to persuade us of it in Boston. There wasn't a word of truth in that claim, and the fact that he doesn't know it is an untruth makes it more irritating. . . . The Master made occasional remarks about your not being here; I tell you now because he will make use of it, of course, later on. I think you are right to stay away from him as much as possible. He is worried by coldness, or lack of response, and I have found it is good to keep him worried.[42]

In his autobiography Guthrie assessed his own participation in *Candide* and assumed some of the blame for its shortcomings. Like Dorothy Parker, he saw the difficulties of working with Bernstein, who, he said, embodied "the stuff of genius." He included himself among the collaborators who "seemed to lose whatever share of lightness and gaiety and dash we might possibly have been able to contribute."[43]

Smith, the production manager, disagreed with an often-repeated claim that too many cooks in the creative kitchen had caused *Candide*'s demise. Bernstein, he noted, had succeeded with equally high-powered collaborators on *West Side Story*. He also suggested that some of the *Candide* collaborators were more relentless and temperamental than others were. Hellman, for instance, "fought tooth and nail with Guthrie over his cuts, denouncing him at one rehearsal. 'You've sold out,' she screamed: 'You're just a whore.' "[44]

According to her biographer Alice Kessler-Harris, Hellman accepted that the weaknesses of *Candide* stemmed from "her own failure at the art of collaboration." As Hellman herself said, "I am not a good collaborator because I am unable to do the kind of pressure work that goes with other people's understandable demands. I am unable to take other people's opinions about writing. I work best on my own for good or bad." Regarding *Candide* specifically, she admitted that she had become "too anxious to stay out of fights," and that she forgot everything she had learned about the theater during the collaboration: "All my instinct went out the window."[45]

Wilbur was protective of his work on the show. He had never minded constructive criticism but was frequently exasperated by Bernstein's tendency to tinker with the lyrics and said he would have quit if he hadn't been strapped for cash. While the collaborators were working on the Vineyard, he found himself needing to leave the island for a few days and asked Hellman to "clip Lenny's piano wires" if she saw him rewriting the lyrics.[46] For his part Bernstein was often impatient with Wilbur's meticulous attention to every word, once snapping that he "shuts himself off in a phone booth and talks to God!"[47]

Some four years after Bernstein's death, as the *Candide* manuscripts were being compiled into a new piano and vocal score, Wilbur's bibliographer, Jack Hagstrom, along with the Amherst College archivist John Lancaster, met Bernstein's agent, Charlie Harmon, at the composer's studio in the Dakota on Central Park West. The agent asked Wilbur's permission to reprint a facsimile of his draft of "Glitter and Be Gay," along with Bernstein's handwritten notes, in the appendix of the new score. Harmon also remarked that lyric writing seemed to be an easy task for Wilbur, judging from the firmness of his handwriting.[48]

A few years later Wilbur found some *Candide* correspondence among a heap of other theater material and sent it to Lancaster along with a brief essay titled "Apropos *Candide*." In the essay he focused entirely on his collaboration with Bernstein and singled out an aspect he thought fans would find particularly amusing:

> In cases where existing music was to be furnished with words, we often devised nonsensical verses which, embodying the music's rhythms in words of a sort, might bring me a little closer to the pertinent verbalizing of Lenny's sound and movement. On one occasion, for example, it occurred to us that a tune Lenny had written for his son Alexander might serve for a number about Candide's departure from Buenos Aires in Act II. The tune—Lenny called it a species of schottische—was tripping and animated in the extreme, and it was therefore especially necessary for me to grope toward some verbal equivalent by way of a provisional or dummy lyric. The reader may be interested to know that the lyric of "Bon Voyage" . . . began with these asinine lines: "Oh what a lovely villager / Oh what a lovely, lovely villager bird."[49]

The opening lines of that chorus ended up being "Bon voyage, dear fellow / Dear benefactor of your fellow man."

Wilbur's thoughts about the show were characteristically rational and measured. "There was no one villain" responsible for *Candide*'s faults, he wrote. "Lillian Hellman really [did not] like musicals, and Lenny's music got more and more pretentious and smashy—the audience forgot what was happening to the characters. Lillian's book got to be mere connective tissue."[50] If there really was any fundamental fault, it lay, in Wilbur's view, in Voltaire's plot, which was "simply one instance of human folly after another."[51]

Despite the problems of its original run, *Candide* has enjoyed numerous reincarnations as both a staged musical and a concert production. Bernstein and Hellman came to agree that the latter format was the better option, as long as it included enough dialogue to prevent it from becoming a series of strung-together songs. Still, the first revival effort—a 1959 performance at London's Saville Theatre—created as much anxiety in Hellman, and sparked as much anger, as the initial collaboration did. The show was scheduled to open on April 30, and she flew to London in February to work with Bobby Lewis, the director, and Michael Stewart, who was helping her revise the book. She wrote to Wilbur on February 11 about an unpleasant week during which she lost her temper because her own edited script—with changes on every single line plus all of Stewart's new lines—came back from Lewis with more than fifty additional adjustments.[52]

The next big production, by the Theatre Group at the University of California at Los Angeles, took place in 1966 and involved even more substantial and contentious revisions of the book. In 1971 the Los Angeles Civic Light Opera put on a version that shuffled some of the musical numbers and included a new song with lyrics by Bernstein. By 1973, when Harold Prince became interested in producing a revival, Hellman was sick of making changes and refused to allow anyone else to alter her words. Prince then asked Hugh Wheeler to write a brand-new book. Although he retained most of Wilbur's lyrics, he brought in Steven Sondheim to add what the opera critic Burton Fisher called "distinctive dazzle."[53]

The cast recording of a performance on December 9, 1956, is all that remains of the original work as staged. Goddard Lieberson lavishly produced it for Columbia Records as if it were a classical album. In the liner notes of its 1991 reissue the Grammy-winning record producer Didier C. Deutsch acknowledged the "runaway" success of the original album, despite the show's theatrical debacle.[54] Ken Mandelbaum, an expert in musical theater, has written that "Bernstein's score is above reproach and the lyrics, whether by Latouche, Wilbur, Sondheim [for revivals in 1973 and 1997], Bernstein, or anyone else, are superb."[55]

In 2011 the producer Ralph Hammann staged a retrospective performance of excerpts from Wilbur's theater work at the restored nineteenth-century

Colonial Theatre in Pittsfield, Massachusetts, where Wilbur came onstage to speak as the guest of honor. A coloratura soprano performed one of *Candide*'s signature songs, "Glitter and Be Gay," a parody of trilling and other operatic techniques. Her extended refrains—"ha ha ha ha ha ha"— interspersed between the stanzas of Wilbur's lyrics, ranged in tone from despair to buoyancy, the latter inflected with a high-pitched maniacal edge.

> Ah, 'twas not to be;
> Harsh necessity
> Brought me to this gilded cage.
> Born to higher things,
> Here I droop my wings,
> Ah! Singing of a sorrow nothing can assuage.[56]

Such mood swings echo the ups and downs and the sense of entrapment that Hellman, Bernstein, and Wilbur all experienced during the collaboration—as well as the fortunes of the show itself.

A Difficult Friendship

In 1957, after Wilbur was hired to teach at Wesleyan, the family moved from Wellesley to Portland, Connecticut. Although Dick and Charlee were now closer to New York, Wilbur's academic circle seldom overlapped Hellman's theater circle, and the couple saw her less frequently. Nonetheless, the three remained close and affectionate friends—so close that they asked her to be the godmother of their fourth child, Aaron, who was born in 1958.

More than twenty years after Hellman's death in 1984, Wilbur spoke about his old friend Lillian, expressing great fondness but also recalling that "she could be a great 'misunderstander' if she interpreted something as an aspersion or a slight." For instance, one day, during the summer of collaboration on Martha's Vineyard, the Wilburs turned down an invitation to dine at Hellman's because they preferred to spend that evening with their family. Several days later, in the middle of Cronig's grocery store in the town of Vineyard Haven, Hellman loudly denounced Charlee as a snob.

Kessler-Harris, who titled her 2012 biography *A Difficult Woman,* wrote that Hellman's "large heart and enormous capacity for warmth and generosity drew people to her even as her irascibility repelled them." Her generosity often surfaced in small but thoughtful gifts. During and after the *Candide* collaborations, letters between the Wilburs and Hellman and the Bernsteins and Hellman show numerous examples of how both couples took pains to reciprocate her kindness. Felicia Bernstein picked up dresses for her in Paris.[57] At Christmas in 1956 Charlee gave her two family heirlooms, a necklace and a matching bracelet that her grandfather had bought in Palestine for her grandmother. She sent the gift, however, without her mother's knowledge and eventually felt compelled to confess, if only because, when Hellman telephoned to thank her, Charlee's mother was in the room and overheard her daughter's awkward response. As Charlee wrote to Hellman later, her mother was glad Hellman had the jewelry for now but suggested she return it to the family by willing it to Ellen Wilbur.[58]

Hellman also lent considerable sums of money to friends. For instance, in February 1961 Charlee sent her a plea for help from Houston, where Wilbur was on sabbatical, with the following disclaimer:

> Only twice since [Dick and I] have been married have we found ourselves in financial difficulties: the terrible year that Nathan was born when he all but died four times in his first year and I had both double pneumonia and peritonitis with not a shred of Blue Cross. The other bad time was when Dick was on leave from Wellesley, without pay, to do CANDIDE and I had taken a job at the Wellesley hospital to pay for Franca whom we had just gotten over from Italy. Just after the first bad year, my mother and Dick's parents each gave us something towards buying our Wellesley house. We have paid them both back, with interest, and have not at any other time accepted any other help from them or anyone else.[59]

Charlee gave a full accounting of how Wilbur's income and professional choices stacked up against the family's unexpected financial burdens. Among other items she included the amount of his teaching salary during the past several years; his plan to take a year off from the reading circuit to devote time to translating Jean Sarment's *Le Pavillon des Enfants* (*The Children's Playhouse*), which never brought him a dime; the illness of three-year-old Aaron, whose autism was yet to be diagnosed; repairs to the Wellesley house that had to be managed long distance; and $1,300 worth of orthodontia for Christopher. Charlee was in a particularly tight bind because she had impulsively given the balance of her personal bank account to her alcoholic cousin's estranged wife so that the woman could afford to feed her children.

Charlee offered elaborate justifications for keeping her husband in the dark about the loan: "Dick becomes tense and anxiety-ridden when he concerns himself with money; household bills appall him; he becomes tense and even sleepless if this is a burden on him." She was willing to assume this burden, but it was imperative, she repeated to Hellman, that he not learn of their financial troubles.

> I am writing now and in a hurry for selfish reasons. March first is Dick's fortieth birthday. He is scheduled to give a reading, the only one of the winter, at the University of St. Louis, and he wants me to go with him. We have planned this for a long time. The school will pay his expenses and not mine. We would be going on Feb. 27th on the train. At the moment I cannot possibly consider going because I cannot simply afford the train nor the expense of a maid overnight and all day for the three days we would be away. All this is most distressing to me, but mainly for Dick's sake. I cannot alarm him about money if I can avoid it. This may seem childish to you, dear, but the one thing I can do for Dick is to create a peaceful, untroubled place within which he can work.[60]

Hellman agreed to lend the Wilburs $1,000 but only if Dick were told the truth, including the backstory about Charlee's gift to her cousin's wife. Charlee agreed, and together the couple sent Hellman a telegram thanking her for arranging to wire the funds. In a separate letter Wilbur again acknowledged his gratitude and thanked her as well for sending a box of suits belonging to her longtime partner Dashiell Hammett, who had died in January.[61]

Though Hellman's generosity to friends was manifest, she could retaliate savagely if she thought someone had crossed her. Mary McCarthy and Hellman had distrusted each other for years, and in 1980 their feud exploded in living rooms across America. During an appearance on *The Dick Cavett Show* McCarthy called Hellman a liar, denouncing her memoirs, especially *Scoundrel Time* and *Pentimento,* as fabrications. When Cavett asked McCarthy to explain, she repeated a statement she had already made in a less public venue: "Every word she writes is a lie, including 'and' and 'the.'"[62]

In March 1984, not long after the McCarthy accusation, Hellman had a falling out with William Wright, who wanted to write a biography of her. She sent telegrams and letters to friends, begging them not to speak to Wright if he sought them out. After receiving one of those telegrams Wilbur tried to talk sense into her. Wright explained the outcome in the epilogue of the biography he eventually published in 1986:

> On his own generous volition, Wilbur wrote Hellman on my behalf, using an argument I had already arrived at to persuade reluctant sources: enemies are only too willing to come forward; if friends withhold positive information, the resulting picture could be unbalanced. Hellman replied

to Wilbur that she might be acting foolishly, and she might be taking herself too seriously, but she wanted him to abide by her wishes.[63]

In 2006 Wilbur reflected on his own curious double standard when he judged Hellman's attitude toward truth:

I was terribly fond of Lillian and never wanted to offend her. Lillian was also the greatest adorer of the truth I ever knew. She equated Dash Hammett with the truth. A very large part of her love for him had to do with his insistence on saying whatever it was he felt. But Lillian, for all her talk about the truth, . . . she used to love to sit around in the evening and talk about some instance of behavior—"why did so and so give that fifty dollar bill to the waitress in the Old Oyster House"—and she wanted to get to the bottom of motivation and she wanted to get to the bottom of the facts. And yet I'm now aware that there was a great deal of fiction in her memoirs. At the time I would have never dared suppose that, and I wouldn't have said it in her presence.[64]

Wilbur was reminiscing about a May 1975 lunch he had shared with Hellman and Eudora Welty at the American Academy of Arts and Letters. At the table he had made a remark that angered Hellman, saying, in essence, that her books were fictions because she had the worst memory of anyone he had ever known. Later that month she wrote to him to clear the air:

The sharpness of your remark has nothing to do with anything: the meaning has. I tried to say that both books came mostly from diaries and I mumbled something about my memory when we were interrupted. I was trying to say that my memory is bad where yours is good, and I believe it is possibly good where yours may not be. I have always known what I could remember and I don't think I ever faked it, although certainly I have found it mistaken where I thought it was good.

It is true that in both books I changed names and places, sometimes to save feelings, more often because my lawyer and Little, Brown insisted upon it. But that does not mean they are fiction: they simply are not. You have a right to think they are fiction, but you picked an unpleasant open table to say so.

Maybe this all has something to do with why two former good friends don't see each other anymore. If that is true, I am sorry. No sense either of us worrying about it any longer.[65]

On June 22, 1984, Hellman wrote to the Wilburs from Vineyard Haven to thank them for remembering her birthday. She was suffering from a cracked rib, she said, and had spent her birthday in bed. She urged them to call next time they came to Martha's Vineyard.[66] She died eight days later.

Candide Residuals and Broadway Repercussions

After the 1966 *Candide* revival at UCLA, the Lantz Agency sent Wilbur a record of the royalties that run had earned, which totaled $75,000. Bernstein, who had been involved in the production only as an observer, had deducted $25,000 off the top for himself, which he'd earmarked as expenses to cover travel and his attendance at performances. Noting this, Wilbur was disturbed, especially because he had not been informed of the revival before it opened. On November 7, 1966, he wrote to Bernstein, saying that he was pleased that the show still had viability but was unhappy to learn of the production as a fait accompli. Although Wilbur's agent Gil Parker had explained that the poet no longer had rights of disposal and that future financial and production arrangements for *Candide* would be made by Hellman and Bernstein alone, he had hoped that they would feel personally, if not legally, bound to consult him about further versions or revivals. His name was on the show, he said. He'd put a lot of sweat into it, and he wanted to be actively involved in any revival.[67]

By 1968, the year that Wesleyan awarded Bernstein an honorary doctorate, Wilbur had become disillusioned with the composer's financial manipulations and with Broadway culture in general. At the Wesleyan ceremony, however, he suppressed his displeasure long enough to escort Bernstein onto the platform. Along with the university's president, Edwin Etheridge, he draped the academic hood that accompanied the degree over Bernstein's crimson Harvard robe.

Candide was not the end of Wilbur's Broadway misadventures. A 1961 production of Sarment's *The Children's Playhouse,* which Wilbur had translated from the French (with Charlee's help), was never staged. The producers, who envisioned the play as a vehicle for older performers, had intended to open it in London and then bring it to Broadway. But Dorothy and Lillian Gish, the sisters who had achieved fame in the silent-film era and who were slated to take the two female leads, refused to go to London. Their excuse ostensibly involved Dorothy's fear that her aged dog, who would have to be boarded, would die in her absence. When the sisters withdrew, the play's financial backers canceled the production, and Gil Parker couldn't find anyone to produce the show who wouldn't require serious cuts. Wilbur declined even to try, saying he had no experience with trimming lines from a script.[68]

Another Broadway disaster followed in 1966. Wilbur and Michel Legrand had been hired to translate the lyrics for Jean Giraudoux's musical play *La Folle de Chaillot* (*The Madwoman of Chaillot*). Maurice Valency, a Columbia University professor with many Broadway credits for both original plays and translations, was simultaneously translating the prose script. Wilbur and Legrand completed their work without realizing that the producer who had hired them no longer owned the American rights to the show; Valency had told the producer to let the rights lapse.

When Wilbur discovered what Valency had done, he was furious. Valency justified his decision in a letter dated April 10, 1967. Jerome Lawrence, Robert Edwin Lee, and Jerry Herman, he said, had conducted an all-out campaign to renew the rights; he couldn't resist the pleasure of surrendering the play to such nice people who wanted it very much. He was sick of agents and gossips, he said; he'd let them have the rights with his blessing. Although Valency knew Wilbur would be angry, self-interest had driven his decision. He had needed a change, he wrote, and he planned to put the whole business behind him.[69]

Wilbur reacted bitterly. Valency had no right, he wrote, to sacrifice the work and hopes of two other men just for the pleasure of surrender. "You know as well as I do what will become of *La Folle* in the hands of the authors of *Hello, Dolly* and *Auntie Mame*. It will be contemptible. It will be the reduction of a subtle and delicate work to lox-and-bagels vulgarity. And that will be your fault." Wilbur used the Latin phrase *corruptio optimi pessima* ("corruption of the best is the worst of all") to describe his utter frustration: "Maurice Valency of Columbia University, who can quote the Chanson de Roland with emotion, and has on occasion brought some taste into our wretched American theater, has behaved as one would never have expected him to do. . . . It's a pity."[70]

Five days later Valency wrote back, claiming he had acted in ignorance—of what he did not say—and accusing Wilbur of misconstruing his intent. He condescendingly addressed Wilbur as "dear boy" (probably a reference to Wilbur's *Candide* lyric, which had been pulled from the New York production) and made himself out to be the victim. Wilbur and Legrand, he said, had had no faith in the three-way collaboration and had seen him as its principle obstacle.[71] Another volley of letters ensued, which included apologies from Valency for relying on hearsay and from Wilbur for not fully articulating the source of his concerns. Finally, on April 25, Wilbur suggested that he and Valency pick up where they had left off and arrange to renew and restore the original partnership. On April 29 Valency said that he feared it was too late.

Like many caught up in Broadway's volatile culture, the three collaborators had become entangled in a web of misunderstanding and accusation. But Wilbur saw the episode as a last straw, and not long afterward he wrote out the following page-long list in his controlled italic handwriting:

Horse Shit
Fuck the following:
Musical theatre.
The public.
Collaboration.
Sweet reasonableness.
"The filtering-down of the best ideas to the great mass." Matthew Arnold
Entertainment industry.
Plot. Story.
"Adaptation" of classics.
Revisions.
Concessions.
Enthralling forward movement and breathtaking timing. Brilliance.
Fear of dullness. Of point.
Money. Gorgeousness.
"Theatre." [72]

Perhaps making this list helped him vent the anger and disappointment brought on by these Broadway debacles. *La Folle* would not be Wilbur's last chance in the theater. He would turn to Molière again and again, then to Racine, and finally to Corneille, the playwright he began to translate during his ninth decade.

10

In the Circle with Lowell, Bishop, and Jarrell

"I should not be conveying competitiveness"

A good poem is a good poem, whatever its technical means, and I cheerfully grant that much of the best work of recent years has been done in "free" forms. It does seem about time, however, to abandon the notion that free verse is daring and progressive, that it is peculiarly suited to conveying present-day experience, and that "experiment" must consist in the abandonment of disciplines.

—RICHARD WILBUR, unpublished draft for a symposium
on the state of poetry, 1972

In June 2007, while browsing in a bookstore in Amherst, Wilbur picked up a recently published volume of Robert Lowell's collected letters. Knowing that he had written letters to Lowell, Wilbur looked in the index for his own name. A week later he spoke to us about what he had found on page 601 and the feelings that his discovery had stirred.

> The whole trouble with Cal Lowell and me was that we felt competitive, and he didn't know he was competitive because he was so utterly lordly about his work, so that he could almost be a bully toward his fellow poet without knowing it. . . . In the letter he was saying to somebody, "Dick and I were almost good friends, and he's a good man." He says that twice. "But his competitiveness"—that wasn't his word, but it was something like that—"is so fierce that I'm aware of it all the time." So funny—a man who could never in any evening's conversation fail to rank all the English and American poets, one two three four, was not aware of his

own competitiveness. It made me feel sad and small to be so transparently competitive as I was.[1]

The words in Lowell's January 24, 1973, letter actually read: "[Wilbur] has really always been a model acquaintance, almost friend to me, though I felt a fragile shell kept his rivalry from muddying me. Still, a good man."[2] When he spoke to us about that letter, Wilbur never mentioned the context of this remark, which included criticism of Wilbur's "Cottage Street, 1953," or that the "somebody" whom Lowell addressed was Elizabeth Bishop.

In 2010 the complete correspondence between Bishop and Lowell was published as *Words in Air.* Ars poetica was not the main focus of their conversation; their letters center instead on their private lives and loves and on the nature of their own relationship. But the correspondence does reveal the solidarity of their alliance in the midst of poets whom they considered both rivals and friends. Wilbur was one such peer, as was Randall Jarrell, the era's most perceptive and caustic critic at a time when competitive and rank-obsessed poets dominated the literary culture.

Jarrell's Retrospective of Poets at Midcentury

In 1962 Jarrell presented a lecture titled "Fifty Years of American Poetry" at the National Poetry Festival in Washington, D.C. His talk, which he published the next year in *Prairie Schooner,* was composed of vignettes of eminent American poets who were working between 1912 and 1962. He began with Edward Arlington Robinson and Edgar Lee Masters but moved quickly to living poets, citing Robert Frost, Wallace Stevens, and T. S. Eliot as the greatest of the century so far. Jarrell characterized and assessed the attributes of Ezra Pound, William Carlos Williams, Marianne Moore, and John Crowe Ransom, among others. He identified Elizabeth Bishop's collection *Poems* as one to which readers would turn as often as they turned to the work of Stevens, Moore, and Ransom. He acknowledged that Theodore Roethke was a forceful and delicate poet whose work was still changing. His main point was that "good American poets are surprisingly individual and independent." For Jarrell, conformity was doom.[3]

Toward the end of his lecture, Jarrell offered a brief assessment of Karl Shapiro ("fresh and young and rash and live") and then made a pointed comparison between Wilbur and Lowell. Did both have the capacity "to write about what is most terrible in the world of the present"? Even the best of poets sometimes lack this ability, he said. Lowell had it, he declared. By implication Wilbur did not.[4]

Jarrell borrowed the phrase "studied felicity," which Petronius used to describe Horace's poetry, to describe Wilbur's work:

> His impersonal, exactly accomplished, faintly sententious skill produces poems that, ordinarily, compose themselves into a little too regular a beauty—there is no eminent beauty without a certain strangeness in the proportion, and yet "A Baroque Wall-Fountain in the Villa Sciarra" is one of the most marvelously beautiful, one of the most nearly perfect poems any American has written, and poems like "A Black November Turkey" and a "A Hole in the Floor" are the little differentiated, complete-in-themselves universes that true works of art are. Wilbur's lyric calling to life of the things of this world—the things rather than the processes or the people—specializes in both true and false happy endings, not by choice but by necessity; he obsessively sees, and shows, the bright underside of every dark thing. What he says about his childhood [in the poem "The Pardon"] is true of his maturity: "In my kind world the dead were out of range / And I could not forgive the sad or strange / In beast or man." This compulsion limits his poems; and yet it is this compulsion, and not merely his greater skill and talent, that differentiates him so favorably from the controlled, accomplished, correct poets who are common nowadays.[5]

Jarrell saw Lowell, however, as "the poet of shock: his effects vary from crudity to magnificence, but they are always surprising and always his own—his style manages to make even quotations and historical facts a personal possession. His variation of Tolstoy's motto 'Make it strange' is 'Make it grotesque.'" Lowell's "astonishing ambition," Jarrell noted, allowed him to compete with the poetry of the past on its own terms. "He bullied his early work but his own vulnerable humanity has been forced in on him." Jarrell articulated his major distinction between the poets:

> It is life that [Lowell] makes into poems instead of, as in Wilbur, the things of life. In Wilbur the man who produces the poems is somehow impersonal and anonymous, the composed conventional figure of The Poet; we know well, almost too well, the man who produces Lowell's poems. The awful depths, the plain absurdities of his own actual existence in the prosperous, developed disastrous world he and we inhabit are there in the poems.[6]

Jarrell's perceptions of Wilbur and Lowell largely prevail today. Wilbur is seen as sensible, sunny, and restrained; Lowell is seen as overwrought, gloomy, and confrontational. How Bishop figured in their relationship is curious, partly because she was much closer to Wilbur in poetic sensibility yet far closer to Lowell emotionally. By examining the friendship and rivalry between Wilbur and Lowell—with Bishop and Jarrell on the sidelines—we also glimpse a boxing ring filled with midcentury poets.

"Come on, *take a chance*"

Wilbur met Robert Lowell, known as Cal, in 1948 at a party hosted by Richard Eberhart, who was teaching at Harvard.[7] Earlier that fall Eberhart had recommended Wilbur's poetry to both Bishop and Lowell. Neither was impressed. Bishop, writing to Lowell on October 23, said she had spent only about fifteen minutes reading the poems but didn't think them very good.[8] In reply, Lowell noted that Wilbur was good at imitating Stevens and, to some extent, Moore, but in his view had nothing much to say.[9]

Lowell and Bishop were both planning to attend the Bard poetry conference during the first weekend of November (see chapter 6). Wilbur would meet Bishop there for the first time; Eberhart would share a room with Lowell. Lowell dubbed the event a "big gang meeting of poets," and Bishop called it a "poetry orgy." Wilbur referred to the "knock-down discussions of poetic form" that ensued after Williams took center stage and insisted that free verse was the only American poetry with a future.[10]

Jarrell was not at the Bard conference, but he astutely predicted that it would begin a "long dreary imaginary war" to decide the future of American poetry. The two sides of that war, as he later wrote in "A View of Three Poets" (published in the *Partisan Review* in 1951), were "America and the Present . . . fighting Europe and the Past."[11] His primary task in this article was to review Wilbur's *Ceremony,* Lowell's *The Mills of the Kavanaughs,* and the first sections of Williams's *Paterson.* His condescending discussion treated Williams as the instigator and organizer of the battle against traditional forms.

Commenting to Lowell about the article, Bishop said nothing about Jarrell's treatment of Williams but was infuriated by his critique of Lowell—though she appreciated Jarrell's demanding and comprehensive approach to criticism in general. What also annoyed her was his excessive admiration for Wilbur's book.[12] Lowell seemed puzzled by her ire: "Don't see how you could think Wilbur flattered by Randall's review; what makes it hurt is R's leaning over backwards to be friendly—caressed by a tiger."[13]

Not long after meeting Jarrell, Wilbur expressed a similar wariness, although he used a different metaphor to describe it: "Jarrell has written poetry reviews of the greatest acerbity: there is none more cutting unless it is Berryman. And yet in person Jarrell is slow, modest, full of well-I-don't-knows and boyish ers and ahs. Of course one must look hard at such people. After two days of quiet talk and 'deference' from Jarrell I noticed a transient glint in his eye, & for a moment glimpsed the tomahawk man."[14]

In "A View of Three Poets" Jarrell explicitly declared that Lowell and Wilbur were capable of distinguished and satisfying work, and in fact both did earn his praise for their subsequent volumes. Nonetheless, he was also blunt about their shortcomings. Lowell was a poet whose "Will" battled with his "Imagination" until the latter began to circle "like a squirrel in a squirrel cage."[15] As for Wilbur:

> The poems [in *Ceremony*] are all Scenes, none of them dramatic; and if the reader is someone who feels that you can't look at the best sunset for more than a few minutes (but that people sometimes last for centuries), he is sure to start longing for a murder or a Character—after thirty or forty pages he would pay dollars for one dramatic monologue, some blessed graceless human voice that has not yet learned to express itself so composedly as poets do.[16]

Perhaps Jarrell's opening sentence—"Richard Wilbur is a delicate, charming, skillful poet—his poems not only make you use, but make you eager to use, words like *attractive* and *appealing* and *engaging*"—had fooled Bishop into thinking that he admired Wilbur too much. Or perhaps she didn't read far enough to recognize that the virtues he attributed to Wilbur—"a skillful use of verbs and kinesthetic words, a relishable relishing texture"—were embodied, he argued, in "a sugar-coated-slap-in-the-face rhetoric" that "produce[d] a real though rather mild pleasure."[17] Similar claims would appear in reviews about Bishop's own work, both during and after her lifetime, as critics assessed and reassessed her achievements.

In 1957, ten years after Lowell won a Pulitzer Prize for *Lord Weary's Castle* and a year after Bishop won hers for *North & South,* Wilbur won his first Pulitzer for *Things of This World.* A few days before the May 6 announcement, Wilbur gave a reading at Amherst, also visiting a modern poetry class taught by C. L. Barber. A student who had searched out a copy of the *Partisan Review* article brashly asked Wilbur what he thought of an analogy Jarrell had made between a play in football and Wilbur's poetic practice:

"There will sometimes be a moment when you can settle for six or eight safe yards, or take a chance and get stopped cold or, if you're lucky, go the whole way. Mr. Wilbur almost always settles for six or eight yards."[18] Wilbur's only response was to say, "No, that was a review by Horace Gregory." He was wrong: Jarrell *had* made the football analogy; Gregory had disparaged Wilbur's poetry in a 1956 issue of the *Partisan Review,* calling it "suburban."[19]

"A View of Three Poets" is filled with insidious analogies. For instance, "So many reviewers have praised [Wilbur] for [playing it safe] that in his second book he takes fewer risks than in his first. (He is one of those Southern girls to whom everybody north of Baltimore has said, 'Whatever you do, *don't* lose that lovely Southern accent of yours': after a few years they sound like Amos and Andy.")[20] Jarrell's accusations have clung to his reputation like barnacles, even as his admirers have tried to scrape them off. Wilbur himself explained sixty years later:

> I was annoyed. So I wrote a note, as one should never do, saying to Randall, "Do you realize that almost all your amusing figures, comparisons, and similes in that article compare me to something feminine? You seem to come close to saying that I'm a sissy." I don't think he intended to do that, and I was being much too touchy. [It] didn't make for a serious breach. We were always close, and he praised me highly at later times, but . . . then without continuing to feel contentious about it, I got sick of people quoting from that damn review. People wrote about it intending to praise me, but they would begin by quoting negative things from Randall. I was just handed a book [at a reading] down at Newburyport, and in the [biographical material about me] was a rehash of Randall's review.[21]

Jarrell zeroed in on what he saw as Wilbur's obvious impersonation of other poets' styles. For example, citing these lines from "The Melongène" (collected in *The Beautiful Changes*)—"Natural pomp! Excessive Nightshade's Prince! Polished potato"—he said that Wilbur "apostrophizes an eggplant" and ridiculed the poem as an apparent effort to evoke Marianne Moore. Yet Jarrell couldn't leave it at that: he remarked how Wilbur no longer seemed to be influenced by Moore, adding, "I wish he were."[22]

Toward the end of the review Jarrell did comment appreciatively on the last few lines of "Grasse: The Olive Trees" (in *Ceremony*):

> Even when seen from near, the olive shows
> A hue of far away. Perhaps for this
> The dove brought olive back, a tree which grows

Unearthly pale, which ever dims and dries,
And whose great thirst, exceeding all excess,
Teaches the South it is not paradise.

For Jarrell these six lines, with their "easy and graceful beauty," represented the apex of *Ceremony*'s achievement. Nothing in that book reached
as high, in his mind, as "Water Walker" did in Wilbur's first collection. Yet
despite his praise, he remained ambivalent about "Grasse," calling it "an
ambitious and felt and thoughtful poem like . . . 'Water Walker'" but also
"a partial failure," although "surely anybody would rather have written it
than some of Mr. Wilbur's slight and conventional successes."[23]

Containing more innuendo and anecdote than analysis, "A View
of Three Poets" may itself be viewed as either a partial failure or a slight
success. Nonetheless, it has had tremendous staying power. According to
Brad Leithauser, who has edited a collection of Jarrell's essays ("A View"
is not included in the volume), reading his work can be "simultaneously
vexing and endearing" because of "his frequent conviction that the point
he's making is self-evident. He's constantly holding up a stanza or a passage
and crying, in effect, 'Nothing more need be said. Only an idiot could be
unmoved!' Which is fine just as long as you share his enthusiasm. When
you don't you're left having to reply, 'As an idiot, I wish you would further
explain to me . . .'"[24]

In a tribute to his friend, Lowell noted that readers have responded to the
power of Jarrell's enthusiasm, which "changed and improved opinions and
values." He remarked that Jarrell "left many reputations [such as Frost's and
Whitman's] permanently altered and exalted."[25] Yet few critics and poets
have been able to excuse or justify Jarrell's gratuitous cruelty. Leithauser
has noted his "hilarious dexterity" in panning verse by poets of "no lasting
interest" and his tendency to spend too much time debating about whether
they were "*thoroughly* bad" or capable of "mediocrity." He "usually managed
to flay rather than flog a dead horse. Still, he might better have left the
corpse to decompose on its own."[26]

According to Bishop, Jarrell's criticism could be "aggrieved" and "unbe-
lievably cruel. . . . He'd take a book of poems, and squeeze." But she seemed
to accept that his cruelty was in service of a higher good. "He hated bad
poetry with such vehemence and so vigorously that it didn't occur to him . . .
[that] a human being [was] also being squeezed."[27] Lowell, eulogizing Jarrell's skill at eulogy, thought his "immense enthusiasms for what he liked"
served to balance his complaints about what he didn't.[28] He remarked on

Jarrell's selflessness, which, as Leithauser has also pointed out, meant that he was usually not only forgiven for his bruising comments but also commended for them. Lowell wrote, "Randall was the only man I have ever met who could make other writers feel that their work was more important to him than his own, . . . and that he cared as much about making the nature and goodness of someone else's work understood as he cared about making his own understood."[29] Bishop acknowledged this intensity when she praised the "minute-to-minute *devotion* to criticism" that Jarrell displayed in "A View of Three Poets."[30] And Wilbur alluded to Jarrell's generosity when he admitted in 2007 that he'd been too touchy about the review.

Jarrell had a demanding and austere conception of the poet and the reading public. He wanted readers to exhibit "the calm and ease and independence that comes from liking things in themselves and for themselves," adding that "if [the public] will read Rilke's and Yeats's and Hardy's poems, [a poet should] bear to have his own poems go unread forever."[31] As Leithauser points out, this selfless ideal was impossible at midcentury, when the literary culture was dominated by competitive and rank-obsessed poets. Yet Jarrell clung to it because he feared an America in which poetry's place would become precarious and the poet culturally irrelevant. He expanded at length on this theme, notably in his essay "The Obscurity of the Poet," in which "obscurity" referred not to vague or dense meaning but to the lack of attention paid to poetry itself.

Leithauser writes, "Time and again, implicitly and explicitly, Jarrell's essays ask, Does poetry matter to the world at large? And his answer is, Less and less."[32] Wilbur, however, disagreed, and he made his case eloquently and vehemently in a 1965 lecture he recorded for the Library of Congress as part of the Voice of America series on poetry.[33] He began by addressing the "social posture" of the poet who stands literally or figuratively before ten, twenty, or even hundreds or thousands of people, "on a platform . . . in a university auditorium, sometimes in an art gallery or community center, sometimes in a nightclub or coffeehouse." Since the war, he said, the poet's visibility had steadily improved and the public's attitude about poetry had "matured," with a recent sign being "the late President Kennedy's readiness to acknowledge and affirm the dignity of the arts."[34] With this affirmation came the poet's choice to remain an alienated artist or be a poet-citizen connected to a community.

> What poetry does with ideas is to redeem them from abstraction and submerge them in sensibility; it embodies them in persons and things,

and surrounds them with a weather of feeling; it thereby tests the ability of any idea to consort with human nature in its contemporary condition. Is it possible, for example, to speak intelligently of angels in the modern world? Will the psyche of the modern reader consent to be called a soul?[35]

Hoping to elicit a resounding yes to both questions, Wilbur offered an example from his own oeuvre, "Love Calls Us to the Things of This World," which addressed a number of concerns that would persist and reappear throughout his career: "All [these themes] have to do (a critic might say), with the proper relation between the tangible world and the intuitions of the spirit. The poems assume that such intuitions are, or may be, true; they incline however, to favor a spirituality which is not abstracted, not dissociated and world-renouncing."[36]

Jarrell's own poems had little connection to "intuitions of the spirit" or to spirituality of any kind. In *Randall Jarrell and His Age* the critic Stephen Burt points to a quality that strikingly distinguishes his poems from Wilbur's: "[They] projected his own needs and the needs he imagined into characters whose lives offered causes, figures, and languages for them. His lifelong preoccupation with loneliness and its remedies, with the self and how it might be changed, gave him his emotional repertoire: expectation, disappointment, pathos, sympathy, nostalgia, half-believed fantasy, mourning, and melancholia."[37] An undated, isolated passage in Wilbur's journal, written nearly a decade after Jarrell's death, both prefigured Burt's assessment and revealed how different Wilbur's sense of the world was from Jarrell's. "Randall: he did not tell all the truth as I see it, but neither did he lie, and he didn't flinch from stating the fact that pain is indeed pain, that in respect of health and looks and animal happiness we are bound to lose."[38]

Given Jarrell's "emotional repertoire," his poems range more widely than Wilbur's do, but they do not share Wilbur's fluency in achieving resonant expression of a powerful vision. Nor was Jarrell able to produce technically perfect poems: in 2014 Wilbur assessed them as "clever, readable, but not deathless" and his use of meter as "slipshod."[39] As Leithauser has noted, Jarrell "was grimly aware that only a fraction of a poet's output was likely to be first-rate."[40] A good poet, he famously said, "is someone who manages, in a lifetime of standing out in thunderstorms, to be struck by lightning five or six times; a dozen or two dozen times and he is great."[41]

As essays such as "Poets, Critics, and Readers" and "The Age of Criticism" show, Jarrell earned a reputation as not only a critic of poets but also a critic of critics.[42] In "A View of Three Poets" he offers advice to those critics who had praised Wilbur for not reaching beyond his poetic grasp: "If I were those reviewers I would quote to Mr. Wilbur something queer and true that Blake said on the same subject: 'You never know what is enough unless you know what's more than enough.'" He concluded:

> In the most serious sense of the word [Wilbur] is not a very satisfactory poet. And yet he seems the best of the quite young poets writing in this country, poets considerably younger than Lowell and Bishop and Shapiro and Schwartz. I want to finish by admiring his best poems, not by complaining about their limitations. But I can't blame his readers if they say to him in encouraging impatient voices: "Come on, *take a chance!*"[43]

Like his football analogy, these remarks raise a question: How is the quality of a poem (that is, its depth and breadth) related to its quantity (that is, its number of lines)? One can imagine Jarrell claiming that, in terms of length, Wilbur did indeed play it safer than many of his peers did. All of his male contemporaries of comparable stature—for instance, Lowell, Merrill, Berryman, Hecht, and Jarrell himself—published long poems or linked sequences of shorter poems.[44] Lowell drew on his obsessions with history, his New England heritage, and his struggles with Christian belief to sustain long and interconnected poems. Merrill wrote an epic account of the contact that he and his partner, David Jackson, had made (using a Ouija board) with souls from the past. Berryman wrote the book-length poem *Homage to Mistress Bradstreet* and developed a three-stanza, inclusive form (lyric, meditative, narrative) that he used exclusively in *Dream Songs* and other late work. Hecht developed a focus on the Holocaust and the pure evil of the Nazis. By 1951, when "A View of Three Poets" came out, Jarrell himself was beginning to extend the length of his poems—a response, Wilbur believed, to Lowell's narratives.[45]

Wilbur had included one long poem, "Water Walker," in *The Beautiful Changes;* as we have discussed, that poem was Jarrell's touchstone for assessing his newer work in *Ceremony*. Wilbur was grateful for Jarrell's praise and in response began to write more long poems—notably "The Mind-Reader," which, like "Water Walker," dramatizes vivid interactions between divine and human awareness. "Walking to Sleep" is a lengthy meditation on the kind of mental journey one takes as wakefulness recedes. It appeared in the collection *Walking to Sleep* (1969), as did "On the Marginal Way," an ambitious long poem whose images of "sea-rocks buried by a wave" and bodies "bulldozed into a common grave" infuse a seascape with Wilbur's awareness of humankind's capacity for evil.[46]

Length aside, these poems represent some of Wilbur's most deeply considered and intellectually incandescent works. But as he has explained, he has preferred, in general, to write shorter poems because he wants each to stand alone without the need for external support or connection.[47] He has been fascinated by epic narratives, yet he has never developed an interest in writing one or in pursuing a single subject complex enough to require such an extended treatment. Instead, he has chosen topics suitable for self-contained meditation, and his subjects have often arisen from his lifelong engagement with natural phenomena that he has animated or located in contexts analogous to human experience. For instance, in "Poplar, Sycamore," a poem from *The Beautiful Changes* that Jarrell admired, he used verbs that not only anthropomorphized their subjects but also resonated in an internal rhyme: poplar branches "trowel" the air in one stanza, and the sun "trawls" light over the trunk of the sycamore in another.

Jarrell praised "Grasse: The Olive Trees," a poem from *Ceremony,* for its "easy . . . beauty," and the poem can be read as a charming rebuke to the edenic pretensions of the Mediterranean climate—when, for instance, the olive tree "teaches the South it is not paradise." But Jarrell did not acknowledge the deeper implication within Wilbur's spiritual vision of the world, where "unearthly pale" olive trees convert their desiccating thirst into a parable: nothing on earth can truly satisfy the human hunger for what true paradise offers.

Wilbur is rare among contemporary poets in his ability to write undoctrinaire but religiously inflected poems that probe and organize both personal and shared cultural experience to arrive at convincing responses to spiritual anxieties. For example, his verse is notably distinct from the doubt-plagued religious poetry of *Lord Weary's Castle,* in which Lowell seemed to be reprising Donne. As Roethke wrote, Wilbur does "not [possess] a graceful mind . . . but a mind of grace, an altogether different and higher thing."[48]

Perhaps Jarrell hoped to push Wilbur into riskier emotional work—the mining of devastating personal loss, of the dramas that illuminate as they ravage human relationships, of the battles with one's own inner demons. In 2005 Charlee Wilbur spoke of her husband's reluctance to write in the first person and how that has contributed, she believed, to misperceptions about his work:

Anyone who reads Dick closely, properly, can see he is as full of pain, at times as full of the difficulties of passing through a lifetime as anyone else. It just comes about differently with him. He does not like to use the word "I"; he says "one" very often, and this is signal with him. He doesn't like to push himself forward; he wants his work to speak for lots of people and . . . to remove [himself] from his own experience. He's always been like that, and he also has always wanted to "unelevate" poetry. To bring it down, *use everything,* as Frost thought you should do as well. Frost was a big influence about language and how "anything goes" in a poem, how anything is justified in a poem. He never wanted to be privy or sage, Dick didn't, or any of those things. That's why the critics have misviewed him, starting with Randall Jarrell; he missed the boat. His was simply too casual a reading, too oversimplified a response.[49]

In recent years Wilbur increased his use of a first-person narrator; about half of the poems in *Anterooms* (2010) speak in his own voice. In 2014 he spoke of his serious and cautious approach to the issue and the slow process of learning to "impersonate" himself: "When we first start to write poems, our impersonations of the person writing is not quite sufficient to write in 'I.' I don't recall becoming more and more capable of 'I,' but I have a feeling that a poet becomes more capable of 'I' as he becomes more capable of the impersonation." Cryptic as that may sound, it echoes an aphorism of Wallace Stevens, which Wilbur copied into his notebook in the early 1970s: "It is said of a man that his work is autobiographical in spite of every subterfuge. It cannot be otherwise."[50]

"Your opinion matters to me"

The archived Wilbur-Lowell correspondence, for the most part warm but professional, is hardly extensive: the collection of Lowell's papers at Harvard's Houghton Library includes five Wilbur letters; the Wilbur papers on deposit at Amherst hold two telegrams and eight letters from Lowell. The final letters from Lowell indicate that his respect for Wilbur's work had increased since his early dismissive comments to Bishop.

Their first exchange began in the fall of 1958, a decade after the Bard conference, when Wilbur asked Lowell to consider editing the selection of Browning's poems that Dell Books was planning to publish in its new Laurel paperback series. Lowell would need to write an introduction of 3,000 to 5,000 words, a one-page chronology, and a one-page bibliography of general works about Browning; he would also need to choose 130 pages of poems and provide notes as necessary. Wilbur had already edited the Poe volume for the series, and his letter lists the other contributors and their subjects: David Ferry, Wordsworth; Leslie Fielder, Whitman; Bob Stange, Coleridge; Howard Nemerov, Longfellow; and Howard Moss, Keats. "I hope that you'll consider it," Wilbur wrote, "as I can think of no one whose opinions on Browning I would hear with greater interest." At the end he added, "Nemerov, by the way, shares our birthday on March 1st. He was born on February 29th, but his parents thought it only fair that he should have a birthday every year."[51]

Lowell, though tempted, declined. The poems he would choose came to mind almost immediately, he told Wilbur, but thoughts of writing the essay stopped him cold. He had little interest or facility in the essay form, and he was also overloaded with books he had already agreed to review, including the complete Dickinson and Mark Twain's letters. In a postscript he said, "What a lot of March hares! Do you suppose someday, old and crooked and in our eighties we will all be given a joint birthday party?"[52] Of the three men only Wilbur reached that age.

A few months earlier, during the summer, Lowell had begun a course of psychoanalytic treatment recommended by his doctors after a fourth hospitalization (this time at McLean) for a major manic episode. It was another in a series of various treatments—including lithium, shock therapy, and sedatives such as Thorazine—that he underwent to counteract bouts of manic behavior and depression complicated by alcoholism. In her introduction to Lowell's collected letters, Saskia Hamilton has noted two underlying and recurring themes within his references to his mental illness in his correspondence: an implicit hope that insight from these treatments might prevent a relapse and an apologetic tone.[53] Although, as Hamilton observes, "Lowell could not control his illness with the power of his will or his understanding," lithium, first prescribed to Lowell in 1967, did relieve him "from suffering the idea that he was morally and emotionally responsible."[54] Yet in a letter to Bishop written in 1959 he wrote: "Five attacks in ten years make you feel rather a basket-case. . . . Maybe when ten years have passed I'll be a sort of monument to the norm—Eberhart and Wilbur combined."[55] Bishop, who was hospitalized a number of times for alcohol abuse and mental exhaustion, could empathize.

Wilbur's and Lowell's social circles overlapped—sometimes frequently, more often tangentially. They met at award ceremonies, readings, and lectures throughout the late 1940s and into the 1970s. Both Wilbur and Bishop visited the Eberharts' Cambridge home during the early 1950s, so Bishop kept Lowell apprised of news in the Wilbur camp. Over the years the men's joint birthdays became an easygoing point of connection and increased their comfort with one another. In 1960, for instance, the Wilburs hosted a celebration for Lowell's forty-third and Wilbur's thirty-ninth birthdays. A month later, Lowell sent a note thanking him for the party but also apologizing. He and his wife Lizzie must have made a poor showing, he said, because they hadn't been able to slow down their frantic New York pace and absorb the hospitable atmosphere of Dick and Charlee's home.[56] That comment recalls Lowell's envy of the grounded qualities he saw in Wilbur's personal life—which to Bishop he had called "the norm."

Lowell perceived a similar grounded, sensible maturity in Wilbur's poetry:

Perhaps the hardest thing you've done [in *Advice to a Prophet*] is to have walked the tight-rope from one part of your life to another, more graying part. So many poets stop, locked in the personality forced upon them by their youthful technique. Of course this has been happening to you for some time in other poems, your translation and in that drowning burst of abundance, your Roman Fountain.[57]

In March 1962 the Wilburs held another joint birthday party for the two men, and Lowell sent another thank-you letter, this time writing about how much he had appreciated the visit, so rich in talk and relaxation.[58] On February 28, 1966, they read together before an audience of 1,500 at the Yale memorial service for Randall Jarrell, this time marking their birthdays with sadness. Lowell wrote on March 8, "You leave me very admiring of the firmness, good spirits and strength of your two appearances when we performed together. I feel you and Charlee are old treasured friends and we must stay in touch."[59]

That sense of treasured friendship is palpable in an exchange that Lowell initiated on Christmas Day 1967. In that note he praised Wilbur's poem "Walking to Sleep," published in the December 23 issue of the *New Yorker*. Lowell thought it one of Wilbur's best and called its blank verse "incredibly beautiful," saying that it evoked for him a deep and haunting sense of déjà vu. The feeling—similar to one Lowell had experienced, he said, when translating the passage about Io's journey in the Greek tragedy *Prometheus Bound*—was a kind of "whisper" that recalled other allusions to myth and literature.[60]

In "Walking to Sleep" the speaker urges readers to "Step off assuredly into the blank of your mind. / Something will come to you." Then, after more prompts, he cautions,

> Try to remember this: what you project
> Is what you will perceive; what you perceive
> With any passion, be it love or terror,
> May take on whims and powers of its own.

Through two more pages of blank verse (without section breaks), the speaker continues to offer ways to avoid unsettling images and insomnia. "What you hope for," he writes,

> Is that at some point of the pointless journey,
> . . .
> The kind assassin Sleep will draw a bead
> And blow your brains out.
>   What, are you still awake?

Here the poem turns, as the reader does, into the dream world and the tensions between the real and surreal; as it draws to a close, some thirty lines later, the speaker holds out the hope that achieving sleep will come from not fighting it:

> Still, if you are in luck, you may be granted,
> As, inland, one can sometimes smell the sea,
> A moment's perfect carelessness, in which
> To stumble a few steps and sink to sleep
> In the same clearing where, in the old story,
> A holy man discovered Vishnu sleeping,
> Wrapped in his maya, dreaming by a pool
> On whose calm face all images whatever
> Lay clear, unfathomed, taken as they came.

Wilbur responded to Lowell's praise nearly two weeks later, in a letter he dated "Epiphany Eve."

Your Christmas note about Walking to Sleep was a fine Christmas present, because your opinion matters to me. I agree with you about the way that journeys—that fine Io speech in your Prometheus, Frost's Directive, Shelley's Alastor, the quest and trials in the Brothers Grimm, Beckford's Vision—seem always to touch something radical, or primitive. What the old fellows chant in phalanx at the plaza, on the day of a Pueblo festival, is a story, or so I am told: how they came up out of the mud, how their heroes encountered the gods, where they traveled, how they came at last to Jemez or Zuni; are their ideas of what they *are* embodied in a string of happenings which at the clearest are parabolic, and are known darkly, not unperplexed as in theology. I wonder whether the first hearers of the Odyssey, sophisticated as it is, said to themselves in so many words that the story is a celebration of Suppleness and Adjustability and Shape-Changing. The journey-account seems not to work when it explains itself—as Shelley does at moments—or reeks of folklore like Yeats' Oisin, or betrays a reading of Jung. However artful the work is, one wants the impression that it is flowing chancily as life and thought flow, simply saying and then and then, and then; believing what it sees; blundering into situations which threaten to mean something.[61]

"Flowing chancily" and "blundering into situations" may at first seem uncharacteristic of both Wilbur and his poems, and Wilbur fans are likely to argue that he rarely stops at *threatening* to mean something. Yet his musings about the "journey-account" and "Walking to Sleep" relate to a statement he made elsewhere about the way in which he writes: "No poem of mine is ever undertaken as a technical experiment; the form which it takes, whether conventional or innovating, develops naturally as the poem develops, as part of the utterance. Nor does my poem ever begin as the utterance of a fully grasped idea. I think inside my lines, and the thought must get where it can amongst the moods and sounds and gravitating particulars which are appearing there."[62] The Epiphany Eve letter to Lowell captures this undercurrent of thought, but its most personally revealing line is his admission: "your opinion matters to me."

Heavyweight Contenders

On May 6, 1957, two months after winning the National Book Award, Wilbur won the Pulitzer for *Things of This World*. The Wilburs and Brinnin celebrated the announcement over drinks and dinner at a steakhouse near Wellesley. Close to midnight Dick and Charlee returned home to find a telegram from John Berryman: "YOUR BEAUTIFUL POEMS WILL LIVE FOREVER."[63] Wilbur sent Berryman a note the next day, thanking him for his good wishes. Although both prize committees had passed over Berryman's *Homage to Mistress Bradstreet,* also published in 1956, Wilbur did not detect any undercurrent of jealously in the message. He was far from naïve when it came to poets' rivalries, but he did tend to assume good intentions rather than veiled resentments.

Later that month Wilbur received a typewritten letter from Berryman.

Dear Richard Wilbur,

A minor apology first for delay: yr letter came slowly but got here Thursday last: I haven't and I often don't open letters until I can answer them, and yrs is unopened. I take it though that it is abt my wire of course, & understandably exasperated, and before I open it I want to say something. That wire was not sent to you but to you-at-Columbia, where I knew you were not (I did not know where you were, whether teaching somewhere or abroad). It was a purely personal gesture of anger; it was not intended to be delivered. And in fact after some hours an operator rang up & said you were not to be found at Columbia, whether among students or faculty, and I said "Kill it then" and she said she wd. But after some more hours, next morning, another operator rang up & said they found you at Wellesley & did I want it to be delivered and I said "*No*" and she said all right, but then she rang up later & said it was too late, it had been delivered. I am sorry for the entirely unintentional insult. I am sorry; I felt like a man who curses in private, as we have a right to do, and finds he's overheard. My anger was this: I do not collect merit badges, but I was informed by competent people that my poem [*Homage to Mistress Bradstreet*] did not receive even an honest consideration for the Natl Bk award and when the Pulitzer went the same way I cd not help feeling briefly that the poem—which whatever its merit, took five years to write—had been twice insulted on its own ground, in its own country; especially since I had that day after my lectures made eleven new lines of a poem [which] is like a slaughterhouse of grief, whereas my impression of yr early work (all I knew) was of work skillful industrious effortless & fireless—I apologize for this unsolicited opinion: I am explaining the occasion of the wire. I thought of wiring you congratulations, but found I cd not do it sincerely, since I had not read yr new book & so cd not say whether you deserved the rewards or not. The two impulses joined, & by accident reached you; to my sorrow.

Well. Now I open yr letter.

But either this is the purest & most savage irony, or I don't remember my wire correctly, or they garbled it as frequently happens.

Anyway: if I offended you, forgive me, and let us be friends. The first thing I am going to do when I get back from India & Spain is get hold of a copy of yr book and read it from cover to cover. Every good luck.[64]

As Wilbur recalled in 2006, Berryman was the most relentlessly competitive of his peers. During a phone conversation in 1970, Berryman asked him which poets he had spoken to at the American Academy of Arts and Letters memorial ceremony for Louise Bogan. When Wilbur named Paddy Colum and John Hall Wheelock, Berryman replied, "Dick, you're consorting with your inferiors." He had, Wilbur continued, "a painful, dreadful sense of who was on his list and who was not. It doesn't take much of a dash of competitiveness to addle a society of poets trying to be conspicuous." He remembered a day in 1962, when Jarrell was delivering the "Fifty Years of American Poetry" lecture. Wilbur said, "I was sitting next to John Berryman in the back of the great auditorium at the Library of Congress . . . and when it became clear that nothing much was going to said about John Berryman, John began to Boo."[65]

In May 1978 Wilbur spoke with Joel Conarroe, whose book on Berryman had just gone to press, about the mental torment common among poets of Wilbur's generation.[66] Berryman had killed himself in 1972, jumping from the Washington Avenue Bridge in Minneapolis after struggling for years with alcoholism and depression. Lowell, Roethke, and Delmore Schwartz suffered from mental illness, and Jarrell's death in 1965 may have been a suicide.[67] Conarroe was curious to know what Wilbur thought a poet needed to sustain stability and normalcy, to be both productive and sane. In response Wilbur told him about a conversation with Stanley Kunitz after Berryman's death, when both survivors decided it was crucial to have interests outside the world of literature. For Wilbur this meant gardening and tennis; for himself, Kunitz joked, it meant bouncing a ball off a wall into a bucket of dirt. In their view poets who lived only inside books had no escape hatch.[68]

Wilbur spoke warmly to Conarroe about Lowell's kindness to his suffering peers. The two poets had been at Johns Hopkins in Baltimore when Roethke was going through a bad time. "Lowell had insisted on calling," Wilbur said, and "knew just the right things to say." Before Lowell's own bad times, he told Conarroe, Cal always talked to him about classifying and ranking their contemporaries. "Cal would say, *You and I know what we're doing, Dick. And Roethke—although I'm not sure about Roethke.*" Evidently, Wilbur said, Roethke also approached writing poetry "as a heavyweight championship" and saw himself and Lowell as the major contenders. As Wilbur and Karl Shapiro were choosing the poems for a revision of Louis Untermeyer's anthology, Roethke called him to complain about his representation: "*You BASTARD, only 4 pages.*"[69]

Lowell's student Kathleen Spivack, who won a fellowship in 1959 to study with him at Boston University and remained close to him until his death in 1977, recalled that "an increased and obsessive classification of other poets" during his seminars became a signal for an impending breakdown. The mood became gloomier in class, she said, as Lowell began to demand that students weigh in: "John Berryman. Major or minor, would you say?" A long pause would ensue, followed by murmuring. Lowell would then prod for an answer, suggesting that *The Dream Songs* might be brilliant, "but what about the other work? . . . He doesn't have the depth of, say, Randall Jarrell." Lowell would relent for a bit and then switch the target, goading the students to similarly classify an author from a different era or literary genre—for instance, Emily Brontë. Then he would circle back: "But Berryman? Major or minor?" One day, when a student worked up the nerve to vote for Berryman as *major,* Lowell triumphantly said, "Wrong!" and moved on to gather a vote on Frost.[70]

At the time of the Conarroe interview Wilbur had just read Donald Hall's attack on Lowell's final book, a collection of sonnets titled *Day by Day.*[71] Wilbur admitted that he, too, got little pleasure from reading Lowell's late books. "In a way," he told Conarroe, "all of Cal's friends had let him down." By this he meant that Lowell had been a better critic of him than he had been of Lowell. In 2007 he was still expressing regret about his 1962 commentary in a *New World Writing* symposium on "Skunk Hour," one of Lowell's most famous poems: "I remember saying to Cal, 'I hope there was some truth in my essay, but it bothers me I wasn't very generous toward your poem.' Cal didn't say anything, but I think he agreed."[72]

Despite his reservations, Wilbur's assessment of "Skunk Hour" had been favorable overall:

> [It] does not afford the reader a kinetic jag, does not dazzle him with its transitions, does not disarm his unbelief by a passionate violence. It cannot be read passively. As with the poems of Elizabeth Bishop . . . one must participate in the lines, discovering their implicit emotional value and generalizing from their relatively dead-pan specificities. . . . There is art enough, and density enough, in "Skunk Hour": it is more flexible poetry than Lowell has ever written; it admits a greater range of feeling, and in particular it liberates the author's excellent sense of humor. With no disrespect to *Lord Weary's Castle,* I should argue that the later poetry, with its objectivity and its demand for collaborative reading, renders Lowell's vision of the world more probable and more readily shared. In any case, "Skunk Hour" is an extremely fine poem.[73]

Bishop preferred Berryman's view of "Skunk Hour," which appeared in the symposium alongside Wilbur's and another by John Frederick Nims. She wrote to Lowell, "Berryman is so much brighter than the other two. I don't like his telegraphic style—but at least it does give the impression that he's right there, reacting, and not having to rack his brain for everything he can say that will show off how much he *knows*. He's the only one who seems to like the skunk! I feel undercurrents of ENVY in the other two, too. To hell with explainers." Lowell had dedicated "Skunk Hour" to Bishop, and she declared, along with her thanks, that the poem "has so much more *life* to it than you'd ever guess from those essays."[74] Whatever he really felt inside, Lowell wrote to Wilbur to say that he was grateful for his "generous and sensitive critique."[75]

In his last letter to Wilbur, dated June 8, 1976, Lowell explained what he felt while reading Wilbur's newly published collection *The Mind-Reader:*

> I was visiting another country, not too distant from mine and with similar flashes—night and waking thoughts: age, though hardly visible in you except in puzzled contrasts etc. with the young; nature and household description.
>
> What struck me as different and enviable is your pace, your way of fixing on some moment in the past, often boyhood. The moment tends to be of no apparent symbolic or passionate interest, but to be just part of the cloth of life. You fix on it slowly and hesitantly—poking and puzzling. Your strict meters speak casually. All this is a good antodote [*sic*] to my narrower intensity. I think we both try for a fairly direct open language—open to experience, and open at times to splurges of rhetoric and intuition. Your style is perhaps a commentary or extension of Frost; or rather you draw on something earlier that he could use but is now almost unavailable to any-one but you—among other things an oblique use of autobiography, scenes peering into meditation.[76]

In this appreciation Lowell articulated his recognition that autobiography may have profound uses beyond the confessional, and he seemed to relax in the notion that he and Wilbur were colleagues in the grand enterprise rather than rivals.

Trouble with Irony

In late 1972 "Cottage Street, 1953," one of Wilbur's most anthologized poems, appeared in the inaugural issue of the *American Poetry Review.* It was advertised on the cover along with Marvin Bell's "Begin Here" and Pablo Neruda's "Love," and it sparked controversy from the start.[77] On the morn-ing of January 14, 1973, Bishop wrote to Lowell complaining that "a very *neat* poem by Wilbur about Sylvia Plath" had made her angry. Although some people, including Frank Bidart, admired it, Bishop did not.

[It was] very bad—really unfeeling. I tried to decide why and think it's because it is supposed to be ironic and isn't—'It is my office to exemplify / The published poet in his happiness'—it's full of words like that. Now Ransom could have written a poem like that, neat rhymes, cliché words, and all—and the irony would have been really there and somehow chilling and deep & sad—this just seems smug, I'm afraid.[78]

Lowell admitted in a January 24 letter that the poem annoyed him as well. He couldn't determine where the irony should be directed: at Wilbur, or Plath, or at a conventional person "much like Dick, yet slashed as his opposite? All, probably." Then he turned to assess Wilbur himself—with the passage Wilbur found in 2007 when he was looking for his name in the index of Lowell's correspondence: "I seem to have run into people lately who are his old friends, and welcome being bitter on him. He has really always been a model acquaintance, almost friend to me, though I felt a fragile shell kept his rivalry from muddying me. Still, a good man. I've always thought, I'm afraid, that Ransom did this kind of poem (Wilbur's) with genius and character."[79] Lowell was probably alluding to Ransom's "Bells for John Whiteside's Daughter," which had been critically acclaimed as an exploration of a man's vexation at life's impartial savagery.[80]

Wilbur wrote "Cottage Street, 1953" in the first person, reconstructing a visit he had paid to Charlee's mother, who was an acquaintance of Aurelia Plath. There he had met Aurelia's daughter, Sylvia, then twenty-one years old and enrolled at Smith College. The poem is set in the summer, and Plath had just spent June in New York City as a guest editor for *Mademoiselle*'s college issue, working alongside several other young women who would be entering their senior years at other schools.[81]

In a letter Plath wrote to herself dated "June . . . July 1953," she addressed herself as an "Over-grown, Over-protected, Scared, Spoiled Baby" and debated the practical and "politic" reasons for deciding against spending $250 in tuition for a course in psychology at Harvard Summer School—essentially, she said, to remain eligible for her Smith scholarship. After her stint at the magazine, she chose to "learn shorthand, typing, and write and read and write and read, and talk to myself about attitudes, and see the Aldriches and neighbors, and be nice and friendly and outgoing, and forget my damn egocentered self in trying to learn and understand about what makes life rich and what is most important." In a journal entry dated July 6, 1953, she expressed the despair that had triggered such resolve: "You are plunged so deep in your own very private little whirlpool of negativism that you can't do more than force yourself into a rote where the simplest actions become forbidding and enormous."[82]

Even though Wilbur's actual visit took place before Plath's suicide attempt on August 24 and her subsequent hospitalization, the young woman's "whirlpool of negativism" must have been palpable in Edna Ward's living room.[83] "Cottage Street" follows in full.

> Framed in her phoenix fire-screen, Edna Ward
> Bends to the tray of Canton, pouring tea
> For frightened Mrs. Plath; then, turning toward
> The pale, slumped daughter, and my wife, and me,
>
> Asks if we would prefer it weak or strong.
> Will we have milk or lemon, she enquires?
> The visit seems already strained and long.
> Each in his turn, we tell her our desires.
>
> It is my office to exemplify
> The published poet in his happiness,
> Thus cheering Sylvia, who has wished to die;
> But half-ashamed, and impotent to bless,
>
> I am a stupid life-guard who has found,
> Swept to his shallows by the tide, a girl
> Who, far from shore, has been immensely drowned,
> And stares through water now with eyes of pearl.
>
> How large is her refusal; and how slight
> The genteel chat whereby we recommend
> Life, of a summer afternoon, despite
> The brewing dusk which hints that it may end.
>
> And Edna Ward shall die in fifteen years,
> After her eight-and-eighty summers of
> Such grace and courage as permit no tears,
> The thin hand reaching out, the last word *love,*
>
> Outliving Sylvia who, condemned to live,
> Shall study for a decade, as she must,
> To state at last her brilliant negative
> In poems free and helpless and unjust.

The situation Wilbur presents in the third and fourth stanzas is steeped in personal irony, though Bishop and Lowell didn't see it. By 1953 Wilbur was already "in [his] office" as a published poet; given his charm, his gracious public persona, and what some critics would later call the "sunny" disposition of his poems, many judged him to be "happy."[84] Yet the poet feels "half-ashamed," "impotent," like a "stupid life-guard," as he watches this young woman who already seems "immensely drowned."[85]

Neither Lowell nor Bishop registered or accepted the irony implied in Wilbur's choice to use a first-person voice for a poem written in formal, rhymed quatrains—a poem in which the narrator finds a suffering young woman "swept to his shallows" and regrets his failure to enter her world and bring her back to his. In the words "his shallows" one may also read another ironic admission: Wilbur had long resisted the confessional mode because of his personal reticence in poetic discourse and thus hadn't ventured nearly so far as Plath had into the sea of feeling. The narrator's play on the relation between the human qualities of shallowness and depth indicates some self-reproach. The shallows may represent the narrator's mental equilibrium and the presumed safety of his surroundings; for Plath, the poem tells us, it was already too late.[86]

Neither commented on or questioned Wilbur's use of the word "unjust" in his final judgment of Plath's poetry. The omission itself seems ironic, given the subsequent Lowell-Bishop correspondence about Plath in which both implicitly acknowledged the aptness of Wilbur's "brilliant negative" epithet to characterize her last poems.[87] Lowell had first brought Plath's work into the conversation in 1963, when he asked Bishop if she had read the ten posthumous Plath poems just published in the October issue of *Encounter.* In a letter dated October 27, he ranked Plath as almost equal to Dickinson, implied that she had emulated not only his work but also Bishop's (for her quiet humor, he said), and suggested that her emotional difficulties had given her the freedom to explore yet control topics he found "searingly extreme." In his view this made Plath a better poet than Anne Sexton or Frederick Seidel.[88]

Apparently Bishop did not write an answer to Lowell's question about reading Plath's poems in *Encounter;* but nearly two years later, after reading the Faber edition of *Ariel,* she told Lowell that Plath was too formless for her taste. Nonetheless, although she could barely stand to read the agony of the last poems, Plath's loss seemed tragic. She wondered if Lowell thought that Plath had talent.[89] Lowell said yes (Plath had been his student at Boston University in 1959, as had Sexton) but expressed reservations about *Ariel.* "Sylvia, I think, had a few perfect poems, but the book as a whole troubles me with its desperation, and even more perhaps by something sprawling, unfinished and disorderly, though poem after poem has flashes that are incredible and make me feel weak."[90]

In his introduction to the American edition of *Ariel,* Lowell tempered some of his reservations by aligning himself with the majority of readers, whose unpleasant reactions he anticipated:

> There is a peculiar, haunting challenge to these poems. Probably many, after reading *Ariel,* will recoil from their first overawed shock, and painfully wonder why so much of it leaves them feeling empty, evasive and inarticulate. In her lines I often hear the serpent whisper, "Come, if only you had the courage, you too could have my rightness, audacity and ease of inspiration." But most of us will turn back.[91]

Whereas Lowell saw Plath as being driven by rightness and audacity to express her pain, Wilbur considered her expression of raw anger and vitriol as unjust, especially in poems such as "Daddy" and "Lady Lazarus." "Daddy," for instance, is a provocative portrait attacking her German-born father, Otto (1885–1940), a biology professor who died when she was eight from untreated diabetes that led to gangrene. The poem likewise indicts Ted Hughes, whom Plath married in 1956: repeated images of both men dissolve into images of Hitler and Nazism.

Plath's fury surely lay at the heart of Wilbur's judgment, and he was not alone in his opinion. Critics then and now have questioned the legitimacy of her harsh portrait of Otto and her use, throughout *Ariel,* of Nazi imagery as a personal weapon.[92] In 2012 the FBI released newly discovered files revealing that Otto Plath had been detained for questioning during World War I but released because agents found no evidence of pro-German disloyalty. Since then, Plath scholars have taken a more complex view of her German heritage.[93]

Several years before the new FBI information surfaced, Wilbur recorded and spoke about a number of his poems, including "Cottage Street, 1953," for the online Web of Stories project:

> I did not write this poem against Sylvia Plath or against any mode of poetry. I hope to do her justice by giving her these several words— *brilliant, free, helpless, unjust.* What is unjust about her poems I think any reader can perceive. But surely they are also brilliant.
>
> Some correspondent asked me a while ago if Edna Ward was not in fact the heroine of the poem. And I must say she is, yes. The poem plays around I notice with dimensions, it plays around with the immensity of Sylvia Plath's suicidal grief, and with other largenesses and smallnesses.

But I hope to balance the poem in favor of showing grace and courage, and ending your life with the word *love*.[94]

Both Lowell and Wilbur used the word *courage* in their assessments of Plath's poetry. For Lowell, courage involved taking risks and registering one's pain in terms so raw that readers may turn away or turn numb. Wilbur defined courage in conjunction with grace, and both depend on a qualification that he specified in the poem: "as permit no tears." Whether or not he meant to reflect and amplify his personal conception of a poet's responsibility or a human's conduct throughout life, he also associated "courage" with both "love" (from its Latin root *cor*) and "uncomplaining." Yet by attempting to find something comparable in each woman's different degree of suffering and despair, he burdened the poem with its own unfairness.[95]

In 2014 Wilbur said that Ward did in fact own an iron fire screen wrought with the image of a phoenix, but he could not have invented a more appropriate symbol in which to frame the view of his mother-in-law. The phoenix imagery suggests a human being who has the ability to rise, to be reborn, from the ashes of defeat and despair, and Ward was an unusually self-reliant woman who had recovered from hardship and dashed hopes.[96] Wilbur described her in life-affirming terms as a "charming, gracious woman who loved to waltz and skate, also a woman of gumption and practical intelligence."[97]

In his introduction to *Ariel* Lowell chose a pair of grotesque metaphors to describe Plath's life-denying choice.

> These poems are playing Russian roulette with six cartridges in the cylinder, a game of "chicken," the wheels of both cars locked and unable to swerve. . . . And yet Sylvia Plath's poems are not celebration of some savage and debauched existence, that of the "damned" poet, glad to burn out his body for a few years of continued intensity. This poetry and life are not a career; they tell that life, even when disciplined, is simply not worth it.[98]

But as Wilbur said in a 1977 *Paris Review* interview, Plath's "brilliant," "helpless" one-sidedness also limited her poetry:

> I suppose she was freed by the onset of her desperate condition of mind to be brilliant in the way the poems of *Ariel* are brilliant. At the same time, she was helpless because it required that condition of mind to bring on those poems. She was unjust because a sick and prejudiced perception of things is—well, that's the limitation on the usefulness of her poetry

to any reader, I think. It gives you some insights into a desperate condition of mind that is *not absolutely foreign* to the rest of us, but that goes farther towards morbidity than I've ever gone, thank God. At the same time there's a lot she can't tell you. She's all wrapped up in herself and her feelings about her children, and herself as a writer, and her fantasies about her dead father, and her arbitrary connections between her dead father and her husband.[99]

. . . I really think Sylvia Plath's later poems, when unfortunately she was at her best, were crazy, and that, whatever virtues they have, they have that limitation. I don't think Lowell's best work is to be described in that way. I think whenever he's been emotionally ill it hasn't enabled him to write. He hasn't written out of illness, but in spite of it. The same story with Roethke, and I'm sure the same with Anne Sexton, whom I didn't know as well. As for pain, it's acceptable and necessary material. One of the jobs of poetry is to make the unbearable bearable, not by falsehood but by clear, precise confrontation. Even the most cheerful poet has to cope with pain as part of the human lot; what he shouldn't do is to complain, and dwell on his personal mischance.[100]

In 2014, when asked if he cared to elaborate on his assertion that Plath's poetry was "unjust," Wilbur said, "I've never been completely happy with that word. But I suppose I would use it again as a distillation of her negativism—not just about her father but of the world."[101]

"The loneliest person who ever lived"

In 2006 Elizabeth Bishop's posthumous volume *Edgar Allan Poe & the Juke-Box* brought to life a debate that Lowell, Berryman, and Roethke would have relished if they had lived to claim a stake in it. To create the book, Alice Quinn, then the poetry editor of the *New Yorker,* had gathered together previously unpublished poems, drafts of poems, and prose pieces (including a series of notes) as well as photographs of manuscript pages with marginalia. Noting that Bishop's reputation had been eclipsed by her mid-twentieth-century male peers, a number of reviewers discussed whether or not she was, in fact, the best poet of her generation. On April 2, David Orr, writing for the *New York Times,* went so far as to declare, "In the second half of the twentieth century, no American artist in any medium was greater than Bishop."[102]

On the following day the critic Helen Vendler published an indignant article about the book in the *New Republic.* She based her ire on a simple fact: "Bishop had years to publish the poems included here, had she wanted to publish them. They remained unpublished (not 'uncollected') because, for the most part, they did not meet her fastidious standards." After defending a poet's posthumous rights versus the rights of literary posterity, Vendler directed a message to prospective literary scavengers: "I am told that poets now, fearing an Alice Quinn in their future, are incinerating their drafts."[103]

In conversation a few days later Wilbur expressed mixed feelings about his old friend Elizabeth's newfound celebrity. He was delighted to see attention lavished on Bishop; he called her one of his "first enthusiasms in mid-twentieth-century poetry" and felt she'd been "wronged by neglect for some time."[104] The rollercoaster highs and lows of a literary career, from praise and visibility to subsequent neglect and dismissal, reminded him that "Frost liked the idea of being crossed off someone's list because then he could make a comeback." Wilbur laughed but went on to question the effects of any wildly inflated claim, especially one based on too much enthusiasm for (or the overvaluing of) work that an author had chosen not to make public. "I would not like to disappear from this world with a trail of inferior poems behind me."[105]

Dick and Charlee had met Bishop in 1948, not long before the Bard conference. Wilbur described her as quiet, approachable, and reserved but with many more definite opinions than one might have initially thought. "In particular, she had a strong notion as to which was Poe's best poem, and I have since come pretty well to agree with her; her favorite was 'Fairy-Land.' "[106] Charlee and Bishop discovered a common dislike: noisy cocktail parties. When the two went to find a quiet place to talk at Bard, Charlee said their conversation turned to Cal Lowell, who had not yet arrived to take his place among the group. They discussed his "curious change of accent," from Boston Brahmin to southern drawl, neither realizing that he had affected the latter while living for three months in a pup tent on Allen Tate's front lawn in Tennessee.[107] Years later, Wilbur remarked that Lowell carried Bishop's poem "Armadillo" in his wallet, "not the way you'd carry the picture of a grandson, but as you'd carry something to brace you and make you sure of how a poem ought to be. I have a feeling that finally she was the poet he most respected which was quite apart from his feelings of great affection for her. He wasn't going to carry anyone else around, not even Randall Jarrell, not even Ted Roethke." He thought, for Lowell, "Elizabeth [was] in some ways the sort of person he would have liked more often to be, in relation to the art, because he had his delicacies and his feelings of what social conversations ought to be, and she talked in his view as a poet ought to talk."[108]

At about the time of the Bard conference, when Wilbur and Bishop were newly acquainted, Wilbur sent her a poem he proposed to dedicate to her. In 2015 he did not remember the poem or recall a draft of it, and Bishop's papers at Vassar do not hold a copy of a Wilbur letter that includes the poem or any mention of it. But Wilbur did save her response to the poem. In a letter dated November 28, 1948, she wrote: "A poem possibly dedicated to oneself is almost impossible to criticize, naturally—and I'm not very good at that sort of thing, anyway. It does remind me of 'Anaphora' [one of her own poems] and it is altogether too much of a compliment for me to cope with at all." But cope she did—in the next paragraph.

> The only suggestion I'm going to make is that I think you could very well omit the first stanza entirely. The image in it seems to me to conflict badly with the later images (maybe you meant it to, of course) and it seems in every way the weakest stanza, with "soft slack breath / and lax tendon," etc. Also I'll say the whole poem could be greatly improved if the line "If sleeping were a way to die" could somehow be made stronger, a real "attack." It sounds too relaxed to me—but then I suppose that suits the sense alright, too—as I said, I'm just no good at this sort of thing.[109]

Bishop, of course, was perfectly good at that "sort of thing." The shyness and insecurity that Wilbur and others noticed at Bard were part of how she projected herself—as dignified and modest. In a 1950 letter to Wilbur from the writing colony at Yaddo, she was again self-deprecating, telling him that she was "just no good at answering questions" about contemporary poets and poetry.[110] Yet the opinionated letters she wrote to Lowell before and after that year disprove this self-evaluation—or perhaps they reveal how unguarded and trusting she was with him.

According to Spivack, however, Bishop did not see herself as others did. By distancing herself from female poets involved in the women's movement and declining to be published in all-female anthologies, she gave her female peers the impression that she was hostile to the feminist movement. In fact she considered herself to be a strong feminist who wanted only to be judged by the quality of her writing.[111] As Wilbur has explained, she "struck . . . the note of loneliness, even when she was in a ménage of some kind or another, but especially when she was not."[112] Bishop once told Lowell, "When you write my epitaph you must say I was the loneliest person who ever lived."[113]

For their book *Remembering Elizabeth Bishop: An Oral History,* Gary Fountain and Peter Brazeau interviewed several sources who describe moments when Bishop turned against Lowell despite their deep bond. In the 1970s, for instance, he published a sonnet in *Notebook* that paraphrased a letter she had sent him and included her name in the title; she considered this act an "unforgivable violation of her privacy." When Lowell drew extensively from his correspondence with Hardwick for *The Dolphin,* published in 1973, Bishop, William Alfred, and Esther Brooks were the only ones who dared to tell him that he couldn't print some of that content. Lowell responded, "You just don't understand. I have to tell the truth, and this is my way of telling the truth."[114]

Wilbur grew used to what he called Bishop's "impatience of untruth in and out of poetry." His poem "Shad-Time," published in the *New Yorker* on May 29, 1978, passed muster with her for its scientific accuracy—the way the shad run in the river and the shad bush blooms on the bank. But a grammatical problem caught her eye: in the center stanza, she said, stood the only incomplete sentence in the poem. Wilbur thought she was disappointed, not because the grammar was wrong but because she didn't expect *him* to get the grammar wrong.[115]

Bishop liked it when her friends saw things the way she did, and she was not shy about confronting those who maintained differing positions. Wilbur's Christian beliefs, for instance, prompted her to challenge him because, as he told Fountain, she was "an unbeliever, even an adamant doubter." At a 1973 party at Brinnin's house in Duxbury, Massachusetts, as the guests were gathering outdoors for drinks and croquet, she became cross when Wilbur mentioned going to church. She asked if he considered himself a Christian, and he said yes, going to church would indicate he was likely to be Christian. When she seemed incredulous, he told her that, like most people, on some days he believed in nothing, on other days in much of Christian doctrine, and on still other days in all of it. But Bishop did not relent and began reciting points of the doctrine she thought were intolerable. "No, no, no," she said. "You must be honest about this, Dick. You really don't believe all that stuff. You're just like me. Neither of us has any philosophy. It's all description, no philosophy."[116]

For a number of years Brinnin's party had been an annual tradition—a weekend celebration in June close to the Wilburs' wedding anniversary— and that year marked their thirty-first. Bishop arrived on Saturday from a semester's teaching at the University of Washington in Seattle, missing the lobster, strawberries, and champagne toasts of the previous evening but in good time for the Sunday afternoon festivities. Brinnin wrote a vivid and detailed account of this party in his journal, including how, to the chagrin of Bishop and Jonathan Aaron, who were both fans of the New York Mets, Vendler interrupted a conversation about the team's pennant chances with a "misdirected discourse" about "how poets bring thoughts to words."[117] A snapshot in Brinnin's archived papers shows Bishop with her hands choked up on a croquet mallet, threatening to conk Wilbur on the head. Meanwhile, Wilbur, in red bathing trunks and oblivious to her, bends over with his backside to the camera, ready to tap his ball through the wicket.[118]

Bishop's dismissal of Wilbur's Christian convictions and her insistence that he was lying to himself suggest she may have grossly misperceived or ignored his religious poetry. Wilbur, however, showed little concern about that possibility; in fact, he perceived a spiritual connection in her work:

> Though she had no orthodox convictions, and wondered at such certainties in others, Elizabeth Bishop had religious concerns and habits of feeling. I think of her poem about St. Peter; I think of the "pure and angelic note" of the blacksmith's hammer in her story "In the Village," and the way the story ends with the cry, "O, beautiful sound, strike again!" . . . Though her world is ultimately mysterious, one of its constants is sorrow, and another is some purity of splendor which, though forever defiled, is also, as her poem "Anaphora" says, perpetually renewed.[119]

Judging by her letters to Wilbur, Bishop was respectful of his poems and often pleased by them, but his translations really excited her. Writing from Brazil in 1963, she praised his *Tartuffe:* "I think you are a *beautiful* translator, also a beautiful rhymer—both in translation and in your own work—and such fastidious workmanship as yours gives one intense pleasure these days."[120]

In Memoriam

A photograph taken at Jarrell's memorial service at Yale on February 28, 1966, shows Wilbur, Kunitz, Berryman, Lowell, and Robert Penn Warren standing with Jarrell's widow, Mary. Lowell appears to have just spoken; the others glance toward him, half smiling, except for Kunitz, who looks straight ahead, and Berryman, who looks down. In a *New York Times* account of the tribute, the five men were identified as the Pulitzer Prize winners among the eleven poets who spoke and read Jarrell's poems during

Pulitzer Prize–winning poets gather with Randall Jarrell's widow, Mary, at his memorial service at Yale on February 28, 1966. Standing from left to right are Robert Penn
Warren, Robert Lowell, Mary Jarrell, John Berryman, Stanley Kunitz, and Richard
Wilbur. *Randall Jarrell Papers, Martha Blakeney Hodges Special Collections and University Archives, The University of North Carolina at Greensboro, North Carolina.*

the service. Bishop, who was in Seattle at the time, did not attend. During
the previous November, a month after Jarrell's death, Lowell had written
to her: "Thank God, we two still breathe the air of the living."[121] In little
more than a decade both would die: Lowell of a heart attack, at age sixty, on
September 12, 1977, and Bishop of a cerebral aneurysm, at age sixty-seven,
on October 6, 1979.

In a March 8 letter to Wilbur written after the Yale tribute, quoted earlier
in this chapter, Lowell expressed how touched he was by his remarks at the
ceremony and by his reading of Jarrell's poems. Those qualities that Lowell
admired—his firmness, good spirits, and strength—were on display again
when Wilbur delivered a eulogy at Lowell's own memorial service at the
American Academy of Arts and Letters:

> Robert Lowell was a dear friend with whom I shared a birthday and much
> else. Despite his fierce ambition, he was always gentle and generous with

friends and fellow-writers. He was also absolutely honest, so that his negative criticism of one's work was truly helpful, and his praise was truly fortifying. I cannot imagine what the poetry of the third quarter of this century would have been without his great and energetic talent. I have some reservations about the confessional in poetry, but in Lowell's work the mode was redeemed, because his life was interesting, his mind wide-ranging, and his gift astonishing.[122]

In 2007, during one of our several conversations with Wilbur about Lowell, he reflected on the poet's fierce ambition in light of his own: "I felt, good God, he's the most competitive of all poets but he's a marvel because he isn't emotionally quite well and he's managed to get on top of it, and I should not be conveying competitiveness to him, but maybe I had."[123]

Wilbur later spoke at Bishop's memorial service, again at the American Academy of Arts and Letters, and shared his perception of her when they first met. She was a woman, he said, "clearly not embarked on anything so pompous and public as a career." He noted her reticence but also her lively enthusiasms. He admired a quality in her autobiographical work in which "she testified to a lifelong sense of dislocation." That is, "she missed from the beginning what some enjoy, an unthinking conviction that things ought to be as they are; . . . that it all makes sense."[124] As an example he referred to "In the Village," a prose account of her early family life. A simple image of a return address in indelible ink—the sanitarium where her mother was sent when Bishop was five—resonated for him, he said, with the understanding of how her world had been shaken so early.

Commenting on Bishop's search for answers, on her wish "that some revelation . . . might have brought all into focus," Wilbur noted, "In and out of her poetry she lamented her want of a comprehensive philosophy; yet I cannot be sorry that so honest a nature as hers refused to force itself into a system, and I question whether system is the only way to go deep into things."[125] This remark reflects his sense of kinship with Bishop, not only as a pair of independent minds but also, as the critic Jonathan Ellis has suggested, in how such independence may extend "to notions of genre and form." Jarrell's 1951 urge to "come on, *take a chance*" has lingered in Wilbur's memory. Wilbur may have "dismissed the criticism," he said in 2007, yet he was "glad to come around later one way or another to write the occasional long poem."[126] He has recognized his own sense of possibility in the midst of what others were interpreting as limitation, even as he has resisted what has not felt true to his nature.

11

Keeping a Difficult Balance

"The time one spends teaching could be spent writing"

After I taught my last class of the year, I drove about doing a few Christmas errands. It was as if I were a tourist in some other and fascinating town. The pressure of my purposes was off me, the blinders of my anxious efforts to know enough about Milton, and to teach him well: I could see things with privilege and wideness and with a happily uncertain sense of relevance.

—RICHARD WILBUR, unpublished journal, December 1970

Richard Wilbur spent thirty-five years balancing his writing career with teaching—at Harvard, Wellesley, and Wesleyan—before retiring in 1985 from his post as a writer in residence at Smith College. In 2008 he returned to the classroom at his alma mater, accepting a John Woodruff Simpson lectureship at Amherst College. As he has explained, teaching has both hindered and enhanced his writing career. The first downside, he said, is obvious: "the time one spends teaching could be spent writing."[1] A second, more curious downside is teaching's potential to diminish verbal agility. "[It] uses the same gray cells, pretty much, that writing does, and so one can come to the job of writing with too little of a sense of rediscovery of the language. That is one reason I like to live out here in the country and lead a fairly physical life—play a lot of tennis, raise a lot of vegetables, go on a lot of long walks." Wilbur has long seen this back and forth movement between the physical and the mental as a way to renew his excitement about language. "It is good," he said, "for a writer to move into words out of the silence as much as he can."[2]

Reading has been the best part of being a "teacher-writer / writer-teacher," Wilbur believes. His use of both terms indicates the delicate balance of these roles. For teachers, reading passively is not an option. They need to move people to recognize and analyze literature, a task that enhances a teaching writer's own ability to articulate. "I know a few writers who don't teach and who, in consequence, do very little reading. This doesn't mean that they are bad writers, but in some cases I think they might be better writers if they read more."[3]

By 1958 Wilbur and Charlee had four children, so his teaching jobs offered him a stable, much-needed salary that did not depend on fluctuating royalties. Yet teaching meant spending not only less time writing but also less time with his family. As his children grew up, he found that integrating the professional with the personal, the public with the private, became increasingly difficult, especially during the tumultuous 1960s.

A Prize-Winning Prof

In May 1957, having already won the Pulitzer for *Things of This World,* Wilbur opened his National Book Award acceptance speech (for the same book) with the assertion that prizes don't motivate "a poet who is at all serious."

> When a poet is being a poet—that is, when he is writing or thinking about writing—he cannot be concerned with anything but the making of a poem. If the poem is to turn out well, the poet cannot have thought of whether it will be saleable, or of what its effect on the world should be; he cannot think of whether it will bring him honor, or advance a cause, or comfort someone in sorrow. All such considerations, whether silly or generous, would be merely intrusive; for, psychologically speaking, the end of writing is the poem itself. As Robert Frost put it, "The fact is the sweetest dream that labor knows."[4]

Wilbur compared the poet to a surgeon or a shoemaker "who must focus on the thing itself." Yet, he said, the poet encounters some reluctance from a public that refuses to see a poem as a necessity.

> Anyone who has participated in public symposia on poetry will know with what curious resentment the psychology of the poetic act is regarded.

People seem to want the poem to be more *transitive* in intention than it is; they would like it to be a direct communication. They don't want the minutes of a meditation; they want oratory. They don't want the love-poem; they want love-making itself. In a society where poetry is little used or understood, this is an understandable and human reaction, but unfortunately it amounts to a repudiation of the art.

Then again, this is the age of the ball-point pen and the plastic toy, of the quick sale and the early replacement; the age of the degradation of the thing. In such a time, it may be hard for some to conceive that any product should be made not to sell, not to please, but for the sake of its own perfection. The poet, in such a time, may well seem guilty of what the Marxists call "commodity fetishism."[5]

Nevertheless, he spoke of poetry "as a deeply social thing—radically and incorrigibly social." It may be indirect, he said, in the sense that the poet does not address a neighbor but "a great congress of persons who dwells at the back of his mind." The poet speaks not of things that are peculiar or personal "but of what in himself is most common, most anonymous, most fundamental, most true of all men, . . . not in private grunts and mutterings but in the public language of the dictionary, of literary tradition, and of the street."

Wilbur expanded on his belief that war poetry should "deal with the one and the many," incorporating into it a position he would carry into the next decade and beyond: "Writing poetry is talking to oneself; yet it is a mode of talking to oneself in which the self disappears; and the product is something that, though it may not be *for* everybody, is *about* everybody." He concluded by returning to the idea of creative independence but not isolation:

> Writing poetry, then, is an unsocial way of manufacturing a thoroughly social product. Because he must shield his poetry in its creation, the poet, more than other writers, will write without recognition. And because his product is not in great demand, he is likely to look on honors and distinctions with the feigned indifference of the wallflower. Yet of course he is pleased when recognition comes; for what better proof is there that for some people poetry is still a useful and necessary thing—like a shoe.
>
> I am grateful for this award; and that it comes from the book industry makes it all the pleasanter to receive.[6]

At the time of the speech, Wilbur was caught up in his final duties at Wellesley. Earlier that spring, Wesleyan, then an all-male institution, had invited Wilbur to join its English department in the following fall. Victor

L. Butterfield (who served as the university's president from 1943 to 1967) wanted to hire a faculty member who would strengthen the department's modern offerings—either an expert on nineteenth- and twentieth-century European literature or a creative person with some engagement in the modern world. According to Fred B. Millett, a soon-to-retire scholar specializing in Shakespeare and the English canon, Butterfield couldn't find anyone in the first category who excited him.[7] Wilbur, however, had been recommended by Henry Allen Moe, a humanist philanthropic administrator affiliated with the American Academy in Rome, the Guggenheim Foundation, and the American Philosophical Association. If Butterfield had any doubts about Wilbur's ability to make an impact on the modern literary world, Wilbur's subsequent sweep of the poetry prizes should have dismissed them.

On April 16 Wesleyan's student newspaper, the *Argus,* heralded Wilbur's arrival with a three-column headline: "National Book Award Recipient to Teach Verse Writing Course." In addition, the article announced, he would teach a first-term Shakespeare class and one on writing narrative prose. The faculty's welcome was enthusiastic. Even before the public announcement, Millett had written to him personally, asking that he take over the first-term Shakespeare course right away rather than wait until Millett had retired. Wilbur saw this as a vote of confidence and agreed.[8]

Wilbur's love of reading undoubtedly affected his preference for teaching subject-matter courses rather than writing courses. They forced him to read epics he may have otherwise overlooked, he has admitted, which did him good. As early as his Wellesley days, he has said, he was never a fan of too much creative-writing teaching at the undergraduate level.[9] When he served on a visiting committee in the 1980s that was advising Harvard's English department, he took issue with the scholars and lawyers in the group who were advocating the launch of a creative major, which would allow students to concentrate for four years on whatever courses they preferred. John Updike, said Wilbur, the only other writer on the committee, made a speech that he agreed with: "Writers have to know something, therefore they have to take geology and know what it is they are standing on."[10]

Nonetheless, Wilbur taught writing in every institution he worked for. It was not time wasted, he said, not for anyone concerned, but it posed challenges:

> The atmosphere of a creative writing class is always kindly, or should be so, and it's necessary of course to be fairly decent to people who are

sticking their necks out and trying to write verse. At the same time . . . if it were possible not to scare people out of writing at all, I think it might be good to begin a creative writing course by saying: *you are proposing to enter the arena in which John Milton wrote and Shakespeare wrote, and so don't be too self-indulgent, be hard on yourself.*[11]

Wilbur found ways to keep the serious, dedicated students interested and to winnow out those who had enrolled on a lark. For instance, by devoting the first two hours in his poetry-writing course to prosody, including detailed discussion of meter and stanzaic forms, he could reduce the class to a manageable size.[12] On the whole, he has found the experience of teaching enjoyable, although he was more depressed by classes that didn't work than elated by classes that did.[13]

In 1962 a Wesleyan colleague named Tom Henney asked Wilbur if he would be willing to make a trade: he wanted to "get rid" of a Milton course he was scheduled to teach and wondered if he could exchange it for a course that Wilbur wanted to unload. Henney just couldn't make the students like it, he told Wilbur. But Henney himself did not like Milton, and that was the source of the problem. Wilbur took on the Milton course, deriving greater pleasure from it year after year.[14] When Wilbur needed to strengthen his own verse or to be prodded or reawakened by another poet, he often turned to Milton, who taught him to see "how expressively and muscularly language can move though verse patterns."[15] Teaching Milton added a traditional and demanding genre to Wilbur's repertoire—extended meditations in blank verse—and a greater focus on the nature and manifestations of divinity. Both were evident in *Walking to Sleep* (1969).

The "University of Verse"

In 1957 a generous gift from an alumnus allowed Wesleyan to establish a university press. Wilbur suggested that rather than compete for scholarly books with existing university presses, the new Wesleyan University Press could make a name for itself with a poetry series, publishing books by new and established poets. In his view one of the press's early triumphs was committing to the poet Robert Francis, who had been rebuffed by the publishing world and was then living in isolation in Amherst. An inquiry from the press had prompted Francis to send the editors a sheaf of poems that had accumulated for years. The manuscript was accepted and they were released in 1960 as *The Orb Weaver.*

The first director of the Wesleyan Poetry Series was Willard Lockwood, a recent Wesleyan graduate who had worked as an editor in New York and at the University of Oklahoma Press. He was not a poet himself, but he worked closely with Wilbur, one of the first members of the poetry series' independent selection board. There were no term limits for the four members of the board, Lockwood said in 2005. "They served until they got sort of tired." (Wilbur estimates that the members read between two hundred and three hundred manuscripts per year.) As Lockwood recalled, they would "sit down and say to one another, 'Well, what do you think?' and sooner or later a name would bubble up. And whatever they picked, we published."[16] Wilbur was on the board from 1958 to 1975, retiring when he became president of the American Academy of Arts and Letters. Donald Hall served from 1958 to 1964; John Hollander, Norman Holmes Pearson, and John Malcolm Brinnin were also early board members. In the 1960s T. S. Eliot, as a roving editor, looked for poets in England and Europe.

In the fall of 1959 the press published its first poetry titles—by Barbara Howes, Hyam Plutzik, Louis Simpson, and James Wright. It eventually published all of James Dickey's early titles, including *Buckdancer's Choice,* which won the National Book Award in 1966. Over the years Wesleyan poets have won five Pulitzers, three National Book Awards, and innumerable prizes in hundreds of contests. The series prompted other university and private publishers to initiate similar programs, and many prospered. The vein they tapped was a rich one, both inside and outside the academy. Today, more than fifty years after its founding, the Wesleyan Poetry Series is respected for its longevity and excellence, even when compared with presses at universities with larger graduate programs and bigger endowments or those with financial backing from the state.

In 1966 Wesleyan established an Honors College in the Russell House, a Greek Revival manse on the east side of High Street, where eighty upperclassmen of academic distinction lived each year and were freed of all curriculum requirements. They studied in small, specialized classes taught by faculty and visiting writers and scholars, and had opportunities to present informal lectures to their group. Wilbur was a fellow of the college in 1968–69, and he spoke to an *Argus* reporter in November 1968 about its benefit to students, despite charges of exclusivity: "There is no reason why it shouldn't have a positive effect on people socially. . . . The isolation of eighty people is better than the isolation of groups of four. Formerly one knew only his roommates and his hi-fi system." He was less hopeful about disposing of curricular requirements altogether: "It might be possible that a great burden has been shifted from the compiler of catalogues to the advisers of students, and that there may be less change, really, than the abolition of requirements might suggest."[17]

A poetry series at the Honors College began in 1966 in conjunction with a nonprofit organization called the Connecticut Poetry Circuit, whose mission was to provide poetry-reading programs for colleges and prep schools and offer Wesleyan students a chance to present their own work to an audience. The list of prominent poets who came to Wesleyan on the reading circuit was long and impressive. Wilbur himself participated for four academic years, both during his time at the university and afterward, and in 1984 he read at the twenty-fifth anniversary celebration of Wesleyan University Press.[18]

Across the River, Then to Houston and Moscow

When Wilbur left Wellesley for Wesleyan, he and Charlee could have moved to the neighborhood in Middletown that skirted the campus, where most of the faculty lived. But Charlee wasn't keen on being pigeonholed as a faculty wife. She wanted no part in the Monday Club, as the wives' formal social enclave was called, and preferred to keep her private life at a literal distance.

The Wilburs found a house for sale at 13 Sunset Terrace in Portland, a ten-minute drive across the Connecticut River. The three-story home, originally called Fairview but renamed Hillcroft by the owners prior to the Wilburs, had been built in 1868. It had a wide central entrance, a wraparound porch, a porte cochere on the side, and two dormer windows looking out onto a lawn with numerous trees and plantings. The house nestled against woods and a line of boulders that separated the property from other homes on the quiet cul-de-sac, and the driveway was lined with maples. The only thing missing, Charlee told Wilbur, was a feature of New England homes that she particularly admired: a large stone to mark the driveway entrance. So several years later, as an anniversary gift, he hired an excavating company to deliver and set in place a huge rock from a nearby quarry.

Hillcroft's double front doors opened onto a hallway with a gleaming brass chandelier. On the right was a sitting room, on the left a formal parlor that adjoined the dining room. Behind the dining room was a large eat-in kitchen with a fireplace. Ellen Wilbur, who was fourteen when the family

Charlee and Dick Wilbur on the porch of Hillcroft, their home in Portland, Connecticut, across the river from Wesleyan University, circa 1965. *Courtesy of Richard Wilbur.*

moved in, remembers how special the place was to her and her younger brothers, Christopher and Nathan, because it symbolized permanence after so many years of moving.[19] Her father's poem "The Writer," which describes her teenage efforts at short-story writing, is set in her bedroom in the right corner of the house.

Soon after the move to Portland Charlee became pregnant with the Wilburs' fourth child. She had experienced several miscarriages between her other pregnancies, and difficulties during the third trimester caused her to fear she would lose this child as well. Lillian Hellman, still a close friend, wrote to her in the autumn of 1958: "Charlee pie: . . . I do hope the baby will come through. It seems to me, all will be well. But you are right: if it doesn't, then you have a fine three, and you are young enough to have another next year. Another called Lily."[20]

On December 12, 1958, Aaron Hammond Wilbur was born after a difficult delivery. On May 22, 1960, he was christened in a ceremony that John Brinnin described in his journal:

> In a white linen suit . . . [I] go with Dick and Charlee and all the children to the Episcopal Church of Portland, hold [Aaron] in a bower of lilies just long enough for the minister to say appropriate words, sprinkle him rather liberally with cold water and make him cry. Thus become a godfather . . . with name in a book and spiritual exercises in my hand. Then we hurry to Bloody Marys, and Lillian Hellman, who's the baby's godmother, phones to hear of the ceremony and we sit down to lunch on the sunny veranda chattering like the squirrels in the trees.[21]

In the fall of 1960 the family left Portland for another sabbatical year. The Ford Foundation had awarded Wilbur a fellowship to spend a year as a resident playwright at the Alley Theater in Houston, writing a play that the company would stage. Charlee waited until November before writing four single-spaced typewritten pages to Brinnin—a self-described "tract about the atmosphere and physical aspect of Houston."[22]

She told him that the family had a season pass to the Houston Symphony Orchestra under Leopold Stokowski and tickets for the Royal Ballet in December; for the first time since Rome, she felt like a city girl. She and Wilbur kept some distance between themselves and the Alley Theater people and spent their weekends exploring with the three older children—at the zoo, at museums and libraries, on the waterfront, watching the Ice Capades, waiting to hear Kennedy and Johnson speak on the campaign trail.[23]

As for the climate, Charlee told Brinnin, "You can take it and shove it. It breeds roaches the size of rats and rats the size of rabbits, plus all sorts of flying, sighing enormous insects that even manage to invade one's bed to say nothing of shoes, sugar bowls, toilet bowls. I found a chameleon turning brown on my bottle of Privine this morning, but I happen to go for chameleons." Her New Englander side noted the charged atmosphere of the city, "an electricity emanating from conscious expansion, from Big Money, a feeling that Houston must contain every cultural advantage." She didn't approve, however, of Texas ostentation:

> The women dress like basement Renaissance whores: in Balenciaga stained-glassed-window dresses with ocelot stoles. *All* hair is dyed, and changes color with the ensemble. The men wear gold string ties (I'm not

kidding. REAL GOLD) in the evening, and wild heavy cuff links and tie clips with brands on them. The people are superficially gracious and polite, even warm toward a northern visitor or toward each other, but they are deeply uneasy socially and have hair-trigger tempers if there is any delay in gratification of senses. . . . Fists clench quite consciously when a waiter is slow to deliver a drink. . . . One rancher who is a member of the Gusher Club (membership limited to those who have made more than a million in oil) has just had his entire family woven into a seventy-five-foot-long tapestry to hang in his "lodge" to the tune of $100,000. Really a mad, mad place and fascinating to observe it.[24]

Wilbur had just returned from two days in New York City, and Charlee wrote a glowing account of his work and his spirits:

Dick has been working like a happy fool here, everything about our life here agreeing with him. No tension as in Rome. He has written four beautiful new poems and sold them all to the *New Yorker* bang bang. He has begun to translate TARTUFFE but with no real pressure whatever. He doesn't expect to finish it any special time and uses it as a pick-up work when he isn't doing something better. . . . He is also toying with a children's book. I feel better than in many years because he is for the first time since I have known him using a year off intelligently instead of desperately. He takes time off with the kids, goes for long walks with Chris [Wilbur], and looks marvelous. In short, I am in love all over again, and this is how it should be in a hot, sensy climate.[25]

In Houston Wilbur wrote seven new poems for his fourth book, *Advice to a Prophet,* which Harcourt was expecting on May 1. Charlee thought they made the collection his best by far. "It is a solid, UN-promising, middle-aged book, by God," she told Brinnin at the end of April 1961. "Dick couldn't care less that Donald Hall isn't going to like it, along with several others who seem to be feeling that Academic Poets are on the way out."[26]

The book's title poem fulfilled a wager that Wilbur had accepted in a London bar at the end of World War II: to write a good poem about the threat of the atom bomb (see chapter 4). Its final lines widen the sense of atomic threat beyond humanity to include the rest of the animal and vegetable kingdoms. Reflecting on the poem, the critic John Gery first quoted another critic, Wendy Salinger, who called it a "moving political poem [that] is at its heart about language," and then offered his own interpretation: "Specifically it is about feeling the *loss* of language (and through that the loss of perception) as our only means of appreciating the dangers of

nuclearism. Annihilation, in other words, is a physical and psychic condition that encompasses the signifiers 'lofty' and 'long standing' together with
whatever they signify, as well as everything else imaginable."[27] Here are the
final eleven lines of the poem, in which the poet identifies "everything else
imaginable" as those qualities that define our humanity:

> Ask us, prophet, how we shall call
> Our natures forth when that live tongue is all
> Dispelled, that glass obscured or broken
>
> In which we have said the rose of our love and the clean
> Horse of our courage, in which beheld
> The singing locust of the soul unshelled,
> And all we mean or wish to mean.
>
> Ask us, ask us whether with the worldless rose
> Our hearts shall fail us; come demanding
> Whether there shall be lofty or long standing
> When the bronze annals of the oak-tree close.

By articulating the ultimate catastrophe held in check by the Cold War,
Wilbur had written one of the era's most eloquent political poems.

When she wrote to Brinnin, Charlee acknowledged the shadow cast on
the future by the threat of nuclear annihilation, but she didn't dwell on
it. Life had been good in Texas, and she was convinced a year spent anywhere else would have meant far less good work for Wilbur. The children
had taken another sabbatical year in stride: Nathan had a role in an Alley
production that ran for twenty-one performances, managed not to miss a
day of school in the process, and thrived on the discipline of working with
a professional company. Ellen was on the honor roll and had had a short
story accepted by the *Transatlantic Review*. Chris made an impression in his
geography class by informing his teacher that Alaska had replaced Texas as
the biggest state in the union. Aaron, now two and a half, was talking like
crazy.[28]

Nonetheless, Charlee was homesick for Hillcroft. When the time came to
leave Houston, Ellen and Aaron flew back separately and waited at Wilbur's
parents' house in North Caldwell for the rest of the family, who returned
by car. But Wilbur had no sooner begun to think about the fall 1961
semester when he left home again, this time for the Soviet Union. During
a diplomatic thaw the U.S. State Department had appointed him, along
with the poet Peter Viereck (like Wilbur, a former G.I. and a Pulitzer Prize

winner), to represent the nation in a cultural exchange program. Hosted by the Soviet Writers' Union, both poets spent the month of September in Moscow and Peredelkino, the writers' enclave on the outskirts of the city. Before the trip they had asked to meet fifty poets and novelists, and by the end of the month they had spent time with all but two.

The visit intensified Wilbur's interest in Russian poetry, which was flourishing in the Soviet Union and had a cultural prominence that its American counterpart never achieved. Soviet poets were national figures who read to huge audiences and sold tens of thousands of books. Yet if their message provoked the ire of the Communist Party, they could be exiled, imprisoned, or killed.

Wilbur learned that the poet Joseph Brodsky, who had taught himself English, in part by translating Frost's poems, was known as the best Russian translator of his work.[29] Brodsky was also one of the many writers targeted by the party, which eventually arrested him in 1963. Charged a year later for the crime of social parasitism (a charge often leveled at dissident intellectuals in that era), he was twice committed to a mental institution (another way of dealing with dissidents). He was then sentenced to five years in a labor camp just south of the Arctic Circle, although he ended up serving only eighteen months.

In 1971, after the government stripped him of his papers and sent him into exile, Brodsky decided to move to the United States, and Wilbur decided to translate his work. "I wanted to do something he would approve of," Wilbur said. "I had heard he was very choosy, very finicky." The first translation took a month to complete, and the second was also a slow process, requiring linguistic counsel and the aid of dictionaries. Wilbur's 2010 collection *Anterooms* includes translations of two Brodsky poems—"Presepio" and "25. XII. 1993"—but he believes his translation of Brodsky's love poem "Six Years Later" to be his best effort.[30]

After the 1961 trip to Moscow Wilbur continued to study new poetry in Russian, often with help from the British expert Max Hayward, who had translated Boris Pasternak's *Dr. Zhivago* (with Manya Harari) as well as the poems of Voznesensky (with Patricia Blake). Blake and Hayward later invited Wilbur to contribute his own translations to a collection of Voznesensky's work. In the meantime, Soviet translators were working on their own versions of Wilbur's and Viereck's poems. In 2008, writing to *Harvard Magazine* in response to an article about Wilbur, Viereck's son and daughter reflected on the pair as cultural ambassadors:

Russian translations of Wilbur's and Viereck's poetry . . . appeared [in 1961] in the *Literaturnaya Gazeta,* along with Yevtushenko's unprecedented "Babi Yar," promoting both aesthetic freedom and human rights.

The popularity of this exchange helped to prompt Khrushchev's November 1962 decision to authorize the uncensored publication of Solzhenitsyn's *One Day in the Life of Ivan Denisovich.* The influence came full circle when Harvard invited Solzhenitsyn to campus as its 1978 Commencement speaker, where he championed "the integral spirit" shared by all humans. . . . Wilbur became a poet instead of writing seventeenth-century European history, but we should remember that Harvard's poets have played no small part in changing the course of world history.[31]

"When you know what is wrong with Aaron"

Neither the carefree atmosphere Brinnin described at Aaron Wilbur's baptismal lunch nor Charlee's excited mention of a son who was "talking like crazy" reveal that the Wilburs were worried about his slow development and lack of emotional response. It took more than seven years for them to learn and eventually understand the cause: Kanner-syndrome autism.

In early 2006 they spoke separately and together about that long process of discovery. Wilbur prefaced his explanation with a description of the Bettelheim theory of autism, which a therapist named Altenburg (Wilbur called him a "volunteer Bettelheimer") reiterated to the couple for years. Altenburg had been recommended to them as an authority on childhood behavior such as Aaron's. "An autistic child has been hated in the womb," he told them. "He has not been wanted, and the mother has conveyed unwillingness and hatred to the child even before it was born."[32] In the 1950s and 1960s the common term for this "cause" of autism was *refrigerator mother,* although Wilbur did not use it.

Charlee explained that neither she nor Wilbur knew where else to seek help. There was no literature that refuted Bettelheim. (Not until 1967, with the publication of *The Siege,* written by the mother of a profoundly autistic child, did an alternate view become available to the general public.)

Aaron was observed in a playgroup while the two of us were seen, for three hours twice a week—so that was six hours—by a child specialist supposedly, who was a Freudian. An extraordinary length of time. The general consensus was that Aaron was schizophrenic and that I had caused it by rejection of him in the womb. And it was suggested that we send him away for a "new finding of himself" by Bruno Bettelheim himself. I was almost destroyed by that therapy as you can imagine.[33]

Charlee acknowledged that Dick, "being the person he is, did not feel that he had to believe an authoritarian figure." Wilbur concurred: "I regarded this [theory] as impossible because Charlee did not have those feelings about Aaron."[34] But Charlee felt vulnerable.

> I am the sort of person who believes what I am told until I find out differently. I didn't want to be an authority in that situation. I wanted someone to tell me what to do and where to go, I was in such misery and confusion. And Dick, in our sessions, gradually became aggressively opposed to Altenburg, and when attacked or queried or questioned by the doctor would say, "I have my own opinion and I think you're wrong." We would leave those sessions in a state of, oh, I can hardly describe the state. It was a terrible time of loneliness, and despair almost, on my part, and division with Dick, which I had not had before. It did not persist in our private life particularly but it was there in those sessions.[35]

Wilbur remembered a fatuous woman who sat in on the sessions and once said with an all-knowing smile, "When you know what is wrong with Aaron, Aaron will be well." Charlee added, "Isn't that horrendous? I went out of there reeling. I didn't even know what she meant."[36]

The Wilburs' private life was difficult in 1963. Charlee was ready to "toss the year into all eternity." Aaron had just turned five, and the family's intense weekly therapy was more strain than support. In addition, Charlee's mother had suffered several strokes and was no longer able to take care of herself.

> Both Dick and I had thought about somehow arranging things in the house in Portland so we could take care of Mother. There was no way, . . . no bedroom or bath downstairs, and she could not go upstairs. There was no way to even put an addition onto the house. And she really didn't want to be with us. She'd had a horror of being dependent upon us. She did go to a couple of nursing homes . . . within twenty minutes of us, and there she had more strokes and became less well. Then she moved in[to] town, where our family doctor had bought a nursing home and was running it, so we felt comfortable with his taking care of Mother. She was not well at all there for a long time. It was tough seeing her like that. [Ward did not die until 1968.] It was very tough going to those two long therapy sessions for Aaron and taking care of the house and the other kids. And

Dick was working so hard, and being out of town traveling at the height of the all the stuff that he was trying to do.[37]

As Charlee recalled, it took several more years before the Wilburs found an autism specialist who had access to more up-to-date research.

I got to be in such bad shape, I was insomniac, I was depressed, I was wondering what to do with Aaron or how to help him, and I finally heard of a psychiatrist in Middletown to whom two of my friends were going, and I made an appointment with her. During the first appointment she said to me, "Write down the answers to a few questions I'm going to ask you," and she gave me a piece of paper and I took a pencil. She asked, "One: Did your child cry early in the morning and did he stop crying when you picked him up? Two: Did he enjoy being held?" A series of questions of that sort. I answered them on paper and she read them. And then she said, "You have no responsibility for the condition of your child. Your child is a Kanner-syndrome autistic child." And I fell on the floor, literally, weeping, and she said, "I'm going to give you a prescription for Valium, and I want you to go home and go to sleep and then come back and see me, but I want you to know you have nothing to berate yourself for." I went home and took [the Valium] and slept for what must have been eighteen straight hours. I couldn't get up the next day. Somebody got up and started the day; I guess Dick did. I was knocked out. Anyway, that's what happened. That was a dreadful period.[38]

The drama and sorrow of these years never seeped into public consciousness until long after they had occurred. Wilbur chose not to make his family's suffering, at this time or any other, a subject for his poetry. Charlee was reticent about the family's misfortunes and defended and protected her husband's position and privacy. Yet that practice sometimes left her emotionally isolated—for instance, when Wilbur was away from home on a reading circuit. In early 1968 Charlee found much-needed support and relief when the Wilburs enrolled Aaron in the newly opened Stonegate School in Durham, Connecticut, a center for mentally challenged children run by an order of nuns called the Daughters of Our Lady of the Garden. Aaron lived part time at the center, which treated him less clinically and more lovingly than the Bettelheim disciples would have, until the family found a residential autism treatment center in Wakefield, Rhode Island.[39]

In 1977 Ruth Sullivan of the National Society for Autistic Children asked Wilbur to contribute some remarks to "Poems on Autism: Beyond Research Data," scheduled to appear in the "Parents Speak" section of the

June issue of the *Journal of Autism and Childhood Schizophrenia.* All of the featured poems were written by parents of autistic children; and "as so often in poetry of all kinds," Wilbur wrote, "[poets] are strongest when they turn upon themselves, endanger themselves, and put themselves under special pressure to be honest or clear." Responding to Catherine Hildyard's poem "Collecting from (Normal) School," Wilbur noted that it "expresses a fierce loyalty to the 'different' child, and accepts—despite the pain of it—a wholly different emotional 'weather' from that which surrounds the normal."[40] At this time Aaron Wilbur was nearly nineteen years old, and Wilbur's comments suggest that he and Charlee had accepted autism's "roadblocks in the brain [as] mysterious and unmovable."[41] As parents, they had come to understand that a child on the autism spectrum cannot be cured but can get better, that their son would always function differently but could learn to communicate with less frustration.

Strife in the Sixties

During the Vietnam War era, Wilbur had to reconcile his personal opposition to the war in Southeast Asia with the national loyalty ingrained in him during World War II—even though before the bombing of Pearl Harbor he had been a pacifist who had opposed entering the conflict. He protested President Johnson's decision to attack and invade North Vietnam by participating in demonstrations and events in Middletown and occasionally elsewhere—for instance, at a program to promote peace in mid-November 1967, held at the Town Hall in New York City, where he read "On the Marginal Way." Although at the time he had questioned the efficacy of savage indignation in political poetry and art, he said, speaking in 2007, that in retrospect he saw the 1960s as his angriest period.

> One reason . . . for my bad temper was that I had been opposed to the Vietnam War when the French were fighting it, and I was at all times opposed to our involvement in it, and I belonged to all the wrong organizations in the view of our [government's] security people, but I felt that the presence of the Vietnam War did not entitle my students to cut classes or come to class full of drugs, and in general be anarchic, ugly-looking, and self-indulgent in every way. The people who had it easiest during the Vietnam War were our students, and they took the occasion in the name of protest to indulge themselves in every possible way. That infuriated me, and I was infuriated by so many of my colleagues at Wesleyan who took the occasion to have delayed adolescences and join the kids, as they were

called. I expressed these opinions, I was quite a loudmouth about it, and I wasn't loved for it.[42]

In January 1967 Robert Gottlieb of Simon and Schuster invited Wilbur to contribute to the American edition of *Authors Take Sides on Vietnam,* and Wilbur began to draft his statement directly onto Gottlieb's letter: "I am opposed to our involvement in Vietnam, to our pretense that it was and is an ideological war, to our use of inhumane weapons and methods, to the secrecy with which our efforts have been expanded, and to our continued defiance of the opinion of mankind." The draft he ultimately submitted, however, did not include that sentence. Instead, he wrote a far more specific and nuanced argument, which begins: "The new weapons have insured that the final stage of any big war must now be indiscriminate and suicidal. It is therefore time to consider abolishing the old Augustinian distinction between just and unjust warfare."[43]

Wilbur's antiwar and anti-Johnson positions culminated in "A Miltonic Sonnet for Mr. Johnson on His Refusal of Peter Hurd's Official Portrait," dated January 6, 1967. The specific subject of the sonnet was the unveiling of Peter Hurd's portrait of the president and Johnson's crass public denunciation of it: he called the painting the "ugliest thing I ever saw." Johnson complained that the Capitol dome in Hurd's painting was too bright, implying that it upstaged his own face.[44]

The descriptor "Miltonic" refers both to the sonnet's rhyme scheme and its political content. Here, Wilbur points to the stark contrast between Thomas Jefferson's conduct of the presidency and Johnson's:

> Heir to the office of a man not dead
> Who drew our Declaration up, who planned
> Range and Rotunda with his drawing-hand
> And harbored Palestrina in his head,
> Who would have wept to see small nations dread
> The imposition of our cattle-brand,
> With public truth at home mistold or banned,
> And in whose term no army's blood was shed,
>
> Rightly you say the picture is too large
> Which Peter Hurd by your appointment drew,
> And justly called that Capitol too bright
> Which signifies our people in your charge;
> Wait, Sir, and see how time will render you,
> Who talk of vision but are weak of sight.

During Jefferson's term America fought no wars, and Jefferson exemplified a distinguished and intellectual notion of leadership. He drafted the Declaration of Independence; he not only founded the University of Virginia but was also the architect of two of its main buildings; he was an expert in the arts. During Johnson's term, however, the president's hesitant and duplicitous handling of the Vietnam War tarnished the early bold promise of his "Great Society," and the intensity of Wilbur's disgust for Johnson's willingness to sacrifice tens of thousands of American lives is palpable.[45]

On May 4, 1970, National Guardsmen at Kent State University in Ohio fired sixty-seven rounds at antiwar demonstrators, killing four students and injuring nine others in a matter of thirteen seconds. After the shootings tensions ran high on college campuses across the United States. Wesleyan students and faculty members, like many others, declared strikes to protest the massacre and demonstrate their solidarity with both student and nonstudent activists.

On May 6 Wilbur submitted his poem "For the Student Strikers" to the *Middletown Strike News,* a mimeographed, student-run daily that covered efforts, by strikers and other activists on campus and in the town, to further support and coordinate antiwar protests, draft resistance, and door-to-door canvassing. As he explained in an endnote, the poem "did not flatter the students in the manner to which they were accustomed." Instead, it urged them to open their ears and minds to other voices, to find a common ground rather than raise fists, and be open to "changes of heart." Its final and most affecting lines encouraged empathy for the "grey wife of your nightmare sheriff / And the guardsman's son."[46] Unsurprisingly, given its tone, a *Strike News* staffer tossed Wilbur's submission into a wastebasket. But someone else pulled it out, and on May 8 the poem appeared in the paper.

In 2001 the New Formalist critic David Mason published a short essay on "For the Student Strikers" in *The Dark Horse,* prompting the following comment on the *Eratosphere* blog:

> Among Wilbur-worshipers, there is a hierarchy of poems that they generally admire. One of the few poems they tend to quietly look down upon is one of my favorites, "For the Student Strikers." David singled this poem out for praise, and I think he is absolutely right to do so. Poetry should be a public act about something important to readers, and a poem that makes an important, nonobvious political point should be a cherished item instead of something relegated to the wastelands outside of our lyrical/confessional playgrounds.

We have largely lost the ability to write great political poetry since Auden and Yeats were in their prime, and "For the Student Strikers" is one of the great exceptions to the generalization.[47]

Wilbur's opposition to the war was put to the test when his older sons went to college—Christopher to Harvard, Nathan to Amherst. Charlee recalled:

> Dick and I split apart again briefly . . . because of what was happening. To me the decade was a highly overdue and exciting period when women's rights were being recognized for the first time, where people opposed the Vietnam War en masse and political activism seemed to be having some effect, where homosexual rights seemed like they were going to improve. The kids were in college and a part of all that, and for Dick it was an extremely frightening period. In the academy the mode of teaching that had been accepted for his length of time as a teacher, the convention of the classroom, all suddenly overturned. In the classroom equality began. Suddenly, in the English department, someone Dick respected very much—he was a well-mannered, well-behaved sort of person, that sounds silly but you know what I mean, a very bright and marvelous lecturer and marvelous conveyer of facts and ideas to students, a marvelous talker to students—suddenly, and this is what Dick said to me, threw off his jacket and tie and began being called by his first name and began saying "shit" and "fuck" in the classroom. Dick just felt that was an outrageous accommodation and inappropriate.[48]

Charlee had been in the thick of student life at Wesleyan for several years, auditing courses of several kinds, some with Ellen, who transferred from Bennington to Wesleyan in 1965. She didn't care how outrageously the professor was behaving in the classroom, but Dick, she said, took his behavior as an affront:

> Change on campus was agonizing to him; he suffered over it. And not just the superficial things I mentioned but what was happening in general. The president's house was invaded by a black contingent in the middle of the night making demands and that sort of thing. He felt the way people were going about change was all wrong. Also he thought that his sons should register and go to this war. Dick was marching in antiwar parades and was part of the antiwar movement at Wesleyan, but where his sons were concerned, that was different. He felt that they did not have the right to be conscientious objectors, that they should undergo whatever came to them in the way of a draft. . . . I on the other hand was going to take them to Canada if necessary. So we were at serious loggerheads in the family about that.[49]

The Wilburs were spared such drastic actions because, in the end, both Christopher and Nathan drew high draft numbers, which kept them out of the military.

When the war ended, Wilbur continued to be uneasy with the shifting Zeitgeist in the academy—for instance, as black studies programs made their way into colleges and universities. In 1995 he reflected on the changes he'd seen in the teaching of humanities:

> The word *tragic,* so often sloppily used, applies very well to what has lately occurred in some of our academies, where a conflict of good motives has produced a sorry outcome. There is, no doubt, some kindness and generosity in the idea of reshaping the curriculum so as to represent the backgrounds of minority students. Yet if people are to be truly at home in America, they need to study the best of that Western culture which has informed our people and our institutions. Any other program is a deprivation for all concerned, and not least for the minorities who are its supposed beneficiaries.[50]

Stone Walls, Streams, and a Silo Study

By 1969 Wilbur was looking ahead to his retirement from Wesleyan. Charlee's mother had died in the nursing home, so they were less tied to the Portland area than they had been. Ellen was on her own, the older boys were in college, and Aaron was in Wakefield. Once the house had been a hub of social activity, both small and grand; for more than a decade Charlee's dinner parties had been renowned among the Wesleyan faculty as well as the Wilburs' writer friends. But Charlee found that managing Hillcroft had become daunting, and after a last big party in the spring to celebrate the March publication of *Walking to Sleep,* the Wilburs put the house on the market.

They decided to purchase a nearly ninety-acre tract in Cummington, a hill town in the Berkshire Mountains of Massachusetts, not far from the house where the poet William Cullen Bryant had once lived. Situated on a quiet winding road, the property lay directly across from a dairy farm and a quarter mile away from a sugarhouse.[51] Stone walls delineated old property divisions; streams and brooks ran through the landscape. From the house Dick and Charlee looked out over the fields and watched the changing cycles of the grasses and weeds. All of these details, even to the sundial outside the sitting room window, eventually found a place in Wilbur's poems.

For instance, "Hamlen Brook," from his *New and Collected* (1987), evokes the walks that Wilbur took around the property, alone or with friends. He discovered the brook's name on an early nineteenth-century map drawn by Bryant's brother, which specified the now mostly forgotten names of old bodies of water in the town. The poem, Wilbur has said, is "an old-fashioned nineteenth-century nature poem, which builds up to a moral. . . . The central sentence is terribly long and is sometimes challenging to read . . . but that's because there are so many things perceptible at once in the brook."[52] The narrator's basic question "How can I drink all this?" culminates in a moral that is also a response:

> Joy's trick is to supply
> Dry lips with what can cool and slake,
> Leaving them dumbstruck also with an ache
> Nothing can satisfy.

Wilbur had researched the Cummington property's history. A family named York had owned the place in the 1920s; the husband was a sculptor and the wife a painter, which accounted for the elongated ceiling windows in the original structure, part of which they had used as a studio. After much of that structure burned to the ground in the 1930s, new owners added rooms, and the place became a summer retreat for a succession of owners and their friends.[53]

The Wilburs left the existing structure intact and decided to build a new home for themselves on a different section of the property, a place that would incorporate large picture windows framing views of the woods and fields. Charlee planned to oversee the construction from afar, and in the autumn of 1969 the couple rented a small apartment in Middletown, where they continued to lead busy lives. In Charlee's case this included auditing a course in William Blake's poetry and spending six hours a week in an African dance class.[54]

The Wilburs' new house fit themselves and the property well. It was also adaptable—for instance, in 1976 they were able to renovate the ground floor so that Dick's mother, Helen, could live with them after Lawrence died. Charlee enjoyed reading and sunning herself on the deck beside an in-ground pool. She also had a small study on the second floor, where over the years she surrounded herself with so many framed family photos that she ran out of wall space. Though she continued to entertain in the house's

A converted silo at Richard Wilbur's home in Cummington, Massachusetts, circa 1980. Wilbur used the space as a study until a tornado demolished it in May 1995. *Courtesy of Richard Wilbur.*

large formal dining and living rooms, and the home was always open to friends, the pace was less demanding.

Wilbur planted a substantial vegetable garden and became absorbed in weeding and pruning; Charlee often had to coax him inside out of the summer heat. To the right of the driveway, along the path to the old house, was a converted silo that he used as a study: an "ivory tower," Charlee joked. When a tornado demolished it in May 1995, they built a more traditional structure that included a reading room and a writing room, each lined with bookshelves. Charlee called it "the Saint Teresa of studies."[55] They also put in a tennis court, surfaced with a unique clay-gravel mixture to which visiting players had to adjust. In 2011 Wilbur resurfaced the court with a more traditional substance. But by then he was ninety years old, and he conceded that it was no longer prudent for him to play.

Between 1969 and his retirement from Wesleyan in 1975–76, Wilbur taught only in the fall semester. He had arranged this schedule shift to

accommodate an annual winter sojourn to Key West, and the Wilburs purchased a home there in 1975. Yet after retirement he found that he missed
teaching. In 1977 Smith College appointed him as a writer in residence, and
he taught there during the fall semesters until 1985, thus maintaining his
writer-teacher balance.

Official reports of his "on leave" accomplishments, which he submitted
to the Wesleyan provost each year, reflect that balance. The reports list readings and public appearances, essays written, and poems drafted and sold.
They note translations started, completed, and polished; honorary degrees
received; and committees chaired. All included some element of humor.
For instance, "In the course of my spring leave in 1972, I underwent two
longish spells of influenza, during which I did little else but grow a beard.
In lucid intervals, however, certain things did get accomplished. I finished
the poems and illustrations for a book called *Opposites,* designed to amuse
children and others."[56]

During the same leave, however, he also published "The Mind-Reader"
in the *New York Review of Books;* expected to publish "other and subsequent
efforts" in the *New Yorker,* the *American Scholar,* and the *American Poetry
Review;* read at Madison Square Garden with Yevgeny Yevtushenko; read
alone at the National Institute of Arts and Letters, MIT, and Amherst;
delivered a lecture titled "Poetry's Debt to Poetry" at the University of
Minnesota; served on a visiting committee convened by Harvard's English
department; translated poems by Voznesensky and Nikolai Morshen; and
wrote an introduction for a limited edition of his poem "Seed Leaves,"
which was illustrated with a drawing by Charles Wadsworth.[57]

Wilbur's accomplishments during the spring of 1975 were no less diverse
and demanding. They included his new duties as president of the American Academy of Arts and Letters. He and Charlee also took a two-week
archaeological cruise of the Mediterranean; soon after that he read a poem
at Wesleyan's commencement. "As for my tennis game," he wrote at the end
of the report, "it is slower but more intelligent."[58]

12

Overstressed and Overmedicated

"No stranger to what is dark in life"

There is almost a difference in kind between the self which vegetates and deludes itself with "contentment" and the self-overcoming self which drives toward creation and service.

—RICHARD WILBUR, unpublished journal, May 1973

On October 5, 1987, Wilbur began a one-year appointment as the second poet laureate of the United States, following Robert Penn Warren.[1] Although Wilbur was sixty-six years old, he still possessed an accessible, youthful charm, and his credentials were impressive: in addition to a Pulitzer (he won a second during his laureate year), he now had a Bollingen for translation. Daniel Boorstin, the librarian of Congress who announced the appointment, praised him as "a poet for all of us, whose elegant words brim with wit and paradox."[2]

Nonetheless, since the 1960s, Wilbur had been fielding questions from interviewers who saw his formalism as rigid and his poetic voice as detached; in a 1977 *Paris Review* interview, he admitted, "I've begun to crumble a bit, and write more shamelessly of what is near to me." He was still far from embarking on the confessional mode. "It is the thing, and not myself," he explained, "that I set out to explore."[3] Yet his choice of the word *crumble* hints at mounting tensions and stress. Wilbur held himself to high standards in all endeavors, but he had begun to feel the strain of meeting his own expectations. He spoke of needing to escape from the blinkered compulsiveness that goes hand in hand with readying poems for publication—what Stanley Kunitz called being in "poetry prison."[4] During a phone conversation after John Berryman's suicide, the two agreed about the importance of enjoying things apart from reading and not succumbing to the public's (or one's own) pressures.[5]

In 2006 Charlee explained how her husband's career had affected their home life:

> Dick is, as I said many times, a perfectionist, someone who is stoic, who is very much a controller, in a good sense, sometimes in not such a good sense for him, someone who never wants to ask for help. . . . He used to say when we moved to Portland—and his life had gotten very complex by then—"Charlee, do everything. Do everything." And this became a family joke. . . . Well, he meant by that, *Take care of everything around the bones of my life because my professional life is just about eating me up.* So I did. I took care of everything.[6]

A Cantata for Liberty

Like Wilbur, the composer William Schuman had an optimistic and abiding love for America as a country of freedom and promise. The pair knew each other well, having worked together closely in the mid-1970s to consolidate the American Academy of Arts and Letters and the National Institute of Arts and Letters. Their collaboration to create *On Freedom's Ground: An American Cantata for Baritone, Chorus, and Orchestra* (1986) grew from these bonds.

Schuman was a visionary in the world of performing arts and musical education, and in early 1984 he was rediscovering his vigor after recovering from triple bypass surgery. He was looking for a way to reprise the patriotic themes that had moved him to compose his major works, including *American Festival Overture* (1939) and *Prayer in Time of War* (1943). In 1980 he had secured a commission from the New York Philharmonic; now he wanted to fulfill it with a major orchestral chorale commemorating the centennial of the 1886 arrival and assembly of the Statue of Liberty on Bedloe's Island.[7]

Schuman was accustomed to working with verse. For *A Free Song,* winner of the inaugural Pulitzer Prize for Music in 1943, he had adapted two of Whitman's patriotic poems. He had also used Archibald MacLeish's poetry for the chorale *Time to the Old* (1980) and had set eight more Whitman poems to music for the choral cycle *Perceptions* (1982). That same year he had also used his own poetry in the four-section chorale *Esses* (so named because each section's title begins with the letter *s*).

For the Statue of Liberty project, which would be thirty or forty minutes long, Schuman wanted poetry with "heft," so he turned to Wilbur, who had already demonstrated his affinity for the Liberty theme.[8] In 1962 he had asked Wilbur to write a dedicatory poem for the opening of Philharmonic (later Avery Fisher) Hall, the first of the Lincoln Center renovations that marked a cultural rejuvenation in New York City.[9] The poem summons the ancient Greek Muses, evoking their lineage as Memory's daughters as they cross waters traveled by pilgrims and slavers to arrive at a city where Liberty lights the roadways.[10] The poem was printed in the souvenir booklet distributed to concertgoers and published in the *New York Times*.

When Schuman's centennial commission was made public in early 1984, Wilbur sent him a brief note of congratulation and expressed curiosity about the project. Schuman answered with three pages detailing his imagined cantata and asked an unsolicited, unanticipated question: Would Wilbur consider writing the libretto?[11] Wilbur accepted, saying that he was honored by the offer and the challenge. Schuman was envisioning a five-part piece, and on April 5 Wilbur sent the composer drafts of the first two sections, along with a reminder that he could dissolve the partnership at any time. By mid-May the first section was finished (Schuman had requested minor revisions in only five lines), and on July 11 Wilbur forwarded the polished second section.

By the end of July, as work on the third section began, the project showed signs of becoming more complicated. At first Schuman had asked Wilbur to write a poem sequence that would move through a variety of moods—slow and musing, then stirring, then mournful—with the idea that the shift in mood would suggest the music to him. But now Schuman was developing an elaborated musical logic—varying or restating certain motifs—that Wilbur worried would not fit with his own vision of the unwritten remainder of the text.

As Schuman understood, Wilbur's poetic structure required "a reprise with a difference."[12] In section 1 a New York harbor scene that opens the libretto, Wilbur evoked the land before colonial settlement, portraying elements of the natural world using the language of servitude. But in section 5 those same elements of nature "rise" and "wheel" freely in the modern harbor where the Statue of Liberty "has been holding sway." Using images of flight and motion, Wilbur symbolized the country's change in perspective in the way it fought for, achieved, experienced (or not), and thus embodied both the nature and the evolution of freedom. In a 1986 interview Schuman stressed that the idea of change had been central to *On Freedom's Ground:*

"Basically, the subject is America, all the things that are right about it, and all the things that are wrong. It is a land with the possibility of change."[13]

To embody and articulate that theme, Wilbur created a series of images drawn from U.S. history. In section 2 he celebrated the American War of Independence as a catalyst for the French Revolution that began thirteen years later. In the opening of section 3, the longest movement of the cantata and itself subdivided into three parts, he suggested a way to humanize, in an individual rather than a collective way, the process of mourning "the dead who died for this country." As he advanced from one part to the next in this section, he described territorial expansion and the divisions that arose while acts of humiliation, violence, and oppression took hold in the land. The final part of section 3 begins: "Praise to this land and our power to change it, / To confess our misdoings, to mend what we can." Wilbur went on to liken the American people to the Statue of Liberty itself: "Its hammered copper bolted together, / Anchored by rods in the continent's rock, / With a core of iron, and a torch atop it." Schuman's response to the section was "glorious—repeat, glorious."[14]

Thus far, Wilbur's collaboration with Schuman did not exhibit the tensions that had existed between Wilbur and Bernstein during their work on *Candide*. Schuman's initial feedback had cleared the way for what by all accounts was a seamless and swift process.[15] For instance, as soon as Wilbur mentioned his desire to allude to the 1963 March on Washington and Martin Luther King Jr.'s 1968 "I Have a Dream" speech in section 3, Schuman told Wilbur he had retrieved the Negro spiritual "Free at Last" from his recording library.[16]

Now all that remained uncertain was how to handle Schuman's idea of incorporating the iconic Emma Lazarus lines "Give me your tired, your poor" into the cantata. In his initial letter to Wilbur, the composer had wondered if it would be "too corny" to sing the lines in different languages—first consecutively, then in unison.[17] In a letter to Brinnin, Wilbur revealed slight misgivings about the idea but remained open to other possibilities: "Bill now feels, however—and musically I am sure that he's right—that once some splendid baritone has belted out 'Free at last' we need for variety some light, fast, short, high-spirited thing, as a breather before the peroration. So far I have no notions whatever beyond tra-la-la and derry-derry-down, but I suppose something will happen, after which I will feel that it is fun to do."[18]

For this "breather" in section 4, Schuman envisioned a light, swift passage, four or five minutes long. "The word 'Dance' occurs to me," he wrote to Wilbur. "American ethnic groups have almost all kept their traditional dances. Is it worth a thought?"[19] In response Wilbur conjured what he called "an artless ditty."[20]

> Now in our lady's honor
> Come dance on freedom's ground,
> and do the waltz or polka,
> Whatever spins around,
>
> Or let it be the raspa,
> The jig or Lindy hop,
> Or else the tarantella,
> Whatever doesn't stop,
>
> The Highland fling, the hornpipe,
> The schottische or the break,
> Or if you like the cakewalk,
> Whatever takes the cake,
>
> But end it with the John Paul Jones,
> Invented in this land,
> That each of us may circle round
> And take the other's hand.

Wilbur agreed to segue from this verse (if Schuman liked it) to the Lazarus lines in whatever language the composer might fancy. But Schuman now thought it was unnecessary to resurrect them.[21]

For nearly half a year Wilbur's focus on the Statue of Liberty libretto eased the pressure of translating Racine's *Phèdre,* which he had begun in late 1983. The play, he said, was full of characters "just asking for trouble," so working with Schuman offered the "pleasures of English and of comparative serenity."[22] But with the libretto well underway, work on the second act of *Phèdre* loomed. Following an impetus similar to the one that had led him, in 1952, to spend his Guggenheim year translating Molière in New Mexico, Wilbur applied for and received a Camargo Foundation grant. In Cassis, France, he would be free to immerse himself in Racine.

Breeze from the Cassis Harbor

Dick and Charlee planned to arrive in Cassis in January 1985 and stay through May. In the last six months of 1984, however, Charlee became ill with tendonitis. Increasingly weak, she eventually underwent surgery on her leg and a subsequent skin graft to repair the flesh. By mid-November she was facing at least another month of recuperation.

The Camargo fellowship did not give her much hope for rest and relaxation, yet she had no interest in wintering alone in Key West. Charlee was still intimately involved with Wilbur's translation work; and though the projects were sometimes exasperating—and not just because of the demanding work required to find *les mots justes*—she understood that translation itself was integral to Wilbur's sense of his literary vocation, even when the work interrupted his own creative projects.

Unlike the Guggenheim fellowship, the Camargo fellowship came with strings attached. Not only were grant recipients required to reside at Camargo's study center on the harbor at Cassis, just east of Marseilles, but they also had to remain there for the duration (except for brief spells to visit nearby cities) and participate in weekly discussions with other scholars and artists in residence. According to Charlee, the Wilburs' cohort included a Lithuanian scholar who was having trouble settling into her project on "first person singular novels written by women between 1975 and 1985." Other residents included "a Harvard couple working together on a book about suicide in the eighteenth century, and a young man doing a Marxian and Freudian interpretation of Molière's plays." A woman in her forties was focusing on sex in the work of Colette, Anaïs Nin, and Simone de Beauvoir; and a Brandeis scholar was writing a psycho-historical novel about Europe. Other areas of research included pigments used in sixteenth- and seventeenth-century painting as well as an obscure literary form called "leonine hexameters" used in eighteenth-century church inscriptions. Two painters rounded out the group. By mid-February, when Charlee was describing the residents to Brinnin, allegiances among them had already formed, broken, and reformed, seemingly with no hard feelings or unwelcome dropping by for drinks. Nonetheless, her impatience with grant-funded residential life hadn't changed since 1954–55, when the Wilburs spent a year at the American Academy in Rome.[23]

The Wilburs' rented Peugeot had battery problems that prevented them from leaving Cassis during their break week in February, but Charlee seemed content to stay in town. Her daily routine included reading in French for several hours (her letters mention Benjamin Constant's *Adolphe*) and taking walks, including an afternoon jaunt into the port for a newspaper, a citron pressé, and cigarettes. She found the citizens to be friendly, polite, and full of humor, much like the Italians, but stingy—and more impressed by America's president Ronald Reagan than by their own president François Mitterand.[24]

By mid-March Charlee and Wilbur had gotten to see the coast from Cassis west to La Ciotat, the largest shipbuilding site in France. In a letter to Brinnin, who was on Key West, she described Bandol as "a mini old timey Cannes with splendid groomed villas, [and] mimosa trees cascading down the cliffs into the sea." The Wilburs wandered through "narrow, medieval back streets where tall weathered stone houses containing far too many families are minutes away from branches of Dior, Vuitton, and Hermès." She said they "found a tiny place for lunch never viewed by a tourist in its ten-year life, and ate magnificently in an enclosed garden under a huge sycamore tree."[25] As always, she kept an eye on local fashion:

> I have come to know every status symbol of [Cassis]. *All* females between 18 and 30 wear a uniform of black leather tight pants, black leather jacket, black leather gauntlets, high-heeled black leather boots, Vuitton shoulder bags, [and] very small lap dogs on very fancy leashes. Men of the same age bracket wear faded jeans and good black leather jackets, boots. All older men and women wear various kinds of fur or fur-collared coats with high-heeled boots. The men's are cowboy boots. Oddly enough, everyone seems to own a Burberry scarf. We are *in* since we each have one with us. . . . There's enough black leather here to satisfy every gay leather freak in the States. As I may have already said, Key West looks like a slum by comparison.[26]

In her first three letters to Brinnin, Charlee maintained a breezy tone, barely hinting at the stress of Wilbur's work on *Phaedra*. Meanwhile, institutional obligations mounted. Russell Young, Camargo's semi-retired director, was due to arrive in mid-April for a trustees' meeting, the first to be held at the study center, at which time the new director, Michael Pretina, was scheduled to take over officially. Wilbur was enlisted to entertain them with a report of his doings. Charlee told Brinnin, "I must say that there has been something of a 'stir' in these parts over Dick's presence; professors from Nice, Marseilles, Aix, and Nîmes have all been in touch, including French TV to which a prompt NON was the response."[27]

By mid-March Wilbur had completed the fourth act of *Phaedra*, despite being flattened for a week by a stomach virus that had made the rounds among the residents. April had been "miserable with almost steady *mistral*, which brings in the chill and causes various angst and vapors," Charlee reported to Brinnin. Still, Wilbur had "wowed" the trustees with a pre-sentation that had "consisted of a few words about translation, the reading of four short well-known French poems translated by Dick, a balletic and an operatic aria speech from Molière, and finally the first two scenes of [*Phaedra*]." She noted that "Dick is now a scant thirty lines from the end of the play and has promised me on a French bible that he won't do another. I've worked *hours* this winter with him on this and am completely fed up with heroic couplets." Although May promised a full card of luncheons and "winding-down farewell parties," Charlee was already eager to leave.[28]

The Alexandrine Dilemma

For his version of *Phèdre* Racine had adapted a legend that had also appealed to Euripides and Seneca, one that explores the ramifications of illicit passion. Phaedra, the second wife of the heroic king Theseus of Athens, is in love with her stepson Hippolytus, a chaste young man who himself is secretly in love with Aricia, whose family members are political rivals of Theseus. The classical playwrights depicted men and women who succumb to desires and hatred, who neglect moral and social responsibility for the sake of passions, and whose lives come to unhappy and violent ends. In contrast, Racine's Phèdre recognizes and abhors the evil inside her and does what she can to act against it. In his introduction to the play, Wilbur noted that she is a Greek woman with a Christian conscience.[29]

By the time Wilbur began to think about translating the play, Robert Lowell's version of *Phèdre* had already been in print for two decades, meaning that he had already contended with Racine's poetic form: six-beat lines called syllabic alexandrines, a meter that is not "native" to English verse.[30] In the introduction to his translation Lowell emphasized "the general and correct assessment" of the play as "untranslatable":

> We cannot reproduce the language, which is refined by the literary artifice of [Racine's] contemporaries, and given a subtle realism and grandeur by the spoken idiom of Louis the Fourteenth's court. Behind each line is a, for us, lost knowledge of actors and actresses, the stage and the moment. Other qualities remain: the great conception, the tireless plotting, and perhaps the genius for rhetoric and versification that alone proves that the conception and plotting are honest. Matisse says somewhere that a reproduction requires as much talent for color as the original painting. I have been tormented by the fraudulence of my own heavy touch.[31]

Rather than replicating the alexandrine, Wilbur chose to reduce it to "our corresponding English meter, the pentameter." His translation includes the same number of lines (1,654) that Racine's original does—"no triumph," Wilbur wrote, "but an indication that the thought and the tone of Racine's line, even at its most compressed, can pass into our traditional dramatic measure."

> Where I have used slightly more enjambment than Racine, it is mostly because English meters are more emphatic and less flowing than the French: too long a sequence of end-stopped English lines, especially if rhymed, can sound like the stacking of planks in a lumberyard. . . . Since French does not sound like English, a translator who sought to duplicate the "music" of certain famous lines in *Phaedra* would in the first place fail, and, in the second, would doubtless slight the meter and tone, which are primary in all writing. What one must do, I think, is to try throughout for equivalent effects of significant sound and pacing in the key of English, and remember always that one is seeking to be worthy of a magnificent ear.[32]

Lowell based the pentameter of his translation on the styles of Pope and Dryden, using "run on" couplets but "avoid[ing] inversions and alliteration" and "loosen[ing] the rhythm with shifted accents and occasional extra syllables."[33]

A comparison of lines from act 3, scene 6 show how each poet found his way into the sound of the lines. In this scene Hippolytus is worried that King Theseus will continue to believe the false accusation made by Phaedra's nurse and confidante: Hippolytus, she has declared, is guilty of an attempt to seduce the virtuous queen. The speech confessing his love for Aricia is aimed at his father, but only the young man's tutor overhears it. Lowell's translation follows:

> What now? His anger turns my blood to ice.
> Will Phaedra, always uncertain, sacrifice
> herself? What will she tell the King? How hot
> the air's becoming here! I feel the rot
> of love seeping like poison through this house.
> I feel the pollution. I cannot rouse
> my former loyalties. When I try to gather
> the necessary strength to face my father,
> my mind spins with some dark presentiment . . .
> How can such terror touch the innocent?

> I LOVE ARICIA! Father, I confess
> my treason to you is my happiness!
> I LOVE ARICIA! Will this bring you joy,
> our love you have no power to destroy?[34]

Here is Wilbur's version of the same passage:

> How her words chilled me! What was in her thought?
> Will Phaedra, who is still her frenzy's prey,
> Accuse herself, and throw her life away?
> What will the King say? Gods! What love has done
> To poison all this house while he was gone!
> And I, who burn for one who bears his curse,
> Am altered in his sight, and for the worse!
> I've dark forebodings; something ill draws near.
> Yet surely innocence need never fear.
> Come, let's consider now how I may best
> Revive the kindness in my father's breast,
> And tell him of a love which he may take
> Amiss, but all his power cannot shake.[35]

Lowell's version is in tune with his own emphatic and muscular poetic style but is less literal than Wilbur's; the end rhymes don't totally erase the "stacking planks" sound that Wilbur cautioned against, even though Lowell was careful to enjamb several of the lines rather than use rhymed end stops. But the rhyme words themselves are heavier and reverberate more than Wilbur's do. Moreover, Lowell's naturally raw and self-accusatory tone is more forceful than Wilbur's, and those prone to autobiographical interpretation may posit that it derived from Lowell's own history. Twenty years earlier, when he had told his father that he was in love with a girl that his father disapproved of, the pair began a shoving match that ended in a fistfight. Lowell's punch knocked his father back against a grandfather clock.[36] By having Hippolytus exclaim, twice, "I love Aricia," a declaration not in Racine's original, Lowell raised the decibels of Racine's text. Whether he did so unconsciously to echo his own fury or overtly to intensify the tragic plot, he heightened the drama and its emotional impact. In contrast, Wilbur stressed Hippolytus's impulse to explain patiently and rationally that he is in love with a girl who, unluckily, happens to be a mortal danger to his clan.

Lowell died before Wilbur's *Phaedra* was published; but given his propensity to rank himself against his rivals, he would have relished the opportunity to measure his translation against Wilbur's. Nonetheless, both poets did agree that the great scenes of Racine's play belong to Phaedra. If we compare their translations of her soliloquy in act 4, scene 5, we see that the notable differences in style, tone, and word choice are astonishing but not surprising. Lowell's version follows:

> Hippolytus is not insensible,
> only insensible to me! His dull
> heart chases shadows. He is glad to rest
> upon Aricia's adolescent breast!
> Oh thin abstraction! When I saw his firm
> repugnance spurn my passion like a worm
> I thought he had some magic to withstand
> the lure of any woman in the land,
> and now I see a schoolgirl leads the boy
> as simply as her puppy or a toy.
> Was I about to perish for this sham,
> this panting hypocrite? Perhaps I am
> the only woman that he could refuse![37]

The French words for *puppy* and *toy* do not appear in Racine's original, but Lowell's less literal translation allowed him to insinuate an age-based rivalry between Phaedra and Aricia. Adolescent hormones rage, even in the older woman, and Phaedra throws a young person's tantrum.

Such a dynamic doesn't mesh with either Racine's or Wilbur's vision of Phaedra:

> Hippolytus can feel, but not for me!
> Aricia has his love, his loyalty!
> Gods! When he steeled himself against my sighs
> With that forbidding brow, those scornful eyes,
> I thought his heart, which love-darts could not strike,
> Was armed against all womankind alike.
> And yet another's made his pride surrender;
> Another's made his cruel eyes grow tender.
> Perhaps his heart is easy to ensnare.
> It's me, alone of women, he cannot bear!
> Shall I defend a man by whom I'm spurned?[38]

In *Wilbur's Poetry: Music in a Scattering Time,* Bruce Michelson analyzed and compared the Lowell and Wilbur versions of one of Phaedra's later soliloquies (act 4, scene 6), in which Wilbur slows and steadies the pace with prepositional phrases and several single-line sentence constructions.

Michelson's observation also applies to the soliloquy in scene 5. The syntax and pace of Wilbur's translation, at once intense, modern, and noble, "maintain the impression that Phaedra, for all her torment, has not slipped over the precipice into pure hysteria. . . . For Racine, for Wilbur, a mad queen is still a queen." According to Michelson, "the conversation between two major American poets about this antique and rarely staged French tragedy has much to do with identity as we struggle to define it now, about the affirmations which language achieves, in the very act of probing the turmoil of the self."[39] The comparison between the two poets' translations of this scene characterizes, in simple terms, their different poetic identities—Wilbur's sensible restraint, Lowell's impetuous emotional abandon.

From the Mistral to the Valley of the Shadow

After returning from the Camargo fellowship at the end of May 1985, the Wilburs kept a low profile. As Charlee explained to Brinnin in mid-September, they "grounded" themselves in Cummington for the summer, where they slowly began to realize the after-effect of their work on *Phaedra* and their five months in Cassis.

> For the last two clean-up months, I was working right along with Dick checking alternative lines and other small work. Dick was at it the whole time, with only two very brief breaks, seven days a week, ten hours a day. That schedule, coupled with our fight against extreme cold in the apartment, combined to wear us down severely. . . . I had just discovered that the painful joint aches I was having were the result of a condition called polymyalgia rheumatica, a very painful but curable disease caused by stress. Then Dick began to have intermittent insomnia and hypertension. When he was wakeful, I became so too.[40]

Even if Brinnin had read between the lines, he might not have understood the implication of the word *grounded*. As the Wilburs' stress and insomnia had worsened in France their attempts at self-medication had escalated. Wine and cognac hadn't helped, so a local French doctor prescribed two drugs in the benzodiazepine family: Valium (diazepam) and Dalmane (flurazepam). "It was an open prescription," Wilbur said in 2006, "and we just kept taking it."

> When we got back to the States, of course, we were no longer applying to a French drugstore, and it occurred to us to just cut it off. We *were* sleeping better. But as soon as we set those drugs aside we were climbing

the walls, having feelings unlike anything we had had before. We had no idea what was the matter with us. I had a semester to teach at Smith and I couldn't do that. We just came apart.[41]

The Wilburs consulted an American doctor, who recommended the sleep aid Halcyon, but a second doctor told them Halcyon was dangerous and that withdrawal feelings would start almost as soon as they were awake. Instead, he put them on a routine of self-control and exercise. Charlee catalogued the changes for Brinnin:

> We both have gone off all booze, tobacco, medications, and we are on a strict diet as well as a Nautilus exercise regime. I have lost 18 pounds, Dick 10. The delights of becoming slim again are somewhat mitigated by the withdrawal we are still experiencing with all the goodies removed after so many years of gluttony. Dick has been really ill, close to a crack-up, it seemed to me, and he will have to learn to put less pressure on himself. . . . We are not allowed by the doctor to do anything more than our daily responsibilities require of us. My earlier troubles have subsided, but I am still having trouble sleeping as long as Dick does. You certainly are the one to understand this kind of helpless identification as you suffered identically with Bill [Read, Brinnin's partner, who died in 1977]. It goes without saying that I don't want anyone to know about us. Dumb pride, I guess, but there it is.[42]

In 2006 Wilbur admitted:

> That was a very jumbled period, which I can't restore very well. I called a psychiatrist we knew over at the Riggs Institute in Stockbridge. I didn't have the word "depression" in my mind, and I didn't know why I was so jumpy and so sleepless . . . but he was not helpful. We went to a psychologist in Northampton and finally had to ask her, "Where can we go to simply fall to pieces and be treated competently?"[43]

Charlee did not write to Brinnin again until December 22, 1985. "Darling John," she began, "I have been passing through the Valley of the Shadow . . . . . . for three months and am finally coming back to a new life. All of this is too complicated to write; I want to tell you all of it in Key West. Until then, please don't worry, my silence was enforced by circumstance."[44] *Circumstance* referred to the Wilburs' recent ninety-day stay at the Brattleboro Retreat, a drug and alcohol treatment center in Vermont, an hour's drive from Cummington. The psychologist in Northampton had arranged admission. Those three months began a period of revelation, despair, and frustration that the couple experienced in different degrees. In May 1986 Charlee began describing it to Brinnin as "our on-going story."[45]

The Wilburs discussed the ramifications of withdrawal and hospitalization during several interviews in 2006, but the story begins with two entries Wilbur recorded in his journal, the first on September 19, 1985.

> Driven by Chris and Ellen from Cummington to Brattleboro Retreat, Charlee and I were both given private rooms in Ripley House. My vital signs taken by the "AT" Dave: fever of 99.6. After last night's sleep of six hours, prompted by the drug Halcyon, felt somewhat relieved of yesterday's tension. Talked on admission, as I forgot to mention, with a pleasant woman, Barbara _____, Wellesley graduate, former alcoholic. She had lived in Ann Arbor, near Don and Kirby Hall. Dr. Percy Ballantine, the [Amour] Craigs' son-in-law and a psychiatrist, questioned me for a long period about my medical history and other matters, asked me to repeat, memorize and reverse various words and numbers. I seemed to get most of them, but astonishingly was unable to remember the date (I got it wrong by one day) or the current president, Mr. Reagan. Ballantine inclines to push aside my claim that my symptoms are the result of sedatives mistakenly taken for the sake of sleep, at a time (Cassis) when we were nervously frayed and insomniac. That is, he inclines toward the notion that I am psychologically dependent on drugs or alcohol. He has taken me off Halcyon; we shall see if slow breathing will allow me any sleep. We go to the cafeteria between 5 and 6 for whatever a bad tummy will permit us to eat. Then perhaps we'll see "60 Minutes" in the living room. Did I have, as Dr. Ballantine may believe, depression before the onset of what I have considered withdrawal? Charlee thinks so. Am I out of touch with my feelings? Repeated testing of vital signs by nurses Paula and Shawna. Librium to correct blood pressure, etc. Many questionnaires to complete.[46]

On October 3, Wilbur wrote in the journal again. His frustration was measured but palpable. "The Retreat's program is primarily for alcoholics, and they rather want me to fit in with what they can give. Since alcoholics do not readily break down and admit addiction, they are ready to think that I have a convenient confession to make." Wilbur continued to resist being described as an alcoholic. "One taste of a drink does not lead [me] to another and another," he insisted. "Nor have C. and I abused sedatives as alcoholics are described as doing—to calm the morning jitters and mask hangover. We simply wanted to sleep, and overdid it with Valium and Dalmane." Wilbur acknowledged the retreat's "good exercise program" but thought the "groups and meetings during the day rather tiresome on the whole." He deemed the "cafeteria food excellent; fellow patients amiable, from all ranks of society" and noted that "the male nurse Gene declared without prompting that what we were 'withdrawing' from was sedatives, not alcohol. I wish that all of the staff would accept that and adjust to *us*."[47]

Wilbur's journal entries echo several passages in the beginning of *Recovery*, John Berryman's semi-autobiographical novel, incomplete when he died and published posthumously in 1973. The author's thinly disguised personality permeates the main character, Alan Severance, a scholar and a "Nationally Famous Drinker" whose credentials Berryman "qualifies" from the start: "ALAN SEVERANCE, M.D., LITT. D., formerly Professor of Immunology and Molecular Biology, now the University Professor, Pulitzer Prize winner, etc.—twice-invited guest on the Dick Cavett Show (stoned once, and a riot)."[48] The book opens with Severance back in the hospital after his second alcohol relapse, wandering down an unlit hallway in early morning.

> A verse from [the Old Testament Book of] Joel drifted through his mind . . . "Awake ye drunkards, and weep . . . for it is cut off from your mouth." Even so; "Sanctify ye and fast." Light was pouring from a doorway with a black sign "SNACK ROOM" dim on the white wall beside it. A tiny kitchen was all, with four bodies in it. He went confidently in. Greetings, smiles all round. . . . The coffee was bad as ever. . . . Discussion of this fact. Data traded.[49]

Recovery's unflinching view of institutional treatment for addiction, as grounded in the twelve-step recovery program of Alcoholics Anonymous, offers a sense of what Wilbur was encouraged to experience at Brattleboro—if only he could make the "convenient confession" of his alcoholism.[50] Severance reveals that his own first treatments "were not exactly rest cures." He spent a "whole week in Intensive Care," carried out the "'fearless and self-searching' scrutiny of the Fourth Step," applied the "damned Serenity Prayer" to his situation, and owned up to a long list of "vices and shortcomings" as well as to the "up-to-scratch's, if any," as required in the Fifth Step. Yet sobriety wouldn't stick. When a group leader asks him why he has relapsed, Severance answers, "One, I'm damned if I know, Louise. Two, I must have conned Gus Larson [his first sponsor] with my First Step."[51]

Charlee and Dick took different approaches to their Brattleboro recovery. Not only were they in different programs with different doctors, but she welcomed talk therapy while Dick resisted it. "Charlee is more suggestible than I," he said in 2006. "It has something to do with the fact that she has a soft spot in her heart for group therapy. Whatever its purpose she has liked that sort of thing. And I am a total resistor of group therapy. So we found ourselves somewhat estranged. Oh, that's too violent a word. We found ourselves going about it very differently."[52]

Charlee spoke openly in 2006 about the way in which her treatment at Brattleboro had triggered memories of her father's death. She was ten years old.

> I'd sashay back and forth between anger at my mother for surviving him and anger at my father for dying, and not forgiving either one of them. I didn't get over those feelings until we were at Brattleboro [Retreat] and I was in therapy there, a grieving group. I wasn't directed to go by a doctor, I just elected to go, and I found out I could forgive both of them, that they'd both done the best they could do under the circumstances. I came out of that hospital experience much better off than when I first came in, whereas Dick came out much worse off; he had a horrible experience in that hospital because he was in an alcoholic ward, told that he was an alcoholic in denial.[53]

In fact, after a brief period in a closed detox ward, Dick left Brattleboro before Charlee did. "He just got fed up," she said. "He wasn't locked up there, he could leave when he wanted to, and finally one day he said to me 'I'm getting out of here, I can't take it anymore.'" Charlee stayed on for a few more weeks, telling the psychiatrist assigned to her that she would do anything to get better. The withdrawal and its attendant psychological confusion was so painful, she said, that he agreed to work with her for as many hours a week as she needed. "As a result," she admitted, "I said yes to everything, including the alcoholism. I wasn't sure I was an alcoholic, but I could have been. We were heavy drinkers; everybody I knew drank heavily back then." She recalled that Dick's frustration deepened at "being told he was an alcoholic and wasn't while I was accepting treatment regardless of my need for it."[54] As Wilbur acknowledged, "The experience had been very jangling to us, very frazzling. At one point at Brattleboro I got so depressed . . . that if I would sit, for instance, in the lounge to watch Dan Rather give the evening news, I saw the skull beneath his skin. I saw the mortality of everything."[55]

After Charlee left treatment the Wilburs decided to drive slowly south to their home in Key West rather than spend Christmas in Cummington with their children. "We were still looking for help or comfort somewhere," Wilbur explained.

We went as instructed to AA meetings daily. I was just never able to say, "My name's Dick and I'm an alcoholic." Charlee said she was cross-addicted, that's the expression she used which meant that if you had too much Valium as we had had, that you would then be susceptible to drink as if you were an alcoholic. In some sense it may have been useful to go to those meetings, except that I kept feeling it was bullshit.[56]

After one AA meeting, shortly before a somewhat nervous Charlee was scheduled to share her "drunkalog," a group member asked to visit them at their home. Charlee laughed: "[He] told us we didn't belong in AA. Whereupon Dick made a big gin and tonic! And we were out from that horror." In the next breath, however, she admitted, "We did not feel physically well for over two years; it took that long to get over that frightful drug exposure and withdrawal."[57]

Both Wilburs underwent surgery in May 1986: she on her left knee and right elbow, he on his knee. As the month came to a close, Charlee still wasn't ambulatory. Although her bone spur troubles weren't a cause for alarm, they created considerable frustration. In a letter to Brinnin she had little to report except "recovering stages of *me*." Then, almost as an afterthought, she told him about "a curious finale" to the couple's ongoing story: "We are now told to drink moderately if we wish—that it never was a problem; that everything that happened was just the conjunction of potent medicines in France combined with accumulated fatigue."[58] Still, the story wasn't over. Three years later, on November 20, 1988, Charlee wrote to Brinnin from the New England Medical Center Hospital in Boston:

> Here I am as of Thursday last, and I feel hugely grateful that I am already on the road to feeling much better. Dick & I have simply not gotten back to normal since the !85 [*sic*] Trauma. This unit is imminently [*sic*] equipped to help us. There are, thanks to the status as a teaching hospital, five doctors and one special nurse assigned to my team. Dick arrives tomorrow. He's been struggling for three years with no relief for a lot of pain and tension.
>
> Please don't worry. This is just the place that I had hoped to find, and we'll let things follow their own course with no plans yet for Key West.[59]

In 2006 Charlee explained that she and Dick shared a room at the medical center for several weeks. "And then Dick got out of that situation; it turned out to be more AA group stuff, more of the same, which he didn't need. But I proceeded to stay longer to see if I could get somewhere with this."[60]

Charlee was scheduled to "get sprung," as she phrased it, on December 13.

> I must conclude here and be honorably discharged. A *marvelous* hospital, and it turns out the whole family is getting a lot [from it]. All chemical, psychological and attendant problems seem to be behind us. (It never was alcohol.) Dick is better than in years, rested and beginning to be self-aware. I can only be hugely grateful. Since all of the kids have been with us all the way we will be skipping a big family Christmas and we'll have a simple one in the beloved [Key West] compound.[61]

During the next eighteen months Charlee's and Brinnin's steady correspondence lapsed into less frequent notes. Then, on June 30, 1990, she sent him a three-page letter, addressing it to Edgehill Hospital in Newport, Rhode Island, where several days earlier Brinnin had entered an alcohol detox program. "I first of all hope that withdrawal is not too painful," she said. She reminded him that she and Dick had been detoxing from two powerful and dangerous drugs and had already been suffering from clinical depression when they entered Brattleboro Retreat. "The people we knew who were just going off booze were rather quickly over really bad feelings. I pray that this is true of you." She suggested writing about the experience in a journal, saying that she was sorry she hadn't done so herself, and told him how proud she was. "You have accepted this and taken strong action on your own."[62]

On July 10 Charlee wrote to Brinnin again. She and Dick had returned the night before "from a five-day jaunt to Canada—primarily for the world premiere of Dick's *Phaedra* as directed by Brian Bedford at Stratford. We were flown up to Toronto, driven the two hours to S. in limo, put up in Victorian British splendor at 'Birmingham Manor,' and wined and dined elegantly. . . . The *Phaedra* was a smashing success, so far with rave reviews. . . . We are hopeful for the future of the play." She mentioned their relief upon finding two letters from him in the morning mail and promised to send him "the requested stamps and cigs." She also gave him what amounted to "treatment advice" from the vantage of someone who'd been in his shoes. Raising uncomfortable issues relating to his denial and self-destruction, she spoke of what she and Dick had experienced: "I (indeed both of us) occupied hot seats on a number of occasions, and the only way to handle that is with scrupulous honesty."[63]

Charlee later said that the recovery periods that the Wilburs and Brinnin underwent marked a shift in their relationship.

[Dick and I] had that awful experience in the hospital, and then [John] was hospitalized for alcoholism. . . . And first he was drinking and we weren't and then we were drinking and he wasn't. And there was some loss of intimacy at that time, and it was never totally restored, and that just killed me. [John] became attached to several other people in the way he'd been attached to me. That was fine with me, but I was sad that our relationship changed at the end of his life. No lack of affection, but we were just on different wavelengths.[64]

"He doesn't suffer, or if he does he can't express it"

In October 1987 David H. Van Biema, a Wesleyan alumnus, interviewed Wilbur for an article in *People* magazine: "Almost Alone Among His Peers, America's New Poet Laureate Survives." Preoccupied with the theme of burnout, Van Biema prompted Wilbur to recall the ranking wars that Roethke and Lowell had instigated some thirty years earlier. He noted that they and other poets of that generation—Schwartz, Jarrell, Berryman— were now gone and thus "out of the running" for the laureateship. But for forty years, "as poetic fashion changed around him, as his friends flared and collapsed like stars, [Wilbur] continued to write much the same kind of elegant, thoughtful, witty verse he was writing back in 1957."[65]

Van Biema raised the common criticism that Wilbur "doesn't suffer, or if he does he can't express it." Responding indirectly to this charge, Wilbur identified two impulses at work in the creation of poetry. One is "the inclination to celebrate things, the capacity for wonder." ("No reader of his poems would begrudge him this," Van Biema admitted.) Second is "the desire to correct the chaos of oneself and the world." Then Wilbur commented mildly, "I am no stranger to what is dark in life."[66]

There is no doubt that many of Wilbur's peers endured illnesses and addictions that were more debilitating than his own, and many did seek treatment both in and out of mental institutions. Yet unlike poets such as Lowell, Plath, Roethke, Berryman, and Sexton, he did not make his mental suffering a subject of his poetry—with one exception: the poem "At Moorditch," published in *Mayflies* (2000). The title is from Shakespeare's *Henry the Fourth, Part 1* (act 1, scene 2), in which Prince Hal says to Falstaff, "What sayest thou to a hare, or the melancholy of Moor Ditch?" In a note to the poem Wilbur wrote: "Moorditch seemed to me a good name for the sort of hospital where people are treated for depression."[67] To dramatize

such a predicament, he created a dialogue between a first-person narrator
and the building that imprisons him:

> "Now," said the voice of lock and window-bar,
> "You must confront things as they truly are.
>   Open your eyes at last, and see
> The desolateness of reality."
>
> "Things have," I said, "a pallid, empty look,
> Like pictures in an unused coloring book."
>
> "Now that the scales have fallen from your eyes,"
> Said the sad hallways, "you must recognize
>   How childishly your former sight
> Salted the world with glory and delight."
>
> "This cannot be the world," I said. "Nor will it,
> Till the heart's crayon spangle and fulfill it."

Not surprisingly, given his earlier resistance to the Brattleboro Retreat
program, the poem takes issue with modern psychiatric treatment of both
depressive personalities and those who defend or deny their afflictions. The
corroborations of Berryman's *Recovery* come to mind once more, particularly a scene in which Severance describes the tactics of Gus, a treatment
supervisor:

> Gus is fond of glaring at some shivering alcoholic who has just recited his
> sins, leaning forward with his hands on his thighs and elbows out—a bru-
> tal type, coarse with suspicion—and booming at him, "You're a drunken
> *lying* halfassed bum!" Or he leans back, with a tender expression, and says
> gently: "In my opinion, you're not an alcoholic. I don't know what you're
> doing here. If I could drink the way you do—or say you do—friend, I
> *would*."[68]

"At Moorditch" looks toward the creative imagination for a better cure,
an approach reminiscent of the way in which John Stuart Mill read himself
out of a nervous breakdown with the aid of Coleridge's and Wordsworth's
poetry.[69] Though it limns the gloom and depression endemic to mental
breakdown, Wilbur's poem rejects the medical profession's diagnosis of
the condition, affirming instead that such sickness is not "reality." The
"heart"—by which Wilbur likely meant the part of us that engages and
finds meaning, pleasure, and remorse in our existence—perceives true
"reality" and is as well the wielder of the "crayon." "At Moorditch" refuses to
incarcerate the reader, or the poet for that matter, within any mental illness.

In the coda of the poem Wilbur chose "spangle" to convey the shimmer of a world that is responsive to our delight in it.[70] Likewise the word "childishly," which appears in the previous stanza, signifies the narrator's refusal of and triumph over the poem's gloomy institutional voice, which demands an adult acceptance of the world's desolation. Wilbur identified with the way in which children color reality through their instinctive capacity for wonder, but a reader may also hear an echo of Wordsworth's formulation in "Lines Composed a Few Miles above Tintern Abbey": reality is the "mighty world / Of eye and ear,—both what they half create / And what perceive"[71]

In the grown-up world, adults paint reality with the use of intoxicants; and words and images associated with alcohol appear in a number of Wilbur poems, especially in those that use an impasto technique—that is, a thick layering of image upon image. None of these poems is primarily about drunkenness. Nonetheless, alcohol was ubiquitous in mid-twentieth-century social settings; and given the heavy drinking among Wilbur's peers, as well as Dick and Charlee's acknowledged struggles with the combination of alcohol and prescription drugs, the imagery of intoxicants is notable.

"The Terrace," published in *Ceremony* (1950), is one such poem. Here, Wilbur described an alfresco meal:

> We drank in tilted glasses of rosé
> From tinted peaks of snow,
> . . .
> When we were done we had our hunger still;
> We dipped our cups in light;
> We caught the fine-spun shade of clouds
> In spoon and plate;
>
> Drunk with imagined breathing, we inhaled
> The dancing smell of height.

In "Piccola Commedia," published in *The Mind-Reader* (1976), the liquor goes "like an ice pick" into the speaker's mind. Wilbur also used alcohol imagery to imbue objects with color and intensify senses other than sight. "Rocks flush rose" in "On the Marginal Way" (in *Walking to Sleep*, 1969), for instance; and in "Part of a Letter" (in *Ceremony*) an arbor is full of "whiffs of anise, a clear clinking / Of coin and glasses" while the wind creates "shadows in relay races / Of sun-spangles over . . . the drinkers' dazzled faces." These images impart a cinematic, shifting focus to the poems.

Other poems invoke a sense of morphing from the physical to the metaphysical or from a mundane reality to a state of being outside objective experience. For instance, in "Merlin Enthralled" (in *Things of This World*, 1956) Arthur and his heroic knights "leav[e] their drained cups on the table round" to search for the legendary magician, whose imagination "endows the world with purpose and value." Wilbur has said that in this poem, as in so many, he expressed his difference with Poe, who saw imagination as an escape rather than an inspiration.[72]

In the title of "A World without Objects Is a Sensible Emptiness" (in *Ceremony*), Wilbur invoked Thomas Traherne, a seventeenth-century theologian who viewed such a world as a "greater misery than death or nothing."[73] The poem opens with imagery that suggests a retreat from the world: "The tall camels of the spirit / Steer for their deserts . . . / To the land of sheer horizon, hunting Traherne's / *Sensible emptiness.*" The speaker implores the camels—"O connoisseurs of thirst, / Beasts of my soul who long to learn to drink / Of pure mirage"—to guard against what shimmers "on the brink of absence," for "auras, lusters / And all shinings need to be shaped and borne." The "pure mirage" so appealing to the soul is similar to drunkenness, in which one achieves at best a delusional and temporary escape from the messiness of the world and its objects. Initially enhancing feeling and perception, the state leads inexorably to depression and numbness.

"A Voice from under the Table," published in *Things of This World*, evokes a toast, perhaps to Plato's *Symposium*, itself a series of speeches delivered at a drinking party; the title alludes to the place relegated to the loser of a drinking contest. The critic Robert Pack, quick to notice that Wilbur's diction is "as high as his posture is low," also noted the wordplay in "holy [wholly] lucid drunkenness."[74] The speaker tells us that before falling into "low distress" he had "swallowed all the phosphorus of the seas," a nod to the extraordinarily reactive properties of the element and its capacity to create an inner glow.[75] He puns on the word *spirit*—"The end of thirst exceeds experience. / A devil told me it was all the same / Whether to fail by spirit or by sense"—conveying a conviction that thirst is a physiological embodiment of unfilled desire. According to Pack, by "combining the high sense of human aspiration with an allusion to his inebriation," the speaker "acknowledges the contradictory extremes of the human psyche, our proclivity to long for transcendence, to dream of immortality," arrayed against "our creaturely finitude, our construction out of dust."[76] The poem's final image suggests that the drunken speaker does not deny what he calls the foolishness of his condition, yet he is not ready to change it:

> I am a sort of martyr, as you see,
> A horizontal monument to patience.
> The calves of waitresses parade about
> My helpless head upon this sodden floor.
> Well, I am down again, but not yet out.
> O sweet frustrations, I shall be back for more.

Significantly, the phrase "down again, but not yet out" can also suggest the repeated attempts an alcoholic might make to get sober before hitting "bottom"—the so-called last stop before recovery begins.

At some point between 1988 and 1992—that is, between the end of the Wilburs' stay at New England Medical Center and the end of Brinnin's stay at Edgehill—Wilbur summarized in his journal a conversation about depression that he had had with Brinnin:

> John B. tells me that his clinical depression ended, "inexplicably," after the death of Bill. In other words, depression and grieving are not at all the same. Perhaps the death put an end to anxiety—which does have to do with depression. Yet, as he says, the thing about depression is that it seems causeless and unrelated—that unrelatedness is the essence of it. Numbness of mind, withdrawal of affect from the world. Barbara Gordon, in her *I'm Dancing as Fast as I Can,* reports that in depression she could not think rationally, but that her mind was full of associational activity.
>
> Hope and despair are not, I think, based upon reasons. . . . Emily D[ickinson]'s "glee without a cause." Coleridge's unaccountable dejection. The presence or absence of the spirit.[77]

When Wilbur told Van Biema that he was "no stranger to what is dark in life," he did not elaborate on that darkness. There was no mention of addiction or recovery in the *People* article. He may have been referring to his wartime service, when he witnessed the conflict's effects on "the one and the many," or to his brother Lawrie's mental difficulties, which had been exacerbated by wartime posttraumatic stress. *Dark* certainly defined the years after the Wilburs' son Aaron was diagnosed with autism, before the Jungian therapist helped free Charlee from self-blame, and would apply to a time of loss ahead. But as Wilbur said in 2003, "The world is full of wonders." His faith, "that we are in the hands of a good God," offered him reassurance: "whatever happens will quite possibly be all right."[78]

13

Key West Winters

"Isaiah's holy mountain"

What people did about difference [in Key West] was to laugh at it, or laugh with it, laugh not in an unkind manner. And Charlee and I thought, We have found our way to Isaiah's holy mountain. This is where the lion lies down with the lamb. And so it seemed for a long time.

—RICHARD WILBUR, interview, "Discovering Key West," ca. 2005

Wilbur got the idea of going to Key West from the painter Samuel Green, a colleague at Wesleyan, who questioned the wisdom of wasting money on airfare to a remote tropical paradise when America had its own subtropics. Green characterized the island with the same qualities he attributed to the film *Bonnie and Clyde:* beauty and tawdriness. When Wilbur told him he thought the film was morally dubious but delightful, the matter was settled. "Then you'll like Key West," Green replied.[1]

Key West's reputation as a writer's haven began in the late 1920s, when John Dos Passos brought Ernest Hemingway there to fish. During the 1930s Hemingway recruited other writers and celebrities to the island, often through bulletins that emphasized both hard work and play. "Cut a ton of crap from the proofs and spread it around the alligator pear trees which are growing to be enormous. Second crop of limes. 3rd crop of Gilbeys," he wrote to Dos Passos in April 1932. "Caught the biggest tarpon they've had down here so far this season. Sixty-three pounds," he wrote to Maxwell Perkins in April 1928. Hemingway's legacy remains a huge tourist draw today, and visitors still flock to his home (where descendants of his six-toed cats still roam) and to haunts such as Sloppy Joe's.[2]

Tennessee Williams first came to Key West in 1941, and photos and artifacts linked to his stay are collected in an exhibit building on Truman Avenue—the same street where he was baptized (with, according to island lore, encouragement from his brother and a fair amount of alcohol) at the Basilica of Saint Mary Star of the Sea. Between 1945 and 1960 Robert Frost spent winters in a small cottage behind the old colonial home of Jessie Porter, a fifth-generation conch (the local term for a native Key Wester) and island preservationist. Known to everyone as Miss Porter, she entertained Hemingway, Frost, Williams, and Wallace Stevens in her exotic gardens. Elizabeth Bishop came to fish in Key West in 1937, writing to Marianne Moore that she loved the island because it was "inexpensive, wild and dilapidated." Bishop purchased a clapboard house on White Street in 1938 and lived there each winter until 1946, when the U.S. Navy bought up all the properties in the area.[3]

An element of tackiness offset Key West's natural beauty, a combination that appealed to both of the Wilburs.[4] Years later Charlee recalled the island's atmosphere when they first arrived in 1967:

> We went there before anyone else went there, and by anybody I don't mean Tennessee or Hemingway or any of those people. I mean the later influx [of writers]. We went there in the sixties. It was a completely unfound depressing town, very crummy, houses falling down, sidewalks heaving upward, roots of old trees unattended. Everyone got along well there: it was Navy/civilian, gay/straight, black/white, Cubans. This is what attracted us, . . . a kind of a marvelous Garden of Eden, a mixing of everybody without racial tension. Benign funny jokes being told, each group to the other.[5]

By 1991 the Wilburs had been wintering in Key West for nearly twenty-five years, and that summer an article about the island appeared in the *Village Voice*. In it the journalist Andrew Kopkind considered the changes that development had wrought even as he noted that its demographic hadn't much changed since the Wilburs' first visit, despite what Charlee called the "later influx" of writers. Key West was "small enough to bike around in half an hour," Kopkind said, but "has more distinct populations in eight square miles (counting salt ponds and coral sand fill) than many big cities." Nonetheless, his take on this diversity was less idealized than the Wilburs' had been in the late 1960s. "The island," he wrote, "has a tradition of compartmentalizing its communities, . . . [yet in] the general context of tolerance . . . for which Key West is rightly famous, separateness has its certain charms."[6]

Pied Pipers of Windsor Lane

On their first trip to Key West the Wilburs stayed in a motel called the Sun 'n' Surf, on the Atlantic side of the island, at a cost of $25 a night. One Sunday morning, Charlee remembered, they rented two bikes and headed from the motel down South Street. Dick rode in front, and she saw his bike approach a police car parked on the right. Two officers sat inside, and Dick saluted them as he passed. When she passed the car, she saw that the cops were sharing a can of Coca-Cola between them.

> They were just sitting there, jawing. And I rode by slowly and said, "Good morning. What are you two doing, goofing off?" And the man at the wheel leaned over with a perfect Jack Benny expression and said, "No, we're in love." . . . That's the kind of thing, cops make jokes . . . people all living together, all putting up with each other's frailties and foolishness. That all began to change as soon as money came in, that was one thing; developers contributed to the changing aspect of the place.[7]

By 1967, Wilbur had arranged with Wesleyan to teach only in the fall semester, which meant that he and Charlee could extend their stays in Key West beyond holiday and winter breaks. Both were fond of an efficiency apartment facing the sea at the end of the second-floor balcony of the Sun 'n' Surf—"Very crumby [sic] but clean and the best outlook on the Island."[8] Still, after several years the Wilburs decided to buy their own efficiency apartment in a former motel on Elizabeth Street.

Initially, the couple was attracted to the island because it was a place away from writers, yet before long they led their northern friends south— like pied pipers, Charlee often joked. John and Judith Ciardi and John and Barbara Hersey were among the first, followed by Ralph and Fanny Ellison and then James Merrill (first, with his partner David Jackson; later with Peter Hooten). Writers Peter Taylor and Alison Lurie, who were close to Merrill and Jackson, wintered in Key West as well. The novelist Robert Stone and his wife, Janice, arrived somewhat later, and the list grew longer as the years went by.

John Brinnin, who favored the island of Saint Thomas as a winter desti- nation, needed enticement to visit Key West. After much encouragement from Charlee, he and Bill Read finally promised to give the island a try in late winter 1975. (After that visit, Brinnin became a regular.) In February Charlee typed out an annotated list of restaurants and other amenities, knowing that she and Dick would be away the first week of John and Bill's stay. Le Mistral on Duval Street was "GOOD" and an easy two-block walk from Pier House, where she had suggested they stay. The Fourth of July was a Cuban place that served no liquor, only beer and wine; she recommended the shrimp enchilada, flan for dessert, and a glass of sangria. She told them that a friend, identified only as "Anne," owned Luigi's: "Introduce yourselves. T. Williams' favorite spot. Have the veal Français and the house salad dressing." If they wanted to try the Sands, located on the beach at Simonton, they should make a reservation if they expected "to eat on the sand, literally. Only good for freshly caught fish of the day." Logun's Lobster House served "poorish food" but it featured "a GREAT ragtime pianist named Billy Nine Fingers. Give him our love." As for the bars: "You should find out for yourselves. The Hemingway bar, Sloppy Joe's, is nothing but a noisy tourist hangout, with expensive, poor drinks. The small Pier House bar is where, late, you find the old salts of the island." For "filthy flicks," she noted, there was the Munro Theatre on Duval Street.[9]

Charlee gave Brinnin several names and phone numbers to call if he and Bill wanted to socialize. About one couple she wrote: "He's retired from something-or-other to become 'a writer.' . . . They are THRILLED (YEAH) to meet another WRITER." Then there was "a really kooky woman," a perpetual southern belle widowed in her sixties, whom Charlee had met sitting under the hair dryer. "Her current flame is the owner of the Pier House. Tell her that Charlee Wilbur, for whom she is looking for a house and whom she met at Donald's Beauty Shop, advised you to give her a ring. . . . The odd thing about Key West," she told Brinnin, "is that people whom you hardly know expect to be called by friends or kept in touch with. Very nice and informal-like, no?" Then she had one more idea: "Yehuda Guttman is in the telephone book. He is a concert pianist, and his wife Ruth is a puppeteer. They have a theatre in their backyard. . . . Call Mrs. Guttman and ask if her husband is giving any concerts during your stay."[10]

In 1975 a local entrepreneur began to renovate eleven dilapidated properties on Windsor Lane, located on the eastern slope of Solares Hill and running past the cemetery in Old Town. The Wilburs encouraged writer friends to buy up these revamped condominiums. Their effort to fill the units may seem curious, given Wilbur's pleasure in the island as "a place away from writers" as well as the fun Charlee would poke at writer groupies and her later dismay about what developers were doing to change Key West's ambiance. But surrounding herself with close friends, writers or not, was important to her.

The Wilburs themselves bought three properties in the development, which came to be known as Windsor Grove. (Charlee preferred to call it "the Compound.") Two they resold almost immediately, but they kept the dove-blue cottage at 715R Windsor Lane, which they had originally purchased for $17,000. Wilbur tended a variety of tropical flowering plants in pots on the deck. Avocado and grapefruit trees kept the house partially hidden from both the neighbors and a communal swimming pool. To celebrate their fiftieth wedding anniversary in 1992, the Wilburs added a second floor to the house, not only for more living space but also to take advantage of cooling breezes.[11]

In 1983 the novelist David Kaufelt founded the annual Key West Literary Seminar, and a year later he began to conduct walking tours past the homes of writers.[12] In 1990 he led an early morning walk through Old Town, an event that was recorded and later featured on National Public Radio. First, he took the group to Hemingway's house, where he spoke of "Papa" as the "first media star" of Key West. According to Kaufelt, Hemingway came to hate such attention, so he hired a builder to construct a brick wall around his house. Eventually, the group paused at Windsor Grove, and Kaufelt remarked on its modesty, calling it "the first [writer's] compound of its kind." He also warned that his friend John Hersey had promised to hurl a brick at his head if he let any of the tour group inside.[13]

In a 1994 review of Hersey's posthumous story collection, *Key West Tales,* the Florida-based author Les Standiford shared an apocalyptic thought he'd had while scouting for celebrities at a cocktail party associated with that year's Key West Literary Seminar.

> I turned and remarked to a friend that, were a bomb to go off in the place, writerly America would be decimated. In a town the size of Winesburg, thousands of miles from any place that could be called a literary center, there was Richard Wilbur hobnobbing with John Malcolm Brinnin, stepping out of the way of James Merrill, who bumped into John Ciardi, with host Tomas Sanchez across the room holding forth to Ann Beattie and Joy Williams, while Rust Hills rubbed elbows in a group that included Seymour Lawrence, Tom McGuane and Richard Ford. And those were just some of the hometown folks in attendance.[14]

Kaufelt came up with what he called "the Peter Pan theory" to explain the literary draw of Key West: "Freud said that we are at our most creative when we are in our very early youth, before we're five years old. That's where we are here. We wear shorts, we ride bicycles, we have the water, a great symbol of the unconscious, and we're free to be children here and let our spirits go. There's nobody in suits and ties telling us what we have to do."[15] Charlee echoed this rationale in 2005, when she spoke of the island's effect on her husband. She said that it gave him a respite from northern responsibility, from academic life, from other professional duties, from an exhausting reading circuit, and, of course, from the New England cold. But most of all, she saw Key West as a playground that nurtured Wilbur's childlike pleasures—games on the grass with friends and bicycle rides into town.[16]

Serious Fun and Games

Wilbur also relished the times when he and his Key West cohort gathered for anagram competitions. Hersey, Ciardi, Merrill, and Brinnin were his fiercest rivals; in fact, Ciardi and Brinnin had been playing with him since their Cambridge days. When Wilbur was a child, his godmother Helen Pigeon and her mother taught him to play anagrams—"an ur-form of Scrabble," as he has called it. "You have a whole lot of tiles as in Scrabble but no numerical value assigned to them," he explained. Likewise, each set has a "standard distribution of tiles; so many Es and Ts, and so on," but here is where any real similarity to Scrabble ends.[17]

Hersey's short story, "A Game of Anagrams," explains the rules and procedures for "kibitzing readers who are vague about how the game is played." Basically, players take turns forming words of at least three letters and then build longer words by adding one or more letters at a time and rearranging the letters to make new words. "Thus BUN may become BURN, then BRUNT, then perhaps BLUNTER, and so on." Altering one's own words is always possible, but stealing and rearranging the words of one's opponents is a far better strategy. After finishing a turn, the player deposits a leftover letter from his or her pile of tiles into a "hope-giving reservoir of tiles at the center of the table." Players who take a chance on a complex combination of letters may face a challenge from a player who doubts the word's existence. The requisite dictionary on the table decides who's right, and whoever is wrong "loses not only face but also his next turn. To win a player must wind up with eight intact words."[18]

Hersey based the characters in "A Game"—three poets and novelist who play together every Wednesday afternoon—on himself and his real-life rivals, and the story is a subtle but hilarious social satire. "The poets are comfortable with each other," the narrator explains, "because all three have won the Pulitzer Prize and the National Book Award. Two of them, Forester and Drum, have also won the Bollingen. . . . The novelist has also taken the Pulitzer, as readers with good long memories may recall."[19] (Hersey had won his Pulitzer, for *A Bell for Adano* in 1944, more than a decade before the other writers in his real-life group had won theirs.)

The poet named Drum shares some of Merrill's attributes: aside from winning the Bollingen Prize, he has been saddled with a famous surname. Yet "emphatic as [Drum] may be at the podium, he is by nature mild and peaceable." The poet named Forester is a send-up of Wilbur:

> Readers of Forester's poems will recall the profusion of fauna in them. The critic Bouvier has spoken of this poet's exemplifying the possibility that a person's name may come in the long run to shape his bent, and commenting on the woodsiness of Forester's poems, he speaks of "the moral force of the man's bestiary, set so lavishly among the trees." The other three players have come to expect Forester to purloin their own little prize wordlets, again and again, and to rescramble them into the names of very obscure creatures—extant, extinct, mythical. It takes courage to challenge any of the ditsy zoa Forester trots out.[20]

According to Hersey's narrator:

> A bare-bones description of the game [which goes on for a full page] gives no idea of the interminable ponderings we will sit through with these players, the sighs, the yelps like little foxes, and the catacombic moans, and sudden snaps of recognition, and tiles moved into place with trembling fingers, and, after thefts, victims' tightened lips hastily modulating into halfheartedly admiring smiles at inspired outrages of robbery. There are also, it must be said, wonderful bursts of laughter that come from these four, for they do enjoy their follies.[21]

Reading the letters that Wilbur and Brinnin exchanged over the years will allay any suspicion that Hersey stepped up the anxious pulse of real-life anagrams games for literary effect. Writing in 1962 Wilbur announced, "I shall settle with you at our next anagrams session—during which by the way I plan to take your word LOFTY and change it to FYLFOT, thereby breaking your spirit altogether."[22] In 1994 he wrote, "Now we are packing for Key West. . . . I am spoiling of course, for an opportunity to take your DESSERT and change it to STRESSED."[23] In 1998 he mused, "When we start organizing anagrams at our next location, which I suspect will be heaven, we must invite only dumb guys who don't know about dugongs."[24]

The Key West group welcomed newcomers to anagrams, but sometimes underestimated their word skills. Wilbur recalled, "Once Brinnin and Hersey and probably Jimmy Merrill were playing anagrams with me on a table outside of Brinnin's beachfront digs, and Bill [Wilfred] Sheed appeared leaning over the balcony from the second floor. I hadn't met him before. We said, 'Why don't you come down and play a little anagrams with us,' and he said, 'I've never played,' and we said, 'We'll tell you when you win.' We felt pretty superior about his chances, and damn if he didn't win. He took the game."[25]

In Brinnin's diary from the winter of 1981 he recorded the games played and won as routinely as he noted the cocktails downed, the sunsets watched, and the impromptu dinners consumed. Claire's on Duval Street was a favorite last stop on a typical night:

1/14: At four, Ciardis for anags. John H., Dick, Jimmy—Dick winning both games. Eve. Dinner w. David and Jimmy chez Jackson.

3/2: Noon, Jimbo, Del, Larry, my sands. 5. With D. to Wilburs; sunset; Claire's.

3/4: Anags with Dick, Jimmy, John C.—win both games.

3/20: Eve. Call for Jimbo, join David's farewell party for Jimmy where, for the first time, see an actual transaction of Ouija board dictation. On hand, Herseys & Brook; Frank & Steve; Joe Lash; Evan Rhodes; Ilse & Gibson; Fanny Ellison; Ciardis & Ben—then on to Claire's.[26]

For years Merrill and Jackson, often in the presence of literary friends, had been consulting a Ouija board and its guide-spirit, whom Merrill called Ephraim. According to Merrill, Ephraim was a Greek Jew once in the court of Tiberius. Merrill and Jackson frequently used the board to receive messages, which were spelled out a letter at a time as their hands guided the planchette. In his ninety-page narrative poem "The Book of Ephraim," published in *Divine Comedies* (1976), Merrill interwove personal memories with chronicles of the communications that Ephraim facilitated with shades and spirits, including Plato and W. H. Auden. *Mirabell: Books of Number* (1979) continued to chronicle Ephraim's contacts with spectral beings; and both books were absorbed into his enormous epic poem, *The Changing Light at Sandover* (1982), which was released a year after Brinnin witnessed the Ouija demonstration mentioned in his diary.

Merrill's later style was rife with involuted language and astonishingly allusive imagery. It was the opposite extreme of the everyday American idiom championed by William Carlos Williams, which, he argued, should be so direct and colloquial that "cats and dogs" could read it.[27] The critic August Kleinzahler called Merrill "a hopeless voluptuary when it comes to language; . . . addicted to wordplay, cleverness with form, ingenious rhymes."[28] Such talents made him not only an ideal anagrams player but also a formidable epigrammatist; his birthday on March 3, just two days after Wilbur's, became an opportunity for an annual verse exchange between the poets. For example, to accompany a silly sun hat that he gave to Merrill on one birthday, Wilbur wrote the following explanation on a card:

> James Merrill is a much-belaurelled chap
> Whose feathers are too many for his cap.
> That he may wear them all, we offer him
> A bit of head gear with a spacious brim.[29]

Not long after Wilbur completed "Sir David Brewster's Toy"—a poem celebrating the kaleidoscope's "sixfold gaudiness," which in his view evokes "Heaven's" infinite repertoire of joys—he gave Merrill a small kaleidoscope as a birthday gift, along with this verse:

> Jimmie, we know that you are fond
> Of trafficking with the Beyond,
> Where blinding light includes the spectrum
> And immaterial bow and plectrum
> Make sounds too sweet for mortal ears.
> Still, for your earthlier moments, here's
> A thing to dangle in the sun
> Of Key West or of Stonington,
> Whereby in broken hues you'll see
> The radiance of eternity.[30]

Wilbur and Merrill were the featured readers at "An Evening with Two Great Poets," a benefit for the Florida Endowment for the Humanities that was held at Key West's Waterfront Playhouse on March 13, 1991. The poet J. D. McClatchy wrote in the program's biographical notes, "Between them, Wilbur and Merrill have more medals on their chests than the Joint Chiefs of Staff," and over the years such awards and accolades had been opportunities for frequent gifts of occasional verse.[31] Merrill celebrated the announcement of Wilbur's poet laureateship in April 1987 with the following poem:

> Such news from an Easter chick!*
> Henceforth how to be cynical?

See Dick upon his pinnacle!
Congratulations, Dick!

Speak now to multitudes, O Laureate,
And set Parnassus glistening!
The heads of State not listening,
Excoriate![32]

The Wilbur-Merrill correspondence includes a remarkable volley of such poems and riddles, all of which reveal not only mutual respect but also the poets' good humor and ready wit. In February 1994, when Merrill was at home in Stonington, Connecticut, Wilbur sent him a postcard he had saved from a 1964 trip to Stockholm:

This picture [of a reflecting pool at the Millesgarden sculpture garden] shows how swimming-pool algae can take over everything. I've sent the AMPHITRYON to Sandy [McClatchy], who will pass it across Stonington to you. Please try to like the more intricate rhyme-orgies, because I don't want to change them, but do please fix anything fixable. You are missed at the anagrams table, and in the Conch Republic in general.[33]

"A closet of whispers"

In the 1980s Frank Taylor, an old friend who had worked at the publisher Reynal and Hitchcock when it released *The Beautiful Changes* in 1947, became a Key West neighbor. In 1991 he sent Dick and Charlee a copy of Kopkind's *Village Voice* article, highlighting a mention of Wilbur's name in the last paragraph, which described the journalist's glimpse of a group of famous writers partying on Duncan Street outside the locked complex of cottages where Tennessee Williams had once lived. The occasion had been the annual champagne and lemon cake celebration of Williams's birthday, which, on March 26, 1991, marked what would have been his eightieth. Wilbur himself had turned seventy on March 1. In the article Kopkind wrote:

The real point seems to be to take the annual snapshot, which will record who has survived, who is looking older, who is missing. It was blazing hot for March, and the writers, many of whom have been coming to the island since the year one, looked a little wilted. John Hersey tugged at a bucket hat. Alison Lurie stood shyly for photographers from the *Miami Herald*. John Malcolm Brinnin chatted with Richard Wilbur.
Others remarked on the high percentage of Pulitzer winners, and

thought up collective nouns [to describe them]. "A pride of Pulitzers" was aptest. Robert Stone walked in late. Jane O'Reilly raised a plastic cup of soda water. The Conch Train, a tourist ride that chugs through Old Town and adjacent streets, passed near the celebration. Then someone snapped the shot, and the party was over.[34]

By the time the *Voice* article ran, "the party" that had been Key West was beginning to wind down for the Wilburs. The original group of compound friends were disappearing: Ciardi died in 1986, Hersey in 1993, Ellison in 1994. Merrill stopped wintering on the island in 1991 and went instead to Athens. As the developers continued to glamorize the island, many writers lamented the good old days, when things seemed unspoiled, or at least more real.

But what is real to one generation may not ring true for the next. In 1993, for example, just down the street from the site where the Key West Literary Seminar was celebrating the poetry of Elizabeth Bishop, the Parrot Bar was hosting a poetry slam. As Carol Shaughnessy reported in the *Island News,* the slammers were "real-world poets reading the poems of real life." They would remedy, she said, the perception of poetry as too often "bloodless, with little connection to the workaday world."[35]

In his *Voice* article Kopkind intended to raise deeper concerns. As he observed, "The gay population, which burgeoned in the last two decades as the ramshackle 'conch houses' of the poor in Old Town were converted into sleek and sunny getaway houses for the Northern queeroisie, has been devastated and decimated by AIDS."[36] This combination of fatal epidemic and irreversible gentrification had suddenly given a new meaning to Key West. In more ways than one it had become the last stop on America's southernmost inhabited island. He also reported on a recent incident of violence at Miss Ruby's, a well-known guesthouse in Old Town, in which several gay guests had been beaten and hospitalized. While the incident sparked no widespread outrage or organized protest, it lingered in the islanders' consciousness, "not exactly [as] a conspiracy of silence, but perhaps a closet of whispers."[37]

The devastation of AIDS had not yet touched the Wilburs as deeply as it would when Merrill died in 1995.[38] Nonetheless, they were accustomed to the varying lifestyles of their friends and for many years could not imagine that intolerance of homosexuals would ever become an issue in the compound—until an incident occurred involving Ralph and Fanny Ellison, who were among their closest and dearest friends, and Frank

Taylor, a longtime friend of both couples. The situation, which grew more complex amid suspicion and rumor, came to resemble Kopkind's "closet of whispers."

The friendship between the Ellisons and the Wilburs began during the summer of 1959 at the thirty-fourth annual writer's conference at Bread Loaf in Middlebury, Vermont. Charlee told Ellison's biographer Arnold Rampersad that of all the people she and Dick met there, including the Ciardis, they "clicked" most with the Ellisons.[39] As Wilbur explained in 2007, Ellison intuitively understood that he was not a racist: "I had absorbed into my family culture a whole lot of black influence. I knew Count Basie by heart; I played the guitar and sang the blues of Jimmy Rushing and Sister Rosetta Tharpe, which made it easier for us to be friends. That aspect was always very important to Ralph."[40]

Rampersad has suggested that Ellison cultivated relationships with white men and women who wanted to develop ties with black America and thus was considered by some to be every white's favorite black man. But no such race-based assessment accounts for or diminishes the genuine and mutual affection shared by the two couples over several decades. In 1966 the Ellisons bought a summer home in Plainfield, Massachusetts, a small town bordering Cummington. According to official investigations, fire due to faulty wiring destroyed the home in 1967, although the Ellisons at first feared that arson may have been the cause and their race the reason. Only in 1973 did they feel emotionally ready to rebuild on the property, and they then added two new rooms onto a studio building that had survived the fire.

Over the years the Wilburs and the Ellisons became closer than ever; and not long after spending Thanksgiving 1975 in Cummington, Ellison learned that he'd been elected to membership in the American Academy of Arts and Letters. He also learned that Wilbur, supported by Robert Penn Warren, Malcolm Cowley, Allen Tate, and Stanley Kunitz, had recommended him. Rampersad notes that Ellison had craved the honor but feared it would be withheld on the grounds that, after *Invisible Man*, he'd published only a short book of essays.[41]

The Ellisons bought into the Windsor Grove compound in 1976, although the deed for their unit, number 727, named Fanny as sole owner. She intended to rent it more than reside in it. When she did fly south to stay there, Ellison rarely accompanied her. The relaxed tropical customs—for instance, daily gatherings to celebrate the sunset—made him uncomfortable.[42] Wilbur described Ellison as being "conspicuously marginal" on the island and disconnected from local ways; he had little in common with Key West's black residents, who were largely unfamiliar with the black culture that Ellison had absorbed in Harlem and at Yale.[43] "I think that Ralph was used to being a certain kind of figure in the black world in Harlem," Wilbur said, "and he couldn't be [the same] down there because [Key West blacks] didn't know who the hell he was."[44]

The incident involving Taylor began when William and Audrey Kelly Roos, a married couple who co-authored murder mysteries, rented the Ellisons' condo for the 1982 season. According to Rampersad, Ralph and Fannie had never met them but thought they would be good tenants. The following August William Roos, now widowed, arranged to rent the place again for the 1983 season. Unbeknownst to the Ellisons, however, his son Stephen and Stephen's lover Frank Taylor also lived there that winter. Only at the end of the season did the Ellisons find out about the extra occupants, as Ralph explained in a letter to Wilbur. Because William Roos wanted to extend the arrangement with his son and Taylor into the winter of 1984, he had asked Ellison to replace a bed in the study with something more comfortable for them.[45]

Ellison believed that the secrecy about the lovers' presence in the apartment was an outright violation of trust.[46] He had met Frank Taylor in 1943, as a novelist invited into the Reynal and Hitchcock fold, and he had considered the married (i.e., heterosexual) publisher to be a friend. But according to Wilbur, Ralph "was disquieted by the tolerance of homosexuality in Key West and in our compound. He found it difficult to admit . . . the level to which he abhorred homosexuality. It spooked him, and I think it spooked Fanny, too."[47] Charlee told Rampersad in 2000 that Fanny wrote to her about the rental episode, saying that the condo had been "dirtied by Frank Taylor and his lover."[48]

By the winter of 1985, when the Wilburs heard rumors of the rift between the Ellisons and Taylor, they were caught up in their own stress over the *Phaedra* translation and their experiences at the Camargo Foundation. Ellison misinterpreted their lack of communication that year as another betrayal, and he assumed that their choice to rent their Key West condo to Taylor while they were in France was a sign that they wanted a clean break from him and Fanny. He was convinced that Wilbur must have portrayed the pair to others in their circle as "disliking gays."[49]

In early 1987 Wilbur sent Ellison a copy of *Phaedra* with a letter asking how he and Charlee had offended him.[50] On February 15 Charlee sent her own letter, recalling the experiences the couples had shared, both happy and painful (an allusion to the Plainfield fire).[51] On February 24 Ellison responded to Wilbur with a six-page, single-spaced, typewritten letter that justified and defended his position. He began by analyzing the logic of Wilbur's supposed public accusation of homophobia. With great rhetorical skill he offered several tangential analogies to explain why any display of homophobia would be, in his case, as farfetched as an exhibition of racial bias. He disclosed that he'd been hounded out of college by a homosexual dean yet said the experience had not influenced his associations or friendships with homosexuals—at least not with those who avoided forcing an awareness of their sexuality on others. Ellison hoped that Wilbur, after reading his letter, would react with the same sense of catharsis and reconciliation that he himself had achieved by writing it.[52]

The Wilburs eventually blamed Ralph's need to withdraw from all social life for the breech in their friendship. Wilbur compared his isolation to "going into the tin can, as the Japanese say, to finish his next book," which he never did complete.[53] After the mid-1980s Fanny suspended her sporadic solo trips to Key West, and the Ellisons continued to rent out their condo until they sold it in 1993. Brinnin, who seems to have recorded the compound group's every social interaction, mentions her presence on the island only twice in his journal: on January 13, 1976, when she was with Charlee at the site of a house he was considering buying, and on March 20, 1981, when she attended a Ouija board session hosted by Merrill.[54]

In 2014, as he recalled the Ellison-Taylor episode, Wilbur spoke with regret and some embarrassment about how his own preconceptions of homosexuality had tinged his first encounter with Merrill. Although both were Amherst alums (Wilbur of the class of 1942, Merrill of the class of 1947), they had never met until they were invited to give a reading there in November 1948, shortly before the Bard conference. "At that reading Rolf Humphries asked if I had talked with Jimmy Merrill yet, but I said I'm not sure I want to because of his homosexuality. Humphries assured me he was an excellent fellow and very bright, and everyone was quite rightly charmed by him. Jimmy *was* an excellent person, very decent to other people, and of course he was always bright and amusing and very generous."[55]

In 1994 Merrill spoke to McClatchy about Wilbur's *The Beautiful Changes,* which he had first read not long after graduating from Amherst: " 'Those earliest poems by Wilbur, though I hadn't yet met their author, for me was like the first meeting with a lifelong friend. I marveled at their relish for the world, their openness to intimacy, their good humor, and best of all, their unaffected faith in art. In a flash I saw a dozen aspects of my own nature—or what was becoming my nature with every page I turned—given form and voice. It was what art could do.' "[56]

In 2002 the Wilburs spoke to Merrill's biographer, Langdon Hammer, about Merrill and Key West. "Jimmy never got bored with a life of art," Wilbur said. "He'd freed himself from being a rich boy in order to follow poetry, and he always worked at it. He never took it for granted. . . . But he got bored with Key West, and he was unable to work [there]." After attending Merrill's January 1994 reading at the Key West Literary Seminar, Charlee realized he was sick. Suspecting that he had AIDS (though neither of them ever discussed it), she told him she would never forget hearing him that night.[57] He died in Tucson a little more than a year later, on February 6, 1995.

Merrill's sexual preference was well known; even before the Stonewall riots of 1969, it was never the "open secret" that it was for many homosexuals. He claimed never to have thought of it as an issue, and he never became a spokesman for gay rights. "I stood still and the closet disintegrated," he remarked. "I don't believe in being the least militant about it."[58] In 2014 Wilbur said that their friendship "involved a complete overlooking of the sexual components of our lives." In fact, he said, they engaged in no conversation that touched on their personal lives.[59]

Brinnin was different. Since 1947, when he first became friends with the Wilburs, he had confided in Charlee and depended on her counsel in matters of the heart. That openness helped to change Wilbur's earlier preconceptions. In June 1977, after learning that Brinnin's longtime partner, Bill Read, had been diagnosed with terminal cancer, he wrote Read an eloquent letter acknowledging how their friendship had deepened his understanding of "affection between men."

> John's news of you makes us feel rebellious against life, for all the goodness of most of it and for all our training in acceptance. We can't well bear this for you, for John, for so many. And yet I want to tell you that, within our grief at the thought that we may lose you, we have been barraged by memories all of which are happy and kind, and so are somewhat fortified by the knowledge that we are grieving for a man who has given a noble account of himself. How long ago was it that I heard you give a paper on Skelton and Klee in Matty's class! And after that there are so

many pictures which come to the mind's eye. Times of simple pleasure at many tables and beside pools and beaches; the day we found what you later identified as *habernaria orbiculata;* your going to church with me at Duxbury; your tanned, handsome and affectionate presence at Ellen's wedding—there's no end to it. And mixed in with all the good times, and making them better, one's constant sense of your decency, loyalty, modesty, and intelligence. I thank you for your love toward us and all our children, and for teaching me what, for some time, I was stupidly unable to see—that affection between men can be present and true. God bless you.[60]

Brinnin sold his Caribbean house after Read's death, and Key West became his wintertime home, from which he flew, less and less frequently, to New York and Venice. His health began to deteriorate in 1997 when he was diagnosed with terminal lung cancer and then had a stroke. On June 15, 1998, Wilbur wrote his final letter to Brinnin. Looking back on their Cambridge days, he said: "Charlee and I (and Ellen) were on the threshold of everything, and you, though not much older than we, had already arrived. . . . It was delightful that we cottoned to each other at once, Charlee becoming your dear friend and you becoming my dear friend and the generous encourager of my poems."[61]

Charlee said goodbye on the same day: "Through ups and downs, losses, physical set backs, your free flowing generosity and funny lively spirit has warmed and sustained us. Enough of fancy verbiage. What is most important is for you to know that you are the irreplaceable, longest-loved friend that we ever had." Ellen Wilbur also wrote to Brinnin, telling him that she wished she could have flown to Key West to see him one last time: "No friend of my parents has ever meant so much to me as you."[62]

"The crush in Key West is daunting"

When the 1993–94 winter season ended, Charlee left Key West feeling that the island and its literary social scene had lost their magic. As she had learned from the photographer Rollie McKenna, their friends had seen her desire to spend quiet times with her husband as a sign of depression and withdrawal. In fact, for both Charlee and Dick the winter had been one of their happiest and healthiest in recent memory. Not only had they worked together on his translation of *Amphitryon,* but they had also biked together, gone swimming at night off South Beach, listened to music, and read aloud to each other. They saw, of course, their "beloved" older friends, and "local friends," whom Charlee said had almost given them up, as well as newer friends such as Robert and Janice Stone. But as she wrote to Brinnin in April 1994, they could no longer stand to attend parties with writers who brought along their competitive discontents and "shoals of groupies." Time becomes infinitely precious, she said, with the inevitable diminution of energy. And the best times for her were the ones she shared with Dick.[63]

Charlee expressed similar sentiments in a Christmas letter she sent to Merrill and Peter Hooten in late 1994. She and Dick had spent the holiday at Sanibel Beach, a remote spot with more seashells and migratory birds than people. "The crush in Key West is daunting," she wrote, wishing them well in Tucson, where Merrill had quietly gone to seek treatment. Nevertheless, the Wilburs continued to winter on the island until 2001–2, relishing their respite from harsh New England weather and continuing to stay as much as possible out of the public eye.

At the start of the 2003 winter season, Charlee was in the hospital recuperating from complications after knee surgery. Travel to Key West by plane or car had now become too difficult for the Wilburs to consider. Yet as Charlee admitted in 2005, the loss was greater for Dick than it was for her. She spoke to us as she sat in the window of their Cummington home, looking from time to time in the direction of a larch tree whose leaves had just turned gold:

> It's been wonderful, Key West has, not necessarily seeping into his work—one doesn't see an influence on his poems—but it's affected him physiologically, no doubt about it. [Cummington] is the place where he is centered and where a great deal evolves and pours out; he's so connected to these grounds, these trees, these plantings. A spruce was just cut down so we could plant the larch. . . . Dick looks at it every day. But although this is the place both of us feel totally connected to, he is much more disappointed about the end of Key West than I, just because of the aspect of his life it represented: being a kid. That's what he's said.[64]

Charlee died in 2007, and Wilbur returned to the island only one more time: to attend the Key West Literary Seminar held in his honor in 2010. He read "Security Lights, Key West," a new poem published in his 2004 *Collected Poems.* Its tone is elegiac, both mournful and nostalgic. The narrator describes his sense of the "strange glare" that halogen security lights cast over the facades of houses shuttered in sleep, just minutes from the nightlife on Duval Street. He contrasts the glare with his memory of the light in "fantastic day," when "the isle," like Prospero's, seemed alive with summoned spirits: ghosts of figures in drama and history such as Cordelia, Joan of Arc, and Thomas à Becket. Turning further into a "narrow, darker street," he notes there is no light other than what emanates from the sky. "Pitch-black houses loom" like shadows in fog. The narrator realizes the houses are built on sand, and whatever drama remains will exist in the "murk" of uncertainty. While other (and perhaps more successful or reso-nant) Wilbur poems, such as "Year's End," "Running," and "This Pleasing Anxious Being," also focus on mortality and the necessary adjustments one makes in facing death, "Security Lights, Key West" stands out because it mourns a place—and not only because the poet's time there has ended.

security lights, Key west

14

Life without Charlee

"Night after night, my love, I put to sea"

The only moments when I feel the bottom drop out of things are when I imagine being without Charlee. I would have to study it all over again, how to be in the world. And that would be quite a hard thing to do in one's 80s. . . . [But] it seems to me that the world is full of wonders. My feelings are that we are in the hands of a good God, so whatever happens will quite possibly be all right.

—RICHARD WILBUR, interview by Elizabeth Meade Howard, 2003

In late March 2007 Charlee developed pneumonia and pleurisy and was admitted to Cooley Dickinson Hospital in Northampton. For a couple of days it seemed as if she might pull through, but then her condition worsened. She signed a form requesting that no extraordinary measures be taken to save her life.

On April 2, Charlee asked a nurse to phone her husband: "Tell him to come earlier than usual today, and that I've asked for a priest." Wilbur immediately drove the thirty-five minutes to Northampton. He arrived in time for Charlee to look silently into his eyes, just for a moment. "Then," he said, "she peacefully lay back and I scarcely knew she had died."[1]

Charlee's last decade and a half had been fraught with injuries and related complications: breaks and fractures from falls and slips and then, in late 2003, a knee replacement that resulted in a near-fatal systemic infection. Her family did not expect her to survive the infection; an Episcopalian priest administered last rites. But survive she did, undergoing a long rehabilitation in the nursing facilities at Linda Manor, a half-hour drive from Cummington.

Charlee returned home in mid-2004, and the duties of Jeanette Horton and Karen Landry, the Wilburs' part-time housekeepers, expanded to accommodate her personal care. After helping Charlee bathe and dress, Jeanette would turn her attention to ironing, polishing silver, or making sure that flowers in the house were abundant and fresh. Karen sat with Charlee to plan each of the daily meals and then cooked them according to instruction. She also became her beautician, doing her makeup, washing and setting her hair weekly, and wielding a curling iron for touch-ups in between.

As of 2016, both women were still working for Wilbur, seeing themselves as family members more than hired help. Jeanette remembers that, at first, she was intimidated by Charlee's fastidiousness: she wanted *everything* ironed, from sheets to linen jackets, and all the polished silver had to gleam. Yet Jeanette was always grateful for her thoughtfulness and generosity. Five or six times each year, for many years, a courier would deliver both Jeanette and Karen gift packages of fine wool sweaters, which Charlee had ordered from catalogs. On Thanksgiving and Easter, two of her favorite holidays, they received more gifts and bonuses.[2]

Yet during Charlee's hospitalization in 2003 and the several months of nursing home rehabilitation, no amount of care, comfort, and support could ease or free Wilbur's mind from worry about his wife. He wrote little, just a letter here and there, and no poetry at all. Charlee's first concern after coming home had been *when will Dick begin to work?*

Corneille's House of Mirrors

For Wilbur translation had always been both energizing and restorative, satisfying his desire for "something honorable to toil at" between "visits from the muse." Yet he had already translated all but one of Molière's verse plays, "a lemon" he was not willing to try.[3] So in late 2005 he turned to a slightly older contemporary of the playwright, Pierre Corneille, and set to work on *The Theatre of Illusion* (*L'Illusion comique*).[4]

Corneille variously described his play as a "strange monster," a "caprice," and an "extravagant trifle." The French Academy frowned upon it because he had, in his words, "stitched together" unfinished comedic pieces and a swatch of tragedy into a hybrid genre.[5] This freewheeling approach did not conform to the standards the academy had set in 1635, which required

French playwrights to uphold the three unities that Aristotle had specified in *Poetics:* the events in a tragic play must take place within a single day, at one locale, and present a continuous action. Today, however, theater scholars consider *The Theatre of Illusion* a baroque masterpiece. Like other plays of the era (notably Shakespeare's *A Midsummer Night's Dream* and *The Tempest*) it mines the territory in which dreams and real life intersect, projecting the period's sense of theater as a metaphor for the illusory nature of human life.

The plot centers on the tale of a father longing to reunite with a son who has fled his strict rules and unrealistic expectations. The father's solution is to hire a magician who conjures three scenes (the illusions) showing the son's whereabouts, companions, and actions. Corneille developed an ingenious conceit for the play's tragic section: a play within a play that becomes more intense as the action unfolds. Here, the son, in the role of an adulterous husband, dies from a stab wound inflicted by a henchman acting on behalf of the husband's mistress and her own cuckolded husband. But the characters in this performance never identify each other by name, so the father believes he is magically witnessing the actual murder of his son. He watches the curtain fall and then rise to reveal the actors divvying up the proceeds from the gate. Both bewildered and aghast, he sees the "living . . . assemble with the dead."[6]

Wilbur has likened the powers of Alcandre, the magician in *The Theatre of Illusion,* to those wielded by Prospero in *The Tempest.* As Prospero dismisses the actor-spirits he has created for entertainment, he declares that we, too, "are such stuff / As dreams are made on."[7] In *Illusion,* by momentarily closing the curtain on the father's worst nightmare, Alcandre makes a strong case for the powerful, dazzling world of theater: how "uplifting and admired the stage is now," he assures the father.[8] One imagines that Corneille meant for the French Academy to hear these lines:

> One slays, one dies, one causes tears to fall,
> But it's the play alone that governs all.
> . . .
>
>   In that demanding art
> They found a refuge and a world apart,
> And all the things which you have seen of late—
> Your son's adulterous love and bloody fate—
> Were but the sad end of a tragic play

That's acted on the stage this very day
By him and others of his noble calling,
And which the whole of Paris finds enthralling.[9]

Illusion was exactly the kind of play Wilbur needed after Charlee's illness. He had more fun with it, he has said, than he did with any other theatrical translation. Immersing himself in Corneille's "house of mirrors" reminded him of the "socko effect" he had experienced at the Church of Sant'Ignazio in Rome, when he was looking at Andrea dal Pozzo's trompe l'oeil ceiling frescoes in the nave. None of his walks with Augustus Hare's guidebook had prepared him for it; Hare had dismissed the church in a half-sentence.[10] As he noted in his introduction to the play, Sant'Ignazio faced a square suggestive of a theater, so "the departing worshipper might see himself as leaving the realities of the altar for the vain shows of the world."[11]

Wilbur's translation of *Illusion* appeared in 2007 and won the National Translation Award from the American Literary Translators Association in 2008. To date, no acting company has chosen to stage it, although Wilbur said that, as he wrote, he had Brian Bedford in mind to play Matamore, a Gascon soldier who attempts to woo a woman who is already his aide's lover. Wilbur's agent Peter Franklin sent Bedford the script, but the actor felt he was too old to be believable as the character.[12]

Tony Kushner's freely adapted prose version of *Illusion* may have contributed to Franklin's difficulty in getting a company to take on Wilbur's version. Kushner's was first performed as a reading at the New York Theater Workshop in 1988 and then produced by the Hartford Stage Company in 1989, but the huge success of the playwright's Pulitzer Prize–winning *Angels in America* in 1993–94 revived interest in *Illusion* for the world stage. Kushner's elaboration of the plot invites directors to interpret the drama's various meta-theatrical elements, and at least one has opted to stage Alcandre's three illusions in different dramatic styles. As a prose adaptation, Kushner's version also removes the challenge that actors of Wilbur's verse translation would face when speaking his rhymed couplets.

In March 2006, as Wilbur's translation of *Illusion* was still in progress, Charlee observed that his intellectual and philosophical engagement with Corneille had helped him release the tension he had built up during her hospitalization and rehabilitation. Work on the play had eased not just his worry but also the sense of his own mortality, the fear that "he was getting dried up as a poet."

He dove into the Corneille and has been going great guns at it ever since. I am absolutely thrilled about what's happening with that. It's a totally different diction—a high, dramatic diction, that couldn't be more different from Molière. Dick connected with it right away; it's his kind of comic notion. As a result he's sunny and relaxed, and he's himself again.

And this will lead to poems. Dick's lyric gift has gone on longer than any poet I've known, including Frost. Frost began to repeat himself and write much less good stuff in his eighties, and was aware of that, and talked to me about it. This is something that hasn't happened with Dick. Some of his best poems were written when he was close to eighty, or in his eighties, which is very unusual. Usually poets burn out long before this. I'm sure he hasn't, hasn't permanently. I'm doing everything I can to ignite that, believe me. Which isn't much, because that's his business.[13]

Wilbur's work, however, was always very much Charlee's business; and sure enough, translating Corneille led him to write more poems. By mid-July 2006, he had completed a first draft of "A Pasture Poem," later published in *Anterooms* (2010). Drawing once more on the life cycles of the natural world, it describes how butterflies lay their eggs in the thistle plant ("all barb and bristle") at the angled spot where "The leaf meets the stem, / So that ants or browsing cows / Cannot trouble them."[14]

Wilbur had concerns in the first draft about using the word "crown" to describe the thistle, given its flower's round shape. But he was satisfied that "blanches" described the pale and withered look of the bloom just before the wind blows thistledown into the field at summer's end. He noted that there had been a four-year lapse since "The Censor," the last poem he had written before Charlee's hospitalization, and that "Corneille came between. He will again. I think I'm going to do *Le Menteur*."[15]

Wilbur translated two other Corneille plays in quick succession: *Le Cid* and *The Liar* (*Le Menteur*), published together in a single volume in 2009.[16] *Le Cid* had been a smash when it opened in Paris in 1637, securing Corneille's role as a major theatrical force in France despite the academy's reflexive attack on the play on formal and moral grounds. It was so universally admired that the title found its way into French idiom: *beau comme Le Cid* became a common form of praise. The play is based on the life of an eleventh-century Spanish nobleman and military leader known as El Cid, and it belongs to the subgenre known as the heroic play, a Restoration period form that condensed and dramatized classical epics. John Dryden, in his 1672 essay "Of Heroic Plays" (written to introduce one of his own), identified the genre's main themes as "Love and Valour."[17]

Like a comedy of manners, another Restoration subgenre, *Le Cid* (and Molière's plays) required not only witty turns of phrase and rhyme but also dialogue with a menacing edge. For instance, in a late scene in act 1, Don Rodrigue, the play's hero, grapples with his duty to avenge the insults that a wealthy count has made to his father, even though the count is the father of his own betrothed. In the following lines from Wilbur's translation, the rhymes work to confront, provoke, and punish:

> How am I torn apart!
> My honor's what desire would free me of,
> Yet I must take revenge, despite my love.
> One voice commands me, one would sway my heart.
> Forced to renounce what is most sweet to me
> Or live in infamy,
> I'm pierced by thrust and counterthrust.[18]

In January 2013 the Storm Theater and Blackfriars Repertory Theater staged the world premiere of Wilbur's *Le Cid* at the Theater of the Church of Notre Dame in New York City. One critic's pan of the production echoed the French literary establishment's attitude during Corneille's time: he complained about the play's lack of both Aristotelian and stylistic unity. According to the reviewer, several of the actors were unable to deliver satisfactory performances of Wilbur's "accomplished" translation. One lacked emotion, he said, while another punctuated metrical stresses with awkward giggles, and a third vamped it up like a "lust-ridden character from *Sex and the City*."[19]

Most translators see themselves as responsible for providing an actor with the means to successfully deliver lines written in a foreign tongue and encumbered by the culture of a bygone era. This sense of foreignness may be the reason why American audiences and translators haven't embraced Corneille as enthusiastically as they have Molière, "whose idea of what is normal, natural or balanced is very much like our own," Wilbur has said. In a 2009 conversation with the poet Dana Gioia, he compared Corneille's language to Molière's, an idiom that American audiences readily understand, and to Racine's, whose spare nobility is challenging. When "rendering a heroic play like Corneille's *Le Cid*," he explained, "one has to be careful not to slip into the oratorical."[20]

In *The Liar* (1643), which is more farcical than heroic, Corneille created a young character named Dorante who brashly announces in the opening scene:

> At last I've doffed the Robe and donned the Sword;
> This is the life that I've been yearning toward;
> Father has let me follow my desire,
> And so I've thrown my law books on the fire.[21]

Dorante has come to Paris with a plan to find the "sweet company" of a woman; and as he spins increasingly preposterous tales of his military and amatory feats, he reinvents himself. According to theater lore, *The Liar* so charmed female Parisian theatergoers that they clamored to be wooed with something akin to "la fête du *Menteur,*" the banquet Dorante fabricates to bolster his reputation for affluence and panache and thus compete for a young lady's affections.[22]

"Of being and seeming, truth and falsehood, there is no end in this play," Wilbur noted in his introduction; the world is duplicitous, and lines blur between appearance and reality. "Metamorphoses are everywhere," warns one character. But the play does not operate as a moral fable. For the characters, as Wilbur pointed out, the price paid for their deceptions, denials, and impersonations is nothing more than momentary confusion and bewilderment. Theatergoers and readers don't expect to see Dorante punished for his mendacity; rather, they are amused and delighted by it—perhaps because, as Corneille himself explained, Dorante's motive is love.[23] Wilbur believes that Corneille's characters, especially in *The Liar,* "may have pointed the way to those great comedies of character in which Molière studies the impact of a quirky central figure on those around him." Such seamless back and forth— between truth and lies, reality and illusion, being and not being—appealed to him as much as the challenge of the diction itself.[24]

"Dick's conjugal good fortune"

When the *Boston Globe* published Charlee's obituary in early May, the headline writers tagged her name with the phrase "inspired and guided poets."[25] The *Berkshire Eagle*'s notice of her memorial service called her a "friend and supporter to many writers, including Ralph Ellison, Stanley Kunitz, Theodore Roethke, John Malcolm Brinnin, and James Merrill."[26] No doubt the list omitted many more names. As the Wilburs' friend David Sofield said, "Thank god she cared for the amateurs among us. . . . Every writer I've known has been profoundly envious of Dick's conjugal good fortune."[27]

Wilbur himself acknowledged Charlee's remarkable ability for figuring out what worked and didn't work in a poem: "As I went on writing poems, without deliberately trying to do so," he said, "I began to write with her taste and sensibilities, as well as my own. I suppose the muse is thought to be a participator, but she was an unusually participating muse."[28] Charlee appeared in or inspired ten of her husband's poems; taken together, they form a many-faceted portrait of both her and their marriage. Some include unmistakable biographical detail from their lives together, in others Wilbur addressed her directly, and still others draw on elements universal to all lovers.

In their college days and the early years of their marriage, Wilbur had written love poems to Charlee, which were never published. She said in 2005:

> As soon as we met he began sending me love poems, very early on, and you know those were lost in a flood [in 1956]. It just kills me because they are unlike anything he has written since that time. They were brilliant. They were in a box with a lot of other correspondence, war correspondence. Not all but most of it was lost. [The flood occurred] while we were living in South Lincoln, in a house very unfortunately built at the bottom of a sloping driveway. We had a terrible rainstorm, and a geyser of water came down the driveway. The basement soaked before we could get the place pumped out. Books were mildewed; oh, it was dreadful. But the letters of Dick's, the longhand letters, [and those poems] were gone. I wish I'd memorized them all.[29]

In "The Reader," which opens the "New Poems" section of his 2004 *Collected Poems*, Wilbur wrote of Charlee's lifelong custom of rereading favorite books, even heavy ones such as *War and Peace*.[30] He admired her empathy with novelists' troubled and often-doomed characters, acknowledging that "having lived so much herself, perhaps / She meets them this time with a wiser eye." The poem shifts between glimpses of youthful, innocent hope and earned wisdom: "But the true wonder of it is that she / For all that she may know of consequences, / Still turns enchanted to the next bright page."

> Caught in the flow of things wherever bound,
> The blind delight of being, ready still
> To enter life on life and see them through.

In the poem Wilbur's tenderness for his wife is palpable, combining into one image a reference to her younger charmed mind and a view of her at a much older age, sitting near a shaded light that "shines on the nape, half-shadowed by her curls."

Charlee Wilbur at Amherst College's Pratt Field, 1941, the year she met Dick. *Courtesy of Richard Wilbur.*

In a much earlier poem, "Galveston, 1961," Charlee emerges from the surf like a goddess with "spattering hair"—her "brown legs" partly obscured by weeds as she approaches the shore. Wilbur's narrator addresses her directly in the first stanza as she moves toward him:

> You who in crazy-lensed
> Clear water fled your shape,
> By choppy shallows flensed
> And shaken like a cape.[31]

In the fifth of the poem's seven stanzas, the narrator invites his flesh-and-blood wife, who had earlier seemed to be an apparition (a "Sleek Panope no more"), to "sprawl beside me here, / Sharing what we can share."[32] The sixth stanza suggests what that shared thing might be:

> Small-talk and speechless love—
> Mine being all but dumb
> That knows so little of
> What goddess you become.

Wilbur wrote "Galveston, 1961" while he and his family were living in Houston in 1960–61.[33] A letter from Charlee to John Brinnin on March 16, 1961, suggests the origin of the poem's setting: "Our family has been spending every nice Saturday on the Galveston beach. We swim in the Gulf, build huge driftwood fires, and grill steak and roast fresh corn. For once I am browner than you in March, by God. . . . My hair is sexily streaked."[34]

Wilbur submitted an early draft of the poem to the *New Yorker* shortly after he wrote it, but the magazine editors, who objected to a line ending with the word "beer," rejected it. He put the poem aside and forgot about it. After Charlee died, however, he rewrote the problem line without the offending word, adjusted the rhyming lines around it, and resubmitted the poem to the *New Yorker*. It appeared in the May 11, 2009, issue and in *Anterooms* the following year.[35]

"The Catch," published in his 1987 *New and Collected*, opens with a full-length image of Charlee, who is "dangling . . . to one side before my eyes / Like a weird sort of fish" a garment she has just pulled from a shopping bag. The dress is "Limp, corrugated, lank, a catch too rare / Not to be photographed." After the narrator fails to properly acknowledge the dress's fine qualities, Charlee models it in front of "the long mirror, mirror on the wall," adding "lacy shoes, a light perfume," and "two slim golden chains." Captivated, the narrator submits to her aura, and the poem ends as Charlee hangs the dress amid others "in the fragrant dark / Of her soft armory."[36]

Such portrayals of male wonderment at female mystique recall a similar reaction in "Piazza di Spagna, Early Morning":

> How she stood at the top of that long marble stair
> Amazed, and then with a sleepy pirouette
> Went dancing slowly down to the fountain-quieted square.

The critic Robert Richman has noted that such "transfiguring instants" lift "the poet out of his world and himself."[37] Yet Wilbur's poetry also celebrates ordinary moments. Using a day-in-the-life approach in the poems "C

Minor" and "A Late Aubade," he considered the everyday elements of marriage. "C Minor" appeared in *The Mind-Reader* (1976), and its title alludes to a Beethoven string quartet that had been playing on the radio before the narrative begins:

> Beethoven during breakfast? The human soul,
> Though stalked by hollow pluckings, winning out
> (While bran-flakes crackle in the cereal-bowl)
>   Over despair and doubt?

The woman shuts the music off, and the speaker agrees she was right to do so. He speculates how the morning might "begin at hazard, perhaps with pecker-knocks / In the sugar bush, the rancor of a jay." He then wonders how the day might continue to play out—hoeing the garden, breaking a plate, being lonely or "by love consoled"—all of it best left to unfold in the moment.

> How should I know? And even if we were fated
> Hugely to suffer, grandly to endure,
> It would not help to hear it all fore-stated
>   As in an overture.

In "A Late Aubade," published in *Walking to Sleep* (1969), Wilbur set the action close to noon.[38] In bed with his wife, the narrator runs through a list of other ways she might have opted to spend the morning—planting salvia, training an unhappy setter to heel, attending a lecture, shopping—and then tells her he's lucky that she'd "rather lie in bed and kiss / Than anything." When she warns him the morning is almost gone, he urges her to linger, then "slip downstairs":

> And bring us up some chilled white wine,
> And some blue cheese, and crackers, and some fine
> Ruddy-skinned pears.

Pears and their edenic echoes figure as well in "June Light," a meditation on innocent love that Wilbur wrote during the war and published in *The Beautiful Changes* (1947). In the first and second stanzas the narrator recalls how his beloved beckoned him through an open window to come outdoors. The word "location" in the first line—"Your voice, with clear location of June days"—is an unexpected choice, recalling "locution" even as it precisely sets the scene. He remembers how she then tossed him a pear. In "uncontested summer all things raise / Plainly their seeming into seamless air," he tells her, punning on homonyms. "Then your love looked as simple and entire / As that picked pear." He is able to read the love in her face—"legible as pearskin's fleck and trace"—but ultimately sees the pear as "more fatal fleshed than ever human grace."

In the third stanza the metaphoric progression of images continues to evoke the fall of man fatally enraptured by a gift of fruit. But the narrator feels blessed, not only because he had the gift (and now remembers it) but also because he may compare his beloved to Eve:

> And your gay gift—Oh when I saw it fall
> Into my hands, through all that naïve light,
> It seemed as blessed with truth and new delight
> As must have been the first great gift of all.

In "A Simile for Her Smile," from *Things of This World* (1956), the narrator's mind wanders as he anticipates his beloved's arrival. He likens her imagined smile to a drawbridge rising, which stalls "hasty traffic . . . on each side massed and staring." Critics have commented on the seemingly effortless polish and phrasing of the poem, yet some don't count it among Wilbur's finest because it engages no large philosophical idea. Edward Zuk, for instance, notes that for all the *motion* conveyed in the alliteration—the "slip / Slip of the silken river past the sides"—the drawbridge simile and the imagery of highway infrastructure supporting it convey no emotion or sense of what the poet expects after the woman smiles.[39]

In "For C.," from *Mayflies* (2000), Wilbur celebrated his marriage by comparing its constancy and longevity to the sadness and regrets of lovers who part. The poem demonstrates his ability to use words in one context that will resonate with deeper meaning in others. For instance, elevator gates "clash" as they close before the reader knows the lovers do, and "morning's crosstown glare" suggests sterner looks exchanged by a bickering couple, perhaps just after dawn. The narrator presents the drama of these parting lovers as something he and his wife have been "denied." With that word choice he twists the more conventional feeling one might expect from lovers—of being spared such grief (or of being lucky)—away from their sense of superiority. Similarly, Wilbur changed the original line, "On such grand scale do the inconstant say goodbye," to "On such grand scale do lovers say goodbye" in the published version, because his children Ellen and Chris thought "inconstant" made the voice of the poet sound too smug.[40]

Wilbur sent "For C." to John Brinnin in September 1996, the day after he wrote it. He said, "[The poem] may be perfect gibberish for all I know; I'm too close to it to tell. You are not obliged to comment, of course, but if you do have a comment, let me have it between the eyes."[41] Brinnin had "some nit-pickings in the first stanza." Regarding the line "She looks up toward the window where he waits," he thought the word "waits" suggested "more unresolved drama than you intend to a routine & possibly anonymous coupling."[42] Wilbur did not agree; the line did not change. Some "bothersome syntax" caused Brinnin a little trouble in the third stanza—the word "yet" so soon on the heels of "while"—but again Wilbur let the original stand. Brinnin also had a comment about the end of the poem, which follows:

> We are denied, my love, their fine tristesse
> And bittersweet regrets, and cannot share
> The frequent vistas of their large despair,
> Where love and all are swept to nothingness;
> Still, there's a certain scope in that long love
> Which constant spirits are the keepers of,
>
> And which, though taken to be tame and staid,
> Is a wild sostenuto of the heart,
> A passion joined to courtesy and art
> Which has the quality of something made,
> Like a good fiddle, like the rose's scent,
> Like a rose window or the firmament.

His problem lay in the third line of the final stanza:

> "A passion joined to courtesy and art" so instantly evokes Yeats as to blunt
> the effect of your lovely ending, I think. And I'm not sure he hasn't got
> dibs on the conjunction of p. c. & a. for good. I wouldn't want the line
> to turn up as a teaser on an SAT—with everyone guessing WBY except
> those who know you by heart & can cite the debt.
>   Also, I don't want anything to spoil the sweet touch of raunchiness in
> "Like a good fiddle."
>   I love the poem. End of sermon.[43]

In his letter to Wilbur, Brinnin was alluding to Yeats's "The People," from his collection *The Wild Swans at Coole* (1919). In that poem the narrator, a poet himself who dedicates his life to art for its own sake and believes art is a public necessity, asks, "What have I earned for all that work?" The "work" is his involvement in the Irish rebellion in what he calls the "unmannerly town" of Dublin.[44]

> . . . I might have lived,
> And you know well how great the longing has been,
> Where every day my footfall should have lit
> In the green shadow of Ferrara wall;
> . . .
> I might have had no friend that could not mix
> Courtesy and passion into one like those
> That saw the wicks grow yellow in the dawn.[45]

Yeats and Wilbur certainly shared the view that art is a personal and public priority, but Wilbur used and formulated "p. c. & a." much differently from Yeats, whose narrator longs for the kind of companionship that combines courtesy and passion, one that is absent in Dublin, given its political animosities. But the distinction between the two poets' use of "p. c. & a." is less important than the reason behind Wilbur's disagreement with Brinnin's suggestion that a poet "has dibs" on a particular phrase or combination of words and images. In his essay "Poetry's Debt to Poetry" he articulated his belief that "art is a loose collective enterprise, . . . prompted, in the first place, by [an encounter with] other art, and that artists, however original, respond to other artists by . . . borrowing, theft, adaptation, translation, impersonation, parody, and so on."[46]

Brinnin himself acknowledged that his worry about the "p. c. & a." echo did not diminish "For C." as a celebration of Dick and Charlee's long bond. But the critic David Yezzi, in a review of *Mayflies,* noted that the poem is more than just a tribute to marital love: "[It] functions as an *ars poetica* as well, a taking stock of Wilbur's life in art."[47] Yezzi's appreciation of "For C." thus aligns with the view of Yeats's own ars poetica in "The People." "Faced with 'nothingness,'" Yezzi pointed out, Wilbur has always found in the human act of making objects—such as a "good fiddle" and "a rose window"—"a token of divine making ('the rose's scent,' 'the firmament'). A number of his poems, Wilbur has said, have to do 'with the proper relation between the tangible world and the intuitions of the spirit'; for him, one is never free of the other."[48]

On the subject of proper relations, Wilbur believes that the words of poems work harder than the words of prose do to "rescue us from inarticulateness, to convey meaning adequate to the world and to our hearts."[49] He has said, "It's rather a lot to have a love poem soar into the firmament and have 'firmament' be the last word. I think if I do get away with it, I do because 'firmament' is balanced by something as modest and earthly as a good fiddle."[50]

"She got into people's lives, heaven knows"

Charlee's memorial service was held on May 19, 2007, at the Village Congregational Church in Cummington.[51] During the service and at the reception that followed, speakers shared memories of times when she had listened, supported, sympathized, and offered advice. Wilbur once called his wife "the most curious woman there ever was," noting her interest in the lives of others: "Every now and then, I would come away from an occasion where we were talking with friends and I would say to Charlee, 'You were too inquisitorial this evening,' and it would trouble her. But I think she meant no evil, and I think it did good for some of the people she interrogated sometimes. She got into people's lives, heaven knows."[52] Ellen Wilbur described that quality in her mother when she called Charlee "a friend and confidant to many—a woman who could bestow on others her delight in life."[53]

As Wilbur had asked, David Sofield prefaced his remarks at the service by reading "The Reader." Sofield, an Amherst College professor, had been Dick and Charlee's friend, and Wilbur's tennis partner, since the mid-1980s. During one particularly grueling match, Sofield recalled, he and Wilbur had barely held their own against two Northampton attorneys. Then "Charlee came from the house where she must have been reading for the third time a large European novel; Dick and I rallied. Charlee did that to people: they became their best selves in her presence."[54]

Sofield concluded his remarks at the service with these words:

> Charlee was *amor,* was love itself, whether in Cummington or Key West or Corrales, New Mexico. Hundreds of people loved her, "caught," as Dick's poem says she was, in the very "delight of being," and she loved them. Dick's dedication in the 2004 *Collected* reads, "For Charlee, in this and the other kingdom." About the other kingdom I cannot speak, but of this one, the one of which Cummington, Massachusetts, is the capital, she was Queen Charlotte the First and Last. How much we, her subjects, will miss her.[55]

Later that summer the family buried her ashes in Dawes Cemetery in Cummington, opposite a small obelisk dedicated to William Cullen Bryant.

During the days and weeks after Charlee's death, Wilbur received a flood of cards and letters, most of them filled with touching personal remembrances of her. Although reading them was a comfort, they overwhelmed him and reinforced his aloneness. In late spring he had asked a small group of friends gathered in his home, "All these letters I received, condolences, letters of sympathy, must I answer them all? Each and every one? There are so many. It's so difficult."[56] The consensus at the table—"Give yourself a year to do this"—seemed to satisfy him only partially. On the one hand, he wanted to do the right thing on an important occasion. On the other hand, he dreaded exacerbating his pain.

Four months after Charlee's death, Wilbur spoke about how he and his family were beginning to adjust to life without her. A question arose about whether to mark the birthdays of Chris (turning sixty-one) and Nathan (turning fifty-six) with the usual July celebration in Cummington:

> I thought the thing to do was to go ahead with it. But Chris said to me on the phone that he thought this was a time of mourning and we probably shouldn't have celebrations of any kind, including birthdays.
>
> I didn't accept that. Ellen and I felt that it was going to be important for everybody to go ahead with continuous affection and awareness of Charlee—to do what we've done every year. Nathan felt pretty much what we felt, at any rate he came out on that side of things. . . . And we had the fine cake as usual, and we did everything as usual like the swimming and the pétanque. We didn't have as much uproarious singing as usual . . . but I think everybody was glad we'd gone on ahead with [the celebrating].
>
> Of course Aaron had very great trouble absorbing his mother's death. It had to be explained to him that people get old and die, and that had happened to his mother. When Aaron assimilates things he tends to repeat them to people, and he said, "Mommy's dead, Mommy's dead now, because when people get old they die," and so on. He went through a recitation of that sort several times while he was out here.[57]

On the third weekend of August, Chris picked up Aaron in Rhode Island and brought him to Wilbur's house to attend the Cummington Fair, an event the extended family looks forward to every summer. This traditional four-day New England agricultural exposition features oxen pulls as well as livestock, vegetable, and flower exhibitions, a midway with fried dough and corn dog vendors, and live entertainment. A string of prize ribbons from the fair, awarded over a number of years for vegetables and flowers, still hangs in Wilbur's den, alongside Aaron's ribbons for participating in Special Olympics events.

In the autumn Wilbur had a trio of public appearances: on September 11 at the Boston Public Library, reading with Donald Hall and Maxine Kumin in honor of a new book by his Cambridge friend, David Ferry; on September 25 at Memorial Hall at the University of Massachusetts in Amherst, for a reading sponsored by the Five College Episcopal Center; and on September 27 at Bryn Mawr College in Pennsylvania, for a reading in the college's Creative Writing Series. Such public appearances seemed to be a way to remain engaged in the literary world, now that Wilbur had only himself to consider when making travel plans. Yet he was already having second thoughts about scheduling three more events for April 2008, two of which would require extensive travel: in one he would read with Mark Strand and W. D. Snodgrass at Emory University in Atlanta; in the other he would present the Walt Whitman Lecture at Whitman College in Washington State. "I'm beginning to get spooky about air travel," he said. "I don't know what they're going to catch me trying to carry aboard the plane. And at my age one starts to have to take a nap, which is a shameful thing. I must say it distresses me to become a napper but if I don't, I become very much the living dead, and so travel is complicated if you need to get a number of zzzs through the day."[58]

Wilbur's Whitman appearance drew the largest crowd of any reading in the series for the academic year, with audience members coming from the college, the local community, and as far away as Seattle. As he often does to end a reading on a light note, Wilbur closed with some "children's" poems, this time from *The Disappearing Alphabet*. Earlier in the reading, introducing "Two Voices in a Meadow," a poem in which the speakers, a milkweed and a stone, accept their destinies in the God-made universe, Wilbur commented, "It is true that my work has been useful." He cited as an example that "Two Voices" had once been read at the funeral of a nun.[59]

When Elizabeth Meade Howard interviewed a number of her Key West neighbors for *Aging Famously*, a book she was writing about strategies to improve longevity, she'd gotten Wilbur to talk about the usefulness of one's work. "If what you do is regarded as having social value, you have impetus," he told her. "I know people start dying when boredom overtakes them and they don't have that sense of being needed. I wouldn't really know who I was unless I was writing on some front or the other."[60]

In the spring of 2008 Wilbur got a chance to put into action his "teacher-writer / writer-teacher" theory—that teaching keeps a writer sharp and articulate—when Amherst's president Tony Marx asked him to join the faculty as the John Woodruff Simpson lecturer, a post once held by Robert Frost. After more than twenty years away from the classroom, Wilbur was honored but nervous. As he told Sofield, "I always made an anxious business of [teaching], over-prepared all my classes, and sought to seem omniscient."[61] Yet soon Marx's offer morphed into a more attractive option: Wilbur could co-teach classes with Sofield, one fall course on poetry (a different selection each year chosen from the Elizabethan to the contemporary era), one spring course on creative writing. Wilbur agreed. As an added attraction, the job would allow him to reacquaint himself with reading—not passively but to articulate to others how the poems they read could enhance their own creative engagement with poetry.

Unsurprisingly, Charlee had sparked the friendship with Sofield that helped to engage her husband's return to teaching after her death. Although the two men had met at several on-campus occasions in the 1970s, they had never had a real conversation. Then Wilbur brought Charlee to a reading in 1984. Sofield found himself "sitting next to her in an open-windowed alcove of the Lord Jeff dining room":

> The smiles were exceptionally cordial, ideas flew, I expressed the greatest admiration, which I felt and feel, for Dick's poems, and before long she asked me if I happened to play tennis. . . . I answered yes, a bit, and the next thing I knew I was invited to be Dick's partner in what turned out to be a quarter of a century of happily chasing lobs that, because Dick played fearsomely close to the net, sometimes floated over his head. And this mind you, on the most adventuresome court surface in Western Massachusetts, complete with the occasional greyhound dashing straight through the action.[62]

Sofield and Wilbur co-taught with great ease. Beginning in the fall of 2009, they offered a twice-weekly modern poetry course featuring work from 1950 to the present. They started with one class on Auden followed by four on Bishop, three on Lowell, and one (reflecting his modesty) on Wilbur. Two classes in one week covered Berryman, Jarrell, J. V. Cunningham, Anthony Hecht, and Donald Justice. Four classes on Philip Larkin and three on Merrill brought the students to the week before Thanksgiving break, during which they read May Swenson, Denise Levertov, Amy Clampitt, Sylvia Plath, Ted Hughes, and Geoffrey Hill. After the break the students turned to Derek Walcott, Paul Muldoon, Frank O'Hara, John Ashbery, Seamus Heaney, Kay Ryan, and Carol Ann Duffy. For the final paper, Sofield and Wilbur gave students a choice to write about either Mary Jo Salter or Simon Armitage.

In 2010 Wilbur spoke with Sofield about his recent experiences in the classroom: "I find [the students] indubitably brighter than we were; the ones I met have been very lively and well prepared for anything we've had to offer them. The only thing wrong with them is that they use the word 'like' in every sentence."[63] It bothered him that good thinkers, readers, and writers were not necessarily good talkers.

Sofield had observed a change of ethos in Amherst's classrooms, especially after the college became coeducational in 1975: "Students now seem more reluctant to speak eloquently or try to speak eloquently in front of their peers, and it's a disappointment." Both he and Wilbur blamed an increased concern about appearances: compared to the charged and more outspoken campus atmosphere of the Vietnam era, contemporary young men didn't want to seem too aggressive, and the young women didn't want to seem too smart. Or, both men admitted, perhaps their perceptions and expectations of students had changed.[64]

After briefly experimenting with a computer and the Internet, Wilbur decided to forgo electronic media for either classroom or personal use. The college express-mailed him students' essays, poems, and stories or sent them by courier. A student drove to Cummington, brought Wilbur to campus, and then drove him home after class until he retired once more after the fall semester of 2014. Teaching at Amherst helped him rediscover the satisfaction and stimulation he had found earlier at Harvard, Wellesley, Wesleyan, and Smith, and perhaps proved to the ghost of Armour Craig that Wilbur could indeed "work pretty hard at Amherst."[65]

"A Grand Old Man of American Poetry"

The critic David Orr has called Wilbur "a Grand Old Man of American Poetry," one who for decades has been "alternately praised and condemned for the same three things":

> First, he's widely agreed to be a formal virtuoso. One might think this would be an indisputable virtue, but in certain quarters, working in meter can still earn you skeptical looks. Second, Wilbur is, depending on your preference, courtly or cautious, civilized or old-fashioned, reasonable or kind of dull. . . . Finally, Wilbur is sometimes put forward as a model of resistance to certain tendencies in American poetry, most notably the conspicuous self-dramatization associated with Robert Lowell and Sylvia Plath, and the even more conspicuous self-dramatization associated with

Allen Ginsberg. Whether this is entirely true of Wilbur is a complicated question, but it's fair to say that his writing can make even Donald Justice's work seem gushy.[66]

As Orr suggests, it's tough to be a Grand Old Man in any field of endeavor, but Wilbur did work to succeed in that role after Charlee's death. Since 1995, he has several times been both a participant and a subject of study at an annual poetry conference devoted to formalist and narrative poetry at West Chester University in Pennsylvania. He delivered keynote addresses in both 1995 and 2008, and in 2009 traveled to West Chester to read and participate in a one-day workshop panel, "A Conversation with Richard Wilbur," hosted by Dana Gioia. He returned again in June 2011, where, after another panel discussion devoted to his work, a large group of attendees gathered outside on the Alumni House lawn to celebrate his ninetieth birthday. Under a tent the crowd ate cake and toasted him with champagne as they listened to prominent poets share personal reminiscences and anecdotes about him.

Wilbur became selective about such Grand Old Man appearances in subsequent years. Yale awarded him an honorary degree at its commencement ceremony in May 2012. In September 2013 Amherst unveiled an oil portrait of him, painted by Sarah Belchetz-Swenson and hung in the college's Johnson Chapel, whose pews were packed with college and community members.[67] In December of the same year, the Emily Dickinson Museum honored him with its second annual "Tell It Slant" award.[68] When a group of regional writers and artists launched *Stone Walls II* in the fall of 2014—bringing back to life a journal that had thrived from 1975 to 1993 in the hill towns of western Massachusetts—Wilbur and his longtime friend and Cummington neighbor, the poet William Jay Smith, were happy to grant interviews for the inaugural issue and read poems at its opening reception. The journal editors could proudly boast that yes, in one town there were two poet laureates.[69]

In 2010 Houghton Mifflin Harcourt published Wilbur's *Anterooms,* a slender volume including poems (both somber and amusing), translations (from French, Russian, and Latin, including thirty-seven riddles from Symphosius's *Aenigmata*), and a song intended for the musical production of Jean Giraudoux's play *Madwoman of Chaillot* that never made it to the stage. In lieu of a formal dedication to Charlee, a poem titled "The House" precedes the book's individual sections; it sets the tone for the eleven poems in the first section, which connect loosely as expressions of gratitude and hope or contemplations of death—or sometimes as both. In "Psalm," for instance, musical instruments ("the plucked lute, and likewise / The harp of ten strings") celebrate the gift of life itself with its attendant goodness (as conveyed by the horn), pandemonium (drum), and sorrow and grief (cello). In "A Measuring Worm" the repetitive "humping" of a caterpillar's back as it inches across a window screen conjures a series of messages sent by semaphore: "Dark omegas meant / To warn of Last Things." By identifying with the caterpillar's inability to comprehend its life cycle, the narrator acknowledges his own uncertainty of what life beyond death may bring, while at the same time implying a belief in it.[70]

> Although he doesn't know it,
> He will soon have wings,
>
> And I too don't know
> Toward what undreamt condition
> Inch by inch I go.

In "Anterooms," the narrator acknowledges that our perception of time "strains belief . . . How an instant can dilate / Or long years be brief." Yet he also muses:

> Dreams, which interweave
> All our time and tenses, are
> What we can believe:
>
> Dark they are, yet plain,
> Coming to us now as if
> Through a cobwebbed pane
>
> Where, before our eyes,
> All the living and the dead
> Meet without surprise.

The kinship between dreams and an afterlife dominates in both last stanzas of "Anterooms" and "The House," a poem of love and yearning in which Wilbur recalled his wife's fondness for a house she visited in dreams. Dreams, especially daydreams, Charlee once said, had always been crucial in allaying her loneliness as a child:

I grew up with the most romantic notions about marriage and what I wished in that way. From the time I was about five years old I used to dream about the man that I would be with for the rest of my life, who was alive somewhere in the world. I used to be put down for a nap . . . and lie there in bed with my cat sending messages to my husband-to-be. That's how lonely and in need I was. And when I met Dick both of us had a sense of immediate recognition—I profoundly but he too—that we were meant to be together, that it was fated.[71]

Reading "The House," one can imagine how Charlee, after coming so close to death in 2003, might have dreamed of a place that offered comfort and romance, one that she may have glimpsed as a girl, en route with her family from Boston to summer in South Berwick, Maine.

> Sometimes, on waking, she would close her eyes
> For a last look at that white house she knew
> In sleep alone, and held no title to,
> And had not entered yet, for all her sighs.
>
> What did she tell me of that house of hers?
> White gatepost; terrace; fanlight of the door;
> A widow's walk above the bouldered shore;
> Salt winds that ruffle the surrounding firs.
>
> Is she now there, wherever there may be?
> Only a foolish man would hope to find
> That haven fashioned by her dreaming mind.
> Night after night, my love, I put to sea.

The final line of the poem is among the most haunted, moving, and understated expressions of emotion Wilbur has ever written.

In many interviews and essays Wilbur has articulated a belief that his poetry is a conscious celebration of the world—both its bounty and the intimation it gives of the world beyond: "In that sense, a poem is a high moment of control and understanding, of finding the right words . . . to record the transcendent moments as well as . . . the absolutely daily and everyday awareness."[72] In his review of *Anterooms,* Orr touched on this quality, which, he believes, "asks something slightly unusual from the contemporary reader. It asks us to value poetry that is happy to be read as solid and static, rather than unstable and in flux. This is especially tricky if you're writing about death, as Wilbur is in the strongest poems here. Death, like Wilbur's poetry, does not easily admit of divisions; it is 'the total emptiness forever,' as Larkin put it."[73]

At the end of his review Orr invoked the commanding presence of the mid-twentieth century's Grand Old Man of American Literary Criticism:

More than 50 years ago, Randall Jarrell claimed that as a poet, Wilbur "never goes too far, but he never goes far enough." The observation is invariably quoted whenever Wilbur gets reviewed (far be it from me to break the chain). But to write convincingly about death—and also, as Wilbur has increasingly done, about grief—isn't a matter of "going" anywhere. It's a matter of remaining poised in the face of a vast and freezing indifference. And while the strong, spare poems here are unlikely to strike many readers as the illustrious pronouncements of a Grand Old Man—the kind of figure Jarrell had in mind—they are wholly successful in meeting the darkest of subjects with their own quiet light. Which is, surely, a far grander thing.[74]

Since Charlee's death, Wilbur has remained in his home in Cummington, where his children and grandchildren visit often, usually in small groups.[75] In September 2014 a family meeting convened, Wilbur said with amusement, to vote on whether there had been too many recent visits, thus tiring instead of energizing him. In 2015 the family found a happy compromise. Patty Kimura, who had been a literary assistant to William Jay Smith for several years before his death in August of that year, now arrives in the late weekday afternoons, shares dinner with Wilbur, and spends the evening with him. They may chat about their common interests and current events—everything from poetry to politics and religion—but they always look, especially in their weightier conversations, for places to inject humor and share a few laughs. Patty spoke about part of their evening ritual:

> One of the things we do is say Grace, which has always been important to Dick, from childhood. He sometimes says a standard Episcopalian Grace but often he says, "Will you?" Since I am terrible at remembering [the Grace from my childhood] . . . I have often made up my own, which sometimes includes things we are mutually grateful for—the natural world, things of the natural world like "steam rising from this soup," and "the color of moss, different on days of rain," and, always "we are grateful for Leo." (Mentioning Leo [Wilbur's cat] always cheers him a great deal.)[76]

Wilbur now declines to give readings, even at nearby venues, and rarely travels out of western Massachusetts. His days adhere to routine. On balmy mornings he may take the short walk from the house to his studio, where his desk stands in front of a grand picture window with a view of the woods, but in winter he stays safely in the first-floor den of the main house. Only recently has he cut back on the number of letters he once sent in response to notes from admirers of his work; now he prefers to write on postcards only to friends. Jeanette brings Wilbur the *New York Times,* still reserved for him daily at the Creamery, where in the late 1970s he and Smith engaged in a weekly limerick-writing contest: whoever got to the store first on a given Sunday would write a humorous verse directly on the first page of the other person's Sunday paper.[77] The chair once monopolized by Charlee is now his; on a nearby coffee table, and on the floor within reach, books are piled in stacks. For years Wilbur's two blue-eyed Siamese cats, siblings named Mimi and Leo, had perched on the arms of his chair like the lions guarding the New York Public Library. Mimi died in 2014, and now Leo, still missing her, prefers to settle on Wilbur's knee.

Acknowledgments

We began to research Richard Wilbur's life and work in the fall of 2005 at the Archives and Special Collections at Amherst College's Frost Library, where his papers are held. We are grateful to those at the archives who directed and assisted us—especially to the director at the time, Daria D'Arienzo; Mike Kelly, the current director; and Christina Barber, the current deputy archivist—as well as to John Lancaster and Jack Hagstrom, the bibliographers of the large collection of Wilbur's correspondence, manuscript drafts, and other materials.

In addition, we would like to thank the librarians and archivists of special collections at several other institutions we visited, including the University of Delaware, the 36th Texas Division's Military Museum at Camp Mabry in Austin, the Manuscripts and Archives Division at the New York Public Library, the Houghton Collection at Harvard University, the Harry Ransom Center at the University of Texas, Austin, and Wesleyan University Library. We thank Karen Faracci and David Faracci for their kind welcome during our visit to Middletown and Portland, Connecticut, in October 2014. Thanks also to two Wesleyan alumni: William Blakemore, for recreating a sense of campus life in the early to mid-1960s, and Michael Wolfe, for his insightful comments on an early draft of our book.

During the years we spent gathering research material, interviewing our sources, and studying and discussing Wilbur's life and work, we have received advice and inspiration from many people. Listing them and properly acknowledging their contributions would take many pages. Their help has directed, corrected, and enriched our work; we thank each and every one of them.

Sections of our book were published in the *Hopkins Review,* the *Yale Review,* the *Common,* the *Amherst Alumni Magazine,* and the *North Dakota*

Quarterly; we thank the editors for their confidence in these early drafts. We appreciate the support of Brian Halley and everyone else at the University of Massachusetts Press, Amherst, whose various talents and efforts have helped bring this book into readers' hands, especially Jack Harrison, the book's cover and general designer. We are grateful to Dawn Potter and Elaine Coveney, respectively, for copyediting and proofreading that was both exacting and inspired. Diane Brenner, by creating a detailed index, allows readers to locate not only the major points of interest in Wilbur's life but also the nuances and complexities of his life and work. And we thank the National Endowment for the Humanities, whose "For the People" grant in 2007 helped to sustain our work.

We have been heartened by the enthusiastic responses from Wilbur fans, many of whom we met at the West Chester Formalist Poetry Conference in 2011 and 2016, and from those who have contacted us over the years and shown interest in this biography. The cooperation of Wilbur's children and their spouses, who not only shared their memories but also allowed us access to unarchived family correspondence and photos, was invaluable. And we are truly indebted to our own family and friends for their encouragement and support.

Notes

Prologue

1. Louise Bogan, "Verse," *New Yorker,* November 15, 1947, 134.
2. Richard Wilbur (hereafter RW), draft letter to Marianne Moore, February 11, 1948, in Richard P. Wilbur Deposit, Amherst College Archives and Special Collections, Amherst Library (hereafter RPW Deposit, AC). As Wilbur explained in his letter, Harry Levin, a friend and colleague at Harvard, where Wilbur had just finished a five-year term as a lecturer, suggested that he send Moore his translation of La Fontaine's fable "Loves of Cupid and Psyche." Moore was fascinated by the craftsmanship and moral messages of La Fontaine's *Fables choisie, mise en vers* and at the time was struggling in her work to translate the complete volume. Her translation was finally published in 1954, although it is not recognized as her greatest poetic achievement.
3. Marianne Moore, letter to RW, September 18, 1948, RPW Deposit, AC. As Moore was quick to make clear, her sketches were not accompaniments to poems; they only illustrated references to some detail she wished to remember. She also responded favorably to Wilbur's translation of La Fontaine's "Loves of Cupid and Psyche," commending his efforts for their spirit, modesty, and hard-to-achieve smoothness (ibid.).
4. John Malcolm Brinnin (hereafter JMB), journal entry, May 6, 1957, John Malcolm Brinnin Papers, University of Delaware Library, Newark, Delaware (hereafter Brinnin Papers, Delaware). In contrast to the reserved Miss Moore, Wilbur cut a dashing figure on the Wellesley campus. In 2006 Sheila (Owen) Monks, a former student and a member of the class of 1956, wrote to him in an attempt to entice him to appear at her fiftieth class reunion. She recalled an image of him, at about age thirty-five, striding around the campus in a cowboy hat and boots, and she claimed that every woman within a radius of five miles had a crush on him (letter to RW, April 28, 2006, RW's personal papers).
5. JMB, journal entry, May 6, 1957.
6. RW, interview by Robert Bagg and Mary Bagg, January 15, 2006. Hereafter, all of our interviews with Wilbur and his wife, which took place at their home in Cummington, will be cited as "interview by the authors."
7. We base this statement on letters from Bishop and Lowell in the RPW Deposit, AC, and in *Words in Air: The Complete Correspondence of Elizabeth Bishop and Robert Lowell,* ed. Thomas Travisano with Saskia Hamilton (New York: Farrar, Straus and Giroux, 2010).
8. RW, interview by the authors, October 26, 2007.
9. In 1976 the National Institute of Arts and Letters merged with the American Academy of Arts and Letters (AAAL) under Wilbur's leadership, to become a single body known as the AAAL. (He was elected to the AAAL in 1972, becoming its president in 1974 and its chancellor in 1976.) He shared his first Bollingen (awarded in November 1963 for translating

Tartuffe) with Walker Arnt (for translating Alexander Pushkin's *Eugene Onegin*). He shared his second Bollingen, awarded for achievements in poetry in January 1971, with Mona Van Duyn.

10. David Orr, "The Formalist," *New York Times,* January 7, 2011.

11. Dana Gioia, quoted in David Lyle Jeffrey, "God's Patient Stet," *First Things* (June 2011), www.firstthings.com.

12. Bruce Michelson, *Wilbur's Poetry: Music in Scattering Time* (Amherst: University of Massachusetts Press, 1991) ("mannered," 8, 17, 42, 113, 200; "amiable," 36; "safe," 18, 36, 149); Anthony Hecht, "Richard Wilbur: An Introduction," in *Melodies Unheard: Essays on the Mysteries of Poetry* (Baltimore: Johns Hopkins University Press, 2003), 174, 176; William Logan, "America's Laureate," *Chicago Tribune,* July 24, 1988; Joseph Bennett, "Verse," and John Ciardi, "Claims on the Poet," in *Richard Wilbur's Creation,* ed. Wendy Salinger (Ann Arbor: University of Michigan Press, 1983), 40, 54; Leslie Fiedler, *Waiting for the End* (London: Stein and Day, 1964), 219.

13. Orr, "The Formalist."

14. RW, unpublished journal, May 1973, RW's personal papers.

1. Childhood in North Caldwell, New Jersey

1. RW, "This Pleasing Anxious Being," in *Collected Poems, 1943–2004* (New York: Harcourt, 2004), 57–58. Unless otherwise noted, all quoted Wilbur poems can be found in this collected volume. On the first mention of each poem we discuss, we name the book in which it first appeared as well as the year that book was published.

2. In a 2014 e-mail Wilbur's daughter-in-law Christie told us that he is the twelfth generation "descended from Samuel Wilbur who, with other followers of Ann Hutchinson, was kicked out of Puritan Boston for heresy, fled south, and was given land by Roger Williams, in what became Rhode Island. (A non-conforming Non-Conformist in other words, though he later returned to the Puritan fold.) Dick is descended from a branch of the family that moved from Rhode Island to upstate New York in the eighteenth century. It was Dick's fifth great-grandfather, Robert Wilbur, born in Little Compton, RI, in 1715, who moved to Duchess County, NY, where he died in 1782. Dick's great-grandfather was Reuben [and his grandfather] was Henry Wilbur, 1825–1898, who at the outbreak of the Civil War became a 1st Lieutenant in the 102nd NY Volunteer Infantry; he received special commendation for his service at the Battle of Gettysburg, rising to Major and then Lieut. Colonel. He served under General Geary from the Battle of Antietam till the close of the war. The Little Compton Wilburs were Quakers—and probably for a time the upstate New York ones [were], too. They had names like Shadrach, Obadiah, and Freelove. One of the Little Compton Wilburs, John Wilbur, who descended from a line that stayed in Rhode Island, was a prominent Quaker minister and gave his name to a Quaker schism in the nineteenth century (the 'Wilburites')." Supplemental information comes from Wilbur's cousin Ray Wilbur in a letter to RW, July 20, 2009, RW's personal papers. He confirmed life dates for the family's "original NE immigrant, Samuel Wildbore (1585–1656)" and for John Wilbur (1774–1856). He also provided insight about John Wilbur's split from the main body of Quakerism: "The issue seems to have been theological, a denial of the virgin birth of Jesus, the resurrection, etc., defended by the Wilburites. Quakers, as you know, emphasized direct spiritual inspiration rather than by the word of the Scriptures."

3. RW, interview by the authors, January 27, 2006.

4. Ibid.

5. During World War II several of Lawrence Wilbur's posters addressed Uncle Sam's need for working women to support the war effort.

6. From 1940 to 1965, the Rheingold Beer Company sponsored highly popular beauty pageants whose winners appeared in its print and television advertising.

7. RW, interview by the authors, January 27, 2006.

8. RW, interview by the authors, December 9, 2005.

9. RW, interview by the authors, December 19, 2005.

10. RW, interview by the authors, January 27, 2006.

11. RW, interview by the authors, April 4, 2006.

12. RW, interview by the authors, January 27, 2006.

13. Charlee Wilbur (hereafter CW), interview by the authors, March 9, 2006.

14. RW, unpublished draft copy of "Tears," RW's personal papers.

15. RW, interview by the authors, April 4, 2006.

16. RW, interview by the authors, January 27, 2006.

17. Ibid.

18. RW, interview by the authors, April 4, 2006.

19. Ibid.

20. The six poems are "He Was," "The Pardon," "Digging for China," "This Pleasing Anxious Being," "A Summer Morning," and "Running."

21. Robert Frost, "Birches," in *The Poetry of Robert Frost: The Collected Poems, Complete and Unabridged*, ed. Edward Connery Latham (New York: Holt, 1969), 121–22.

22. RW, interview by the authors, January 27, 2006.

23. The word *modesty* is a genuine concern of several Corneille characters and is ironically attributed to others. Corneille was born into a family of modest means and achieved modest renown in his lifetime. *Modesty* was a trait ascribed to him by an astrological horoscope for June 6, 1606 (his birthdate); other traits were *competent, scrupulous, logical,* and *tidy.*

24. RW, interview by the authors, October 29, 2007.

25. Thomas Gray, "Elegy Written in a Country Churchyard," in *The Norton Anthology of Poetry: Shorter Edition,* 3rd ed., ed. Alexander W. Allison, Herbert Barrow, Caesar A. Blake, Arthur J. Carr, Arthur M. Eastman, and Hubert M. English, Jr. (New York: Norton, 1983), 248–51. Lines 85–88 of the "Elegy" read:

    For who to dumb Forgetfulness a prey,
    This pleasing anxious being e'er resigned,
    Left the warm precincts of the cheerful day,
    Nor cast one longing lingering look behind?

26. RW, interview by the authors, April 6, 2006.

27. RW, interview by the authors, July 16, 2006. Essex Fells was an unusually small and unique residential community, originally incorporated as a borough by a charter that explicitly prohibited commercial development. Its zoning restrictions also ensured that its house lots would be irregular and spacious, and its well-off residents were disposed to support a superior school system.

28. Irving Selvage, interview by the authors, November 2, 2006. Selvage was a classmate of Wilbur's in Essex Fells.

29. RW, interview by the authors, July 16, 2006.

30. Ibid.

31. Ibid.

32. RW, interview by the authors, January 27, 2006.

33. RW, interview by the authors, July 16, 2006.

34. RW, "The Difficulty of Getting Out a Newspaper," *Nottingham News,* August 2, 1933, 2, RPW Deposit, AC. The newsletter was associated with Robin Hood Camp in Sargentville-Herricks, Maine.

35. Wilbur reached Star Scout rank and was leader of the Silver Fox patrol when it won a knot-tying contest at a camporee.

36. RW, cartoon of Lincoln and Uncle Sam, [Montclair High School] *Mountaineer,* February 11, 1938, 2; RW, cartoon of wealthy matron, *Mountaineer,* December 17, 1937, 2; both in RPW Deposit, AC.

37. RW, "From *Belmont Blast,*" for English 10-2, RW's personal papers.

38. RW, "He Will Not Tell You This," *Mountaineer,* November 19, 1937, 2, RPW Deposit, AC.
39. RW, "Case for Infancy," *Mountaineer,* October 15, 1937, 2, RPW Deposit, AC.

2. Amherst College

1. Amherst College, "Hurricane of 1938," www.amherst.edu. The text is from a 2005 exhibition in the Amherst College Library, Archives and Special Collections.
2. RW, interview by the authors, July 16, 2006.
3. "*Touchstone* Lacking Talent in First Issue," *Amherst Student,* October 23, 1940, 1, Amherst College Student and Alumni Publications Collections, Amherst College Archives and Special Collections (hereafter AC Student Archives), series 2, box 14. "White hope," used here as a generic epithet, originally denoted a white prizefighter who was expected to defeat a black champion.
4. RW, interview by the authors, December 19, 2005.
5. Morgenthau was the son of President Roosevelt's secretary of the treasury and went on to become a long-serving district attorney for Manhattan.
6. RW, "Back on the Toboggan," *Amherst Student,* March 10, 1941, 2, AC Student Archives, series 2, box 14.
7. RW, "Fraternity Hazing," *Amherst Student,* October 5, 1939, 2; RW, "Lowenstein and Baldwin Debate Issue of Civil Liberties and Fifth Column," *Amherst Student,* October 28, 1940, 1; both in AC Student Archives, series 2, box 14.
8. RW, "Gambolling," *Touchstone* (April 1940): 3, AC Student Archives, series 1, box 13.
9. RW, "The New Seriousness," *Touchstone* (October 1941): 5, AC Student Archives, series 1, box 13.
10. RW, "The New Gloriousness," *Touchstone* (February 1941): 6, AC Student Archives, series 1, box 13.
11. CW, interview by the authors, March 9, 2006.
12. CW, interview by the authors, October 20, 2005.
13. Morris Jastrow, Jr., "William Hayes Ward (1835–1916)," *JSTOR Early Journal Content,* http://archive.org.
14. CW, interview by the authors, October 20, 2005.
15. Published after the Civil War, Phelps's *The Gates Ajar* appealed to the era's hopeful view of an afterlife for the war's dead: its characters reside in the hereafter and retain their physical attributes and personalities. Phelps was an advocate of social reform, temperance, and women's rights, writing in 1874, "Burn up the corsets! . . . No, nor do you save the whalebones. . . . Your emancipation, I assure you, has from this moment begun" (*Phelps Family History in America,* www.phelpsfamilyhistory.com).
16. CW, interview by the authors, October 20, 2005.
17. See chapter 10 for more about the life of Edna Ward.
18. CW, interview by the authors, October 20, 2005.
19. RW, letter to CW, ca. March 1941, RW's personal papers.
20. RW and CW, interview by the authors, March 9, 2006.
21. CW, interview by the authors, October 20, 2005.
22. George Shenk, "Out of South Memphis," *Touchstone* (October 1941): 16, AC Student Archives, series 1, box 13.
23. RW, letter to Theodore Baird, July 5, 1941, Richard P. Wilbur Papers, Amherst College Archives and Special Collections, Amherst College Library (hereafter RPW Papers, AC), series 5, box 4, folder 18.
24. Sterling Lamprecht, marginalia, in RW, "Protestantism in the Light of Its History," undated, RW's personal papers.
25. RW, untitled essay, RW's personal papers.
26. RW, "Now That We Are in It," *Amherst Student,* December 8, 1941, 1, AC Student Archives, series 2, box 14.

27. Stanley King, "Address to Students at Johnson Chapel," *Amherst Student,* December 8, 1941, 1, AC Student Archives, series 2, box 14.

28. RW, interview by the authors, January 27, 2006.

29. CW, interview by the authors, October 20, 2005.

30. Ibid. A studio photo, accompanied by an announcement that Charlee had been chosen to be queen of Amherst College's Harvest Festival and "will probably make her bow over the holidays," appeared in the *Boston Sunday Herald,* November 5, 1939.

31. An undated newspaper clipping, probably from a South Berwick weekly, described the dresses and flowers of the female attendants and the mothers of the bride and groom (from a scrapbook, RW's personal papers).

32. CW, interview by the authors, October 5, 2005.

3. World War II, Stateside and in Italy

1. Allen Tate, "Ode to Our Young Proconsuls of the Air," *Partisan Review,* March 1943, 129–31.

2. RW, letter to Theodore Baird (hereafter TB), April 1, 1943, RPW Papers, AC, series 5, box 4, folder 18.

3. RW, letter to TB, August 5, 1943, RPW Papers, AC, series 5, box 4, folder 18.

4. Wilbur allowed us access to his war records, which he had requested in 2006 from the National Personnel Records Center in Washington, D.C. They document his movement through the ranks from private to sergeant. In January 2007, we visited the Texas Military Forces Museum in Austin, which houses the archives of the 36th Texas Division, and received permission to copy a number of after-action reports covering the division's activity during World War II. We constructed the narratives in chapters 3 and 4 from these materials and from information in the following sources: Fred Walker, *From Texas to Rome: A General's Journal* (Dallas: Taylor, 1969); Matthew Parker, *Monte Cassino: The Hardest-Fought Battle of World War II* (New York: Knopf Doubleday, 2005); David Haven Blake, "Richard Wilbur's World War II Poetry," *War Literature and Arts* 10, no. 1 (1998): 1–36; Joseph Cox, "Versifying in Earnest," *War Literature and Arts* 10, no. 1 (1998): 37–71.

5. RW, letter to TB, May 2, 1943, RPW Papers, AC, series 5, box 4, folder 18. The army did transfer Schwadron to a less sensitive communications unit in California but eventually trusted him enough to put him in charge of extensive telephone networks in both Italy and France. Wilbur's friendship with Schwadron may have reinforced his superiors' judgment that Wilbur had not shed his collegiate sympathy for Soviet communism.

6. RW, letter to Armour Craig, October 4, 1943, RPW Papers, AC, series 5, box 4, folder 25.

7. The events were reported in Studs Terkel's *The Good War: An Oral History of World War II* (New York: Pantheon, 1984), 151–53.

8. Nat Brandt, *Harlem at War: The Black Experience in WWII* (Syracuse, N.Y.: Syracuse University Press, 1996), 137.

9. RW, letter to Tom Wilcox, December 11, 1943, Thomas W. Wilcox (AC 1942) Papers, Amherst College Archives and Special Collections, Amherst College Library (hereafter cited as TWW Papers, AC), box 1, folder 16.

10. RW, interview by the authors, January 27, 2006.

11. The U.S. military's SIGABA code machine (whose name suggests its communication and alphabetical components but is not an acronym) has long been a classified subject. We do know that it enabled orders and information to be disseminated securely via shortwave radio from commanders to their units in war zones. The British were able to crack the Germans' Enigma code after they acquired one of its machines, but apparently the Germans neither captured a SIGABA nor learned to decipher its messages.

12. RW, interview by the authors, November 15, 2015.

13. RW, interview by the authors, January 27, 2006.

14. RW, letter to CW, January 21, 1944, RW's personal papers.

15. RW, typescript of "Maddaloni," RW's personal papers.

16. RW, typescript of "Two Statements," RW's personal papers.

17. Ibid.

18. According to the Texas Military Museum archives, the 36th Division suffered 2,877 casualties, including 1,681 killed ("Rapido River Crossing, 36th Div., Italy, WWII," http://texasmilitaryforcesmuseum.yuku.com).

19. RW, letter to Joe Cox, September 5, 1997, RW's personal papers.

20. Not firing Walker was one of Clark's luckiest personnel decisions; probably no other general would have accomplished what Walker did during the first few days of June 1944.

21. RW, interview by the authors, November 15, 2005.

22. Wilbur recalled a dinner conversation he had years later in Cambridge, England, concerning the controversial decision to bomb. A German officer who had been on the mountaintop (and who later became a war historian), assured him that the Germans had not used the monastery in any way. The general in charge of its defense, Fridolin von Senger und Etterlin, a Prussian aristocrat who despised Hitler and the Nazis, had even forbidden his men, when visiting the abbey or dining with the monks, to look out its windows.

23. RW, "Day After the War," *Foreground* 1, no. 2 (1946): 108–16, 111. The same issue features six other poems by Wilbur—"Water Walker," "Mined Country," "Potato," "Place Pigalle," "The Regatta," and "In a Bird Sanctuary"—all of which were included in *The Beautiful Changes.*

24. RW, letter to Helen Wilbur and Lawrence Wilbur, February 25, 1944, RW's personal papers.

25. RW, letter to Helen Wilbur and Lawrence Wilbur, April 3, 1944, RW's personal papers.

26. RW, letter to Helen Wilbur and Lawrence Wilbur, July 28, 1944, RW's personal papers.

27. Ibid.

28. RW, "Round About a Poem of Housman's," in *Responses: Prose Pieces, 1953–1976,* rev. ed. (Ashland, Ore.: Story Line, 1999), 27–54.

29. Ibid., 54.

30. Ibid.

31. During World War II the U.S. military developed V-mail, short for Victory Mail, to conserve shipping space and reduce the costs of moving mail through the military postal system. Letters were censored, photographed, copied to microfilm, and then printed on paper at 60 percent of their original size.

32. RW, letter to Helen Wilbur and Lawrence Wilbur, May 20, 1944, RW's personal papers.

33. Paul Wells, "History of the 36th Signal Company," in *36th Signal Company History: 1922–1945* (Deniston, Tex.: 36th Signal Company, 1983), 38.

34. RW, interview by the authors, March 9, 2007.

35. RW, letter to CW, June 6, 1944, RW's personal papers.

36. CW, letter to Helen Wilbur and Lawrence Wilbur, dated "Saturday night, June 1944," RW's personal papers.

37. RW, letter to CW, June 11, 1944, RW's personal papers.

38. Walker was ordered back to the United States, where he assumed command of the Army Infantry Training Center at Fort Benning, Georgia.

39. RW, letter to Helen Wilbur and Lawrence Wilbur, July 22, 1944, RW's personal papers.

40. RW, letter to CW, June 16, 1944, RW's personal papers.

41. Polly Tywater Burton, letter to RW, October 7, 1987, RPW Deposit, AC.

42. RW, interview by the authors, January 27, 2006.

43. LST (short for "Landing Ship, Tank") is the naval designation for a World War II vessel that supported amphibious operations by carrying vehicles, supplies, and troops directly to shore.

44. RW, *History of the 36th Signal Company, Message Center Division in France, Germany and Austria* (Camp Mabry, Tex.: 36th Texas Division, n.d.), 7.

45. RW, letter to Helen Wilbur and Lawrence Wilbur, August 8, 1944, RW's personal papers.

4. World War II in France, Germany, and England

1. RW, *History of the 36th Signal Company, Message Center Section in France, Germany and Austria* (Camp Mabry, Tex.: 36th Texas Division, n.d.), 5.
2. RW, letter to Helen Wilbur and Lawrence Wilbur, September 9, 1945, RW's personal papers.
3. RW, *History*, 12.
4. Ibid., 13.
5. RW, interview by the authors, June 28, 2006.
6. RW, *History*, 12.
7. RW, letter to Helen Wilbur and Lawrence Wilbur, September 9, 1945, RW's personal papers.
8. RW, letter to Helen Wilbur and Lawrence Wilbur, September 17, 1945, RW's personal papers.
9. RW, typescript of "Fingers," undated, RW's personal papers.
10. RW, *History*, 16.
11. Ibid., 23.
12. Ibid., 24.
13. Ibid., 30.
14. Ibid.
15. Ibid.
16. CW, interview by the authors, March 9, 2006.
17. CW, letter to RW, November 21, 1945, RW's personal papers.
18. RW, *History*, 35–36. While his unit was at Weilheim, Wilbur wrote, "The infantry captured the German General von Rundstedt, soaking in his bath [twenty miles away] at Bad Tölz, and pleading rheumatism." According to official documents in the 36th Division archives, however, Second Lieutenant Joseph Burke captured von Rundstedt—who was recovering from a leg injury and was distressed at being unable to resist—as he sat with his family before a fire.
19. RW, *History*, 36–37.
20. RW, "The Day After the War," *Foreground* 1, no. 2 (1946): 108–16.
21. RW, letter to TB, July 30, 1945, RPW Papers, AC, series 5, box 4, folder 18.
22. RW, interview by the authors, June 28, 2006.
23. RW, interview by the authors, April 4, 2006.
24. RW, interview by the authors, January 14, 2008.
25. RW, letter to TB, July 30, 1945, RPW Papers, AC, series 5, box 4, folder 18.
26. Ibid.
27. Ibid.
28. RW, editorial, *Robert Reveille,* July 17, 1945, 2.
29. RW, letter to TB, September 17, 1945, RPW Papers, AC, series 5, box 4, folder 18.
30. RW, editorial, *Robert Reveille,* June 27, 1945, 2.
31. RW, editorial, *Robert Reveille,* July 10, 1945, 2.
32. RW, editorial, *T-Patch,* October 28, 1945, 2, 6.
33. RW, letter to TB, August 23, 1945, RPW Papers, AC, series 5, box 4, folder 18.

5. Religion and Wilbur's War Poems

1. RW, letter to TB, April 1, 1943, RPW Papers, AC, series 5, box 4, folder 18.
2. The ten war poems are "Potato," "Place Pigalle," "Caserta Garden," "The Peace of Cities," "First Snow in Alsace," "A Dubious Night," "Water Walker," "Mined Country," "On the Eyes of an SS Officer," and "Tywater." The last seven poems in this list refer to God.
3. Joe Cox, letter to RW, August 29, 1997, RW's personal papers.
4. RW, letter to Joe Cox, September 5, 1997, RW's personal papers.
5. Ibid.

6. Paul Mariani, "A 1995 Interview with Richard Wilbur," *Image* 12 (Winter 1995): 39–51, 46.
7. Adam Kirsch, "Get Happy: Richard Wilbur and the Poetry of Profusion," *New Yorker,* November 22, 2004, 95.
8. Mariani, "A 1995 Interview," 46.
9. Ibid.
10. Terza rima stanzas follow the pattern *aba, bcb, cdc,* and so on; traditionally a terza rima poem ends with a single line that rhymes with the middle line of the last tercet.
11. Paul Mariani, *God and the Imagination: On Poets, Poetry, and the Ineffable* (Athens: University of Georgia Press, 2002), 235.
12. The poem was published as "Cigales" in *The Beautiful Changes,* but Wilbur changed the title to "Cicadas" in later collections to reflect the insect's Latin name.
13. Jewel Spears Brooker, "Interview with Richard Wilbur," *Christianity and Literature* 41, no. 4 (Summer 1992): 517–39, 538–39. In 1992 the Conference on Christianity and Literature awarded Wilbur its Lifetime Achievement Award, citing how his poetry conveys love and sensitivity to his fellow creatures, humility before the natural world, and openness to the supernatural—all marked by a Christian sense of grace.

6. The Cambridge Years

1. RW and CW, interview by the authors, October 20, 2005.
2. In a letter drafted (but possibly unsent) to Armour Craig, Wilbur explained that a friend (probably Brinnin, who would organize Dylan Thomas's first tour in New York in 1950) had asked Jack Sweeney, the curator of the Lamont Poetry Reading Room, to solicit recommenders, including Randall Jarrell, Peter Taylor, and Ridgely Torrence, who might help Thomas gain an academic position in Wales comparable to the one Frost held as a poet in residence at Amherst in the late 1930s. Would Craig be willing to write as well? A guaranteed academic salary would free Thomas from the need to write scripts for the BBC, and Brinnin believed that he would in turn drink less and go back to writing serious poetry. However, Thomas never did get such a position before he died in New York in 1953 (RW, draft letter to Armour Craig, ca. 1949, RW's personal papers).
3. RW, letter to Armour Craig and Peggy Craig, February 25, 1946, RPW Papers, AC, series 5, box 4, folder 25.
4. Ibid.
5. In January 1946 the university had an influx of 3,000 returning veterans, many of them, like Wilbur and Wilcox, not originally Harvard students.
6. Questionnaire, "Evaluations of Harvard English Department, 1943–1948," typescript, 6, 11, Widener Library, Harvard University.
7. Henry Taylor, quoted by RW, interview with the authors, June 27, 2007.
8. JMB, journal entry, September 7, 1947, Brinnin Papers, Delaware.
9. RW, letter to Craig and Craig, February 25, 1947. "Empsonian" refers to literary criticism that is based on close textual reading and excludes social, autobiographical, and political contexts.
10. RW and CW, interview by the authors, October 20, 2005. The story of du Bouchet's pronouncement has become a legend in Wilbur lore and one that Wilbur has shared with a number of interviewers.
11. Ibid.
12. Monroe Engel, letter to RW, March 22, 1946, RPW Deposit, AC.
13. Gerry Gross, letter to RW, September 11, 1947, RPW Deposit, AC. The offending word appears in the first stanza.
14. JMB, letter to RW, November 1, 1997, RPW Deposit, AC. The Stones were Walter Stone and his wife, the poet Ruth Stone. Bill Read was Brinnin's partner.
15. Louise Bogan, "Verse," *New Yorker,* November 15, 1947, 134.
16. F. C. Golffing, "A Remarkable New Talent," *Poetry* 71 (January 1948): 122.

17. RW, unpublished Cambridge notebook, 5–6, RW's personal papers.

18. In psychology the word *canalization* refers to the way in which an organism channels its need into fixed patterns of gratification.

19. William Wordsworth, "Preface [to *Lyrical Ballads*]," in *English Romantic Poetry and Prose,* ed. Russell Noyes (New York: Oxford University Press, 1956), 365; Robert Frost, "Putting in the Seed," in *Collected Poems, Prose, and Plays,* ed. Richard Poirier and Mark Richardson (New York: Library Classics of America, 1995), 120.

20. RW, unpublished Cambridge notebook, 24. Wilbur's offhand comment about "having no patience for suicides" brings to mind the critical outcry regarding "Cottage St., 1953," his poem about meeting Sylvia Plath a decade before she took her own life (see chapter 10). His parenthetical remark about the actor reflects that during the period in which he wrote in this notebook, T. S. Eliot's talk at Harvard inspired him to think about writing verse drama (see chapter 7).

21. Ibid., 39.

22. George C. Homans and Orville T. Bailey, "The Society of Fellows of Harvard University, 1933–1947," in *The Society of Fellows,* ed. Crane Brinton (Cambridge, Mass.: Society of Fellows at Harvard University, 1959), 1–37, 5–6. As Homans and Bailey explained, Trinity conducted a yearly competition among its graduates to identify the men who were most likely to make important advances in the sciences and the great humanistic disciplines, such as classics and philology. Its Prize Fellows program succeeded spectacularly. According to a 1926 report presented at Harvard by a four-person committee (including Lawrence Joseph Henderson, a professor of biological chemistry who was instrumental in shaping the Society of Fellows), "one-half of the British Nobel Prize winners, one-fifth of the civil members of the Orders of Merit, and four of the five Foulerton Research Professors of the Royal Society" were Trinity fellows.

23. In 1947 the newly elected junior fellows were William P. Jacobs, biology; Carl Kaysan, economics; Ivan King, astronomy; I. Herbert Scheinberg, medicine; Peter Schneider, romance languages; Donald H. Shiveley, far eastern languages; James Tobin, economics; and Wilbur in English literature. Other notable junior fellows in English literature have included Cesar Lombardi Barber (1936–1939), Walter Jackson Bate (1942–1946), Donald Hall (1954–1957), John Hollander (1954–1957), Harry Levin (1936–1939), Allen Mandelbaum (1951–1954), and Lowry Nelson, Jr. (1951–1954).

24. RW, "Degas and the Subject," typescript, 2, RW's personal papers.

25. Ibid., 23.

26. Charles Baudelaire, "Mon coeur mis à nu: journal intime" (1887), www.bmlisieux.com.

27. RW, "Degas and the Subject," 8.

28. "Dandy" became Baudelaire's shorthand for a dedicated artist. In 1947 Sartre incorporated aspects of Baudelaire's version of dandyism into a book-length appreciation of the poet's personality.

29. Radcliffe students did not gain access to Lamont until the late 1960s.

30. See, for instance, Richard Wilbur, André du Bouchet, Thomas W. Wilcox, and William B. Whiteside, "To the Editors of the *Crimson,*" *Harvard Crimson,* July 18, 1947. The writers expressed dismay at the editors' failure to take a stand in support of demonstrators (some accused of communist leanings) in the audience of seven hundred people who were listening to a speech by Gerald L. K. Smith. An unabashed racist and anti-Semite, Smith was rebuffed by the America First Committee of noninterventionists before America joined World War II but went on to join the America First Party in 1944 as well as the postwar Christian Nationalist Crusade. Wilbur and the others asked in their letter, "Is it a denial of free speech for the audience to be rather louder than the man who is addressing it?"

31. Steiner, who was, for a time, du Bouchet's partner, studied both poetry and singing after graduation. She went on to perform with various folksingers in the 1950s and later recorded under her married name, Jackie Sharpe.

32. RW, unpublished Cambridge notebook, 36. In March 1949 the Wilburs met Sitwell and her brother Sir Osbert Sitwell at Richard and Betty Eberhart's home.

33. George A. Leifer, "An Evening with the Sitwells," *Harvard Crimson,* March 5, 1949.

34. Peter De Vries to RW, September 25, 1947, *New Yorker* Records, Manuscripts and Archives Division, New York Public Library (hereafter *New Yorker* Records, NYPL), series III (subseries 3.1), box 456, folder 25.

35. Ibid.

36. RW, letter to Peter De Vries, ca. October 3, 1947, *New Yorker* Records, NYPL, series III (subseries 3.1), box 456, folder 25. After Wilbur's lengthy explanation of the art historical conventions that justified his choice, De Vries replied that his use of "Toulouse seems all right" (letter to RW, October 7, 1947, *New Yorker* Records, NYPL, series III (subseries 3.1), box 456, folder 25.

37. De Vries, letter to RW, October 7, 1947.

38. RW, letter to Peter De Vries, October 8, 1947, *New Yorker* Records, NYPL, series III (subseries 3.1), box 456, folder 25.

39. CW, letter to Tom Wilcox, April 13, 1948, TWW Papers, AC, box 1, folder 12.

40. The poem refers to Edmund Burke, the British philosopher whose *Reflections on Revolution in France* (1790) addresses the nature of human rights. Certain animal rights activists have adopted his famous statement "The only thing necessary for the triumph of evil is for good men to do nothing" as a slogan.

41. RW, letter to Tom Wilcox, April 12, 1948, TWW Papers, AC, box 1, folder 19.

42. Ibid.

43. RW, letter to Tom Wilcox and Darlene Wilcox, May 14, 1948, TWW Papers, AC, box 1, folder 19. Wilbur and Wilcox remained close friends until Wilcox's death in 2008, visiting each other when schedules permitted. Their correspondence, however, was never as intense as it was during the war and immediate post-Harvard years. Wilbur spoke at Wilcox's memorial service on March 7, 2009.

44. See chapter 1 for the text of the poem "Tears."

45. Peter De Vries, letter to RW, February 24, 1948, *New Yorker* Records, NYPL, series III (subseries 3.1), box 470, folder 48.

46. Peter De Vries, letter to RW, May 19, 1948, *New Yorker* Records, NYPL, series III (subseries 3.1), box 470, folder 48.

47. Helen Wilbur, letter to Peter De Vries, June 1, 1948, *New Yorker* Records, NYPL, series III (subseries 3.1), box 470, folder 48.

48. RW, quoted in Gary Fountain and Peter Brazeau, *Remembering Elizabeth Bishop: An Oral Biography* (Amherst: University of Massachusetts Press, 1994), 107.

49. David Kalstone, *Becoming a Poet: Elizabeth Bishop with Marianne Moore and Robert Lowell* (Ann Arbor: University of Michigan Press, 1989), 145.

50. Paul Mariani, *Lost Puritan* (New York: Norton, 1996), 172. Hardwick and Lowell married in 1949 and divorced in 1972.

51. Elizabeth Bishop, letter to RW, November 28, 1948, RPW Deposit, AC.

52. John Holmes, "The Visiting Poets," typescript, hand-dated February 1962, included inside a letter to RW, February 23, 1962, RPW Deposit, AC.

53. RW, "The Bottles Become New, Too," in *Responses: Prose Pieces, 1953–1976,* rev. ed. (Ashland, Ore.: Story Line, 1999), 271–81, 271. The title plays on his "The Genie in the Bottle," an earlier poetic manifesto in favor of formalism in which Wilbur concluded that "the strength of the genie comes of his being [so] confined" (in *Mid-Century American Poets,* ed. John Ciardi [New York: Twayne, 1950], 7–14).

54. Ibid., 271–72.

55. Ibid., 281.

56. RW, quoted in Craig Lambert, "Poetic Patriarch," *Harvard Magazine* III, no. 2 (November–December 2008): 36–41, 41.

57. RW, unpublished Cambridge notebook, n.p.

58. RW, "Edgar Allan Poe," in *Responses,* 66.

59. RW, letter to Theodore Baird, August 30, 1951, RPW Papers, AC, series 5, box 4, folder 18. *Borné* means "of limited intelligence."

60. RW, interview by the authors, July 16, 2006. Richards told Wilbur he liked to climb mountains because "one feels so alone." He met the woman he married, also a loner, on a mountaintop.

61. RW, letter to Baird, August 30, 1951.

62. Ibid.

63. The poems Wilbur wrote after arriving in Rome in September 1954 develop this revelation within the context of the city's art and history.

64. RW, unpublished Cambridge notebook, 21–22.

65. Robert Frost, quoted in Lambert, "Poetic Patriarch," 39.

66. Thomas Lovell Beddoes, "The Phantom Wooer," in *Norton Anthology of Literature,* 6th ed., vol. 2, ed. M. H. Abrams et al. (New York: Norton, 1993), 889–90.

67. RW, "Poetry's Debt to Poetry," in *Responses,* 230–31.

68. Ibid., 231.

69. RW, unpublished Cambridge notebook, 18.

70. Ibid., 19.

71. In 1924, when Matthiessen asked his friends in Yale's Skull and Bones Society if he should resist or yield to his love for Cheney, they gave him their blessing. (Skull and Bones and other Yale senior, secret societies require members to share their autobiographies and bare their souls to each other.)

72. JMB, journal entry, April 1, 1950, Brinnin Papers, Delaware. We could not identify V., although he was most likely someone Brinnin knew from his teaching days at Vassar.

73. F. O. Matthiessen, telegram to RW, April 1, 1950, RPW Deposit, AC. In his suicide note Matthiessen wrote that his severe depressions (which he had endured for ten years after a nervous breakdown caused by overwork) had driven him to kill himself. The note went on to imply that the rise of McCarthyism and rabid anti-communism as well as the enslavement of Eastern Europe were secondary causes. Brinnin was correct to assume that the death of Cheney had exacerbated Matthiessen's deep depression.

74. Herschel Baker, letter to RW, October 28, 1953, RPW Deposit, AC.

7. Claiming Molière for His Own Native Tongue

1. Members of the Poets' Theatre also included Donald Hall, John Ashbery, Frank O'Hara, Alison Lurie, Catherine Huntington, Lyon Phelps, Adrienne Rich, Edward Gorey, and many others.

2. Nora Sayre, "The Poets' Theatre," *Grand Street* 3 (Spring 1984): 92–105, 93. In 2014 Wilbur didn't recall why he'd felt the need to make that statement but was quick to correct any impression that members were ashamed of their association with the group.

3. T. S. Eliot, *Poetry and Drama* (London: Faber and Faber, 1950), 11, 21. After Faber and Faber published a first edition of the lecture, the text became part of Eliot's collected essays.

4. Ibid., 12–13.

5. "Casa Gutiérrez—Sandoval—Cordova," in *Corrales Historic Buildings* (Corrales, N.M.: Village of Corrales, Historic Preservation Committee, 2000). The Wilburs rented from John Adair, an anthropologist and an expert on Indian silversmithing, who had bought the house in early 1952.

6. RW, letter to JMB, September 10, 1952, Brinnin Papers, Delaware.

7. RW, letter to JMB, April 9, 1953, Brinnin Papers, Delaware.

8. RW, letter to JMB, May 17, 1953, Brinnin Papers, Delaware.

9. RW, letter to JMB, September 10, 1952.

10. RW, letter to R. A. Brooks, [Fall 1952], RPW Deposit, AC.

11. RW, unpublished Corrales notebook, RW's personal papers.

12. CW, interview by the authors, October 20, 2006.

13. RW, letter to Brooks, [Fall 1952].

14. John Keats, "Ode to a Nightingale," in *The Norton Anthology of Poetry: Shorter Edition,* 3rd ed., ed. Alexander A. Allison, Herbert Barrow, Caesar A. Blake, Arthur J. Carr, Arthur M. Eastman, and Hubert M. English, Jr. (New York: Norton, 1983), 370–71. In the last two lines Keats asks, "Was it a vision, or a waking dream? / Fled is that music:—Do I wake or sleep?"

15. RW, unpublished Corrales notebook.

16. The quotation marks around the passages and the ellipses that interrupt them indicate that he was quoting his own draft letter.

17. RW, unpublished Corrales notebook. Wilbur alludes here to the news that recently released KGB papers had documented that Hiss was in fact a Soviet spy.

18. RW, interview by the authors, March 17, 2014.

19. CW, interview by the authors, October 20, 2006.

20. Eliot, *Poetry and Drama,* 21–22.

21. CW, interview by the authors, October 20, 2006.

22. Eliot, *Poetry and Drama,* 26.

23. RW, "Introduction," in Molière, *"The Misanthrope" and "Tartuffe,"* trans. Richard Wilbur (New York: Harcourt, 1965), 7.

24. RW, "The Bottles Become New, Too," in *Responses: Prose Pieces, 1953–1976,* rev. ed. (Ashland, Ore: Story Line, 1999), 272 (emphasis added). We discuss Wilbur's defense of formalism in chapter 6.

25. Ibid., 273.

26. Ibid., 277.

27. RW, unpublished Corrales notebook (source of all quoted phrases in paragraph).

28. Ibid.

29. William Butler Yeats, "The Circus Animals' Desertion," *The Poems of W. B. Yeats,* ed. Richard J. Finneran (New York: Macmillan, 1983), 347–48.

30. RW, letter to JMB, April 9, 1953.

31. Ibid.

32. See the prologue, at note 12, for a critical overview of this perceived flaw.

33. Adam Kirsch, "Get Happy," *New Yorker,* November 22, 2004, 96.

34. Ibid.

35. RW, "The Bottles Become New, Too," 277.

36. Isabella Wai offers a cogent discussion of "On the Marginal Way," particularly as regards the references to art in Wilbur's poetry (" 'Perfection in a Finite Task': Theme and Form in Representative Poems of Richard Wilbur," PhD diss., McMasters University, 1980). Other examples (among many) include "Looking into History" (with a reference to Mathew Brady's Civil War photographs), "This Pleasing Anxious Being" (with references to a Georges de La Tour nativity scene, Wilbur's father's paintings, and cinema and film as genres), and "Ceremony" (with a reference to Frédéric Bazille's *Family Reunion*).

37. Thomas Lask, "18 Leading Poets and Writers Give Reading Stressing Peace," *New York Times,* November 13, 1967. The reading included five other Pulitzer winners: Kunitz, Lowell, Snodgrass, Arthur Miller, and Mark Van Doren. The phrase "some dirty war" is a quote from "On the Marginal Way."

38. RW, interview by the authors, December 5, 2007.

39. RW, letter to Donald Carne-Ross, February 14, 1968, RPW Deposit, AC.

40. RW, interview by the authors, March 17, 2014.

41. Molière, *"The Misanthrope" and "Tartuffe,"* 38.

42. Eleanor Blau, "New 'Misanthrope' for Brian Bedford," *New York Times,* February 22, 1983.

43. RW, "Introduction," 9.

44. Ibid., 10. Molière drew on a comedic view of human nature that had come to life on the

Elizabethan stage, primarily in the work of Ben Jonson and William Shakespeare. It was based on the theory that a character's behavior was influenced by his or her predominant trait (or humor). The Elizabethans themselves had drawn on the theories of ancient Greek physicians and philosophers, who believed that the four humors (blood, phlegm, yellow bile, black bile) are the metabolic agents of the four elements (correspondingly, air, water, earth, fire) in the human body.

45. Ibid.
46. Dana Gioia, "An Interview with the Translator," in *The American Theatre Reader,* ed. *American Theatre Magazine* staff (New York: Theatre Communications Group, 2013), 2:121 (originally published as "A Translator's Tale," *American Theatre Magazine* [April 2009]).
47. John Popk, "*The Misanthrope* at the Poet's Theatre," *Harvard Crimson,* November 2, 1955.
48. Peter Davison, quoted in Harold Gaarder, "The Droll Master of the Throwaway Line," *Christian Science Monitor,* February 9, 1988, 26. Davison later became poetry editor of the *Atlantic Monthly* and a literary historian.
49. Popk, "*The Misanthrope* at the Poet's Theatre."
50. Ibid.
51. Stephen Porter directed the production. The off-Broadway opening took place several weeks before the Broadway premiere of *Candide,* on which Wilbur collaborated with Leonard Bernstein and Lillian Hellman (see chapter 9).
52. Blau, "New 'Misanthrope.'"
53. George Maksian, "A Man for All Molière's," *Playbill,* January 31, 2003, 44.
54. RW, draft letter to Paul Weidner, undated, RPW Deposit, AC. The production run began on September 28, 1972.
55. RW, "A Note to the Harvest Edition," in Molière, *"The Misanthrope" and "Tartuffe,"* v.
56. RW, draft letter to Weidner.
57. Ibid.
58. RW, "Note to the Harvest Edition," v.
59. Ibid., vi.
60. Donald Roy, "Introduction," in Molière, *Five Plays,* trans. Richard Wilbur (London: Methuen, 1994), 28. The original production had three acts, which scholars believe are the first three acts of the five total acts in the text today.
61. Ibid.
62. Molière, *"The Misanthrope" and "Tartuffe,"* 160.
63. F. W. Dupee, "A Laughing Matter," *New York Review of Books,* February 25, 1965, 25–28, 25.
64. Ibid., 27.
65. William Ball, letter to RW, March 22, 1965, RPW Deposit, AC.
66. William Ball, letter to RW, June 8, 1965, RPW Deposit, AC.
67. RW, draft letter to William Ball, ca. June 1965, RPW Deposit, AC. Ellipses and excisions match the original; italicized passages were underlined.
68. RW, letter to the drama editor, *San Francisco Chronicle,* February 21, 1973.
69. "Secolo Barocco Clash," *San Francisco Chronicle,* January 30, 1973.
70. RW, letter to the drama editor.
71. RW, interview by the authors, December 5, 2007.
72. RW, letter to Robert Lowell, December 8, 1967, Robert Lowell Papers (ms. Am. 1905), Houghton Library Collection, Harvard University, series 1, 1433.

8. Prix de Rome

1. CW, letter to JMB, dated "I have no notion of time" [ca. September 1954], Brinnin Papers, Delaware.
2. CW, letter to JMB, November 8, 1954, Brinnin Papers, Delaware.
3. CW, letter to JMB, "I have no notion."
4. Note to RW from mind reader, trans. Ombretta Frau, RPW Deposit, AC.

5. CW, letter to JMB, "I have no notion."
6. Elizabeth Young, e-mail to Robert Bagg, June 25, 2013.
7. RW, interview by the authors, July 16, 2006.
8. William L. Macdonald and Dale Macdonald, joint diary, transcription of "letter to Drue and Bob," October 3, 1954, Nick Macdonald's personal papers.
9. CW, letter to JMB, November 8, 1954.
10. CW, letter to JMB, "I have no notion."
11. Ibid.
12. Ibid.
13. CW, letter to JMB, November 8, 1954.
14. Ibid.
15. Ibid.
16. Anthony Hecht, "The Motions of the Mind," *Times Literary Supplement,* May 20, 1977, 602.
17. The title refers to a passage from Saint Augustine's *Confessions,* written in the fourth century, in which the saint laments that the beautiful things of the world have created a distance between him and God.
18. The subjects correspond to the poems "A Baroque Wall-Fountain in the Villa Sciarra," "Altitudes," "Love Calls Us to the Things of This World," "For the New Railway Station in Rome," and "The Mind-Reader," respectively.
19. John Andrew Moore, letter to Betty Burford, January 22, 1956, Robert Bagg's personal papers.
20. Paul Mariani, "A 1995 Interview with Richard Wilbur," *Image* 12 (Winter 1995), 39–51, 44.
21. Wilbur spent nearly twenty years thinking about, drafting, and revising "The Mind-Reader." Its first documented draft, four lines long, appears on a sheet of lined paper dated "1968." He sent a later draft of the poem, then titled "Pizzeria Sagrestia, 1954," to his friend William Jay Smith in November 1971. Smith marked some suggestions on a number of lines and replied that it was a lovely poem, although not a breakthrough, but he thought it certainly deserving of publication (letter to RW, November 19, 1971, RPW Deposit, AC).
22. In New Critical literary parlance, *vehicle* is the literal verbal expression in a work; *tenor* refers to the meaning the author intends the reader to perceive.
23. We quote here only those lines from "The Mind-Reader" that carry the argument forward, adding italics for emphasis. The last line echoes T. S. Eliot's "Gerontion," in *American Poetry: The Twentieth Century,* ed. Robert Hass, John Hollander, Carolyn Kizer, Nathaniel Mackey, and Marjorie Perloff (New York: Library of America, 2000), 1:741–43.
24. Thomas F. Gould, conversation with Robert Bagg, ca. 1980. Gould was a professor of classics at Yale.
25. RW, interview by the authors, March 7, 2009.
26. James Thurber, *The Years with Ross* (New York: Little, Brown, 1959), 11, 232, 233. Thurber provides several examples of Ross's insistence that he understand the magazine's content and quotes Alexander Woollcott's description of the editor: "He has the utmost disdain for anything he doesn't understand" (77).
27. Our assessment of a "*New Yorker* poem" comes from reading a good deal of correspondence in the *New Yorker* files, which are archived at the New York Public Library. The prose editors were not nearly so solicitous of their readers' comfort. For instance, the *New Yorker* published complete versions of John Hersey's *Hiroshima* and Hannah Arendt's account of the Adolf Eichmann trial, both of which were highly disturbing.
28. Ezra Pound, "Mr. Nixon," in *Pound: Poems and Translations,* ed. Richard Sieburth (New York: Library of America, 2003), 554–56.
29. CW, letter to JMB, November 8, 1954.
30. RW, letter to Howard Moss, November 27, 1954, *New Yorker* Records, NYPL, series III, (subseries 3.1), box 733, folder 3.

31. Howard Moss, letter to RW, November 30, 1954, *New Yorker* Records, NYPL, series III, (subseries 3.1), box 733, folder 3.

32. Howard Moss, letter to RW, December 10, 1954, *New Yorker* Records, NYPL, series III, (subseries 3.1), box 733, folder 3. By "special" Moss did not mean "specialized." He was euphemistically referring to the poem's religious content.

33. The magazine's name, *Botteghe Oscure,* translates as "the street of dark shops," a reference to the location of Caetani's Roman palace near the Tiber. See Helen Barolini, "The Shadowy Lady of the Street of Dark Shops," *Virginia Quarterly Review* 74, no. 2 (1998), www.vqronline.org.

34. Volume 13 (published in early 1954) included "Looking into History," and Wilbur, W. H. Auden, W. S. Merwin, André Malraux, and Robert Graves were featured on the cover. Volume 16 (published in late 1955) featured "Things of This World" and included stories by Wayland Young and Carson McCullers and poems by André du Bouchet, Anthony Hecht, and Alberto Moravia. In 1959 Caetani published W. D. Snodgrass's long poem "Heart's Needle," which won a Pulitzer Prize after it was published as a book in the United States.

35. CW, letter to JMB, January 20, 1955, Brinnin Papers, Delaware.

36. RW, "Sumptuous Deprivation," in *Emily Dickinson,* ed. Harold Bloom (1960; reprint, New York: Chelsea House, 2008), 10. Not incidentally, Dickinson's brother Austin and his wife Susan were neighbors.

37. Howard Moss, letter to RW, August 23, 1955, *New Yorker* Records, NYPL, series III (subsection 3.1), box 740, folder 18.

38. Wilbur spelled the architect's name "Maderna" so that the sound of the final syllable would preserve the iambic pentameter of the line, which the long *o* ending of "Maderno" would have disrupted. Wilbur was also familiar with Anthony Hecht's poems about Roman fountains. For instance, during his Rome fellowship year (1950–51), Hecht had written "The Gardens of the Villa d'Este," to celebrate the many-breasted goddess portrayed in a fountain there (in *Collected Earlier Poems* [New York: Knopf, 1996], 92–96). He later described the contrasted fountains in Wilbur's "A Baroque Wall-Fountain" as representing alternative aspects of the "spirit, one of relaxed and worldly grace, and the other of strenuous, earth-defying effort" ("Richard Wilbur: An Introduction," in *Melodies Unheard: Essays on the Mysteries of Poetry* [Baltimore: Johns Hopkins University Press, 2003], 174).

39. RW and CW, interview by the authors, March 9, 2006.

40. Ibid.

41. Ibid.

42. CW, letter to JMB, May 26, 1955, Brinnin Papers, Delaware.

43. Spencer was working at the time on the title novella from her collection *The Light in the Piazza and Other Italian Tales* (1960; reprint, New York: McGraw-Hill, 1980).

44. RW, unpublished journal, ca. 1973, RW's personal papers.

45. Ibid.

46. Pope John Paul II beatified Padre Pio in 1999 and canonized him in 2002; Saint Pio's remains were brought to the Vatican during the 2015–16 Extraordinary Jubilee of Mercy.

47. RW, letter to William L. Macdonald, January 24, 2006, Nick Macdonald's personal papers.

48. RW, letter to William L. Macdonald, April 8, 2006, Nick Macdonald's personal papers.

49. CW, letter to JMB, May 26, 1955.

50. CW, interview by the authors, October 20, 2005.

9. *Candide* and Other Broadway Misadventures

1. Voltaire, *Candide,* trans. Lowell Blair (New York: Bantam Classics, 1984), 27.

2. Lillian Hellman (hereafter LH), letter to the House Un-American Activities Committee, May 19, 1952, http://historymatters.gmu.edu.

3. Humphrey Burton, *Leonard Bernstein* (New York: Doubleday, 1994), 236. *The Lark,* starring Julie Harris and Boris Karloff, opened on Broadway in 1955.

4. Ibid.

5. Dana Gioia, "Richard Wilbur on Creating *Candide,*" *Dark Horse* 27 (Summer–Autumn 2011): 48–55, 49.

6. LH, letter to RW, May 28, 1954, RPW Deposit, AC.

7. Latouche's lyrics are primarily limited to two songs: "You Were Dead, You Know" and "My Love." According to Wilbur, he and Latouche should share equal credit for "My Love" (RW, interview with the authors, October 26, 2007).

8. Leonard Bernstein (hereafter LB), letter to LH, March 27, 1955, Harry Ransom Center, University of Texas at Austin (hereafter Ransom Center, Austin), series 2, box 4, folder 8. According to Burton (in *Leonard Bernstein,* 262–63), Reiner, a wealthy New Yorker, had had limited theatrical experience. In 1954 she produced *The Rainmaker,* which ran for 125 performances at the Cort Theatre. She invested about $100,000 of her own money in *Candide* and solicited the rest, nearly $250,000, from other backers. Kanin's career spanned theater, film, and television; and Robert Lewis founded the influential Actors Studio in 1947. Other directors they considered included Gene Kelly and René Clair.

9. LB, letter to LH, March 27, 1955.

10. LH, letters to LB, April 5, 1955, and April 19, 1955, Ransom Center, Austin, series 2, box 4, folder 8.

11. In fact, Parker wrote the few lyrics she contributed to early versions of the play when she was alone in her own apartment.

12. Marion Meade, *Dorothy Parker: What Fresh Hell Is This?* (New York: Villard, 1988), 361.

13. In 1963 Tyrone Guthrie also founded the renowned Guthrie Theater in Minneapolis.

14. RW, letter to LH, December 9, 1955, Ransom Center, Austin, series 2, box 4, folder 8.

15. LH, letter to RW, December 15, 1955, RPW Deposit, AC.

16. RW, letter to LH, December 21, 1955, Ransom Center, Austin, series 2, box 4, folder 8.

17. LH, letter to RW, March 27, 1956, RPW Deposit, AC.

18. RW, "*Candide* Comes to Broadway," *Web of Stories,* ca. 2005, www.webofstories.com.

19. Ibid.

20. Syphilis had reached epidemic proportions during the era in which *Candide* was set.

21. RW, draft letter to LH, March 24, 1956, RPW Deposit, AC.

22. Burton, *Leonard Bernstein,* 260.

23. RW, "Poetry Reading, 'Pangloss's Song,'" *Web of Stories.*

24. Burton, *Leonard Bernstein,* 261.

25. JMB, journal entry, October 29, 1956, Brinnin Papers, Delaware.

26. William Wright, *Lillian Hellman: The Image, the Woman* (New York: Simon and Schuster, 1986), 269–70.

27. In 2003 the Martin Beck was renamed for Al Hirschfeld. *Candide* ran at the 1,437-seat theater from December 1, 1956, to February 2, 1957. Wilbur's translation of *The Misanthrope* ran at the 120-seat Theatre East from November 12, 1956, to February 17, 1957.

28. Brooks Atkinson, "The Theatre: 'Candide,'" *New York Times,* December 3, 1956.

29. Walter Kerr, "Candide," *New York Herald Tribune,* December 3, 1956.

30. Mary McCarthy, "The Reform of Dr. Pangloss," *New Republic,* December 17, 1956, 20–21.

31. Ibid.

32. Burton, *Leonard Bernstein,* 265.

33. Foster Hirsch, *Harold Prince and the American Musical Theatre* (Cambridge: Cambridge University Press, 1989), 149.

34. Burton, *Leonard Bernstein,* 265.

35. CW, letter to LH, December 27, 1956, Ransom Center, Austin, series 2, box 56, folder 2.

36. CW, letter to LH, January 10, 1957, Ransom Center, Austin, series 2, box 56, folder 2.

37. Ibid.

38. Burton, *Leonard Bernstein,* 263.
39. Wright, *Lillian Hellman,* 269–70.
40. LH, letter to RW, ca. February 5, 1957, RPW Deposit, AC.
41. Ibid.
42. LH, letter to RW, ca. December 3, 1956, RPW Deposit, AC.
43. Tyrone Guthrie, *A Life in Theater* (New York: McGraw-Hill, 1959), 241.
44. Burton, *Leonard Bernstein,* 263.
45. Alice Kessler-Harris, *A Difficult Woman* (New York: Bloomsbury, 2012), 91.
46. Burton, *Leonard Bernstein,* 263. Wilbur later admitted, "There was, on the whole, no need to be protective of my verbal domain; in our planning and making of numbers, Lenny did his best to rein in his versatility, and we had an agreeable division of labor" (draft of "Apropos *Candide*").
47. Wright, *Lillian Hellman,* 268. Although no real script conferences were held in such close quarters, one during the Boston run of the show took place in theater's men's room.
48. Charlie Harmon, letter to RW, July 28, 1994, RPW Deposit, AC. Harmon was vice president of the Amberson Group, and the meeting took place four years after Bernstein's death.
49. RW, draft of "Apropos *Candide.*"
50. Burton, *Leonard Bernstein,* 263.
51. RW, interview by the authors, August 3, 2007.
52. LH, letter to RW, February 11, 1959, RPW Deposit, AC.
53. Michael H. Hutchins, "*Candide:* A Chronology," *The Stephen Sondheim Reference Guide,* www.sondheimguide.com.
54. Didier C. Deutsch, liner notes, *Candide: Original Cast Recording* [reissue] (New York: Sony, 1991), CD.
55. Ken Mandelbaum, *Not Since Carrie: Forty Years of Broadway Musical Flops* (New York: St. Martin's, 1992), 335.
56. RW, "Glitter and Be Gay," in *Collected Poems, 1943–2004* (New York: Harcourt, 2004), 468.
57. Kessler-Harris, *A Difficult Woman,* 71.
58. CW, letter to LH, December 27, 1956.
59. CW, letter to LH, February 15, 1961, Ransom Center, Austin, series 2, box 77, folder 5.
60. Ibid.
61. RW, letter to LH, February 28, 1961, Ransom Center, Austin, series 2, box 77, folder 5.
62. McCarthy's charge that Hellman's memoirs were complete fabrications was hyperbolic and would never have stood up in court, although they did contain falsehoods, as witnesses eventually agreed. McCarthy's accusation provoked Hellman to file a lawsuit, which ended only with Hellman's death on June 30, 1986. A judgment would have left McCarthy penniless.
63. Wright, *Lillian Hellman,* 439.
64. RW, interview by the authors, August 3, 2007.
65. LH, letter to RW, May 23, 1975, RPW Deposit, AC.
66. LH, letter to RW, June 22, 1984, RPW Deposit, AC.
67. RW, draft letter to LB, November 7, 1966, RPW Deposit, AC.
68. CW, interview with the authors, October 20, 2005. Wilbur's translation of *The Children's Playhouse* is so tightly constructed that cutting any speeches, let alone scenes or characters, would render it unintelligible.
69. Maurice Valency, letter to RW, April 10, 1967, RPW Deposit, AC.
70. RW, to Maurice Valency, April 14, 1967, RPW Deposit, AC.
71. Maurice Valency, letter to RW, April 19, 1967, RPW Deposit, AC.
72. RW, undated list, RW's personal papers.

10. In the Circle with Lowell, Bishop, and Jarrell

1. RW, interview by the authors, June 18, 2007. Lowell's nickname was a shortened version of both Caliban and Caligula and dated back to his days at St. Mark's School in Southborough, Massachusetts.

2. Robert Lowell, *The Letters of Robert Lowell*, ed. Saskia Hamilton (New York: Farrar, Straus and Giroux, 2007), 601.

3. Randall Jarrell, "Fifty Years of American Poetry," *Prairie Schooner* 37, no. 1 (1963): 23. In several disclaimers Jarrell acknowledged a lack of space and noted that he should also have discussed Léonie Adams, Louise Bogan, John Berryman, John Peale Bishop, James Dickey, Horace Gregory, Katherine Hoskins, Howard Nemerov, Adrienne Rich, Muriel Rukeyser, Delmore Schwartz, Louis Simpson, W. D. Snodgrass, Louis Untermeyer, Mark Van Doren, Theodore Weiss, and James Wright. In addition, he had a knack for stringing together adjectives, a dozen or more at a time, to characterize the individuality of his chosen poets. For instance, the list for Williams includes "outspoken, warmhearted, generous, fresh, sympathetic, enthusiastic, spontaneous, impulsive, emotional, observant, curious, rash, courageous, undignified, unaffected humanitarian, experimental, empirical, liberal, secular, democratic. One is rather embarrassed," Jarrell concluded, "at the necessity of calling him original; it is like saying a Cheshire cat smiles" (11). As for Bishop, "her poems are quiet, truthful, sad, funny, [the] most marvelously individual poems." He added, "They have a sound, a feel, a whole moral and physical atmosphere; . . . they are honest, modest, minutely observant, masterly; even their most complicated or troubled or imaginative effects seem, always, personal and natural" (20).

4. Jarrell, "Fifty Years," 26. Jarrell never mentioned Allen Ginsburg, who certainly wrote often and passionately about (in Jarrell's words) "what is most terrible in the world at present." According to Ian Hamilton, Lowell credited Ginsburg with inspiring him to loosen the lines in the poems in *Life Studies* (see Hamilton, *Robert Lowell: A Biography* [New York: Vintage, 1983], 236).

5. Jarrell, "Fifty Years," 25–26.

6. Ibid., 27.

7. In 1934 Eberhart had been newly hired to teach poetry at St. Mark's when he met Lowell, who was a senior there. That year Eberhart also published "The Groundhog," the poem that launched his literary reputation. Eberhart remained something of a mentor, despite periods of mutual antagonism during Lowell's college years, until Lowell gained acclaim and the men became peers.

8. Elizabeth Bishop (hereafter EB), letter to Robert Lowell (hereafter RL), October 23, 1948, in *Words in Air: The Complete Correspondence between Elizabeth Bishop and Robert Lowell*, ed. Thomas Travisano and Saskia Hamilton (New York: Farrar, Straus and Giroux, 2010), 64.

9. RL, letter to EB, October 25, 1948, in *Words in Air*, 65.

10. RL, quoted in Mariani, *Lost Puritan*, 171; EB, letter to RL, October 23, 1948, in *Words in Air*, 64; RW, "The Bottles Become New, Too," in *Responses: Prose Pieces, 1951–1976*, rev. ed. (Ashland, Ore.: Story Line, 1999), 271.

11. Randall Jarrell, "A View of Three Poets," *Partisan Review* 18, no. 6 (1951): 700.

12. EB, letter to RL, November 26, 1951, in *Words in Air*, 130.

13. RL, letter to EB, February 26, 1952, in *Words in Air*, 132.

14. RW, unpublished Cambridge notebook, n.d., RW's personal papers.

15. Jarrell, "A View of Three Poets," 697.

16. Ibid., 691.

17. Ibid., 691, 693, 692.

18. Ibid., 693. According to Jarrell, an "unusually reflective halfback" had explained to him how a run in football develops.

19. Horace Gregory, "The Poetry of Suburbia," *Partisan Review* 23 (Fall 1956): 545–53. The student in the classroom was Robert Bagg, an Amherst senior at the time.

20. Jarrell, "A View of Three Poets," 693.

21. RW, interview by the authors. October 26, 2007. Wilbur gave two readings at the 2007 Newburyport [Massachusetts] Literary Festival—one on October 12 at his grandson Liam's high school, the other on October 13, at the public library. The annual festival awards a prize for poetry in Wilbur's name.

22. Jarrell, "A View of Three Poets," 692.

23. Ibid.

24. Brad Leithauser, ed., "Introduction," in Randall Jarrell, *No Other Book: Selected Essays* (New York: HarperCollins, 1999), xx.

25. RL, quoted in ibid., xiv.

26. Ibid., xx.

27. EB, quoted in Stephen Spender, "Randall Jarrell's Complaint," *New York Review of Books*, November 23, 1967, 26–30, 26. Spender was reviewing *Randall Jarrell: 1914–1965*, a memorial volume of essays by Jarrell's peers, edited by Lowell, Peter Taylor, and Robert Penn Warren.

28. RL, quoted in ibid., 27.

29. Leithauser, "Introduction," xvi.

30. EB, letter to RL, November 26, 1951, in *Words in Air*, 130.

31. Leithauser, "Introduction," xvi.

32. Ibid., xii.

33. Howard Nemerov, Consultant in Poetry at the Library of Congress, had invited Wilbur and about twenty other poets to participate in the project by considering four "stimulating or irritating questions as spurs to the spirit": the poet's change in character or style since first beginning to write; the poet's thoughts on whether a revolution in poetry had taken place in the century (or ever) and, if applicable, what it was like to participate; how the changing world during the century had preoccupied the poet's vision; and, finally, how the poet saw the "proper function of criticism" and which genre of poetry the poet did not admire or tolerate. The resulting lectures appeared in Nemerov's edited volume *Poets on Poetry* (New York: Basic Books, 1965).

34. Wilbur's original Voice of America essay is reprinted as "On My Own Work," in *Responses*, 148–62, 148–49.

35. Ibid.

36. Ibid.

37. Stephen Burt, *Randall Jarrell and His Age* (New York: Columbia University Press, 2002), 20. Burt's comment that Jarrell projected his need onto imagined characters is exemplified by the way in which he used southern belles and halfbacks as foils to further his criticism of Wilbur's poetry.

38. RW, unpublished notebook, undated entry [ca. 1969–1975], RW's personal papers.

39. RW, interview by the authors, July 18, 2014.

40. Leithauser, "Introduction," xx.

41. Brooke Allen, "Criticism and the Age: A Biography and a Collection of Essays Celebrate the Writer Randall Jarrell," *New York Times*, August 1, 1999.

42. Both essays appear in Jarrell, *No Other Book*.

43. Jarrell, "A View of Three Poets," xx.

44. Comparable female poets writing in that era—those who were slightly older (such as Bogan and Bishop) as well as those who were younger (such as Sexton, Plath, and Levertov)—did not produce long poems, which did not seem to concern or worry them.

45. In a 1964 interview with Robert Frank and Stephen Mitchell, Wilbur speculated that Jarrell's canard derived from his own abandonment of formal poetry in favor of "longer narrative poems in comparatively relaxed rhythms" and that he had accused Wilbur of "settling for 'short gains'" because Wilbur wasn't "running on" at Jarrell's length (William Butts, ed., *Conversations with Richard Wilbur* [Jackson: University of Mississippi Press, 1990], 22).

46. The other long Wilbur poems are "Lying," "A Baroque Wall-Fountain in the Villa Scia-rra," "On Freedom's Ground," "Giacometti," "Castles and Distances," "In the Field," and "Running."

47. "I have an aversion to sonnets," Wilbur admitted in an interview with us on July 18, 2014. "I am grateful for their existence but not drawn to writing in that demanding form. I would find it confining." Nonetheless, four sonnets (or sonnet-length poems) appear in his 2004 *Collected Poems;* the most notable is "A Miltonic Sonnet for Mr. Johnson on His Refusal of Peter Hurd's Official Portrait."

48. Roethke seems to use *grace* in an aesthetic rather than a religious sense. His comment about Wilbur is well known, but it's difficult to track down where or when he actually said it. According to William Pitt Root, who met Roethke at Washington University in early 1963, "Of his near contemporary, Richard Wilbur, he declared no man that hand-some could be taken seriously, no one that accomplished at tennis could possibly be as good at poetry, and that it was quite unforgivable how effortlessly his charm drew young Ivy League women around him in such swarms. He managed to mock Wilbur and himself at the same time" ("'This Is a Junior': On Meeting Roethke," *Basalt,* June 25, 2013, www.eou.edu).

49. CW, interview by the authors, October 20, 2005.

50. RW, interview by the authors, July 18, 2014; RW, unpublished notebook, RW's personal papers.

51. RW, letter to RL, October 31, 1958, Robert Lowell Papers (ms. Am. 1905), Houghton Library, Harvard University, series 1, 1429.

52. RL, letter to RW, November 1, 1958, RPW Deposit, AC. Joint birthday parties became a regular part of the winter in Key West for Wilbur and James Merrill, born on March 3, and they occasionally also celebrated with Ralph Ellison, born on March 1.

53. Saskia Hamilton, "Introduction," in RL, *The Letters of Robert Lowell,* ed. Saskia Hamilton (New York: Farrar, Straus and Giroux, 2007), xv. Lowell's first hospitalization for a major manic episode was in Baldpate Hospital in Massachusetts in 1949, followed some months later by a stay at Payne Whitney Clinic in New York City for depression. His final stay was in 1976 at St. Andrew's in Northampton, England.

54. Ibid., xv–xvii.

55. RL, letter to EB, July 24, 1959, in *Words in Air,* 303.

56. RL, letter to RW, April 6, 1960, RPW Deposit, AC.

57. RL, letter to RW, January 8 [1962], RPW Deposit, AC.

58. RL, letter to RW, March 8, 1966, RPW Deposit, AC.

59. Ibid.

60. RL, letter to RW, dated "Christmas Day" [1967], RPW Deposit, AC.

61. RW, letter to RL, dated "Epiphany Eve" [1968], Robert Lowell Papers (ms. Am. 1905), Houghton Library, Harvard University, series 1, 1433.

62. RW, "On My Own Work," in *Responses,* 148–62, 151.

63. John Berryman, telegram to RW, May 6, 1956, RPW Deposit, AC.

64. John Berryman, letter to RW, May 25, 1956, RPW Deposit, AC.

65. RW, interview by the authors, June 28, 2006. In this interview Wilbur spoke about Berry-man's attitudes toward other poets with more detachment than he did when remembering Lowell's competitiveness.

66. Conarroe had just completed work on *John Berryman: An Introduction to the Poetry* for Columbia University Press. He went on to become president of the Guggenheim Foundation from 1985 to 2002.

67. Accounts of Jarrell's death usually attribute it to suicide rather than accident. He was struck by a car near a highway underpass. Although his widow did not believe he pur-posely stepped into the car's path, most of his friends disagreed. For Lowell's account, see RL, letter to EB, October 28, 1995, in *Words in Air,* 592.

68. RW, interview by Joel Conarroe, May 3, 1978, 1, RW's personal papers.

69. Ibid., 3.

70. Kathleen Spivack, *With Robert Lowell and His Circle* (Boston: Northeastern University Press, 2012), 164.

71. Donald Hall's review of Lowell's *Day by Day* is included in his essay "Robert Lowell and the Literature Industry," *Georgia Review* 32 (Spring 1978): 7–12. Charles Molesworth's "Lowell's Last Book" summarized Hall's review in preparation for his own defense of the collection. Hall, he wrote, "argued that Lowell's work had declined in quality at least since *For the Union Dead* (1964), and that his reputation was kept at a falsely high mark through friends and appreciators who lacked the nerve to face what Hall considered the obvious weakness of the latest work. Hall pointed especially to the *Notebook,* and the three volumes Lowell published in 1973, which contained revised versions of the sonnets of *Notebook.* In particular, Hall objected to Lowell's slack metaphors, his discontinuities of form, and an overall incoherence" (*Salmagundi* 44/45 [Spring–Summer 1979]: 242–52).

72. RW, interview by the authors, June 18, 2007.

73. RW, "Robert Lowell: 'Skunk Hour,' " in *The Contemporary Poet as Artist and Critic,* ed. Anthony Ostroff (Boston: Little, Brown, 1964), 84–87.

74. EB, letter to RL, June 17, 1963, in *Words in Air,* 465.

75. RL, letter to RW, January 8, 1962, RPW Deposit, AC.

76. RL, letter to RW, June 8, 1976, RPW Deposit, AC.

77. The inaugural issue (*American Poetry Review* 1, no. 1 [1972]) also included work by David Ignatow, Joyce Carol Oates, Donald Hall, David Antin, Denise Levertov, Donald Justice, Cesar Vallejo, Allen Ginsberg, C. K. Williams, Philip Levine, Norman O. Brown, John Sonne, Louis Simpson, Armand Schwerner, Richard Howard, and Diane Wakoski.

78. EB, letter to RL, January 14, 1973, in *Words in Air,* 737.

79. RL, letter to EB, January 24, 1973, in *Words in Air,* 738.

80. Kieran Quinlan, *John Crowe Ransom's Secular Faith* (Baton Rouge: Louisiana State University Press, 1989), 30–31.

81. During Plath's stint on the magazine, she interviewed not only the novelist Elizabeth Bowen but also Hecht and Wilbur (for an article called "Poets on Campus"). Wilbur could not recall if the meeting at Ward's house had been prompted by that interview. Moreover, according to Bruce Michelson (see note 97), it's unclear if Charlee accompanied him or if he went alone. In our interviews Wilbur could not document the date of the visit or clarify the events.

82. Sylvia Plath, "Letter to an Over-grown . . . Spoiled Baby," dated "June . . . July 1953," and journal entry, July 6, 1953, in *The Unabridged Journals of Sylvia Plath,* ed. Karen V. Kukil (New York: Anchor, 2000), 543, 185.

83. Plath was sufficiently stable to return to Smith for the spring semester of 1954.

84. Jay Parini, "The Poet As Heliotrope," *Guardian,* March 24, 2006.

85. If one can extrapolate from Plath's autobiographical novel *The Bell Jar* (originally published in the United States in 1963), which draws on events of her life during the summer of 1953, she was obsessed with committing suicide in water. (We cite page numbers for the following chapters from the 2005 HarperCollins paperback edition.) In chapter 12 (140–53), the main character, Esther, finds that she is unable to slit her wrists in the warm water of her bathtub and can't immerse more than her ankles in the frigid waters of the sea. In chapter 13 (154–69), when Esther and her friends go to the lake, she swims farther from the shore than her date is willing to go and tries, again unsuccessfully, to drown. The mantra *"I am I am I am"* haunts her, and each time she tries to dive beneath the water's surface her body bobs to the top. Neither Lowell nor Bishop seemed to connect Wilbur's lifeguard simile to Plath's novel. In our interview on July 6, 2014, Wilbur told us he had no recollection of reading *The Bell Jar* or making any intentional allusions to its images of drowning.

86. In the top margin of a journal entry Plath defined *shallow* as "low in frequency and amplitude" and *deep* as "high in frequency and amplitude." The context for these qualifications involves an "excitement curve," which she used to describe how "admittedly some people live more than others." Plath ranked Willa Cather, Lillian Hellman, and Virginia Woolf among the women she would like emulate and thus "listen, observe, and feel, and try to live more fully" (journal entry, "[no.] 47," dated between July 1950 and July 1953, in *Unabridged Journals*, 44).

87. Jim Long, "On Sylvia Plath," *Sylvia Plath Info Blog*, May 26, 2009, http://sylviaplathinfo.blogspot.com. According to Long, "While the poem may be legitimately critiqued as being somewhat mannered and laborious, it puzzles me greatly that Bishop and Lowell seem so oddly dense about the import of the poem, seeing it as unfeeling and lacking in irony. It suggests to me that there is some personal animus behind their criticism of Wilbur's poem, which, curiously, Lowell himself hints at with his mention of 'his rivalry' and in the line about 'people . . . who are his old friends and welcome being bitter on him.'"

88. RL, letter to EB, October 27, 1963, in *Words in Air*, 513.

89. EB, letter to RL, August 2, 1965, in *Words in Air*, 583.

90. RL, letter to EB, August 16, 1965, in *Words in Air*, 586.

91. RL, "Foreword," in Sylvia Plath, *Ariel* (New York: Harper and Row, 1966), viii. Lowell told Bishop that he'd "been through agonies hammering out a three-page introduction to Sylvia Plath," which was published in the *New York Review of Books* on May 12, 1966, and reprinted in *Ariel* as the foreword. He complained that such writing was "laborious" and "a bit harsh and perverse" (RL, letter to EB, February 25, 1966, in *Words in Air*, 601).

92. Jacqueline Rose noted, "For a writer who has so consistently produced outrage in her critics, nothing has produced the outrage generated by Sylvia Plath's allusions to the Holocaust in her poetry, and nothing the outrage occasioned by 'Daddy'" (*The Haunting of Sylvia Plath* [Cambridge, Mass.: Harvard University Press, 1992], 242). George Steiner asked, "Are these final poems entirely legitimate? In what sense does anyone, himself uninvolved and long after the event, commit a larceny when he invokes the echoes and trappings of Auschwitz and appropriates an enormity of ready emotion to his own private design?" ("Dying Is an Art," in *Language and Silence: Essays on Language, Literature, and the Inhuman* [1967; reprint, New Haven: Yale University Press, 1998], 301).

93. Sylvia Plath Symposium, Indiana University, Bloomington, October 2012.

94. RW, "Poetry Reading: 'Cottage Street, 1953,'" *Web of Stories*, ca. 2005, www.webofstories.com.

95. Early in 1959, while Plath was studying with Lowell in Boston, she wrote a notebook entry in which she compares reading Wilbur's poems to reading Lowell's: "Wilbur a bland turning of pleasaunces, a fresh speaking and picturing with incalculable grace and all sweet, pure, clear, fabulous, the maestro with the imperceptible marcel. Robert Lowell after this is like a good strong, shocking brandy after a too lucidly sweet dinner wine, dessert wine" (January 27, 1959, in *Unabridged Journals*, 465).

96. As Charlee explained in our interview with her on March 9, 2006, her mother earned a law degree but never practiced. After Edna graduated she went back to her hometown in Edwardsville, Illinois, to help her father recoup losses from a partner who had absconded with money and left him in bad shape financially. When Charlee's father died in 1931, Edna used her considerable business acumen during the Depression and afterward to support herself and her daughter.

97. Bruce Michelson, *Wilbur's Poetry: Music in a Scattering Time* (Amherst: University of Massachusetts Press, 1991), 156.

98. RL, "Foreword," viii.

99. Ted Hughes and Wilbur corresponded briefly and also had a professional connection as national poets laureate, which may have influenced Wilbur's sense of Plath's characterization of her husband.

100. Helen McCloy Ellison, Elessa Clay Hugh, and Peter A. Stitt, "Richard Wilbur: The Art of Poetry, No. 22," *Paris Review* 72 (Winter 1977): 68–105, 90.

101. RW, interview by the authors, July 28, 2014.

102. David Orr, "Rough Gems," *New York Times,* April 2, 2006.

103. Helen Vendler, "The Art of Losing," *New Republic,* April 3, 2006, 33–37.

104. RW, interview by the authors, April 6, 2006. Wilbur's sense of friendship for Bishop was grounded by both his admiration for her and their bonds in the literary world. Her gender kept her male contemporaries from including her in their ranking obsessions, although her correspondence with Lowell reveals that she possessed the same competitive spirit.

105. Ibid.

106. Gary Fountain and Peter Brazeau, *Remembering Elizabeth Bishop: An Oral Biography* (Amherst: University of Massachusetts Press, 1994), 106.

107. Ibid., 107. Lowell spoke about living in the pup tent in a 1961 *Paris Review* interview, and the story is often repeated in biographical accounts (Frederick Seidel, "Robert Lowell: The Art of Poetry, No. 3," *Paris Review* 25 [Winter–Spring 1961]).

108. Fountain and Brazeau, *Remembering Elizabeth Bishop,* 108.

109. EB, letter to RW, November 28, 1948, RPW Deposit, AC.

110. EB, letter to RW, November 13, 1950, RPW Deposit, AC.

111. Spivack, *With Robert Lowell,* 106.

112. Fountain and Brazeau, *Remembering Elizabeth Bishop,* 308.

113. RL, letter to EB, August 15, 1957, in *Words in Air,* 225. In this letter Lowell asked Bishop whether she remembered asking him to write the epitaph in 1948, when they were in Stonington, Connecticut, visiting Betty Eberhart's parents, not long before the Bard conference. He had considered proposing to her there but felt the setting wasn't right, so he put it off. Then at Bard he met Hardwick. His reminiscence in this long letter is regretful but resigned ("asking you is *the* might have been for me"), because by this time he was in love with Hardwick and Bishop was in love with Lota de Soares.

114. Fountain and Brazeau, *Remembering Elizabeth Bishop,* 309. See also Colm Tóibín, *On Elizabeth Bishop: Writers* (Princeton: Princeton University Press, 2015), 154.

115. Fountain and Brazeau, *Remembering Elizabeth Bishop,* 106–7. The line originally appeared as "Buckles the current, a green glare" (RW, "Shad-Time," *New Yorker,* May 29, 1978, 30), and was later revised to "Buckles the surge is a green glare" for his 1987 *New and Collected Poems.*

116. Fountain and Brazeau, *Remembering Elizabeth Bishop,* 348.

117. JMB, journal entry, [June 1953], Brinnin Papers, Delaware. Jonathan Aaron won the Amy Lowell Traveling Scholarship in 1975–76, and both Wilbur and Bishop had served as judges.

118. JMB, photograph, [June 1953], Brinnin Papers, Delaware. Wilbur mentioned this snapshot in his memorial tribute to Bishop, American Academy of Arts and Letters, December 6, 1979.

119. RW, "Elizabeth Bishop," in *Elizabeth Bishop and Her Art,* ed. Lloyd Schwartz and Sybil P. Estess (Ann Arbor: University of Michigan Press, 1983), 266.

120. EB, letter to RW, October 13, 1963, RPW Deposit, AC. In a later letter Bishop responded to the recently published *Walking to Sleep* but steered clear of comment on the long title poem—unlike Lowell, who had been deeply affected by it and had told Wilbur so in early 1968 (see note 61). Instead, she mentioned "Miltonic Sonnet," the detail of what she called his "nature poems," and his admirable translations of poems by François Villon and Andrei Voznesensky (EB, letter to RW, March 19, 1969, RPW Deposit, AC).

121. RL, letter to EB, November 24, 1965, in *Words in Air,* 596.

122. RW, draft of eulogy to RL, undated, RPW Deposit, AC.

123. RW, interview by the authors, October 26, 2007.

124. RW, "Elizabeth Bishop," 264. Orr (in "Rough Gems") wrote, "Her father died when she was a baby; her mother vanished into an insane asylum when Bishop was five; her college

boyfriend committed suicide when she refused to marry him and sent her a parting post-card that said, 'Go to hell, Elizabeth'; and the great love of her life [Lota de Soares], with whom she spent many years in Brazil, fatally overdosed in Bishop's apartment."

125. RW, "Elizabeth Bishop," 263–64. See also Jonathan Ellis, *Art and Memory in the Work of Elizabeth Bishop* (New York: Routledge, 2006), 169.

126. RW, interview with the authors, June 18, 2007.

11. Keeping a Difficult Balance

1. Helen McCloy Ellison, Ellesa Clay High, and Peter A. Stitt, "Richard Wilbur: The Art of Poetry, No. 22," *Paris Review* 72 (Winter 1977): 68–105, 71.
2. Ibid.
3. Ibid.
4. RW, National Book Award acceptance speech, 1957, *National Book Foundation,* www.nationalbook.org. The quoted line is from Frost's poem "Mowing." Judges for the award were Louise Bogan, Edward Davidson, Horace Gregory, Louis Simpson, and Yvor Winters.
5. Ibid.
6. Ibid.
7. Fred Millett, letter to RW, April 2, 1957, RPW Deposit, AC.
8. Ibid.
9. RW, "Teaching Writing Courses," *Web of Stories,* ca. 2005, www.webofstories.com.
10. Ibid. Updike wrote several books on geology, so his example was apt.
11. Ibid.
12. Ibid.
13. Ellison et al., "Richard Wilbur," 71.
14. RW, "Teaching Writing Courses."
15. RW, "Poets Who Inspire Me," *Web of Stories.*
16. Jane Gordon, "University of Verse," *New York Times,* October 16, 2005.
17. Mark Tratner, "Richard Wilbur Discusses Poetry, Parietals, and Politics," *Wesleyan Argus,* November 1, 1968.
18. Wilbur participated in 1967–68, 1971–72, 1974–75, and 1981–82.
19. Ellen Wilbur, interview with the authors, March 23, 2006.
20. LH, letter to CW, [1957], RPW Deposit, AC.
21. JMB, journal entry, May 22, 1960, Brinnin Papers, Delaware.
22. CW, letter to JMB, November 3, 1960, Brinnin Papers, Delaware.
23. Ibid.
24. Ibid.
25. Ibid.
26. CW, letter to JMB, April 27, 1961, Brinnin Papers, Delaware.
27. John Gery, *Ways of Nothingness: Nuclear Annihilation and Contemporary American Poetry* (Gainesville: University Press of Florida, 1996), 109.
28. CW, letter to JMB, March 16, 1961, Brinnin Papers, Delaware.
29. Frost visited the Soviet Union in 1962, not long before he died, with Secretary of the Interior Stewart L. Udall and the poet Franklin Reeve, a friend of Wilbur's who served as Frost's interpreter (Stewart L. Udall, "Robert Frost's Last Adventure," *New York Times,* June 11, 1972).
30. RW, interview by the authors, August 12, 2011.
31. Valerie Viereck Gibbs and John Alexis Viereck, "Richard Wilbur's World" [letter to the editor], *Harvard Magazine* 111, no. 3 (2009): 8. If Wilbur had turned to writing history, it would have been art history of the nineteenth century, specifically the work of Degas.
32. CW and RW, interview by the authors, March 9, 2006.

33. CW, interview by the authors, December 12, 2005.
34. CW and RW, interview by the authors, March 9, 2006.
35. CW, interview by the authors, December 12, 2005.
36. CW and RW, interview by the authors, March 9, 2006.
37. CW, interview by the authors, December 12, 2005.
38. Ibid.
39. CW, letter to JMB, January 25, 1966, Brinnin Papers, Delaware.
40. "Poems on Autism: Beyond Research Data," *Journal of Autism and Childhood Schizophrenia* 7 (December 1977): 404–5.
41. Cammie McGovern, "The Parent Trap," *New York Times,* June 5, 2006. McGovern was responding to three current news stories about parents who were accused of killing their autistic children. As a parent of an autistic child herself, she cautioned against the unrealistic expectations for a cure (and thus for a "normal life") conveyed in inspirational books she called "bibles of hope." Support of this kind did not exist when the Wilburs struggled to find help for Aaron in the early 1960s, but McGovern suggests that "to aim for full recovery—for the person your child might have been without autism—is to enter a dangerous emotional landscape."
42. RW, interview by the authors, August 3, 2007. Wilbur reiterated his belief that poetry is most moving and useful when it reflects the true complexity of things; poems that aimed to provoke a rallying cry of indignation after Kent State lost sight of the fact that the events there were tragedy, not melodrama.
43. RW, draft and galley proof of a contribution to *Authors Take Sides on Vietnam* [New York: Simon and Schuster, 1967], RPW Deposit, AC.
44. Lyndon B. Johnson, quoted in the front-page article "LBJ Calls Portrait of Him 'Ugliest Thing I Ever Saw,'" *Spokesman Review,* January 6, 1967.
45. When he wrote the sonnet, Wilbur may not have known that Jefferson owned slaves, but he correctly predicted that historians would condemn Johnson's entrance into the Vietnam War. In fact, however, historians such as Doris Kearns Goodwin and Johnson's biographer, Robert Caro, would also honor Johnson's civil rights initiatives and his Great Society policies, both of which sharply improved the lives of millions of Americans and reclaimed some of the world's good opinion, which the Vietnam War had badly damaged.
46. RW, "For the Student Strikers," *Middletown Strike News,* May 8, 1970. Wilbur included the unrevised poem in *The Mind-Reader* (1976).
47. Michael Juster, "Mason on Wilbur," July 1, 2001, *Eratosphere,* www.ablemuse.com.
48. CW, interview by the authors, December 12, 2005.
49. Ibid.
50. RW, quoted in Robert Greer Cohn, Robert Conquest, Réne Girard, Czeslaw Milosz, Ricardo J. Quinones, George Steiner, Richard Wilbur, and James Q. Wilson, "The Humanities, in Memorium," *Academic Questions* 8, no. 1 (1995): 60.
51. For many years during sugaring season Charlee helped the family who owned the sugar-house by driving the tractor that transported the sap buckets (Jeanette Horton, interview with the authors, October 16, 2014).
52. RW, "Poetry Reading, 'Hamlen Brook,'" *Web of Stories.*
53. RW, interview by the authors, March 9, 2006.
54. CW, letter to JMB, October 23, 1969, Brinnin Papers, Delaware.
55. CW, interview by the authors, March 9, 2006.
56. RW, report on spring semester leave, 1972, Special Collections and Archives, Wesleyan University.
57. Ibid.
58. Ibid.

12. Overstressed and Overmedicated

1. Warren (1905–1989), a poet, novelist, and critic, was associated with the Fugitives, a post–World War I literary movement that included Ransom, Jarrell, and Allen Tate.
2. Daniel Boorstin, quoted in Irvin Molotsky, "Richard Wilbur Is Named Nation's Poet Laureate," *New York Times,* April 18, 1987.
3. Helen McCloy Ellison, Ellesa Clay High, and Peter A. Stitt, "Richard Wilbur: The Art of Poetry, No. 22," *Paris Review* 72 (Winter 1977): 68–105, 87.
4. Stanley Kunitz, quoted in RW, interview by the authors, October 26, 2007.
5. Ellison et al., "Richard Wilbur," 88.
6. CW, interview by the authors, March 9, 2006.
7. Steve Swayne, *Orpheus in Manhattan: William Schuman and the Shaping of America's Musical Life* (New York: Oxford University Press, 2011), 512. The Crane School of Music and several symphony orchestras became partners in funding the project.
8. Swayne, *Orpheus,* 513.
9. More recently, the performance space has been renamed David Geffen Hall.
10. RW, "A Poem of Dedication for Lincoln Center," *New York Times,* September 24, 1962.
11. William Schuman, letter to RW, February 2, 1984, RPW Deposit, AC.
12. RW, letter to JMB, July 23, 1984, Brinnin Papers, Delaware.
13. Nan Robertson, "A Musical Collaboration in Homage to America," *New York Times,* January 2, 1986.
14. Swayne, *Orpheus,* 515.
15. Ibid., 512.
16. Ibid., 515.
17. Ibid.
18. RW, letter to JMB, July 23, 1984, Brinnin Papers, Delaware.
19. William Schuman, letter to RW, June 19, 1984, quoted in Swayne, *Orpheus,* 515–16.
20. RW, letter to William Schuman, June 26, 1984, quoted in Swayne, *Orpheus,* 516.
21. Schuman, letter to RW, August 26, 1984, quoted in Swayne, *Orpheus,* 516.
22. RW, letter to JMB, July 23, 1984, Brinnin Papers, Delaware.
23. CW, letter to JMB, February 18, 1985, Brinnin Papers, Delaware.
24. Ibid.
25. CW, letter to JMB, March 17, 1985, Brinnin Papers, Delaware.
26. Ibid.
27. Ibid.
28. CW, letter to JMB, May 1, 1985, Brinnin Papers, Delaware.
29. RW, "Introduction," in Jean Racine, *Phaedra,* trans. Richard Wilbur (New York: Harcourt, 1986), ix, xv.
30. Wilbur believed that Lowell's translation of *Phaedra* was a response to his own translations of Molière and was consistent with Lowell's habit of directly challenging his peers. He also said that Lowell mistakenly credited him with a broad knowledge of French literature (RW, interview by Joel Conarroe, May 3, 1978, RW's personal papers).
31. RL, "On Translating *Phèdre,*" in *Jean Racine's Phèdre,* trans. Robert Lowell (New York: Farrar, Straus and Cudahy, 1960), 7.
32. RW, "Introduction," xv–xvi.
33. RL, "On Translating *Phèdre,*" 7–8.
34. RL, *Jean Racine's Phèdre,* 58–59.
35. RW, *Phaedra,* 66.
36. Paul Mariani, *Lost Puritan: A Life of Robert Lowell* (New York: Norton, 1996), 301.
37. RL, *Jean Racine's Phèdre,* 69–70.
38. RW, *Phaedra,* 76.
39. Bruce Michelson, *Wilbur's Poetry: Music in a Scattering Time* (Amherst: University of Massachusetts Press, 1991), 186.

40. CW, letter to JMB, September 17, 1985, Brinnin Papers, Delaware. Polymyalgia rheumatica predominately affects Caucasian women older than age fifty and is common among those who suffer from arthritis, as Charlee did. It is treated with corticosteroids such as prednisone.

41. RW, interview by the authors, January 5, 2006. Wilbur's contract with Smith required him to teach during the fall semester only; he resigned the day before classes began in September 1985.

42. CW, letter to JMB, September 17, 1985.

43. RW, interview by the authors, January 5, 2006.

44. CW, letter to JMB, December 22, 1985, Brinnin Papers, Delaware. The six ellipses are Charlee's.

45. CW, letter to JMB, May 24, 1986, Brinnin Papers, Delaware.

46. RW, journal entry, September 19, 1985, RW's personal papers.

47. RW, journal entry, October 3, 1985, RW's personal papers.

48. John Berryman, *Recovery* (New York: Thunder's Mouth Press, 1973), 7. Throughout the book, Berryman indulges in wordplay with *qualify*—the short disclaimer of prior drunkenness or alcoholic behavior that has given way to recovery, as made by an AA member to justify his or her role as chairperson or speaker at an AA meeting. Regarding the facts behind Severance's television appearances: in 1970 Berryman read "The Song of the Tortured Girl" on television and did appear to be drunk or stoned.

49. Ibid., 8.

50. RW, journal entry, October 3, 1985.

51. The First Step is "We admitted our life is powerless over alcohol and that our lives had become unmanageable"; the Fourth Step is "Made a searching and fearless moral inventory of ourselves"; the Fifth Step is "Admitted to God, to ourselves, and to another human being the exact nature of our wrongs" (Alcoholics Anonymous, *Twelve Steps and the Twelve Traditions* [New York: Alcoholics Anonymous World Services, 2012], 21, 42, 55).

52. RW, interview by the authors, January 5, 2006.

53. CW, interview by the authors, March 9, 2006.

54. Ibid.

55. RW, interview by the authors, January 5, 2006. "The skull beneath the skin" is a reference to the playwright John Webster, Shakespeare's contemporary, and appears in T. S. Eliot's poem "Whispers of Immortality," in *American Poetry: The Twentieth Century*, ed. Robert Hass, John Hollander, Carolyn Kizer, Nathaniel Mackey, and Marjorie Perloff (New York: Library of America, 2000), 1:740–41.

56. RW, interview by the authors, January 5, 2006.

57. CW, interview by the authors, March 9, 2006.

58. CW, letter to JMB, May 22, 1986, Brinnin Papers, Delaware.

59. CW, letter to JMB, November 20, 1988, Brinnin Papers, Delaware. The hospital is now called Tufts Medical Center. Although Brinnin did not save the letter's envelope and Charlee did not mention the hospital by name, "New England Medical Center" appears in the November 1988 journal entries of Christie Wilbur (Chris's wife), and family members have confirmed the name's accuracy.

60. CW, interview by the authors, March 9, 2006.

61. CW, letter to JMB, December 13, 1988, Brinnin Papers, Delaware.

62. CW, letter to JMB, June 30, 1990, Brinnin Papers, Delaware. Wilbur kept a record of his Brattleboro experience on several loose sheets of paper, which were tucked into his bound journal notebook. We are not certain if Charlee knew about these pages because she died before her husband gave us access to them.

63. CW, letter to JMB, July 10, 1989, Brinnin Papers, Delaware.

64. CW, interview by the authors, February 23, 2006.

65. David H. Van Biema, "Richard Wilbur," *People*, October 5, 1987, 91–99, 92. The date 1957 refers to the year that Wilbur won his first Pulitzer Prize.

66. Ibid.

67. Regarding Prince Hal's remark: scholars posit that Shakespeare made reference to the hare because of its melancholy look and note that Moor Ditch was a general term for the open sewer ditches surrounding London. See "The First Part of Henry the Fourth," in *The Riverside Shakespeare,* ed. G. Blakemore Evans (New York: Houghton Mifflin, 1974), 843 [act 1, scene 2, note 78].

68. Berryman, *Recovery,* 9.

69. John Stuart Mill, "A Crisis in My Mental History: One Stage Onward," in *The Norton Anthology of English Literature,* 6th ed., ed. M. H. Abrams (New York: Norton, 1993), 2:1022–30.

70. Wilbur used "spangle" with similar implications in "A Baroque Wall-Fountain in the Villa Sciarra" (*Things of This World*) and "Part of a Letter" (*Ceremony*).

71. William Wordsworth, "Lines Composed a Few Miles above Tintern Abbey," in *Norton Anthology of Poetry: Shorter Edition,* 3rd ed., ed. Alexander A. Allison, Herbert Barrow, Caesar A. Blake, Arthur J. Carr, Arthur M. Eastman, and Hubert M. English, Jr. (New York: Norton, 1983), 275.

72. Wilbur explicitly discusses his "public quarrel" with Poe's aesthetics in his essay "Edgar Allan Poe," in *Responses: Prose Pieces, 1953–1976,* rev. ed. (Ashland, Ore.: Story Line, 1999), 55–89. See also Isabella Wai, "Wilbur's 'Merlin Enthralled,'" *Explicator* 62 (Summer 2004): 231.

73. Thomas Traherne (1638–1674), "Introduction," *Centuries of Meditations,* ed. Bertram Dobell (London: Bertram Dobell, 1903), xxvii. A reader might see Wilbur's "A World without Objects" as a precursor to his later "Love Calls Us to the Things of This World," which makes a case against the biblical warning "Love not the world, neither the things that are in the world" (1 John 2:15).

74. Robert Pack, "God Keep Me a Damned Fool," *Dartmouth Alumni Magazine* 87, no. 2 (1994): 34–43, 42.

75. Dana Ullman notes not only the reactive properties of phosphorus but also the effects of too much and too little phosphorus on the balance of other minerals in the human body. Heavy drinkers, he says, often suffer from a depletion of the mineral ("Understanding Nature to Learn Materia Medica," *Homeopathic Educational Services,* www.homeopathic.com).

76. Pack, "God Keep Me," 42.

77. RW, undated journal entry, RW's personal papers. We've estimated a date range of 1988–1992 because of the loose-leaf entry's placement among other dated material in Wilbur's bound journal.

78. RW, interview by Elizabeth Meade Howard, March 2003, quoted in Howard's "Aging Famously: Follow Those You Admire to Living Long and Well," unpublished manuscript, 2016, 274.

13. Key West Winters

1. RW, "Discovering Key West," *Web of Stories,* ca. 2005, www.webofstories.com.

2. Arlo Haskell, "David A. Kaufelt, 1939–2014," *Littoral,* www.kwls.org; "The Poet Homes of Key West, FL," *Academy of American Poets,* www.poets.org.

3. Matt Jordon, "Elizabeth Bishop, Geographer of Dreams," *Island Life,* January 13, 1994.

4. Arlo Haskell and RW, "A Great Wonder: Richard Wilbur in Conversation," 2011, *Academy of American Poets,* www.poets.org.

5. CW, interview by the authors, October 20, 2005.

6. Andrew Kopkind, "End of the Line," *Village Voice,* July 16, 1991.

7. CW, interview by the authors, October 20, 2005. The Wilburs also shared this story with Langdon Hammer, Merrill's biographer (RW and CW, interview by Hammer, December 17, 2002, RW's personal papers).

8. CW, letter to JMB, February 25, 1975, Brinnin Papers, Delaware.

9. Ibid.
10. Ibid.
11. RW and CW, interview by Hammer.
12. For a history of the Key West Literary Seminars, see Haskell, "David A. Kaufelt."
13. Ibid.
14. Les Standiford, "A Celebration of Key West with John Hersey," *Chicago Tribune,* March 13, 1994.
15. Haskell, "David A. Kaufelt."
16. CW, interview by the authors, October 6, 2005.
17. RW, interview by the authors, August 3, 2007.
18. John Hersey, "A Game of Anagrams," in *Key West Tales* (New York: Random House, 1994), 113.
19. Ibid., 109–10.
20. Ibid., 109–11. Merrill's father was Charles Merrill, a famous investment banker. The reference to "ditsy zoa" alludes to Wilbur's fascination with odd animal species; in 1955, for instance, Pantheon published *A Bestiary* (reissued in 1993) comprising literary quotations compiled by Wilbur along with wire-form illustrations by Alexander Calder.
21. Ibid., 113–14.
22. RW, letter to JMB, May 15, 1962, Brinnin Papers, Delaware. A fylfot is a swastika.
23. RW, letter to JMB, October 31, 1994, Brinnin Papers, Delaware.
24. RW, letter to JMB, April 27, 1998, Brinnin Papers, Delaware. A dugong is an aquatic mammal found on the coasts of the Indian Ocean from eastern Africa to northern Australia and distinguished from a manatee by its forked tail.
25. RW, interview by the authors, August 3, 2007.
26. JMB, diary entries, 1981 and 1982, Brinnin Papers, Delaware.
27. William Carlos Williams, *The Autobiography of William Carlos Williams* (New York: New Directions, 1951), 172.
28. August Kleinzahler, "Changing Light," *New York Times,* November 7, 2008.
29. RW, letter to James Merrill (hereafter JM), with unpublished poem, undated, James Merrill Papers, Washington University Libraries, Special Collections Department (hereafter Merrill Papers, Washington University).
30. RW, letter to JM, with unpublished poem, undated, Merrill Papers, Washington University.
31. J. D. McClatchy, "Seeing Through Us, Seeing Us Through," broadsheet on the occasion of "An Evening with Two Great Poets," Waterfront Playhouse, Key West, Florida, March 13, 1991.
32. JM, letter to RW, with unpublished poem, April 19, 1987, RPW Deposit, AC. The asterisk in the verse footnoted Alfred Korn, who had told Merrill about the appointment.
33. RW, letter to JM, February 12, 1994, Merrill Papers, Washington University.
34. Kopkind, "End of the Line."
35. Carol Shaughnessy, "Poetry of the Real World—at the Parrot," *Island Life,* January 14, 1993.
36. Kopkind, "End of the Line."
37. Ibid.
38. For a number of years Merrill's fatal heart attack was not publicly attributed to complications associated with AIDS, but as early as 1994 Charlee and other friends in their circle suspected the reason for his debilitated condition.
39. Arnold Rampersad, *Ralph Ellison: A Biography* (New York: Knopf, 2007), 334.
40. RW, interview by the authors, June 18, 2007. Ralph and Fanny Ellison were among the two hundred guests at the Wilburs' 1969 black-tie bash to celebrate the release of *Walking to Sleep,* where Lionel Hampton's band played till well past midnight.
41. Rampersad, *Ralph Ellison,* 503–4. Other mutual literary friends with homes in the Berkshires included Russell Lynes, a former publisher who was chair of the MacDowell artists' colony, and his wife Mildred; and the scholar and critic John Kouwenhouven and his wife

Joan. Rampersad notes that Ellison's essays, *Shadow and Act,* established him as a serious man of letters but did not sell as well as or achieve the recognition of James Baldwin's 1963 *The Fire Next Time* (409).

42. Ibid., 559.

43. RW, interview by the authors, June 18, 2007; Rampersad, *Ralph Ellison,* 407–8. At Yale Ellison had held a Rockefeller Foundation fellowship for the academic year of 1964–65.

44. RW, interview by the authors, June 18, 2007.

45. Ralph Ellison, letter to RW, February 24, 1987, RPW Deposit, AC.

46. Ibid.

47. RW, interview by the authors, June 18, 2007.

48. Rampersad, *Ralph Ellison,* 559. Wilbur elaborated on Fanny's comment as Rampersad quoted it, saying that she had mentioned to Charlee that she had needed to wash the sheets several times. Both Wilburs considered the comment homophobic (RW, interview by the authors, January 5, 2006).

49. RW, interview by the authors, January 5, 2006.

50. Ellison, letter to RW, February 24, 1987. In this letter Ellison answered Wilbur's question, which he acknowledged receiving in addition to the translation of *Phaedra.*

51. Rampersad, *Ralph Ellison,* 560.

52. Ellison, letter to RW, February 24, 1987.

53. RW, interview with the authors, January 5, 2006. Having been reconstructed and completed by an editor, Ellison's second novel was published posthumously as *Juneteenth* (New York: Random House, 1999).

54. JMB, diary entry, January 13, 1976, Brinnin Papers, Delaware.

55. RW, interview by the authors, July 18, 2014.

56. JM, quoted in J. D. McClatchy, "Seeing Through Us, Seeing Us Through."

57. RW and CW, interview by Hammer.

58. William H. Pritchard, review of *Collected Poems* by James Merrill, *Amherst Magazine* (Summer 2001).

59. Ibid.

60. RW, draft of letter to Bill Read, June 15, 1977. RPW Deposit, AC. *Habernaria orbiculata* is a type of orchid.

61. CW, letter to JMB, June 15, 1998, Brinnin Papers, Delaware.

62. Ibid.; Ellen Wilbur, letter to JMB, June 14, 1998, Brinnin Papers, Delaware.

63. CW, letter to JMB, April 22, 1994, Brinnin Papers, Delaware.

64. CW, interview by the authors, October 20, 2005.

14. Life without Charlee

1. RW, interview by the authors, April 18, 2007.

2. Jeanette Horton, interview by the authors, October 16, 2014.

3. RW and Arlo Haskell, "A Great Wonder: Richard Wilbur in Conversation," *Academy of American Poets,* www.poets.org.

4. *L'Illusion comique* opened in Paris at the Théâtre du Marais in 1636 and remained popular on the stage for about fifty years. Over the centuries it has been sporadically revived, most successfully in a 1937 production starring the famed actor Louis Jouvet at the Comédie Française. See RW, "Introduction," in Pierre Corneille, *The Theatre of Illusion,* trans. Richard Wilbur (New York: Harcourt, 2007), vii.

5. Ibid.

6. Corneille, *Illusion,* 128.

7. RW, "Introduction," in ibid., x.

8. Corneille, *Illusion,* 131.

9. Ibid., 128–29.

10. RW, interview by the authors, July 16, 2006.

11. RW, "Introduction," in Corneille, *Illusion,* x.

12. RW, interview by the authors, July 16, 2006.

13. CW, interview by the authors, March 9, 2006.

14. RW, "A Pasture Poem," draft copy, RW's personal papers.

15. RW, interview by the authors, July 16, 2006.

16. Pierre Corneille, *"Le Cid" and "The Liar,"* trans. Richard Wilbur (Boston: Houghton Mifflin Harcourt, 2009).

17. "England: Restoration Drama," in *The Reader's Encyclopedia of Drama,* ed. John Gassner (New York: Courier Dover, 2002), 221.

18. Corneille, *"Le Cid" and "The Liar,"* 28.

19. Mark Dundas Wood, "'Le Cid' Lacks a Unity of Style," *Backstage,* January 13, 2013, www.backstage.com.

20. Dana Gioia, "An Interview with the Translator," in the *American Theatre Reader,* ed. *American Theatre Magazine* staff (New York: Theatre Communications Group, 2013), 2:122.

21. Corneille, *"Le Cid" and "The Liar,"* 129.

22. RW, "Introduction to *The Liar*," in Corneille, *"Le Cid" and "The Liar,"* 121.

23. Ibid., 121–23. Wilbur's take here on lying and its consequences (or the lack thereof) will resonate with anyone familiar with the first six lines of his poem "Lying" (from *New and Collected,* 1987).

24. Ibid., 123.

25. "Charlee Wilbur, 85, Inspired and Guided Poets," *Boston Globe,* May 6, 2007.

26. "Charlotte Wilbur: Obituary," *Berkshire Eagle,* April 10, 2007.

27. David Sofield, remarks at CW's memorial service, May 19, 2007, RW's personal papers.

28. RW, interview by Elizabeth Meade Howard, March 2003, quoted in Howard's "Aging Famously: Follow Those You Admire to Living Long and Well," unpublished manuscript, 2016, 274.

29. CW, interview by the authors, October 20, 2005.

30. At readings Wilbur often prefaced the "The Reader," a perennial audience favorite, with anecdotes about Charlee's book choices.

31. RW, "Galveston, 1961," in *Anterooms* (New York: Houghton Mifflin Harcourt, 2010), 19. *Flense* means to strip the skin or the fat from a carcass, especially a whale's.

32. Panope is a sea nymph. Milton alluded to her in "Lycidas."

33. David Orr, "The Formalist," *New York Times,* January 7, 2011.

34. CW, letter to JMB, March 16, 1981, Brinnin Papers, Delaware.

35. Orr, most likely unaware that the Wilburs had spent that sabbatical year in Texas, called the poem "the strangest" in the book, thinking it depicted a "drowning victim of the great Galveston hurricane, now rising back from the ocean as a combination of deity and vision" ("The Formalist"). The 1961 hurricane, however, did not occur until September 1961, months after the Wilburs had returned to Connecticut.

36. The first sentence of the *Boston Globe* obituary alludes to "The Catch": "Captured in verse by her husband, the everyday gestures of Charlee Wilbur achieved a measure of immortality as she tried on a new dress in front of a mirror long ago" ("Charlee Wilbur, 85, Inspired and Guided Poets").

37. Robert Richman, "Benevolent Possessions: New and Collected Poems by Richard Wilbur," *New York Times,* May 29, 1988.

38. *Aubade,* from Middle French, is an early morning amorous poem or serenade.

39. Christopher Beach, ed., "New Criticism and Poetic Formalism," in *The Cambridge Introduction to Twentieth-Century American Poetry* (Cambridge: Cambridge University Press, 2003), 146; Edward Zuk, "Richard Wilbur: A Marvel of Our Time," *EP & M Online Review,* www.expansivepoetryonline.com.

40. RW, interview by the authors, August 3, 2007.

41. RW, letter to JMB, September 12, 1996, Brinnin Papers, Delaware.

42. JMB, letter to RW, October 13, 1996, RPW Deposit, AC.

43. Ibid.

44. M. L. Rosenthal, *Running to Paradise: Yeats's Poetic Art* (New York: Oxford University Press, 1994), 17.

45. William Butler Yeats, "The People," in *The Poems: A New Edition,* ed. Richard Finneran (New York: Macmillan, 1983), 150.

46. RW, "Poetry's Debt to Poetry," in *Responses: Prose Pieces, 1953–1976,* rev. ed. (Ashland, Ore.: Story Line Press, 1999), 204–32; 210, 232.

47. David Yezzi, "A Passion Joined to Courtesy and Art," *Poetry* 177 (February 2001): 337–44, 344.

48. Ibid., 344.

49. RW, quoted in Howard, "Aging Famously," 274.

50. RW, "Poetry Readings, 'For C.,'" *Web of Stories,* ca. 2005, www.webofstories.com.

51. For many years the Wilburs were communicants of St. Stephen's Church in Pittsfield, Massachusetts.

52. RW, interview by the authors, August 3, 2007.

53. "Charlotte Wilbur: Obituary."

54. Sofield, remarks.

55. Ibid.

56. Michael Wolfe, personal communication, February 23, 2015.

57. RW, interview by the authors, August 3, 2007.

58. RW, interview by the authors, June 25, 2007. The September and April dates had been in place since early June 2007.

59. Sophie Johnson, "Wilbur Reads Celebrated Poetry at Annual Walt Whitman Lecture," *Pioneer,* April 17, 2008, http://whitmanpioneer.com.

60. RW, interview by Howard.

61. RW and David Sofield, interview, "Richard Wilbur, 1942," www.amherst.edu/library/about/support/friends/interviews/wilbur.

62. Sofield, remarks. The greyhound was the Wilburs' dog.

63. RW and Sofield, interview.

64. Ibid.

65. When Wilbur was first at Wellesley, he had hinted to Armour Craig that he would be open to an offer to teach at Amherst. In response, Craig alluded not only to the rivalry between Harvard's and Amherst's English departments but also to the fact that Amherst assigned each student in its freshman writing course three papers per week. Each section had eighteen to twenty students, and each faculty member taught at least one section per semester. The workload for faculty members, therefore, was quite rigorous. Craig had warned him, "Dick, we work pretty hard at Amherst." RW, interview by the authors, August 3, 2007.

66. Orr, "The Formalist."

67. The portrait hangs among the paintings of past college presidents, including Calvin Coolidge, and next to another portrait, also painted by Belchetz-Swenson, of Rose Richardson Olver, L. Stanton Williams '41 Professor of Psychology and Sexuality, Women's and Gender Studies, Emerita, who taught at Amherst for fifty years.

68. Wilbur felt suddenly shaky and unwell the day before the presentation; his doctors attributed his symptoms to an imbalance in the dosage of his medications. Missing the ceremony, something that has rarely happened in more than sixty years of public appearances, bothered him more than his physical symptoms did. However, a number of local poets and writers agreed to hold a panel discussion in lieu of the reading. They included Susan Snively, Peggy O'Brien, Christopher Benfey, David Sofield, Ilan Stavans, and Robert Bagg.

69. William Jay Smith (1918–2015) served a two-year appointment (1968–1970) as the poetry consultant to the Library of Congress, a position now known as the U.S. Poet Laureate. The author of more than fifty books (including poems, translations, literary criticism, children's verse, and memoirs), he published his first and second poetry collections in 1947

(*Poems*) and 1950 (*Celebration of Dark*), the same years in which Wilbur's first two books appeared. The men's paths crossed because of the coincidental timing and the attention their first books garnered—from Louise Bogan in the *New Yorker* (for Wilbur) and from Marianne Moore, whose praise of Smith's book resulted in a *New York Times* review by Milton Crane. Thus began their long relationship as friends and as critical readers of each other's poems. In the early 1950s, after Smith completed his Rhodes Scholarship at Oxford, he and his wife, the poet Barbara Howes, settled in Pownal, Vermont; Smith taught across the border at Williams College in Williamstown, Massachusetts. In the mid-1960s, after Smith and Howes divorced, Charlee invited Smith to a dinner party at Hillcroft, hoping he would enjoy the company of another guest, Sonja Haussmann, a woman she had met through a mutual friend from Wesleyan. Smith and Haussmann married in 1966 and soon settled in West Cummington, on property that had once been part of the William Cullen Bryant homestead, just miles away from the property the Wilburs would buy in 1969.

70. When Wilbur submitted the manuscript, he intended "A Measuring Worm" to be the book's title poem, but a friend warned that it might be off-putting or misleading.
71. CW, interview by the authors, March 9, 2006.
72. RW, interview by Howard.
73. Orr, "The Formalist."
74. Ibid.
75. Wilbur has three grandchildren—Gabriel, Amelia, and Liam—and two great-grandchildren. (Gabriel is the father of twins.)
76. Patty Kimura, personal communication, May 8, 2016.
77. In 1978 Sonja Haussmann Smith printed some of these verses on a pamphlet to share with friends on her husband's sixtieth birthday ("Verses on the *Times*," by Richard Wilbur and William Jay Smith, RW's personal papers, and courtesy of William Jay Smith). An example from Smith to Wilbur:

> Patricia Hearst has shocked the nation
> By listing her occupation
> When arrested: "Self-employed urban guerrilla."
> If Richard Wilbur had to fill a
> Similar blank when booked one day
> For occupation what would he say?
> Something that sounded much sublimer?
> "Self-employed Cummington country rhymer?"
> Or given that chance, would he just blow it
> And put down simply: "Sunday poet?"

An example from Wilbur to Smith:

> Bill Smith went to Hungary,
> Wearing one dungaree.
> The people of Buda, aghast
> At seeing him look so half-assed,
> Cried, "Get out of Buda, you pest!
> You're improperly dressed!"

Index

Bate, Walter Jackson, 105, 329n23
Baudelaire, Charles, 115–16, 329n28
The Beautiful Changes (Wilbur): "The Beau-
tiful Changes," 55, 110; Bogan's review,
120; "Cicadas," 97–98; "On the Eyes of
an SS Officer," 80–81; "First Snow in
Alsace," 61; as gift of to Sitwell, 119; "June
Light," 304–5; launch party, 109; Merrill's
response to, 289–290; "Poplar, Sycamore,"
208; publication, 1, 108–9, 285; response of
De Vries and White, 124; reviews, 109–10;
sales and impacts, 110; themes in, 92; title
for, 109; "Water Walker," 98, 207
Beck, Brooks, 36
Beddoes, Thomas Lovell, 130–31
Bedford, Brian, 151–52, 270, 297
Belchetz-Swenson, Sarah, portrait of RW,
313, 352n67
The Bell Jar (Plath), 341n85
"Bells for John Whiteside's Daughter"
(Ransom), 218
Benedictine abbey bombing, Cassino, Italy,
58–59, 326n22
Bennett, Joseph, 5
"Beowulf" (Wilbur), 117
Bernstein, Leonard: appeal of the *Candide*
story to, 179; collaboration with, 4, 178,
187–89, 337n46; CW's frustration with,
185–86; financial manipulations, 195;
response to *Candide* reviews, 185
Berryman, John: competitiveness, 214–17;
criticisms of psychiatric treatment, 272;
death, 215; long poems and three-stanza
inclusive form, 207; Lowell's critiques, 216;
response to RW's Pulitzer, 2–3, 213–14;
writings about alcoholism, 267, 347n48
A Bestiary (Wilbur and Calder), 349n20
Betjeman, John, 87
bipolar disorder, manic depression:
Lawrie Wilbur's diagnosis, 86–87; Lowell's
hospitalizations for, 210, 340n53. *See also*
mental illness
"Birches" (Frost), 16, 130
birthday celebrations, 210–11, 228, 284, 309,
313, 340n52
Bishop, Elizabeth: agnosticism, 226–27;
alcohol abuse, 210; background and
experiences, 343–44n124; at the Bard

poetry conference, 125, 201; Brinnin's
recollections of, 227; competitiveness,
343n104; death, 228; friendship with CW,
224; Jarrell on, 199, 338n3; in Key West,
277; loneliness, 225; personality, 225–26;
posthumous reassessments, 223–24;
relationship with Lowell, 216–17, 225–26,
343n113; responses to Jarrell's critiques,
201–2, 204–5; on Plath's poetry, 220; RW's
descriptions, 223, 229; on RW's poetry,
201, 217–18, 220, 225, 343n120; on RW's
Pulitzer, 3; RW's spiritual connection and
friendship with, 211, 227, 343n104; on
RW's translations, 227; views on femi-
nism, 225; *Words in Air* (correspondence
with Lowell), 199
Bizerte, Tunisia, 51
"A Black November Turkey" (Wilbur), 200
black studies programs, RW's response to,
249
Blake, William, 207
blank verse, 211–12, 234
blues music, RW's enjoyment of, 122, 287
Bogan, Louise, 1, 4, 109–10, 120, 214–15
"Bon Voyage" (*Candide* lyric), 189
"The Book of Ephraim" (Merrill), 283
Boorstin, Daniel, 253
Boothbay Harbor, Me., honeymoon, 45
Botteghe Oscure (journal), 170, 335nn33–34
"The Bottles Become New, Too" (Wilbur),
126–27, 330n53
boxing, 30
Bramante, architecture of, 168–69
Brattleboro Retreat, Brattleboro, Vt.,
Wilburs' detox experience, 265–68, 270,
272
Bread Loaf writers' conference, Middlebury,
Vt., 286–87
Briggs-Copeland Assistant Professor of
Creative Writing, Harvard University, 133
Brinnin, John Malcolm: alcoholism, 270;
annual parties, 226–27; as contributor to
Foreground, 119; critique of *Candide,* 183;
depression, 275; on "For C.," 306–7; as
godfather to Aaron Wilbur, 238; homo-
sexuality, 290; on impact of Wilburs in
Cambridge, 106; in Key West, 278–79,

God (*continued*)
275, 315, 327n2; RW's faith in, 275, 294.
See also imagination/creativity; religious/
spiritual beliefs, Christian faith
Goering, Hermann, 81
Goethe, Johann Wolfgang von, 162
golf, golfing, 8, 26
Golffing, Francis, 109–10
Gottlieb, Robert, 246
"Grace" (Wilbur), 110
grammatical precision. *See* technical virtuosity
grandchildren, 353n75
Grasse, France, excursion to, 122
"Grasse: The Olive Trees" (Wilbur): Jarrell's
appreciation for, 203–4, 208; publication
in *New Yorker,* 124
Gray, Thomas ("Elegy Written in a Country
Churchyard"), 21, 323n25
Great Britain: adulation for, during RW's
childhood, 7, 9; production of *Candide* in,
156, 190; RW's postwar experiences in, 85,
87, 91
Green, Samuel, 276
Gregory, Horace, 203, 338n3
grief/mourning: depression vs., 275;
inadequate human responses to, 112–13,
and mourning for CW, 294; RW's poems
about, 315–16. *See also* death
Grolier Poetry Book Shop, 104
Grose, Joan, 36
group therapy, 267–68
Guggenheim Foundation fellowship, 135
Guthrie, Tyrone: as a collaborator, 182; cuts
to *Candide,* 182–83; Guthrie Theater,
336n13; hiring as director for *Candide,* 180;
London production of *Tartuffe,* 156; on
role in *Candide's* shortcomings, 188
Gutiérrez, Francisco, 136
Guttman, Yehuda and Ruth, 279

Habberton family, 9–10
Hagstrom, Jack, 189
Halcyon, prescription for, 265–66
Hall, Donald: as American Academy of Arts
and Letters president, 235; in Cambridge
with RW, 103; as critic of RW's poetry, 239;
on *Day by Day* (Lowell), 216, 341n71; as
junior fellow at Harvard, 329n23; public

appearances with, 310; on Wesleyan Poetry
Series selection board, 235
Hamilton, Saskia, 210
"Hamlen Brook" (Wilbur), 250
Hammer, Langdon, 290
Hammett, Dashiell, 193–94
Hammann, Ralph, 190–91
"Hand-Dance" (Wilbur), 55
Harcourt Publishers/Houghton Mifflin
Harcourt: *Advice to a Prophet,* 239;
Anterooms, 305; recording of reading by
RW, 186; royalties from, 141
Hardwick, Elizabeth, 124–25, 183, (Lizzie)
211, 226, 330n50, 343n113
Hare, Augustus, 160, 297
Harmon, Charlie, 189
Hartford Stage Company, production of
Kushner's *Phaedra,* 297
Harvard Crimson, review of production of
The Misanthrope, 150
Harvard Magazine: Lambert interview with
RW, 127; on RW and Viereck as cultural
ambassadors, 241–42
Harvard University, Cambridge, Mass.:
Amherst College competition with, 105;
application of coursework to poetry,
116–17; appointment as Briggs-Copeland
Assistant Professor of Creative Writing,
133; course work, 104; criticisms of
graduate English program, 106; develop-
ment of public persona at, 106; doctoral
exam system, 104–5; hiring policies, 105;
homosexuality at, 117–18; junior fellowship program, 5, 113–14; poets among
fellow students at, 103; and postwar
fears about Communism, 118; Spencer
Memorial Series, 135; studies under the GI
Bill, 91, 102–3, 105; teaching assistantships,
129, 131; unequal treatment of women, 117;
visiting literary celebrities, 119
Hayward, Max, 241
"Heart's Needle" (Snodgrass), 335n34
Hecht, Anthony: on "A Baroque Wall-
Fountain in the Villa Sciarra," 335n38;
friendship with the Wilburs in Rome,
159; long poems, 207; response to RW's
poetry, 4
Hélion, Jean, 122

Hellman, Lillian: on challenges of working with Bernstein, 187–88; collaboration with on *Candide,* 4, 178, 181, 188; conflicts with Reiner, 186–87; dramatic success prior to *Candide,* 179; feud with McCarthy, 193; final contacts with the Wilburs, 194–95; friendship with CW, 185–87, 237–38; as godmother to Aaron Wilbur, 238; investigation of by HUAC, 178–79; loan from, 192–93; on London production of *Candide,* 190; personality, 188, 191–92; relationship with Hammett, 194; relationship with Wright, 193–94; response to *Candide* reviews, 185; RW's reminiscences about, 191, 194

Helmbrecht le Fermiêr, 70, 107–8

Hemingway, Ernest, 276–77, 279–280

Henney, Tom, 234

Herman, Jerry, 196

heroic plays, 298–99

"Of Heroic Plays" (Dryden), 298

Hersey, Barbara, 278

Hersey, John, 278, 280–83, 285–86

"He Was" (Wilbur), 15–16, 55–56

Hildyard, Catherine, 245

Hillcroft, Portland, Conn.: CW and RW on porch at, *237;* CW's homesickness for, 240; decision to sell, 249; purchase and description, 236–37

History of the 36th Signal Company, Message Center Section (Wilbur), 71–73, 75–77, 80–81

Hitler, Adolf, 41, 221

Hi-Y (YMCA), 25

Hoenig, Ed, 135

"A Hole in the Floor" (Wilbur), 200

Hollander, John, 235, 329n23

Holmes, John, 125–26

Holocaust: continuation of atrocities after V-E Day, 89; and doctrine of Aryan superiority, 80–81; Hecht's focus on, 207; Plath's references to, 342n92; RW's references to, 146

Homage to Mistress Bradstreet (Berryman), 2–3, 207, 213–14

"Home Burial" (Frost), 164

homosexuality: Brinnin's, 290; and homophobia in midcentury America, 117–18; and homophobia in Key West, 286–88;

Matthiessen's, 289, 331n71; Merrill's, 290; RW's preconceptions about, 289

Honors College, Wesleyan University, 235–36

Hooten, Peter, 278, 292

Hopkins, Gerard Manley, 95, 97–98, 109, 111–12

Horthy, Miklós, 80

Horton, Jeanette, 295, 317

"The House" (Wilbur), 313

House Un-American Activities Committee (HUAC), 118, 178–79, 182

Housman, A. E., 61

Houston, Tex., sabbatical in, 238–39, 303

Howard, Elizabeth Meade, interview with, 294, 310

Howes, Barbara, 235, 353n69

Hubbard, Gene, 31

Hughes, Ted, 221, 311, 342n99

human nature, humanity: complexity of, RW's lessons, 93, 175, 206; defining, 239–40; Giacometti's view, 122; Molière's view, 332–33n44

humor: Bishop's, 220; Frost's, 131; in letters about accomplishments, 252; in letters during the war, 50, 54; and life in Key West, 277, 291; in postcards to Baird, 39; pranks, practical jokes, 5, 25–26, 33; RW's fondness for American humorists, 28

Hurd, Peter, portrait of Johnson, 246

hurricane of 1938, impacts of in Amherst, 30

Hutchinson, Ann, 322n2

The Illusion (*L'Illusion comique*) (Corneille, Kushner version), 297–98

L'Illusion comique (*The Theatre of Illusion*) (Corneille), 18, 295, 350n4. See also *The Theatre of Illusion*

imagination, creativity: and artistic vision, 146; and the artist's ability to set a scene, 20; as cure for mental suffering, 272; and the divine-human collaboration, 163, 167–69, 171, 173; imaginary games during childhood, 23; importance of for giving world meaning, 274; and the innate sense of wonder, 273; Poe's concept, 93, 128, 274; RW's evolving views on, 122–24; as source of purpose, 274

New York Times: review of *Candide,* 184;
RW's poem for opening of Philharmonic
Hall, 255
"Nightingales" (Wilbur), 24
Nims, John Frederick, 216–17
Nixon, Richard, 144
normality/normalness: and balancing
physical and mental exertion, 215, 230–31;
as basis for criticism of RW's poems, 4–5,
17, 132, 145–46, 203, 207–8; and maintain-
ing outside interests, 254
North & South (Bishop), 202
North Caldwell, N.J. *See* Armitage estate
North of Boston (Frost), 164
Nottingham News (Boy Scouts), 25
"NOW THAT WE ARE IN IT" (Wilbur),
42

"The Obscurity of the Poet" (Jarrell), 205
"Ode to a Nightingale" (Keats), 140
"On the Eyes of an SS Officer" (Wilbur),
80–81, 113
"On the Marginal Way" (Wilbur), 146–48,
207–8, 245, 273
"the one and the many," as subject for war
poetry, 47, 56, 232, 275
One Day in the Life of Ivan Denisovich
(Solzhenitsyn), 242
opinion pieces in the Army press, 85–86
opposite poems: for Amherst College 50th
reunion, 29; *More Opposites,* 24; *Opposites,*
24, 252
opposites/paradoxes, lifelong fascination
with, 24, 40–41, 92, 95–97, 271
The Orb Weaver (Francis), 234
Orr, David: on *Anterooms,* 4–5; critical
reassessment of Bishop, 223; on RW as the
"Grand Old Man" of American poetry,
312–13; on RW's poems about death and
grief, 5, 315–16
Osterman, Lester, 183–84, 186–87
Ostia Antica, Italy, excursion to, 162
Ouija board consultations, 283
Oxford, England, postwar visit to, 87

pacifism. *See* anti-interventionist, antiwar
views
Pack, Robert, 274

Packard, Laurence, 33, *34*
Padre Pio, 176, 335n46
Paestum, Italy, excursion to, 66–67
painting. *See* art/painting
paradox. *See* opposites/paradoxes, lifelong
fascination with
"The Pardon" (Wilbur), 15
Paris, France: impact on RW's thinking
about creativity, 122–24; support for
the arts and artists in, 121–22; postwar
nightlife, 121. *See also* Corneille; Molière;
Racine
Paris Review interview, 145–46, 222, 253
Parker, Dorothy, 120, 180, 188
Parker, Gil, 195–96
Partisan Review, 47, 201–2
"Part of a Letter" (Wilbur), 117, 273
"A Pasture Poem" (Wilbur), 298
Paterson (Williams), 201
Paul, Saint: and command to rejoice in
God, 101; metaphors for in "Water
Walker," 99–100; ministry, RW's
fascination with, 98
Le Pavillon des Enfants (*The Children's
Playhouse*) (Sarment, Wilbur translation),
192, 195–96
Pearl Harbor attack, 42–43
Pearson, Norman Holmes, 235
Pentimento (Hellman), 193
PEN translation award, 156
"The People" (Yeats), 306–7
People magazine interview, 271
Perceptions (Schuman), 254
perfectionism: as form of worship, 115; Helen
Wilbur's, 11; RW's, impact on family life,
254
Perkins, Maxwell, 276
Phaedra (Racine, Wilbur translation):
Bedford's production of, 270; language
in, comparison with Lowell's translation,
261–64; stress of working on, 257, 259–60,
288. See also *Phèdre*
"The Phantom Wooer" (Beddoes), 130–31
Phèdre: Lowell's translation, 260–63; Racine's
original version, 260, 346n30
Phelps, Elizabeth Stuart, 36–37, 324n15
Philbrick, Herbert, 118
phosphorus, properties, 274, 348n75

from teaching, 312; teaching assistantships at Harvard, 129, 131; teaching position at Wellesley College, 1, 177, 181. *See also* Wesleyan University

"Tears" (Wilbur), 11–14, 123–24

technical virtuosity: critical recognition of, 312–13; criticisms of RW's poetry, 110–11; criticisms of RW's poetry for, 4, 132; and elegant rigor, 116; and grammatical precision, 19–20, 226; and the importance of discipline, 198; and linguistic precision, 19–21; and perfectionism, 115; "Tywater" example, 67. *See also* poetic forms; rhyme, rhyming

"Tell It Slant" award (Emily Dickinson Museum), 313

tennis: at the Armitage estate, 9–10, 14, 17; exposure to, as a child, 26; lifelong enjoyment of, 26, 230, 251–52; physicality of, as balance to writing, 30, 174, 215; skill at, 252, 340n48; at the Wilbur home in Cummington, 251, 308

"The Terrace" (Wilbur), 273

"Terza Rima" (Wilbur), 65. *See also* Dante

Theater of the Church of Notre Dame, New York, 299

The Theatre of Illusion (*L'Illusion comique*) (Corneille, Wilbur translation), 295–99

Things of This World (Wilbur): and the emotional intensity of RW's response to nature, 111; "Love Calls Us to the Things of This World," 129, 162–63, 170, 206; "Merlin Enthralled," 140, 274; National Book Award for, 231; "A Plain Song for Comadre," 140–41; Pulitzer Prize for, 2–3, 202, 213–14; "A Simile for Her Smile," 305; "A Voice from under the Table," 137, 274–75

36th Texas Division: casualties, 57–58, 326n18; and the deaths of Tywater and Barton, 64; description of Texans in, 59–60; RW's assignment to, 3; wartime maneuvers, 56, 58–63, 65–70, 73–76, 80–81. *See also* Signal Company, 36th Texas Division

"This Pleasing Anxious Being" (Wilbur), 7–8, 13, 18–21, 293, 332n36

Thomas, Dylan, 104, 328n2

Thommen, Edward, 150

Thurber, James, 334n26

Time to the Old (Schuman), 254

Touchstone (Amherst literary magazine), RW's writings for, 31–35

T-Patch (army newspaper), RW's editorials for, 71–72, 90

Traherne, Thomas, 274

Transatlantic Review, Ellen Wilbur story in, 240

translations: appeal of to RW, 134, 258; of Brodsky's poetry, 241; CW's help with, 149, 195; of Pichette's poetry, 122; praise and awards for, 156, 227; respect for original cadence and meaning, 152–56; and RW's fluency in French, 72; success of, pluses and minuses for the Wilburs, 156; and translators' responsibility to actors, 299. *See also* Corneille; Molière; Racine

Truscott, Lucien, 62, 65, 68–69, 71

Tufts, Cathleen, 23

Turner, Stansfield, 118

"25.XIII.1933" (Brodsky, Wilbur translation), 241

"Two Statements" (Wilbur), 55–56, 113

"Two Voices in a Meadow" (Wilbur), 310

"Tywater" (Wilbur), 67–68, 108, 113

Tywater, Lloyd, 64, 68

UCLA, Los Angeles, *Candide* revival at, 190, 194–95

Untermeyer, Louis, 215

Updike, John, 233, 344n10

Valency, Maurice, 196–97

Valium/Dalmane addiction: CW's vs. RW's approach to treatment, 267–68; detox efforts, 6, 264–65; initial prescription for, 244; time needed to recover from, 269, 273

Van Biema, David H., interview with, 271, 275

Van Doren, Mark, 332n37, 338n3

Variety, review of *Candide* in, 183

Velletri, Italy, wartime experience in, 62

verse plays: characteristics of Molière's dialogue, 149; challenges of writing, 141–42; Eliot's Harvard lecture on, 135; interest in during the early 1950s, 134–35, 137; and the

ROBERT BAGG graduated from Amherst College (AB 1957) and the University Connecticut (PhD 1965). He has received fellowships from the American Academy of Arts and Letters (Rome Prize) and the Guggenheim and Rockefeller (Bellagio) foundations, as well as grants from the NEA and NEH. He taught at the University of Washington in Seattle from 1963 to 1965, then at the University of Massachusetts Amherst from 1965 to 1996. There he served as graduate director (1982–86) and chair (1986–92) of the Department of English. He has published six books of poetry and twenty-one literary essays. His nine translations of Greek plays by Sophocles and Euripides have been staged in seventy-two productions worldwide. His translations of *Antigone* and *Oedipus the King*, which were first published by the University of Massachusetts Press and later (along with *Oedipus at Kolonos, Elektra*, and *The Women of Trakhis*) by HarperCollins in *The Complete Plays of Sophocles*, are included in the third edition of the *Norton Anthology of World Literature*. He lives with his wife, Mary, in Worthington, Massachusetts.

MARY BAGG, a graduate of the University of Massachusetts Amherst, first collaborated with Robert Bagg in the late 1990s, coauthoring the notes and introductions for his translations of Sophocles in *The Oedipus Cycle*, published by the University of Massachusetts Press in 2004. She has been a freelance editor of nonfiction for more than a decade.

Made in the USA
Las Vegas, NV
16 August 2022